# Learning C# by Deve[illegible] Games with Unity 2021

*Sixth Edition*

Kickstart your C# programming and Unity journey by building 3D games from scratch

**Harrison Ferrone**

Packt>

BIRMINGHAM – MUMBAI

# Learning C# by Developing Games with Unity 2021

*Sixth Edition*



**Producer:** Caitlin Meadows, Manish Nainani
**Acquisition Editor – Peer Reviews:** Saby Dsilva
**Project Editor:** Namrata Katare
**Content Development Editor:** Edward Doxey
**Copy Editor:** Safis Editing
**Technical Editor:** Aniket Shetty
**Proofreader:** Safis Editing
**Indexer:** Sejal Dsilva
**Presentation Designer:** Ganesh Bhadwalkar

First published: September 2013
Second edition: March 2016
Third edition: December 2017
Fourth edition: March 2019
Fifth edition: August 2020
Sixth edition: October 2021

Production reference: 1271021

Published by Packt Publishing Ltd.
Livery Place
35 Livery Street
Birmingham
B3 2PB, UK.

ISBN 978-1-80181-394-5

www.packt.com

*"If people reach perfection, they vanish, you know."*

- *T.H. White, The Once and Future King*

# Contributors

## About the author

**Harrison Ferrone** was born in Chicago, Illinois and was raised all over. He's worked at Microsoft, PricewaterhouseCoopers, and a handful of small start-ups, but most days you can find him creating instructional content for LinkedIn Learning and Pluralsight or tech editing for the Ray Wenderlich website.

He holds various fancy looking pieces of paper from the University of Colorado at Boulder and Columbia College Chicago. Despite being a proud alumnus, these are stored in a basement somewhere.

After a few years as a full-time iOS and Unity developer, he fell into a teaching career and never looked back. Throughout all of this, he's bought many books, been owned by several cats, worked abroad, and continually wondered why *Neuromancer* isn't on more course syllabi.

*Completing this book wouldn't have been possible without loving support from Kelsey, my wife and partner in crime on this journey.*

# About the reviewers

**Simon Jackson** is a long-time software engineer and architect with many years of Unity game development experience, as well as the author of several Unity game development titles. He loves to both create Unity projects as well as lend a hand to help educate others, whether it's via a blog, vlog, user group, or major speaking event.

His primary focus at the moment is with the XRTK (Mixed Reality Toolkit) project, which is aimed at building a cross-platform mixed reality framework to enable both VR and AR developers to build efficient solutions in Unity and then build/distribute them to as many platforms as possible.

**Joshua Steinhauer** is a game developer by day, indie developer by night. Having picked up programming at a young age, Joshua has stuck to his passion ever since, and has shown no signs of stopping. He loves building tools to speed up development and help make others' jobs easier.

His favorite games are *The Elder Scrolls III: Morrowind* and *Fallout: New Vegas*, and he has spent the past four years developing an open world RPG in Unity and leading a team to make it possible. His dream is to start his own game studio!

# Table of Contents

# Preface

Unity is one of the most popular game engines in the world, catering to hobbyists, professional AAA studios, and cinematic production companies. While known for its use as a 3D tool, Unity has a host of dedicated features supporting everything from 2D games and virtual reality to post-production and cross-platform publishing.

Developers love its drag-and-drop interface and built-in features, but it's the ability to write custom C# scripts for behaviors and game mechanics that really takes Unity the extra mile. Learning to write C# code might not be a huge obstacle to a seasoned programmer with other languages under their belt, but it can be daunting for those of you who have no programming experience. That's where this book comes in, as I'll be taking you through the building blocks of programming and the C# language from scratch while building a fun and playable game prototype in Unity.

## Who this book is for

This book was written for those of you who don't have any experience with the basic tenets of programming or C#. However, if you're a competent novice or seasoned professional coming from another language, or even C#, but need to get hands-on with game development in Unity, this is still where you want to be.

## What this book covers

*Chapter 1, Getting to Know Your Environment*, starts off with the Unity installation process, the main features of the editor, and finding documentation for C# and Unity-specific topics. We'll also go through creating C# scripts from inside Unity and take a look at Visual Studio, the application where all our code editing takes place.

*Chapter 2, The Building Blocks of Programming*, begins by laying out the atomic-level concepts of programming, giving you the chance to relate variables, methods, and classes to situations in everyday life. From there, we move on to simple debugging techniques, proper formatting and commenting, and how Unity turns C# scripts into components.

*Chapter 3, Diving into Variables, Types, and Methods*, takes a deeper look at the building blocks from *Chapter 2*. This includes C# data types, naming conventions, access modifiers, and everything else you'll need for the foundation of a program. We'll also go over how to write methods, add parameters, and use return types, ending with an overview of standard Unity methods belonging to the `MonoBehaviour` class.

*Chapter 4, Control Flow and Collection Types*, introduces the common approaches to making decisions in code, consisting of the `if-else` and `switch` statements. From there, we move on to working with arrays, lists, and dictionaries, and incorporating iteration statements for looping through collection types. We end the chapter with a look at conditional looping statements and a special C# data type called enumerations.

*Chapter 5, Working with Classes, Structs, and OOP*, details our first contact with constructing and instantiating classes and structs. We'll go through the basic steps of creating constructors, adding variables and methods, and the fundamentals of subclassing and inheritance. The chapter will end with a comprehensive explanation of object-oriented programming and how it applies to C#.

*Chapter 6, Getting Your Hands Dirty with Unity*, marks our departure from C# syntax into the world of game design, level building, and Unity's featured tools. We'll start by going over the basics of a game design document and then move on to blocking out our level geometry and adding lighting and a simple particle system.

*Chapter 7, Movement, Camera Controls, and Collisions*, explains different approaches to moving a player object and setting up a third-person camera. We'll discuss incorporating Unity physics for more realistic locomotion effects, as well as how to work with collider components and capture interactions within a scene.

*Chapter 8, Scripting Game Mechanics*, introduces the concept of game mechanics and how to effectively implement them. We'll start by adding a simple jump action, create a shooting mechanic, and build on the previous chapters' code by adding logic to handle item collection.

*Chapter 9, Basic AI and Enemy Behavior*, starts with a brief overview of artificial intelligence in games and the concepts we will be applying to Hero Born. Topics covered in this chapter will include navigation in Unity, using the level geometry and a navigation mesh, smart agents, and automated enemy movement.

*Chapter 10, Revisiting Types, Methods, and Classes*, takes a more in-depth look at data types, intermediate method features, and additional behaviors that can be used for more complex classes. This chapter will give you a deeper understanding of the versatility and breadth of the C# language.

*Chapter 11, Introducing Stacks, Queues, and HashSets*, dives into intermediate collection types and their features. Topics covered in this chapter include using Stacks, Queues, and HashSets and the different development scenarios that each is uniquely suited for.

*Chapter 12, Saving, Loading, and Serializing Data*, gets you ready to handle your games information. Topics covered in this chapter include working with the filesystem and creating, deleting, and updating files. We'll also cover different data types including XML, JSON, and binary data, and end with a practical discussion on serializing C# objects directly into data formats.

*Chapter 13, Exploring Generics, Delegates, and Beyond*, details intermediate features of the C# language and how to apply them in practical, real-world scenarios. We'll start with an overview of generic programming and progress to concepts such as delegation, events, and exception handling.

*Chapter 14, The Journey Continues*, reviews the main topics you've learned throughout the book and leaves you with resources for further study in both C# and Unity. Included in these resources will be online reading material, certification information, and a host of my favorite video tutorial channels.

# To get the most out of this book

The only thing you need to get the most from your upcoming C# and Unity adventure is a curious mind and a willingness to learn. Having said that, doing all the code exercises, Hero's trials, and Quiz sections is a must if you hope to cement the knowledge you're learning. Lastly, revisiting topics and entire chapters to refresh or solidify your understanding before moving on is always a good idea. There is no sense in building a house on an unstable foundation.

You'll also need a current version of Unity installed on your computer – 2021 or later is recommended. All code examples have been tested with Unity 2021.1 and should work with future versions without issues.

| Software/hardware covered in the book |
|---|
| Unity 2021.1 or later |
| Visual Studio 2019 or later |
| C# 8.0 or later |

Before starting, check that your computer setup meets the Unity system requirements at `https://docs.unity3d.com/2021.1/Documentation/Manual/system-requirements.html`.

# Download the example code files

The code bundle for the book is hosted on GitHub at `https://github.com/PacktPublishing/Learning-C-by-Developing-Games-with-Unity-Sixth-Edition`. We also have other code bundles from our rich catalog of books and videos available at `https://github.com/PacktPublishing/`. Check them out!

# Download the color images

We also provide a PDF file that has color images of the screenshots/diagrams used in this book. You can download it here: `https://static.packt-cdn.com/downloads/9781801813945_ColorImages.pdf`.

# Conventions used

There are a number of text conventions used throughout this book.

`CodeInText`: Indicates code words in text, database table names, folder names, filenames, file extensions, pathnames, dummy URLs, user input, and Twitter handles. For example; "Select the `Materials` folder."

A block of code is set as follows:

```
public string firstName = "Harrison";
```

When we wish to draw your attention to a particular part of a code block, the relevant lines or items are highlighted:

```
accessModifier returnType UniqueName(parameterType parameterName)
{
    method body
}
```

**Bold**: Indicates a new term, an important word, or words that you see on the screen, for example, in menus or dialog boxes. For example: "Click on **Create** | **3D Object** | **Capsule** from the **Hierarchy** panel."

# Get in touch

Feedback from our readers is always welcome.

**General feedback**: Email `feedback@packtpub.com`, and mention the book's title in the subject of your message. If you have questions about any aspect of this book, please email us at `questions@packtpub.com`.

**Errata**: Although we have taken every care to ensure the accuracy of our content, mistakes do happen. If you have found a mistake in this book we would be grateful if you would report this to us. Please visit, `http://www.packtpub.com/submit-errata`, selecting your book, clicking on the Errata Submission Form link, and entering the details.

**Piracy**: If you come across any illegal copies of our works in any form on the Internet, we would be grateful if you would provide us with the location address or website name. Please contact us at `copyright@packtpub.com` with a link to the material.

**If you are interested in becoming an author**: If there is a topic that you have expertise in and you are interested in either writing or contributing to a book, please visit `http://authors.packtpub.com`.

# Share your thoughts

Once you've read *Learning C# by Developing Games with Unity 2021, Sixth Edition*, we'd love to hear your thoughts! Scan the QR code below to go straight to the Amazon review page for this book and share your feedback.

`https://packt.link/r/1801813949`

Your review is important to us and the tech community and will help us make sure we're delivering excellent quality content.

# 1

# Getting to Know Your Environment

Pop culture often markets computer programmers as outsiders, lone wolves, or geeky hackers. People possessing extraordinary mental gifts for algorithmic thought, little social IQ, and the odd anarchic bent. While this is not the case, there is something to the idea that learning to code fundamentally changes the way you look at the world. The good news is your naturally curious mind already wants to see these kinds of patterns in the world, and you may even come to enjoy this new way of thinking.

From the moment your eyes snap open in the morning to the last glimpse of your ceiling fan before you go to sleep, you're unconsciously using analytical skills that translate to programming—you're just missing the right language and syntax to map those life skills into code. You know your age, right? That's a variable. When you cross the street, I presume you look down the road in both directions before stepping off the curb like the rest of us. That's evaluating different conditions, better known as control flow in programming terminology. When you look at a can of pop, you instinctively identify that it has certain properties like shape, weight, and contents. That's a class object! You get the idea.

With all that real-world experience at your fingertips, you're more than ready to cross over into the realm of programming. To kick off your journey, you'll need to know how to set up your development environment, work with the applications involved, and know exactly where to go when you need help.

To those ends, we're going to begin by delving into the following C# topics:

- Getting started with Unity 2021
- Using C# with Unity
- Exploring the documentation

Let's get started!

# Technical requirements

Sometimes it's easier to start with what a thing isn't, rather than what it is. The goal of this book *isn't* to teach you everything there is to know about the Unity game engine or game development. By necessity, we'll cover these topics at a basic level at the beginning of our journey, and in more detail in *Chapter 6, Getting Your Hands Dirty with Unity*. However, these topics are included to provide a fun, accessible way to learn the C# programming language from the ground up.

Since this book is aimed at complete beginners to programming, if you have no previous experience with either C# or Unity, you're in the right place! If you've had some experience with the Unity Editor but not with programming, guess what? This is still the place to be. Even if you've dabbled in a bit of C# mixed with Unity, but want to explore some more intermediate or advanced topics, the later chapters of this book can provide you with what you're looking for.

> If you're an experienced programmer in other languages, feel free to skip the beginner theory and dive right into the parts you're interested in, or stick around and refresh your fundamentals.

In addition to running Unity 2021, you'll also be using C# 8.0 and Visual Studio to write your game code.

# Getting started with Unity 2021

If you don't have Unity installed, or are running an earlier version, follow these steps to set up your environment:

1. Head over to `https://www.unity.com/`.
2. Select **Get started** (shown in the following screenshot):

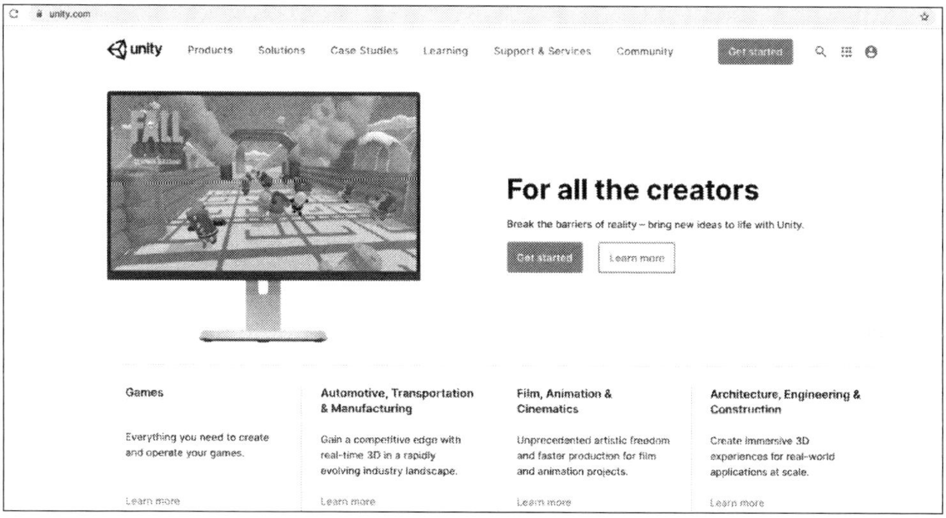


Figure 1.1: Unity homepage

This will take you to the Unity store page. Don't feel overwhelmed by this—you can get Unity completely for free!

> If the Unity homepage looks different for you than what you can see in *Figure 1.1*, you can go directly to `https://store.unity.com`.

3. Select the **Personal** option. The other paid options offer more advanced functionality and services, but you can check these out on your own:

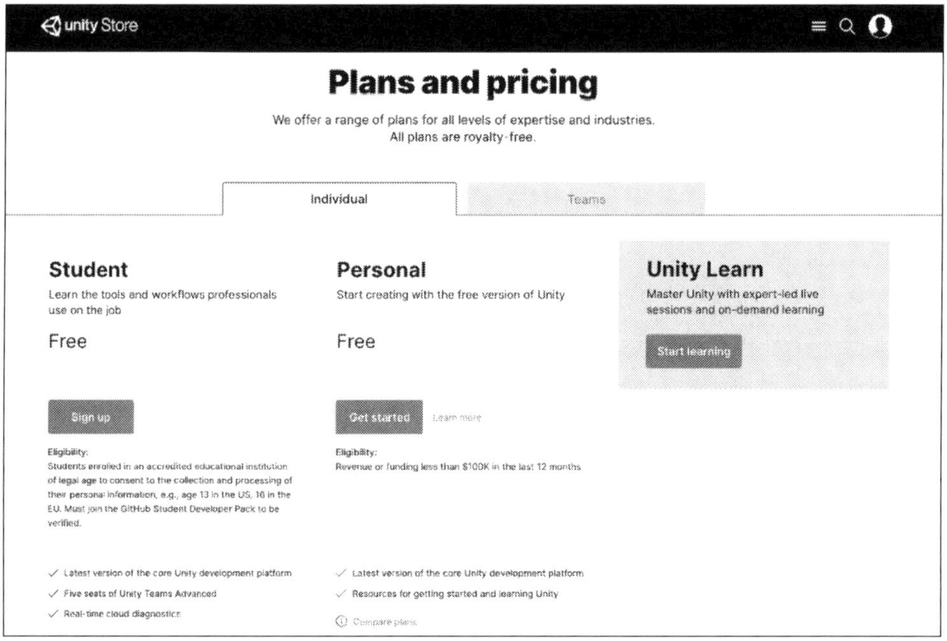


Figure 1.2: Unity plans and pricing

4. After selecting the **Personal** plan, you'll be asked if you're a first-time or returning user. Select **Start here** under **First-time users**:

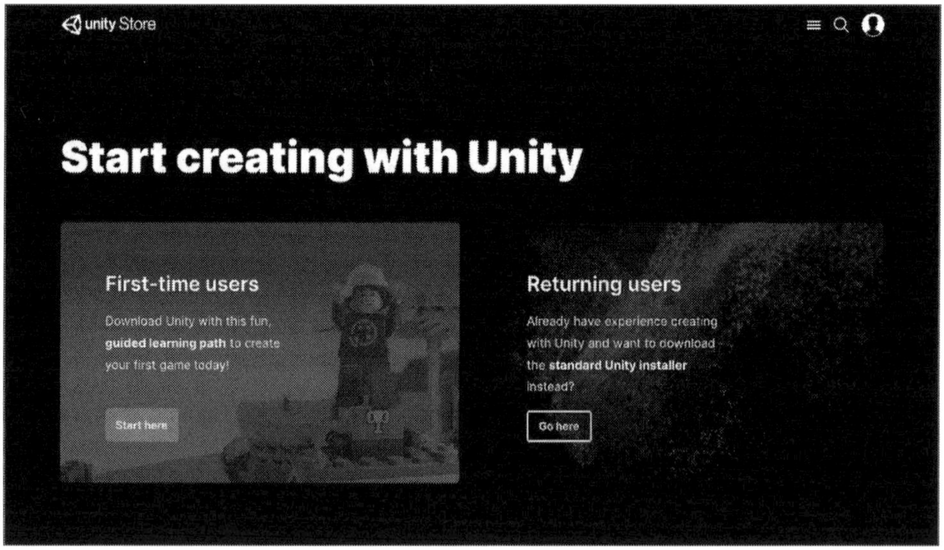


Figure 1.3: Start creating with the Unity portal

5. Select **Agree and download** to get your copy of Unity Hub:

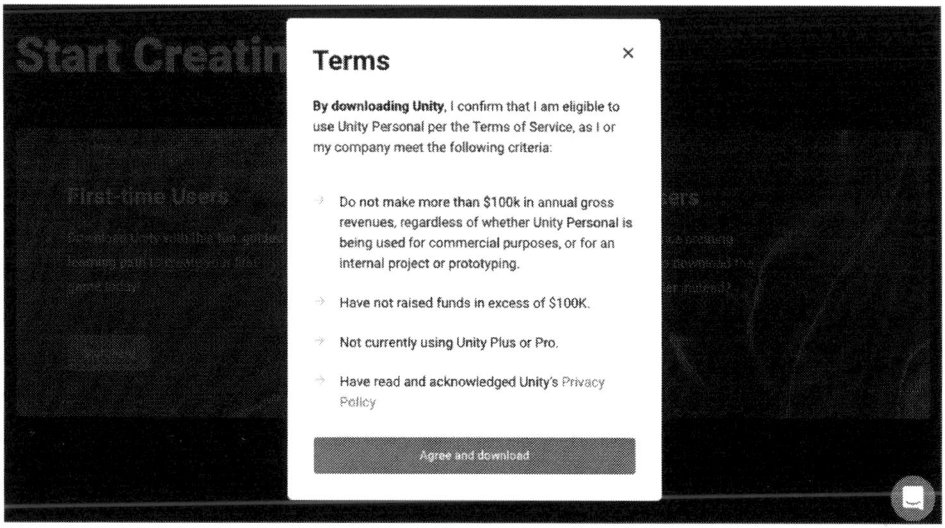


Figure 1.4: Unity terms and conditions

Once the download is complete, follow these steps:

1. Open up the installer (by double-clicking it)
2. Accept the user agreement
3. Follow the installation instructions

When you get the green light, go ahead and fire up the Unity Hub application!

> The newest version of Unity Hub will offer an install wizard when you first open the application. If you'd like to follow that, feel free.

The following steps show you how to start a new project without any help from the application:

1. Select **Skip Install Wizard** in the lower left, then confirm **Skip Wizard**:

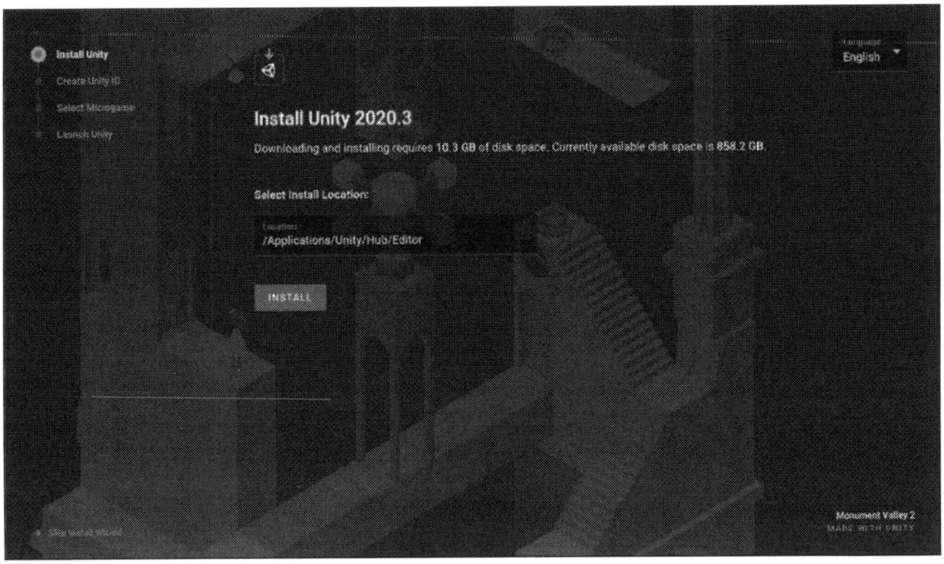


Figure 1.5: Install wizard

2. Switch to the **Installs** tab from the left-hand menu, and select **ADD** to choose your Unity version:

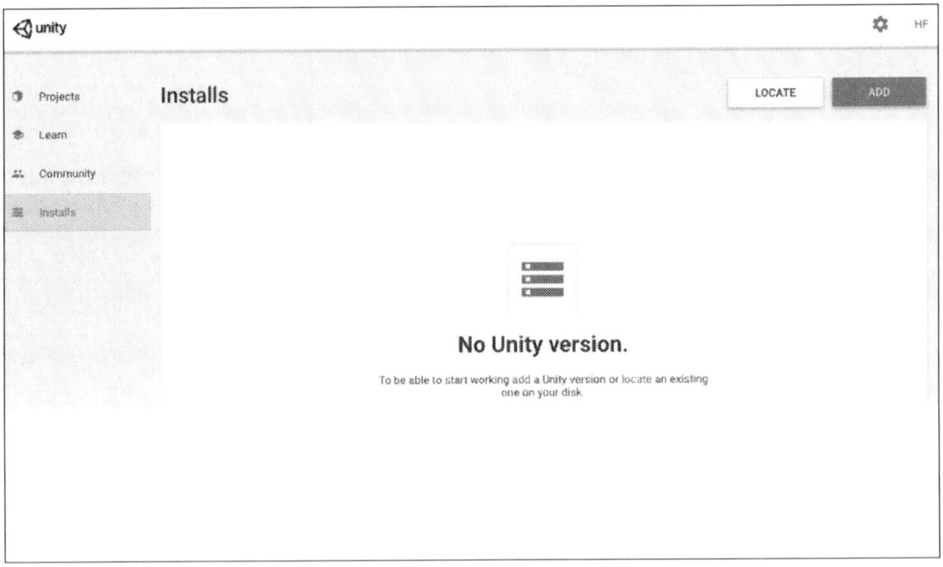


Figure 1.6: Unity Hub Installs panel

3. Select your desired version of Unity, then click **NEXT**. At the time of writing, Unity 2021 is still in pre-release, but you should be able to select a 2021 version from the **Official Releases** list by the time you're reading this:

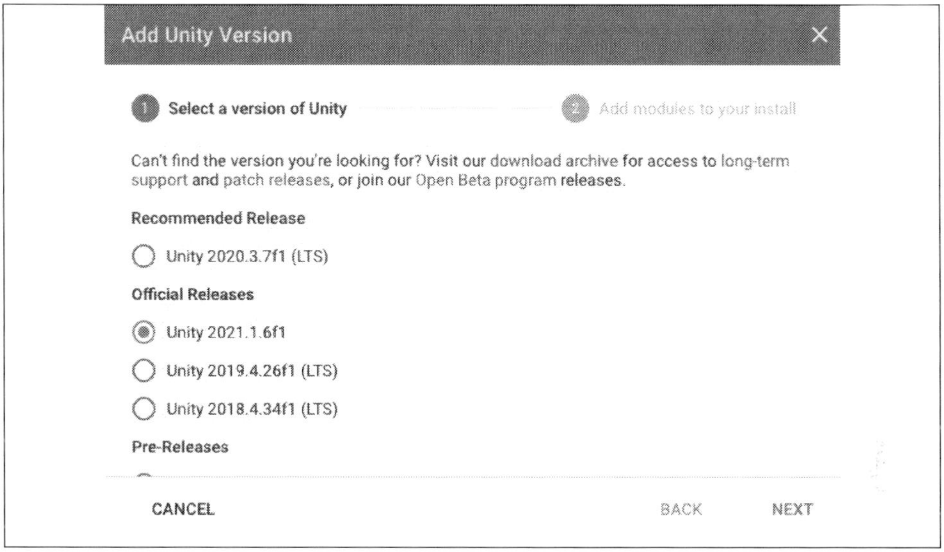


Figure 1.7: Add Unity Version pop-up window

4. You'll then be given the option to add various modules to your installation. Make sure the Visual Studio module is selected and click **NEXT:**

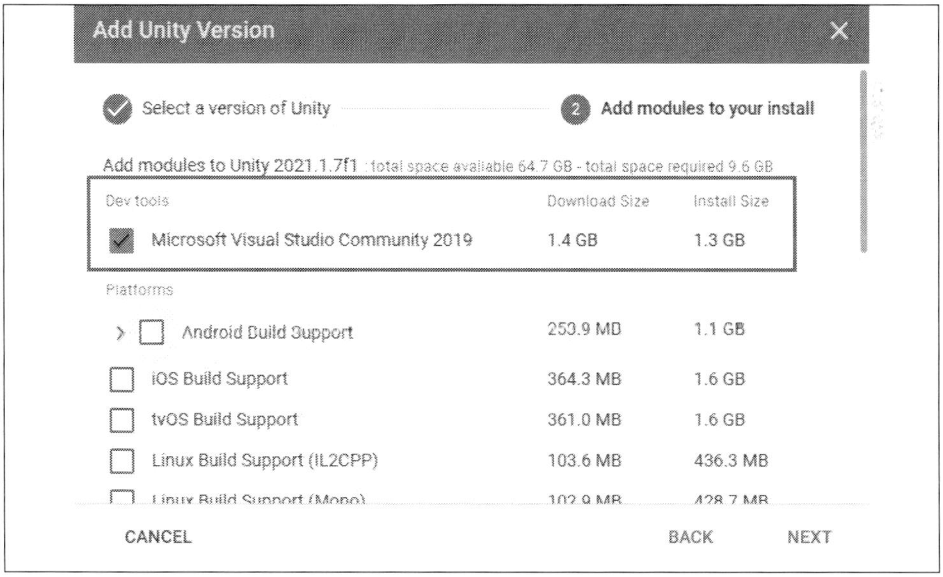


Figure 1.8: Adding install modules

> If you want to add any modules later, you can click the **More** button (three-dot icon) at the upper right of any version in the **Installs** window.

When the installation is complete, you'll see a new version in your **Installs** panel, as follows:

Figure 1.9: Installs tab with Unity versions

> You can find additional information and resources about the Unity Hub application at `https://docs.unity3d.com/Manual/GettingStartedInstallingHub.html`.

There's always a chance of something going wrong, so be sure to check the following section if you're using macOS Catalina or later, which has been known to throw up issues.

# Using macOS

If you're working on a Mac with OS Catalina or later, there is a known issue when using some versions of Unity Hub to install Unity. If that's the case for you, take a deep breath, go to the **Unity download archive**, and grab the 2021 version you need (`https://unity3d.com/get-unity/download/archive`). Remember to use the **Downloads (Mac)** option instead of the Unity Hub download:

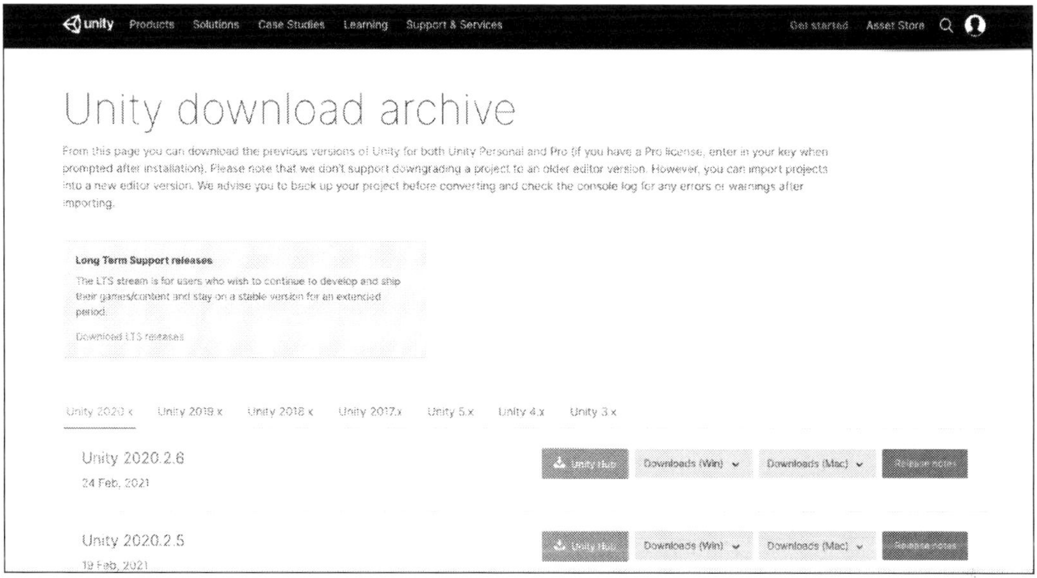


Figure 1.10: Unity download archive

> If you're working on Windows and run into similar install issues, downloading an archived copy of Unity will also work just fine.

The download is a normal application installer since it's a `.dmg` file. Open it up, follow the instructions, and you'll be ready to go in no time!

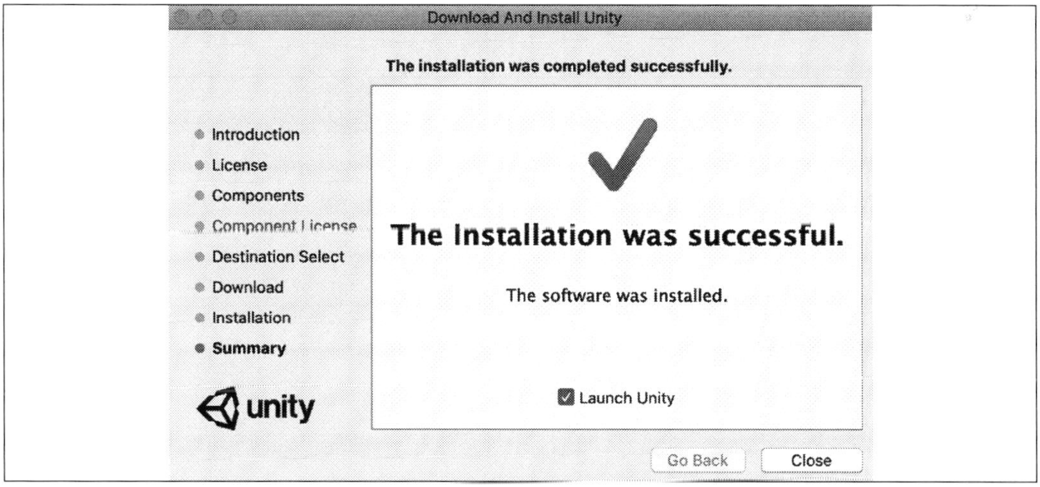


Figure 1.11: Successful Unity installation from the download manager

All of the examples and screenshots for this book were created and captured using Unity 2021.1.0b8. If you're using a newer version, things might look slightly different in the Unity Editor, but this shouldn't affect your following along.

Now that Unity Hub and Unity 2021 are installed, it's time to create a new project!

# Creating a new project

Launch the Unity Hub application to start a new project. If you have a Unity account, go ahead and sign in; if not, you can either create one or hit **Skip** at the bottom of the screen.

Now, let's set up a new project by selecting the arrow icon next to the **NEW** button in the top right corner:

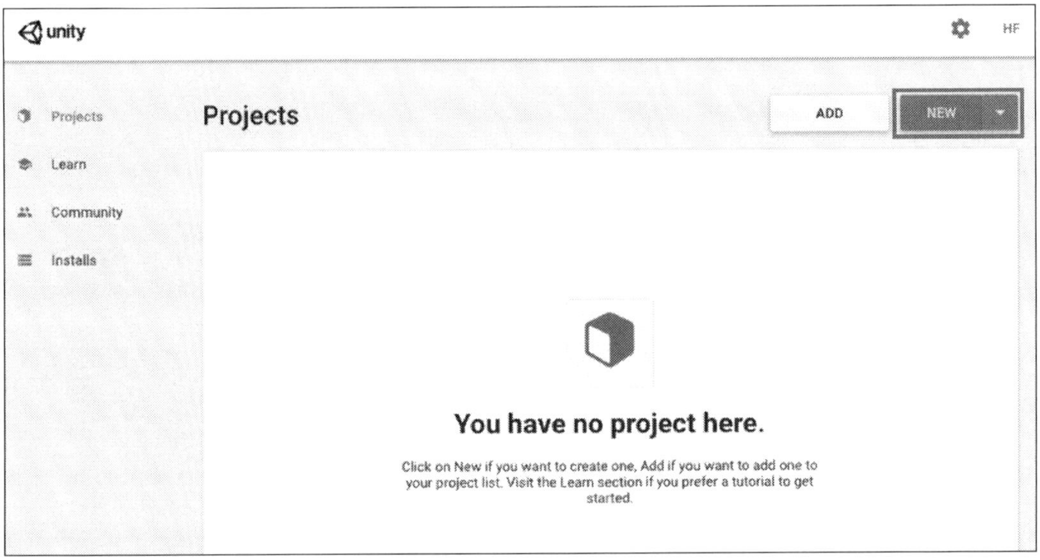


Figure 1.12: Unity Hub Projects panel

Choose your 2021 version and set the following fields:

- **Templates**: The project will default to **3D**
- **Project Name**: I'll be calling mine `Hero Born`
- **Location**: Wherever you'd like the project to be saved

Once the settings have been configured, hit **CREATE**:

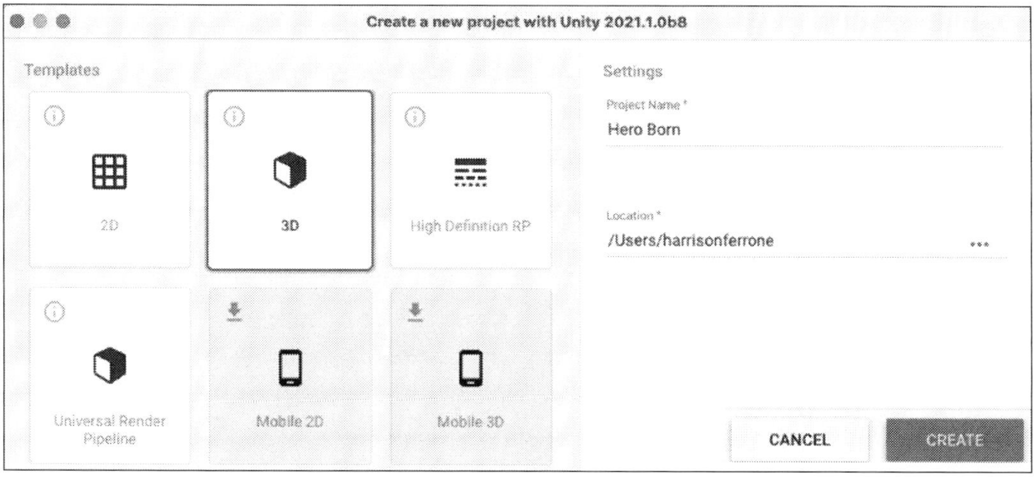


Figure 1.13: Unity Hub with new project configuration popup

With the project created, you're all set to explore the Unity interface! You can re-open your project anytime from the **Projects** panel in Unity Hub.

# Navigating the editor

When the new project finishes initializing, you'll see the glorious Unity Editor! I've marked the important tabs (or panels, if you prefer) in the following screenshot:

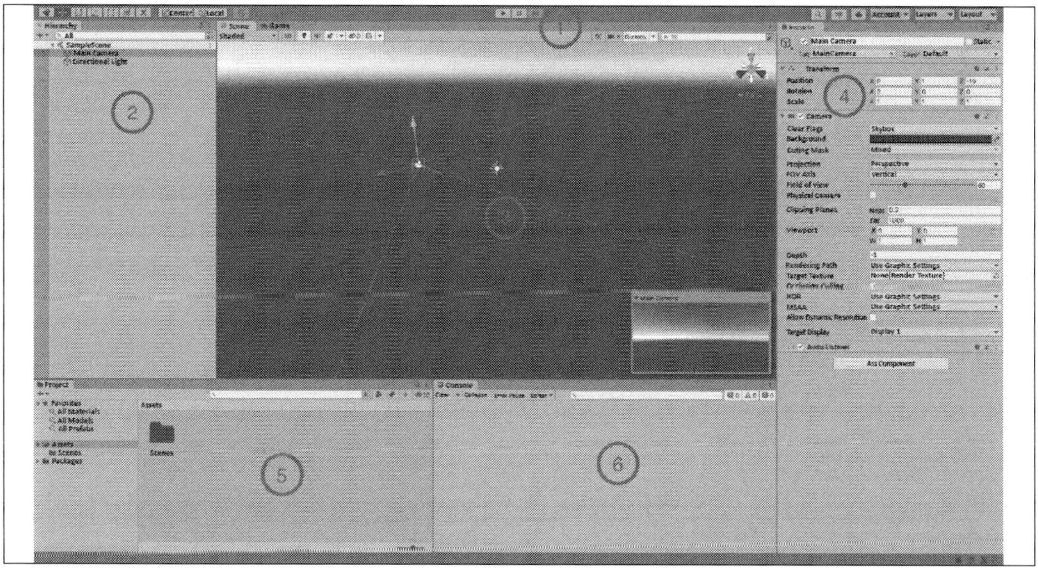


Figure 1.14: Unity interface

This is a lot to take in, so we'll look at each of these panels in more detail:

1. The **Toolbar** panel is the topmost part of the Unity Editor. From here, you can manipulate objects (far-left button group) and play and pause the game (center buttons). The rightmost button group contains Unity services, **LayerMasks**, and layout scheme features, which we won't be using in this book because they don't apply to learning C#.
2. The **Hierarchy** window shows every item currently in the game **scene**. In the starter project, this is just the default camera and directional light, but when we create our prototype environment, this window will start to get filled in.
3. The **Game** and **Scene** windows are the most visual aspects of the editor. Think of the **Scene** window as your stage, where you can move and arrange 2D and 3D objects. When you hit the **Play** button, the **Game** window will take over, rendering the **Scene** view and any programmed interactions.
4. The **Inspector** window is your one-stop shop for viewing and editing the properties of objects in the scene. If you select the **Main Camera GameObject** in the **Hierarchy**, you'll see several parts (Unity calls them components) are displayed—all of which are accessible from here.
5. The **Project** window holds every asset that's currently in your project. Think of this as a representation of your project's folders and files.
6. The **Console** window is where any output we want our scripts to print will show up. From here on out, if we talk about the console or debug output, this panel is where it will be displayed.

> If any of these windows get closed by accident, you can re-open them anytime from **Unity** | **Window** | **General**. You can find more in-depth breakdowns of each window's functionality in the Unity docs at `https://docs.unity3d.com/Manual/UsingTheEditor.html`.

Before continuing, it's important that Visual Studio is set up as the script editor for your project. Go to the **Unity menu** | **Preferences** | **External Tools** and check that **External Script Editor** is set to Visual Studio for Mac or Windows:

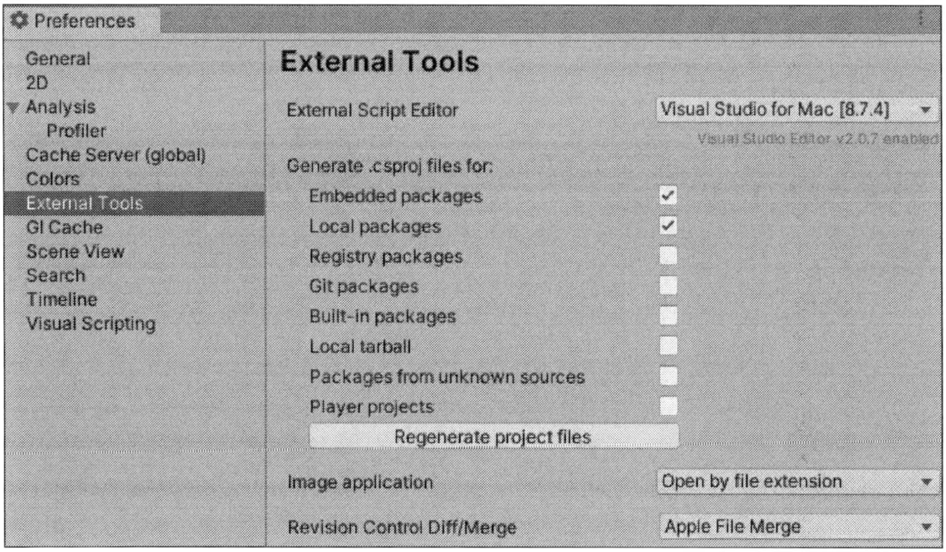


Figure 1.15: Changing the External Script Editor to Visual Studio

As a final tip, if you want to switch between light and dark modes, go to the **Unity menu** | **Preferences** | **General** and change the **Editor Theme**:

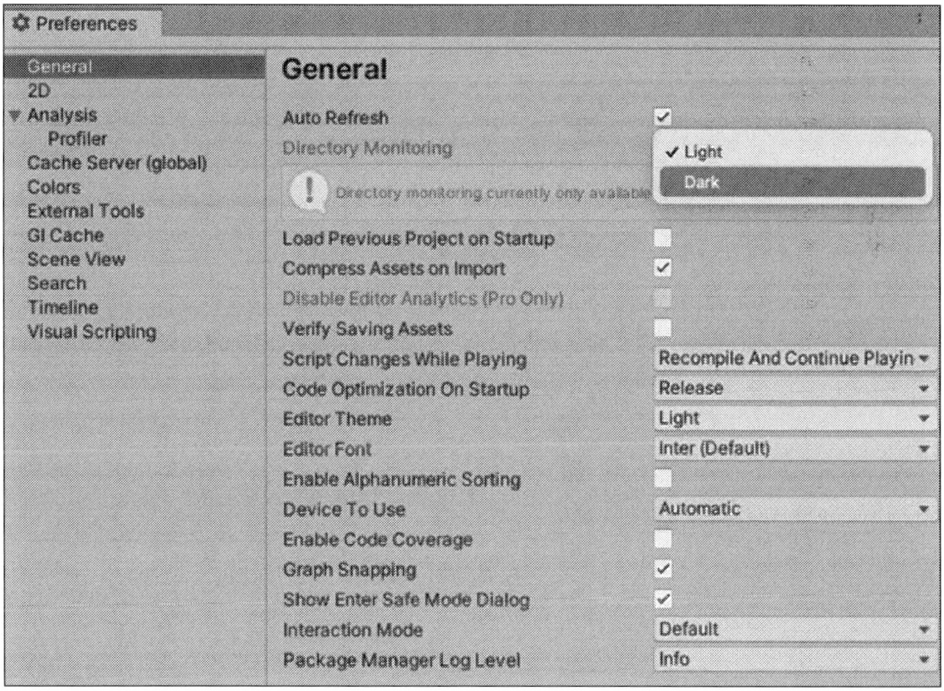


Figure 1.16: Unity general preferences panel

I know that was a lot to process if you're new to Unity, but rest assured that any instructions going forward will always reference the necessary steps. I won't leave you wondering what button to push. With that out of the way, let's start creating some actual C# scripts.

# Using C# with Unity

Going forward, it's important to think of Unity and C# as symbiotic entities. Unity is the engine where you'll create scripts and game objects, but the actual programming takes place in another program called Visual Studio. Don't worry about that right now—we'll get to that in a moment.

## Working with C# scripts

Even though we haven't covered any basic programming concepts yet, they won't have a home until we know how to create an actual C# script in Unity. A C# script is a special kind of C# file in which you'll write C# code. These scripts can be used in Unity to do virtually anything, from responding to player input to creating game mechanics.

There are several ways to create C# scripts from the editor:

- Select **Assets** | **Create** | **C# Script**
- Right under the **Project** tab, select the **+** icon and choose **C# Script**
- Right-click on the **Assets** folder in the **Project** tab and select **Create** | **C# Script** from the pop-up menu
- Select any GameObject in the **Hierarchy** window and click **Add Component** | **New Script**

Going forward, whenever you're instructed to create a C# script, please use whichever method you prefer.

> Resources and objects other than C# scripts can be created in the editor using the preceding methods. I'm not going to call out each of these variations every time we create something new, so just keep the options in the back of your mind.

For the sake of organization, we're going to store our various assets and scripts inside their marked folders. This isn't just a Unity-related task—it's something you should always do, and your coworkers will thank you (I promise):

1. From the **Project** tab, select **+** | **Folder** (or whichever method you like best—in *Figure 1.17* we've selected **Assets** | **Create** | **Folder**) and name it `Scripts`:

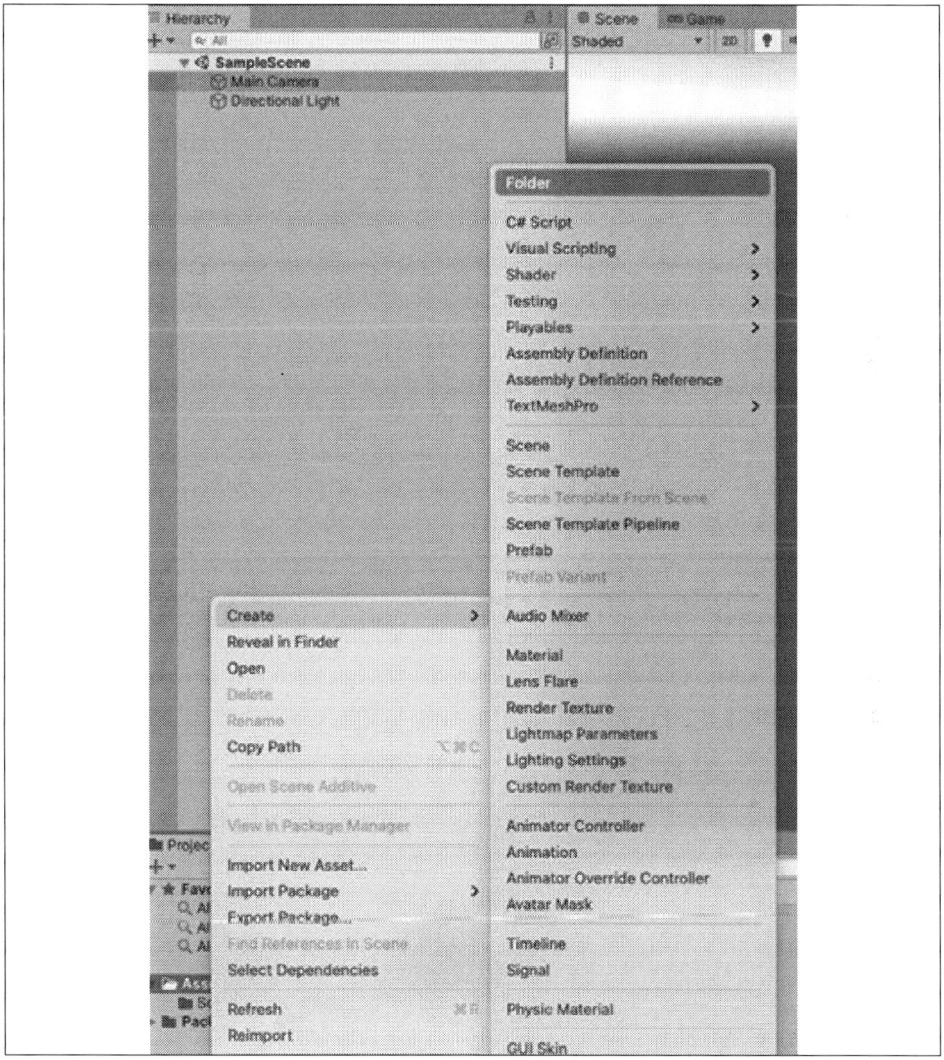


Figure 1.17: Creating a C# script

2. Double-click on the **Scripts** folder and create a new C# script. By default, the script will be named `NewBehaviourScript`, but you'll see the filename highlighted, so you have the option to immediately rename it. Type in `LearningCurve` and hit *Enter*:

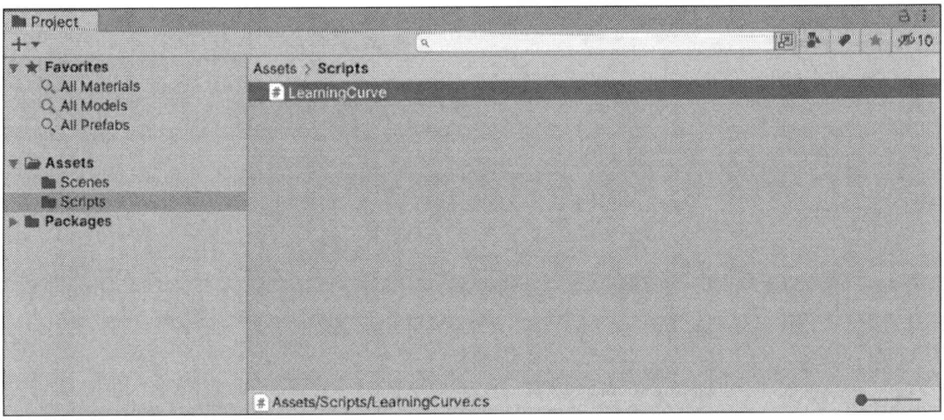


Figure 1.18: Project window with the Scripts folder selected

> You can use the small slider in the bottom right of the **Project** tab to change how your files are displayed.

So, you've just created a subfolder named `Scripts`, as shown in the preceding screenshot. Inside that parent folder, you created a C# script named `LearningCurve.cs` (the `.cs` file type stands for C-Sharp, in case you were wondering), which is now saved as part of our *Hero Born* project assets. All that's left to do is open it up in Visual Studio!

# Introducing the Visual Studio editor

While Unity can create and store C# scripts, they need to be edited using Visual Studio. A copy of Visual Studio comes pre-packaged with Unity and will open up automatically when you double-click any C# script from inside the editor.

## Opening a C# file

Unity will synchronize with Visual Studio the first time you open a file. The simplest way to do this is by selecting the script from the **Project** tab.

Double-click on `LearningCurve.cs`, which will open up the C# file in Visual Studio:

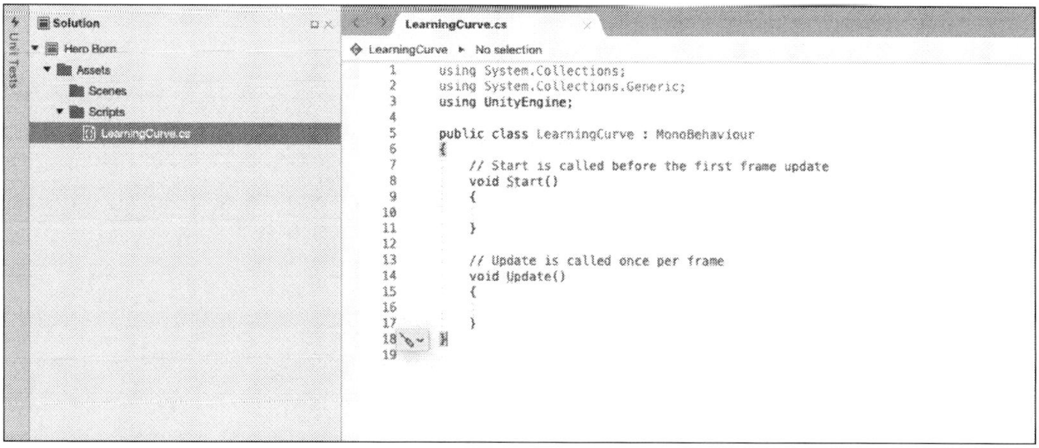


Figure 1.19: LearningCurve C# script in Visual Studio

> You can change the Visual Studio tabs at any time from **Visual Studio** | **View** | **Layout**. I'll be using the **Design** layout for the rest of the book so we can see our project files in the left-hand side of the editor.

You'll see a folder structure on the left-hand side of the interface that mirrors the one in Unity, which you can access like any other. On the right-hand side is the actual code editor where the magic happens. There are far more features to the Visual Studio application, but this is all we need to get started.

> The Visual Studio interface is different for Windows and Mac environments, but the code we'll be using throughout this book will work equally well with both. All the screenshots in this book have been taken in a Mac environment, so if things look different on your computer, there's no need to worry.

# Beware of naming mismatches

One common pitfall that trips up new programmers is file naming—more specifically, naming mismatches—which we can illustrate using line 5 from *Figure 1.19* of the C# file in Visual Studio:

```
public class LearningCurve : MonoBehaviour
```

The `LearningCurve` class name is the same as the `LearningCurve.cs` filename. **This is an essential requirement**. It's OK if you don't know what a class is quite yet. The important thing to remember is that, in Unity, the filename and the class name need to be the same. If you're using C# outside of Unity, the filename and class name don't have to match.

When you create a C# script file in Unity, the filename in the **Project** tab is already in **Edit** mode, ready to be renamed. It's a good habit to rename it then and there. If you rename the script later, the filename and the class name won't match.

If you were to rename the file at a later point, the filename would change, but line 5 would be as follows:

```
public class NewBehaviourScript : MonoBehaviour
```

If you accidentally do this, it's not the end of the world. All you need to do is go into Visual Studio and change `NewBehaviourScript` to the name of your C# script, as well as the name of the `.meta` file on your desktop. You can find the `.meta` file in the project folder under **Assets** | **Scripts**:

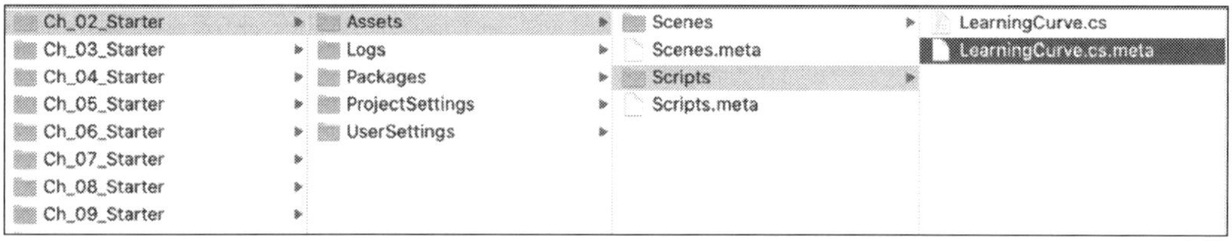


Figure 1.20: Finding the META file

# Syncing C# files

As part of their symbiotic relationship, Unity and Visual Studio communicate with each other to synchronize their content. This means that if you add, delete, or change a script file in one application, the other application will see the changes automatically.

So, what happens when Murphy's Law, which states that "*anything that can go wrong will go wrong*," strikes and syncing just doesn't seem to be working correctly? If you run into this situation, take a deep breath, select the troublesome script in Unity, right-click, and select **Refresh**.

You now have the basics of script creation under your belt, so it's time we talk about finding and efficiently using helpful resources.

# Exploring the documentation

The last topic we'll touch on in this first foray into Unity and C# scripts is documentation. Not sexy, I know, but it's important to form good habits early when dealing with new programming languages or development environments.

## Accessing Unity's documentation

Once you start writing scripts in earnest, you'll be using Unity's documentation quite often, so it's beneficial to know how to access it early on. The *Reference Manual* will give you an overview of a component or topic, while specific programming examples can be found in the *Scripting Reference*.

Every game object (an item in the **Hierarchy** window) in a scene has a **Transform** component that controls its **Position**, **Rotation**, and **Scale**. To keep things simple, we'll just look up the camera's **Transform** component in the Reference Manual:

1. In the **Hierarchy** tab, select the **Main Camera** game object
2. Move over to the **Inspector** tab and click on the information icon (question mark) at the top right of the **Transform** component:

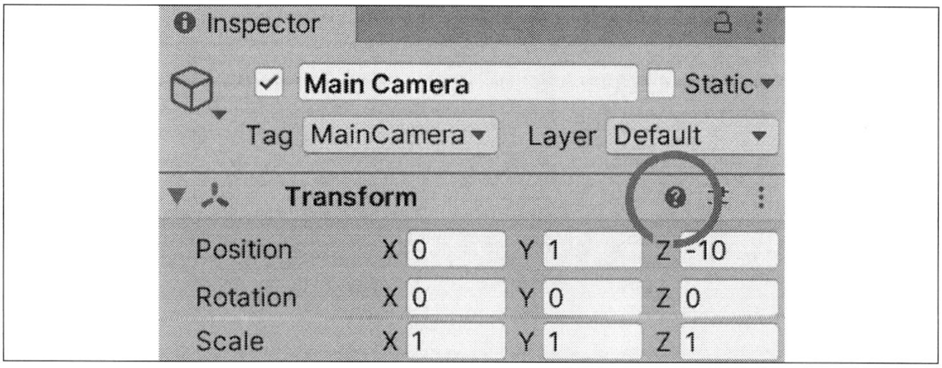


Figure 1.21: Main Camera game object selected in the Inspector

You'll see a web browser open on the **Transforms** page of the Reference Manual:

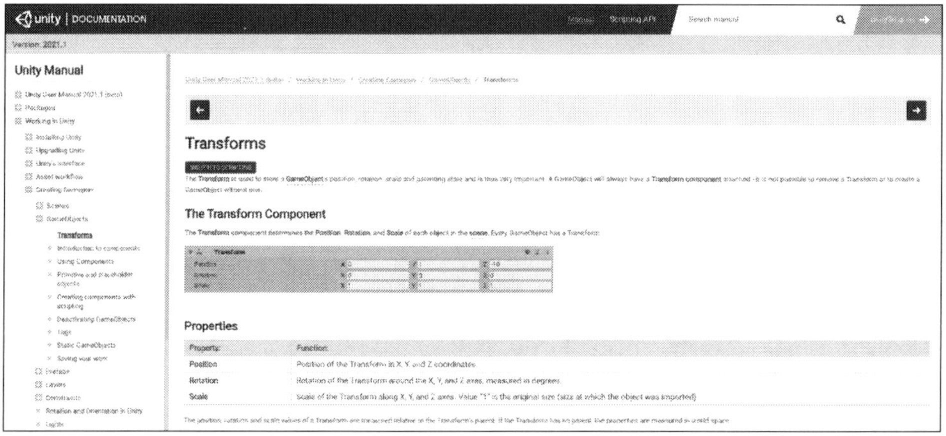


Figure 1.22: Unity Reference Manual

All the components in Unity have this feature, so if you ever want to know more about how something works, you know what to do.

So, we've got the Reference Manual open, but what if we wanted concrete coding examples related to the **Transform** component? It's pretty simple—all we need to do is ask the Scripting Reference.

Click on the **SWITCH TO SCRIPTING** link underneath the component or class name (**Transform**, in this case):

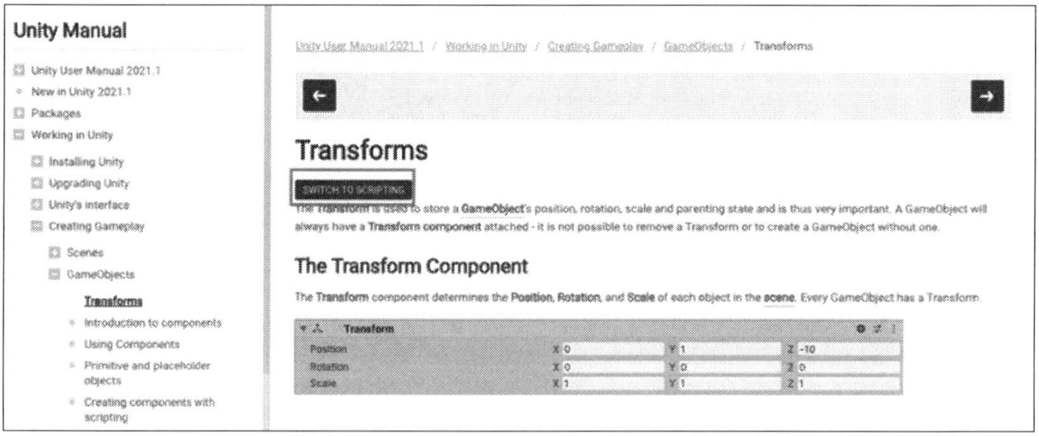


Figure 1.23: Unity Reference Manual with the SWITCH TO SCRIPTING button highlighted

By doing so, the Reference Manual automatically switches to the Scripting Reference:

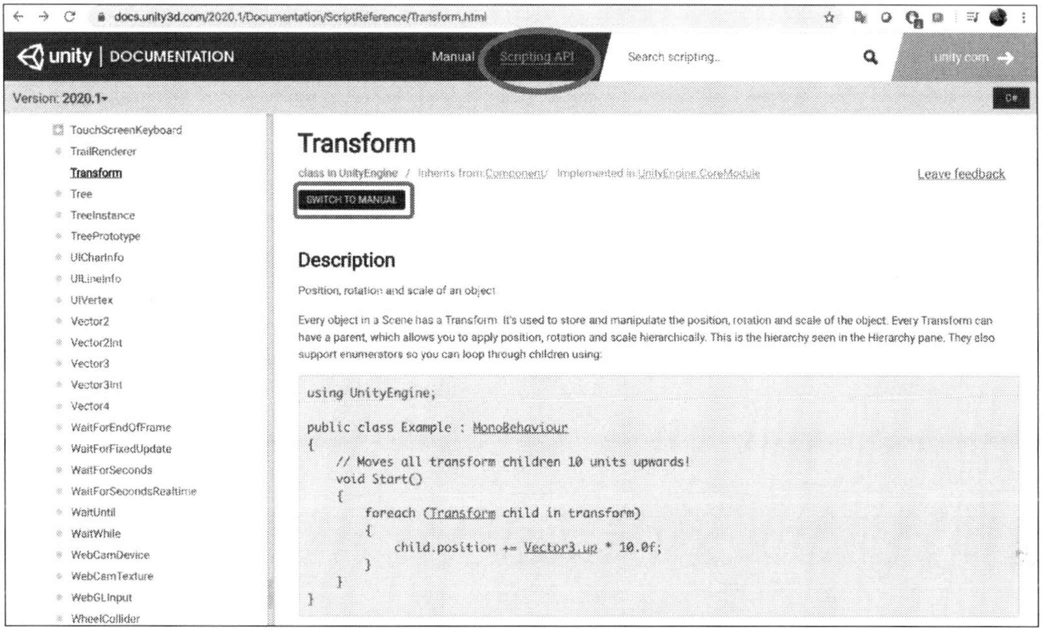


Figure 1.24: Unity scripting documentation with SWITCH TO MANUAL highlighted

As you can see, as well as coding help, there is also an option to switch back to the Reference Manual if necessary.

> The Scripting Reference is a large document because it has to be. However, this doesn't mean you have to memorize it or even be familiar with all of its information to start writing scripts. As the name suggests, it's a reference, not a test.

If you find yourself lost in the documentation, or just out of ideas regarding where to look, you can also find solutions within the rich Unity development community in the following places:

- Unity Forum: `https://forum.unity.com/`
- Unity Answers: `https://answers.unity.com/index.html`
- Unity Discord: `https://discord.com/invite/unity`

On the other side of things, you'll need to know where to find resources on any C# question, which we'll cover next.

# Locating C# resources

Now that we've got our Unity resources taken care of, let's take a look at some of Microsoft's C# resources. For starters, the Microsoft Learn documentation at `https://docs.microsoft.com/en-us/dotnet/csharp` has a ton of great tutorials, quickstart guides, and how-to articles. You can also find great overviews of individual C# topics at `https://docs.microsoft.com/en-us/dotnet/csharp/programming-guide/index`.

However, if you want detailed information on a specific C# language feature, the reference guides are the place to go. These reference guides are an important resource for any C# programmer, but since they aren't always the easiest to navigate, let's take a few minutes to learn how to find what we're looking for.

Let's load up the programming guide link and look up the C# `String` class. Do either of the following:

- Enter `Strings` in the search bar in the top-left corner of the web page
- Scroll down to **Language Sections** and click on the **Strings** link directly:

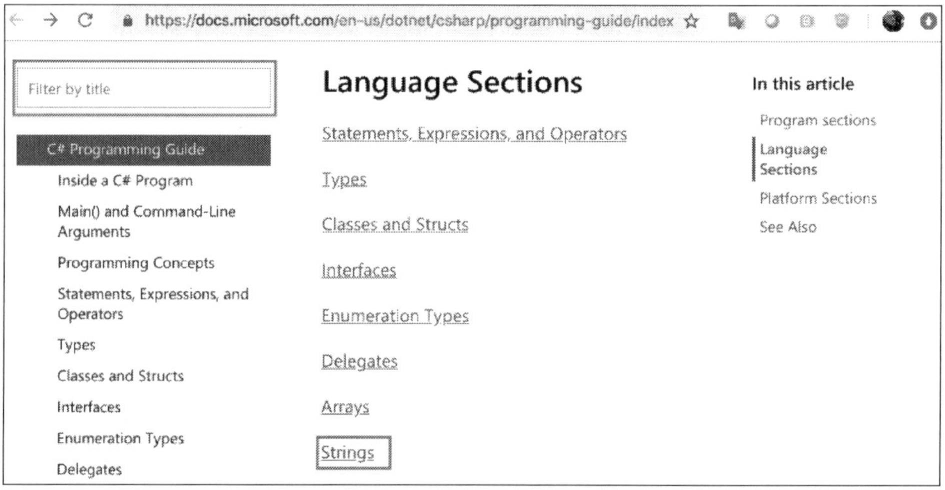


Figure 1.25: Navigating Microsoft's C# reference guide

You should see something like the following for the class description page:

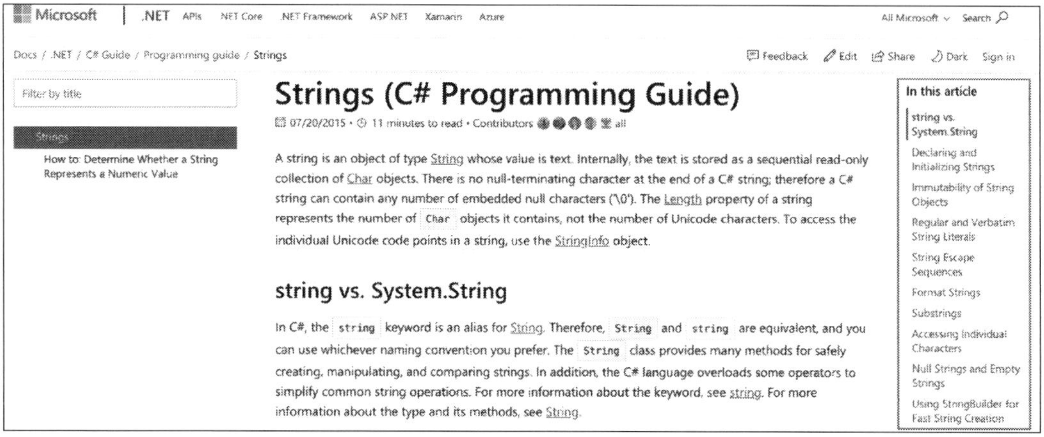


Figure 1.26: Microsoft's Strings (C# Programming Guide) page

Unlike Unity's documentation, the C# reference and scripting information is all bundled up into one, but its saving grace is the subtopic list on the right-hand side. Use it well! It's extremely important to know where to find help when you're stuck or have a question, so be sure to circle back to this section whenever you hit a roadblock.

# Summary

We covered quite a bit of logistical information in this chapter, so I can understand if you're itching to write some code. Starting new projects, creating folders and scripts, and accessing documentation are topics that are easily forgotten in the excitement of a new adventure. Just remember that this chapter has a lot of resources you might need in the coming pages, so don't be afraid to come back and visit. Thinking like a programmer is a muscle: the more you work it, the stronger it gets.

In the next chapter, we'll start laying out the theory, vocabulary, and main concepts you'll need to prime your coding brain. Even though the material is conceptual, we'll still be writing our first lines of code in the `LearningCurve` script. Get ready!

# Pop quiz – dealing with scripts

1. What type of relationship do Unity and Visual Studio share?
2. The Scripting Reference supplies example code in regards to using a particular Unity component or feature. Where can you find more detailed (non-code-related) information about Unity components?
3. The Scripting Reference is a large document. How much of it do you have to memorize before attempting to write a script?
4. When is the best time to name a C# script?

# 2

# The Building Blocks of Programming

Any programming language starts off looking like ancient Greek to the unaccustomed eye, and C# is no exception. The good news is beneath the initial mystery, all programming languages are made up of the same essential building blocks. Variables, methods, and classes (or objects) make up the DNA of conventional programming; understanding these simple concepts opens up an entire world of diverse and complex applications. After all, there are only four different DNA nucleobases in every person on earth; yet, here we are, every one of us a unique organism.

If you are new to programming, there's going to be a lot of information coming at you in this chapter, and this could mark the first lines of code that you've ever written. The point is not to overload your brain with facts and figures; it's to give you a holistic look at the building blocks of programming using examples from everyday life.

This chapter is all about the high-level view of the bits and pieces that make up a program. Getting the hang of how things work before getting into the code directly will not only help you new coders find your feet, but it will also solidify the topics with easy-to-remember references. Ramblings aside, we'll focus on the following topics throughout this chapter:

- Defining variables
- Understanding methods
- Introducing classes

- Working with comments
- Putting the building blocks together

# Defining variables

Let's start with a simple question: what is a variable? Depending on your point of view, there are a few different ways of answering that question:

- **Conceptually**, a variable is the most basic unit of programming, as an atom is to the physical world (excepting string theory). Everything starts with variables, and programs can't exist without them.
- **Technically**, a variable is a tiny section of your computer's memory that holds an assigned value. Every variable keeps track of where its information is stored (this is called a memory address), its value, and its type (for instance, numbers, words, or lists).
- **Practically**, a variable is a container. You can create new ones at will, fill them with stuff, move them around, change what they're holding, and reference them as needed. They can even be empty and still be useful.

> You can find an in-depth explanation of variables in the Microsoft C# documentation at `https://docs.microsoft.com/en-us/dotnet/csharp/language-reference/language-specification/variables`.

A practical real-life example of a variable is a mailbox—remember those?

Figure 2.1: Snapshot of a row of colorful mailboxes

They can hold letters, bills, a picture from your aunt Mabel—anything. The point is that what's in a mailbox can vary: they can have names, hold information (physical mail), and their contents can even be changed if you have the right security clearance. Similarly, variables can hold different kinds of information. Variables in C# can hold strings (text), integers (numbers), and even Booleans (binary values that represent either true or false).

# Names are important

Referring to *Figure 2.1*, if I asked you to go over and open the mailbox, the first thing you'd probably ask is: which one? If I said the Smith family mailbox, or the sunflower mailbox, or even the droopy mailbox on the far right, then you'd have the necessary context to open the mailbox I was referencing. Similarly, when you are creating variables, you have to give them unique names that you can reference later. We'll get into the specifics of proper formatting and descriptive naming in *Chapter 3, Diving into Variables, Types, and Methods*.

# Variables act as placeholders

When you create and name a variable, you are creating a placeholder for the value that you want to store. Let's take the following simple math equation as an example:

```
2 + 9 = 11
```

Okay, no mystery here, but what if we wanted the number `9` to be its variable? Consider the following code block:

```
MyVariable = 9
```

Now we can use the variable name, `MyVariable`, as a substitute for `9` anywhere we need it:

```
2 + MyVariable = 11
```

> If you're wondering whether variables have other rules or regulations, they do. We'll get to those in the next chapter, so sit tight.

Even though this example isn't real C# code, it illustrates the power of variables and their use as placeholder references. In the next section you'll start creating variables of your own, so keep going!

Alright, enough theory—let's create a real variable in the `LearningCurve` script we created in *Chapter 1, Getting to Know Your Environment*:

1. Double-click on `LearningCurve.cs` from the Unity project window to open it in Visual Studio.
2. Add a space between lines 6 and 7 and add the following line of code to declare a new variable:

   ```
   public int CurrentAge = 30;
   ```

3. Inside the `Start` method, add two debug logs to print out the following calculations:

   ```
   Debug.Log(30 + 1);
   Debug.Log(CurrentAge + 1);
   ```

Let's break down the code we just added. First, we created a new variable called `CurrentAge` and assigned it a value of `30`. Then, we added two debug logs to print out the result of `30 + 1` and `CurrentAge + 1` to show how variables are storage for values. They can be used the exact same way as the values themselves.

It's also important to note that `public` variables appear in the Unity Inspector, while `private` ones don't. Don't worry about the syntax right now—just make sure your script is the same as the script that is shown in the following screenshot:

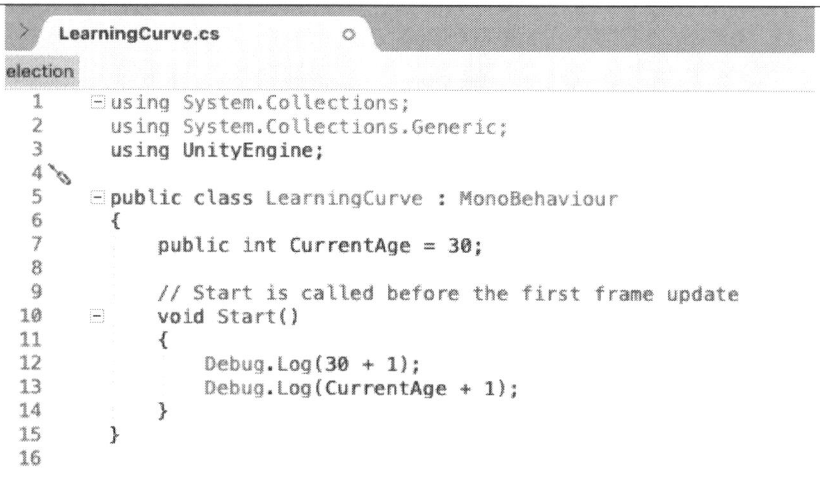


Figure 2.2: LearningCurve script open in Visual Studio

To finish, save the file using **Editor** | **File** | **Save**.

For scripts to run in Unity, they have to be attached to *GameObjects* in the scene. The sample scene in *Hero Born* has a camera and directional light by default, which provides the lighting for the scene, so let's attach `LearningCurve` to the camera to keep things simple:

1. Drag and drop `LearningCurve.cs` onto the **Main Camera**.
2. Select the **Main Camera** so that it appears in the **Inspector** panel, and verify that the `LearningCurve.cs` (Script) component is attached properly.
3. Click play and watch for the output in the **Console** panel:

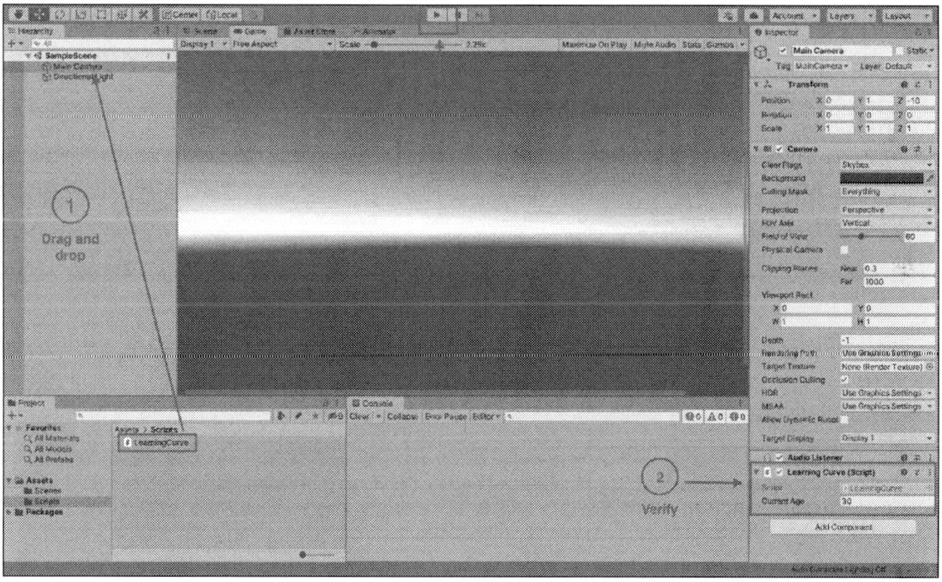


Figure 2.3: Unity Editor window with callouts for dragging and dropping scripts

The `Debug.Log()` statements printed out the result of the simple math equations we put in between the parentheses. As you can see in the following **Console** screenshot, the equation that used our variable, `CurrentAge`, worked the same as if it were a real number:

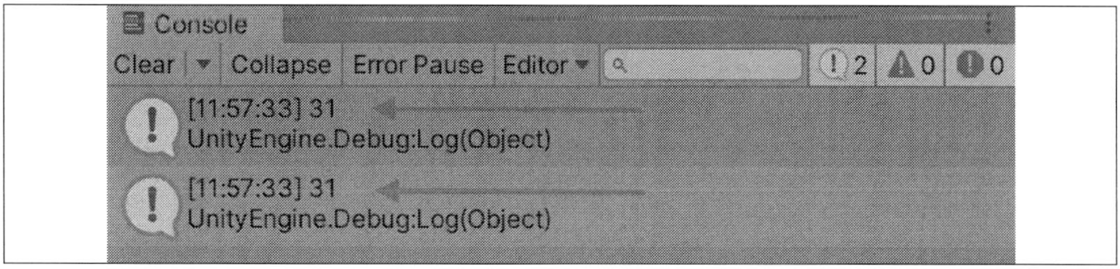


Figure 2.4: Unity console with debug output from the attached script

We'll get into how Unity converts C# scripts into components at the end of this chapter, but first, let's work on changing the value of one of our variables.

Since `CurrentAge` was declared as a variable on line 7 as shown in *Figure 2.2*, the value it stores can be changed. The updated value will then trickle down to wherever the variable is used in code; let's see this in action:

1. Stop the game by clicking the **Pause** button if the scene is still running
2. Change **Current Age** to `18` in the **Inspector** panel and play the scene again, looking at the new output in the **Console** panel:

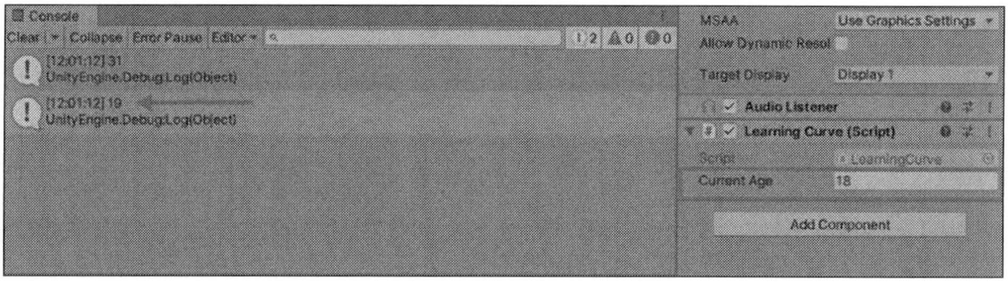

Figure 2.5: Unity console with debug logs and the LearningCurve script attached to Main Camera

The first output will still be `31` because we didn't change anything in the script, but the second output is now `19` because we changed the value of `CurrentAge` in the Inspector.

> The goal here wasn't to go over variable syntax but to show how variables act as containers that can be created once and referenced elsewhere. We'll go into more detail in *Chapter 3, Diving into Variables, Types, and Methods.*

Now that we know how to create variables in C# and assign them values, we're ready to dive into the next important programming building block: methods!

# Understanding methods

On their own, variables can't do much more than keep track of their assigned values. While this is vital, they are not very useful on their own in terms of creating meaningful applications. So, how do we go about creating actions and driving behavior in our code? The short answer is by using methods.

Before we get to what methods are and how to use them, we should clarify a small point of terminology. In the world of programming, you'll commonly see the terms *method* and *function* used interchangeably, especially in regards to Unity.

Since C# is an object-oriented language (this is something that we'll cover in *Chapter 5, Working with Classes, Structs, and OOP*), we'll be using the term *method* for the rest of the book to conform to standard C# guidelines.

> When you come across the word function in the Scripting Reference or any other documentation, think method.

# Methods drive actions

Similarly to variables, defining programming methods can be tediously long-winded or dangerously brief; here's another three-pronged approach to consider:

- **Conceptually**, methods are how work gets done in an application.
- **Technically**, a method is a block of code containing executable statements that run when the method is called by name. Methods can take in arguments (also called parameters), which can be used inside the method's scope.
- **Practically**, a method is a container for a set of instructions that run every time it's executed. These containers can also take in variables as inputs, which can only be referenced inside the method itself.

Taken all together, methods are the bones of any program—they connect everything and almost everything is built off of their structure.

> You can find an in-depth guide to methods in the Microsoft C# documentation at `https://docs.microsoft.com/en-us/dotnet/csharp/programming-guide/classes-and-structs/methods`.

# Methods are placeholders too

Let's take an oversimplified example of adding two numbers together to drive the concept home. When writing a script, you're essentially laying down lines of code for the computer to execute in sequential order. The first time you need to add two numbers together, you could just add them like in the following code block:

```
SomeNumber + AnotherNumber
```

But then you conclude that these numbers need to be added together somewhere else.

Instead of copying and pasting the same line of code, which results in sloppy or "spaghetti" code and should be avoided at all costs, you can create a named method that will take care of this action:

```
AddNumbers()
{
    SomeNumber + AnotherNumber
}
```

Now AddNumbers is holding a place in memory, just like a variable; however, instead of a value, it holds a block of instructions. Using the name of the method (or calling it) anywhere in a script puts the stored instructions at your fingertips without having to repeat any code.

> If you find yourself writing the same lines of code over and over, you're likely missing a chance to simplify or condense repeated actions into common methods.
>
> This produces what programmers jokingly call spaghetti code because it can get messy. You'll also hear programmers refer to a solution called the **Don't Repeat Yourself** (**DRY**) principle, which is a mantra you should keep in mind.

As before, once we've seen a new concept in pseudocode, it's best if we implement it ourselves, which is what we'll do in the next section to drive it home.

Let's open up LearningCurve again and see how a method works in C#. Just like with the variables example, you'll want to copy the code into your script exactly as it appears in the following screenshot. I've deleted the previous example code to make things neater, but you can, of course, keep it in your script for reference:

1. Open up LearningCurve in Visual Studio.
2. Add a new variable to line 8:

   ```
   public int AddedAge = 1;
   ```

3. Add a new method to line 16 that adds CurrentAge and AddedAge together and prints out the result:

   ```
   void ComputeAge()
   {
       Debug.Log(CurrentAge + AddedAge);
   }
   ```

4. Call the new method inside `Start` with the following line:

```
ComputeAge();
```

Double-check that your code looks like the following screenshot before you run the script in Unity:

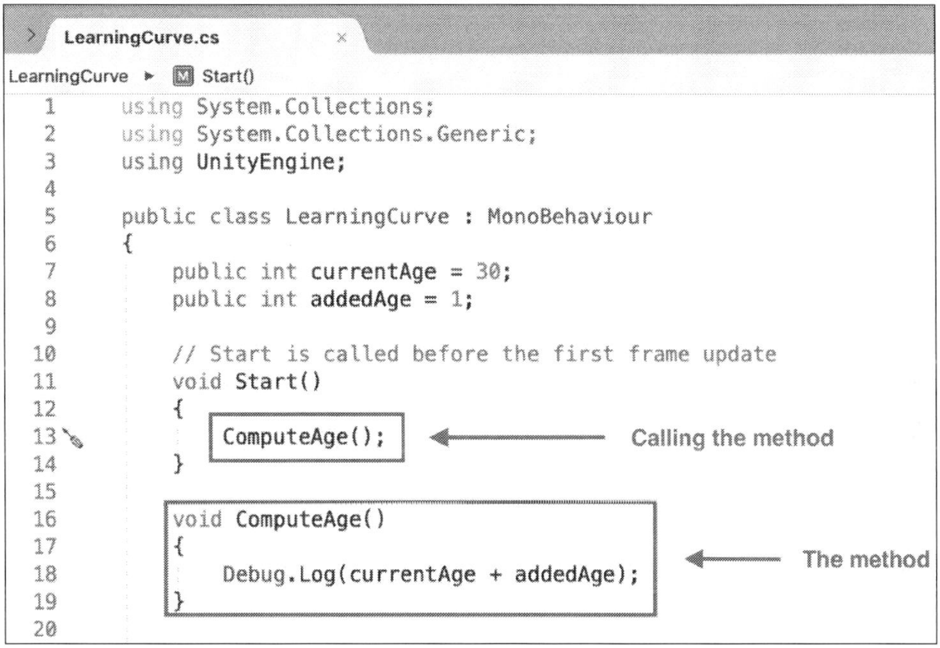


Figure 2.6: LearningCurve with new ComputeAge method

5. Save the file, and then go back and hit play in Unity to see the new **Console** output.

You defined your first method on lines 16 to 19 and called it on line 13. Now, wherever `ComputeAge()` is called, the two variables will be added together and printed to the console, even if their values change. Remember, you set `CurrentAge` to `18` in the Unity Inspector, and the Inspector value will always override the value in a C# script:

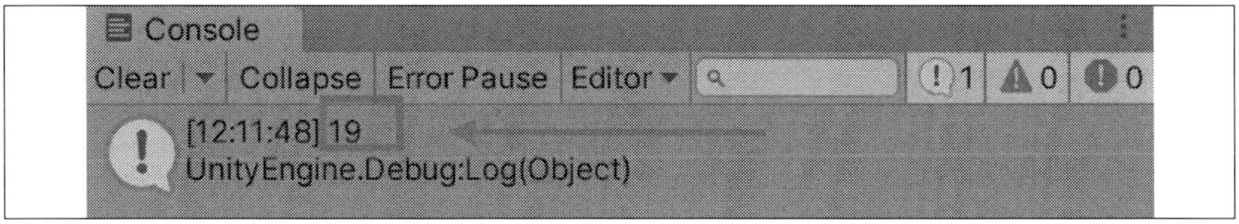


Figure 2.7: Console output from changing the variable value in the Inspector

Go ahead and try out different variable values in the **Inspector** panel to see this in action! More details on the actual code syntax of what you just wrote are coming up in the next chapter.

With a bird's-eye view of methods under our belts, we're ready to tackle the biggest topic in the programming landscape—classes!

# Introducing classes

We've seen how variables store information and how methods perform actions, but our programming toolkit is still somewhat limited. We need a way of creating a sort of super container, containing variables and methods that can be referenced from within the container itself. Enter classes:

- **Conceptually**, a class holds related information, actions, and behaviors inside a single container. They can even communicate with each other.
- **Technically**, classes are data structures. They can contain variables, methods, and other programmatic information, all of which can be referenced when an object of the class is created.
- **Practically**, a class is a blueprint. It sets out the rules and regulations for any object (called an instance) created using the class blueprint.

You've probably realized that classes surround us not only in Unity but in the real world as well. Next, we'll take a look at the most common Unity class and how classes function in the wild.

> You can find an in-depth guide to classes in the Microsoft C# documentation at `https://docs.microsoft.com/en-us/dotnet/csharp/fundamentals/types/classes`.

## A common Unity class

Before you wonder what a class looks like in C#, you should know that you've been working with a class this whole chapter. By default, every script created in Unity is a class, which you can see from the `class` keyword on line 5:

```
public class LearningCurve: MonoBehaviour
```

`MonoBehaviour` just means that this class can be attached to a GameObject in the Unity scene.

Classes can exist on their own, which we'll see when we create standalone classes in *Chapter 5, Working with Classes, Structs, and OOP*.

> The terms script and class are sometimes used interchangeably in Unity resources. For consistency, I'll be referring to C# files as scripts if they're attached to GameObjects and as classes if they are standalone.

# Classes are blueprints

For our last example, let's think about a local post office. It's a separate, self-contained environment that has properties, such as a physical address (a variable), and the ability to execute actions, such as sending out your mail (methods).

This makes a post office a great example of a potential class that we can outline in the following block of pseudocode:

```
public class PostOffice
{
    // Variables
    public string address = "1234 Letter Opener Dr."

    // Methods
    DeliverMail() {}
    SendMail() {}
}
```

The main takeaway here is that when information and behaviors follow a predefined blueprint, complex actions and inter-class communication become possible. For instance, if we had another class that wanted to send a letter through our `PostOffice` class, it wouldn't have to wonder where to go to fire this action. It could simply call the `SendMail` function from the `PostOffice` class, as follows:

```
PostOffice().SendMail()
```

Alternatively, you could use it to look up the address of the post office so you know where to post your letters:

```
PostOffice().address
```

If you're wondering about the use of periods (called dot notation) between words, we'll be diving into that in the next section—hold tight.

# Communication among classes

Up until now, we've described classes and, by extension, Unity components as separate standalone entities; in reality, they are deeply intertwined. You'd be hard-pressed to create any kind of meaningful software application without invoking some kind of interaction or communication between classes.

If you remember the post office example from earlier, the example code made use of periods (or dots) to reference classes, variables, and methods. If you think of classes as directories of information, then dot notation is the indexing tool:

```
PostOffice().Address
```

Any variables, methods, or other data types within a class can be accessed with dot notation. This applies to nested, or subclass, information as well, but we'll tackle all those subjects when we get to *Chapter 5, Working with Classes, Structs, and OOP*.

Dot notation is also what drives communication between classes. Whenever a class needs information about another class or wants to execute one of its methods, dot notation is used:

```
PostOffice().DeliverMail()
```

> Dot notation is sometimes referred to as the `.` operator, so don't be thrown off if you see it mentioned this way in documentation.

If dot notation doesn't quite click with you yet, don't worry, it will. It's the bloodstream of the entire programming body, carrying information and context wherever it's needed.

Now that you know a little more about classes, let's talk about the tool you'll use the most in your programming career—comments!

# Working with comments

You might have noticed that `LearningCurve` has an odd line of text (**10** in *Figure 2.6*) starting with two forward slashes, which were created by default with the script.

These are code comments! In C#, there are a few ways that you can use to create comments, and Visual Studio (and other code editing applications) will often make it even easier with built-in shortcuts.

Some professionals wouldn't call commenting an essential building block of programming, but I'll have to respectfully disagree. Correctly commenting out your code with meaningful information is one of the most fundamental habits a new programmer can develop.

## Single-line comments

The following single-line comment is like the one we've included in `LearningCurve`:

```
// This is a single-line comment
```

Visual Studio doesn't compile lines starting with two forward slashes (without empty space) as code, so you can use them as much as needed to explain your code to others or your future self.

## Multi-line comments

Since it's in the name, you'd be right to assume that single-line comments only apply to one line of code. If you want multi-line comments, you'll need to use a forward slash and an asterisk, (/* and */ as opening and closing characters respectively) around the comment text:

```
/* this is a
      multi-line comment */
```

> You can also comment and uncomment blocks of code by highlighting them and using the *Cmd* + / shortcut on macOS and *Ctrl* + *K* + *C* on Windows.

Visual Studio also provides a handy auto-generated commenting feature; type in three forward slashes on the line preceding any line of code (variables, methods, classes, and more) and a summary comment block will appear.

Seeing example comments is good, but putting them in your code is always better. It's never too early to start commenting!

# Adding comments

Open up `LearningCurve` and add in three backslashes above the `ComputeAge()` method:

```
        /// <summary>
        /// Time for action - adding comments
        /// Computes a modified age integer
        /// </summary>
        void ComputeAge()
        {
            Debug.Log(CurrentAge + AddedAge);
        }
    }
```

Figure 2.8: Triple-line comment automatically generated for a method

You should see a three-line comment with a description of the method generated by Visual Studio from the method's name, sandwiched between two `<summary>` tags. You can, of course, change the text, or add new lines by hitting *Enter* just as you would in a text document; just make sure not to touch the `<summary>` tags or Visual Studio won't recognize the comments correctly.

The useful part about these detailed comments is clear when you want to know something about a method you've written. If you've used a triple forward slash comment, all you need to do is hover over the method name anywhere it's called within a class or script, and Visual Studio will pop your summary:

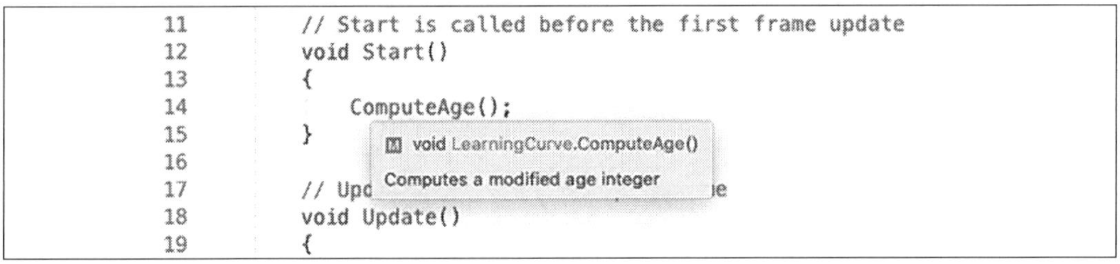


Figure 2.9: Visual Studio pop-up info box with the comment summary

Your basic programming toolkit is now complete (well, the theory drawer, at least). However, we still need to understand how everything we've learned in this chapter applies in the Unity game engine, which is what we'll be focusing on in the next section!

# Putting the building blocks together

With the building blocks squared away, it's time to do a little Unity-specific housekeeping before wrapping up this chapter. Specifically, we need to know more about how Unity handles C# scripts attached to game objects.

For this example, we'll keep using our `LearningCurve` script and Main Camera GameObject.

# Scripts become components

All GameObject components are scripts, whether they're written by you or the good people at Unity. The only difference is that Unity-specific components such as `Transform`, and their respective scripts just aren't supposed to be edited by users.

The moment a script that you have created is dropped onto a GameObject, it becomes another component of that object, which is why it appears in the **Inspector** panel. To Unity, it walks, talks, and acts like any other component, complete with public variables underneath the component that can be changed at any time. Even though we aren't supposed to edit the components provided by Unity, we can still access their properties and methods, making them powerful development tools.

> Unity also makes some automatic readability adjustments when a script becomes a component. You might have noticed in *Figures 2.3* and *2.5* that when we added `LearningCurve` to Main Camera, Unity displayed it as `Learning Curve`, with `CurrentAge` changing to `Current Age`.

We looked at how to update a variable in the **Inspector** panel in the *Variables act as placeholders* section, but it's important to touch on how this works in more detail. There are three situations in which you can modify a property value:

- In **Play Mode** in the Unity Editor window
- In **Development Mode** in the Unity Editor window
- In the Visual Studio code editor

Changes made in Play Mode take effect in real time, which is great for testing and fine-tuning gameplay. However, it's important to note that any changes made while in Play Mode will be lost when you stop the game and return to Development Mode.

When you're in Development Mode, any changes that you make to the variables will be saved by Unity. This means that if you were to quit Unity and then restart it, the changes would be retained.

> The changes that you make to values in the **Inspector** panel while in Play Mode do not modify your script, but they will override any values you had assigned in your script when in Development Mode.

Any changes made in Play Mode will always reset automatically when you stop Play Mode. If you need to undo any changes made in the **Inspector** panel, you can reset the script to its default (sometimes called initial) values. Click on the three vertical dots icon to the right of any component, and then select **Reset**, as shown in the following screenshot:

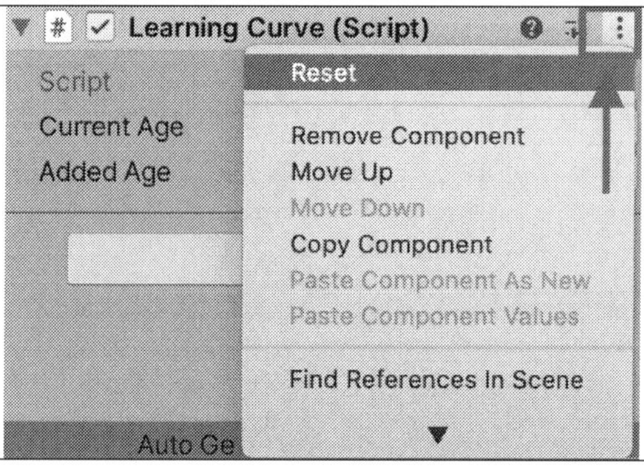


Figure 2.10: Script reset option in the Inspector

This should give you some peace of mind—if your variables get out of hand, there's always the hard reset.

# A helping hand from MonoBehaviour

Since C# scripts are classes, how does Unity know to make some scripts components and not others? The short answer is that `LearningCurve` (and any script created in Unity) inherits from `MonoBehaviour` (a default class provided by Unity). This tells Unity that the C# class can be transformed into a component.

The topic of class inheritance is a bit advanced for this point of your programming journey; think of it as the `MonoBehaviour` class lending a few of its variables and methods to `LearningCurve`. *Chapter 5, Working with Classes, Struct, and OOP*, will cover class inheritance in practical detail.

The `Start()` and `Update()` methods that we've used belong to `MonoBehaviour`, which Unity runs automatically on any script attached to a GameObject. The `Start()` method runs once when the scene starts playing, while the `Update()` method runs once per frame (depending on the frame rate of your machine).

Now that your familiarity with Unity's documentation has gotten a nice bump, I've put together a short optional challenge for you to tackle!

## Hero's trial – MonoBehaviour in the Scripting API

Now it's time for you to get comfortable using the Unity documentation on your own, and what better way than to look up some of the common `MonoBehaviour` methods:

- Try searching for the `Start()` and `Update()` methods in the Scripting API to gain a better understanding of what they do in Unity, and when
- If you're feeling brave, go the extra step and have a look at the `MonoBehaviour` class in the manual for a more detailed explanation

# Summary

We've come a long way in a few short pages, but understanding the overarching theory of fundamental concepts such as variables, methods, and classes will give you a strong foundation to build on. Bear in mind that these building blocks have very real counterparts in the real world. Variables hold values like mailboxes hold letters; methods store instructions like recipes, to be followed for a predefined result; and classes are blueprints just like real blueprints. You can't build a house without a well-thought-out design to follow if you expect it to stay standing.

The rest of this book will take you on a deep dive into C# syntax from scratch, starting with more detail in the next chapter on how to create variables, manage value types, and work with simple and complex methods.

# Pop quiz – C# building blocks

1. What is the main purpose of a variable?
2. What role do methods play in scripts?
3. How does a script become a component?
4. What is the purpose of dot notation?

# 3

# Diving into Variables, Types, and Methods

The initial steps into any programming language are plagued with a fundamental issue—you can understand the words being typed out, but not the meaning behind them. Normally, this would be cause for a paradox, but programming is a special case.

C# is not its own language; it's written in English. The discrepancy between the words you use every day and the code in Visual Studio comes from missing context, which is something that has to be learned all over again. You know how to say and spell the words used in C#, but what you don't know is where, when, why, and, most importantly, how they make up the syntax of the language.

This chapter marks our departure from programming theory and the beginning of our journey into actual coding. We'll talk about accepted formatting, debugging techniques, and putting together more complex examples of variables and methods. There's a lot of ground to cover, but by the time you reach the last quiz, you'll be comfortable with the following high-level topics:

- Writing proper C#
- Debugging your code
- Understanding variables
- Introducing operators
- Defining methods

Let's get started!

# Writing proper C#

Lines of code function like sentences, meaning they need to have some sort of separating or ending character. Every line of C#, called a statement, *must* end with a semicolon to separate them for the code compiler to process.

However, there's a catch that you need to be aware of. Unlike the written word we're all familiar with, a C# statement doesn't technically have to be on a single line; whitespace and newlines are ignored by the code compiler. For example, a simple variable could be written like this:

```
public int FirstName = "Harrison";
```

Alternatively, it could also be written as follows:

```
public
int
FirstName
=
"Harrison";
```

These two code snippets are both perfectly acceptable to Visual Studio, but the second option is highly discouraged in the software community as it makes code extremely hard to read. The idea is to write your programs as efficiently and clearly as possible.

> There will be times when a statement will be too long to reasonably fit on a single line, but those are few and far between. Just make sure that it's formatted in a way someone else could understand, and don't forget the semicolon.

The second formatting rule you need to drill into your coding muscle memory is the use of curly brackets or braces: {}. Methods, classes, and interfaces all need a set of curly brackets after their declaration. We'll talk about each of these in-depth later on, but it's important to get the standard formatting in your head early on.

The traditional practice in C# is to include each bracket on a new line, as shown in the following method:

```
public void MethodName()
{

}
```

However, you might see the first curly bracket located on the same line as the declaration out in the wild. It's all down to personal preference:

```
public void MethodName() {

}
```

While this isn't something to tear your hair out over, the important thing is to be consistent. In this book, we'll stick with "pure" C# code, which will always put each bracket on a new line, while C# examples that have to do with Unity and game development will often follow the second example.

Good, consistent formatting style is paramount when starting in programming, but so is being able to see the fruits of your work. In the next section, we'll talk about how to print out variables and information straight to the Unity console.

# Debugging your code

While we're working through practical examples, we'll need a way to print out information and feedback to the **Console** window in the Unity editor. The programmatic term for this is debugging, and both C# and Unity provide helper methods to make this process easier for developers. You already debugged your code from the last chapter, but we didn't go into much detail about how it actually works. Let's fix that.

Whenever I ask you to debug or print something out, use one of the following methods:

- For simple text or individual variables, use the standard `Debug.Log()` method. The text needs to be inside a set of parentheses, and variables can be used directly with no added characters; for example:

  ```
  Debug.Log("Text goes here.");
  Debug.Log(CurrentAge);
  ```

  This will produce the following in the **Console** panel:

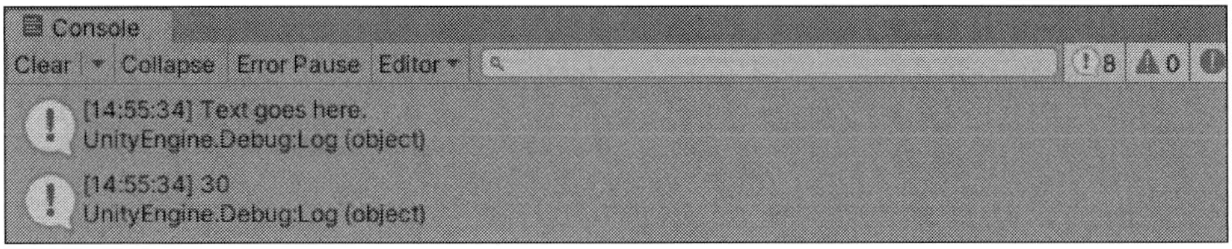


Figure 3.1: Observing Debug.Log output

- For more complex debugging, use `Debug.LogFormat()`. This will let you place variables inside the printed text by using placeholders. These are marked with a pair of curly brackets, each containing an index. An index is a regular number, starting at 0 and increasing sequentially by 1. In the following example, the `{0}` placeholder is replaced with the `CurrentAge` value, `{1}` with `FirstName`, and so on:

```
Debug.LogFormat("Text goes here, add {0} and {1} as variable
  placeholders", CurrentAge, FirstName);
```

  This will produce the following in the **Console** panel:

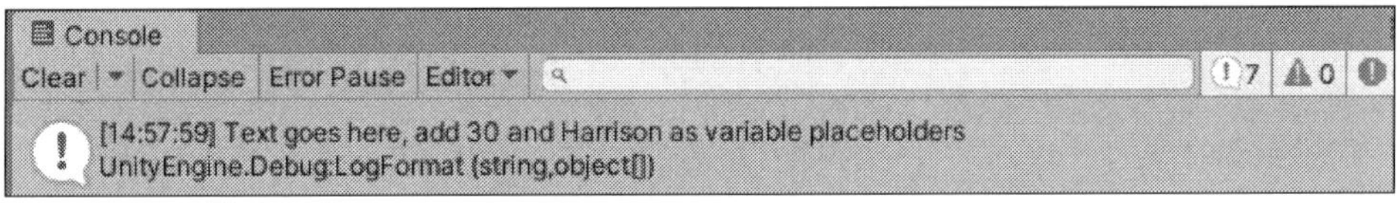


Figure 3.2: Observing Debug.LogFormat output

You might have noticed that we're using **dot notation** in our debugging techniques, and you'd be right! Debug is the class we're using, and `Log()` and `LogFormat()` are different methods that we can use from that class. More on this at the end of this chapter.

With the power of debugging under our belts, we can safely move on and do a deeper dive into how variables are declared, as well as the different ways that syntax can play out.

# Understanding variables

In the previous chapter, we saw how variables are written and touched on the high-level functionality that they provide. However, we're still missing the syntax that makes all of that possible.

# Declaring variables

Variables don't just appear at the top of a C# script; they have to be declared according to certain rules and requirements. At its most basic level, a variable statement needs to satisfy the following requirements:

- The type of data the variable will store needs to be specified
- The variable has to have a unique name
- If there is an assigned value, it must match the specified type

- The variable declaration needs to end with a semicolon

The result of adhering to these rules is the following syntax:

```
dataType UniqueName = value;
```

> Variables need unique names to avoid conflicts with words that have already been taken by C#, which are called keywords. You can find the full list of protected keywords at `https://docs.microsoft.com/en-us/dotnet/csharp/language-reference/keywords/index`.

This is simple, neat, and efficient. However, a programming language wouldn't be useful in the long run if there was only one way of creating something as pervasive as variables. Complex applications and games have different use cases and scenarios, all of which have unique C# syntax.

## Type and value declarations

The most common scenario for creating variables is one that has all of the required information available when the declaration is made. For instance, if we knew a player's age, storing it would be as easy as doing the following:

```
int CurrentAge = 32;
```

Here, all of the basic requirements have been met:

- A data type is specified, which is `int` (short for integer)
- A unique name is used, which is `CurrentAge`
- `32` is an integer, which matches the specified data type
- The statement ends with a semicolon

However, there will be scenarios where you'll want to declare a variable without knowing its value right away. We'll talk about this topic in the following section.

## Type-only declarations

Consider another scenario—you know the type of data you want a variable to store and its name, but not its value. The value will be computed and assigned somewhere else, but you still need to declare the variable at the top of the script. This situation is perfect for a type-only declaration:

```
int CurrentAge;
```

Only the type (`int`) and unique name (`CurrentAge`) are defined, but the statement is still valid because we've followed the rules. With no assigned value, default values will be assigned according to the variable's type. In this case, `CurrentAge` will be set to `0`, which matches the `int` type. As soon as the actual value of the variable becomes available, it can easily be set in a separate statement by referencing the variable name and assigning it a value:

```
CurrentAge = 32;
```

> You can find a complete list of all C# types and their default values at `https://docs.microsoft.com/en-us/dotnet/csharp/language-reference/builtin-types/default-values`.

At this point, you might be asking why, so far, our variables haven't included the `public` keyword, called an *access modifier*, which we saw in earlier scripting examples. The answer is that we didn't have the necessary foundation to talk about them with any clarity. Now that we have that foundation, it's time to revisit them in detail.

# Using access modifiers

Now that the basic syntax is no longer a mystery, let's get into the finer details of variable statements. Since we read code from left to right, it makes sense to begin our variable deep dive with the keyword that traditionally comes first—an access modifier.

Take a quick look back at the variables we used in the preceding chapter in `LearningCurve` and you'll see they had an extra keyword at the front of their statements: `public`. This is the variable's access modifier. Think of it as a security setting, determining who and what can access the variable's information.

> Any variable that isn't marked `public` is defaulted to `private` and won't show up in the Unity Inspector panel.

If you include a modifier, the updated syntax recipe we put together at the beginning of this chapter will look like this:

```
accessModifier dataType UniqueName = value;
```

While explicit access modifiers aren't necessary when declaring a variable, it's a good habit to get into as a new programmer. That extra word goes a long way toward readability and professionalism in your code.

There are four main access modifiers available in C#, but the two you'll be working with most often as a beginner are the following:

- **Public**: This is available to any script without restriction.
- **Private**: This is only available in the class they're created in (which is called the containing class). Any variable without an access modifier defaults to private.

The two advanced modifiers have the following characteristics:

- **Protected**: Accessible from their containing class or types derived from it
- **Internal**: Only available in the current assembly

There are specific use cases for each of these modifiers, but until we get to the advanced chapters, don't worry about **protected** and **internal**.

> Two combined modifiers also exist, but we won't be using them in this book. You can find more information about them at `https://docs.microsoft.com/en-us/dotnet/csharp/language-reference/keywords/access-modifiers`.

Let's try out some access modifiers of our own! Just like information in real life, some data needs to be protected or shared with specific people. If there's no need for a variable to be changed in the **Inspector** window or accessed from other scripts, it's a good candidate for a private access modifier.

Perform the following steps to update `LearningCurve`:

1. Change the access modifier in front of `CurrentAge` from `public` to `private` and save the file.
2. Go back into Unity, select the Main Camera, and take a look at what changed in the `LearningCurve` section:

Figure 3.3: LearningCurve script component attached to the Main Camera

Since `CurrentAge` is now private, it's no longer visible in the **Inspector** window and can only be accessed within the `LearningCurve` script in code. If we click play, the script will still work exactly as it did before.

This is a good start on our journey into variables, but we still need to know more about what kinds of data they can store. This is where data types come in, which we'll look at in the next section.

# Working with types

Assigning a specific type to a variable is an important choice, one that trickles down into every interaction a variable has over its entire lifespan. Since C# is what's called a *strongly-typed* or *type-safe* language, every variable has to have a data type without exception. This means that there are specific rules when it comes to performing operations with certain types, and regulations when converting a given variable type into another.

## Common built-in types

All data types in C# trickle down (or *derive*, in programmatic terms) from a common ancestor: `System.Object`. This hierarchy, called the **Common Type System** (**CTS**), means that different types have a lot of shared functionality. The following table lays out some of the most common data type options and the values they store:

| Type | Contents of the variable |
|---|---|
| int | A simple integer, such as the number 3 |
| float | A number with a decimal, such as the number 3.14 |
| string | Characters in double quotes, such as, "Watch me go now" |
| bool | A boolean, either **true** or **false** |

Figure 3.4: Common data types for variables

In addition to specifying the kind of value a variable can store, types contain added information about themselves, including the following:

- Required storage space
- Minimum and maximum values
- Allowed operations
- Location in memory
- Accessible methods
- Base (derived) type

If this seems overwhelming, take a deep breath. Working with all of the types C# offers is a perfect example of using documentation over memorization. Pretty soon, using even the most complex custom types will feel like second nature.

> You can find a complete list of all of the C# built-in types and their specifications at `https://docs.microsoft.com/en-us/dotnet/csharp/programming-guide/types/index`.

Before the list of types becomes a sticking point, it's best to experiment with them. After all, the best way to learn something new is to use it, break it, and then learn to fix it.

Go ahead and open up `LearningCurve` and add a new variable for each type in the preceding chart from the *Common built-in types* section. The names and values you use are up to you; just make sure they're marked as public so we can see them in the Inspector window. If you need inspiration, take a look at my code:

```
public class LearningCurve : MonoBehaviour
{
    private int CurrentAge = 30;
    public int AddedAge = 1;

    public float Pi = 3.14f;
    public string FirstName = "Harrison";
    public bool IsAuthor = true;

    // Start is called before the first frame update
    void Start()
    {
        ComputeAge();
    }

    /// <summary>
    /// Time for action - adding comments
    /// Computes a modified age integer
    /// </summary>
    void ComputeAge()
    {
        Debug.Log(CurrentAge + AddedAge);
    }
}
```

> When dealing with string types, the actual text value needs to be inside a pair of double quotes, while float values need to end with a lowercase `f`, as you can see with `FirstName` and `piFirstName`.

All our different variable types are now visible. Take note of the `bool` variable that Unity displays as a checkbox (true is checked and false is unchecked).

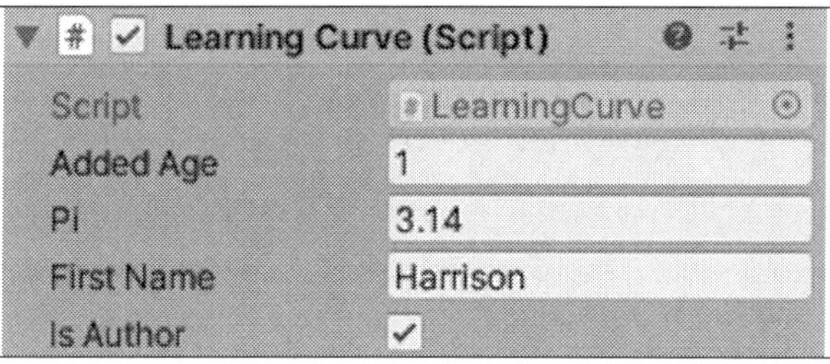


Figure 3.5: LearningCurve script component with common variable types

Remember, any variables you declare as private won't show up in the Inspector window. Before we move on to conversions, we need to touch on a common and powerful application of the string data type; namely, the creation of strings that have variables interspersed at will.

While number types behave as you'd expect from grade school math, strings are a different story. It's possible to insert variables and literal values directly into text by starting with a `$` character, which is called string interpolation. You've already used an interpolated string in your `LogFormat()` debugging; adding the `$` character lets you use them anywhere!

Let's create a simple interpolated string of our own inside `LearningCurve` to see this in action. Print out the interpolated string inside the `Start()` method directly after `ComputeAge()` is called:

```
void Start()
{
    ComputeAge();

    Debug.Log($"A string can have variables like {FirstName} inserted
directly!");
}
```

Thanks to the `$` character and curly brackets, the value of `FirstName` is treated as a value and is printed out inside the interpolated string. Without this special formatting, the string would just include `FirstName` as text instead of the variable value.

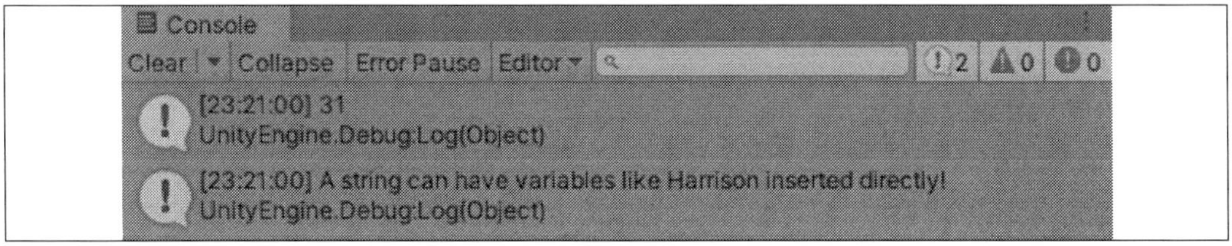


Figure 3.6: Console showing debug log output

It's also possible to create interpolated strings using the + operator, which we'll talk about in the *Introducing operators* section.

# Type conversions

We've already seen that variables can only hold values of their declared types, but there will be situations where you'll need to combine variables of different types. In programming terminology, these are called conversions, and they come in two main flavors:

- **Implicit** conversions take place automatically, usually when a smaller value will fit into another variable type without any rounding. For example, any integer can be implicitly converted into a `double` or `float` value without additional code:

  ```
  int MyInteger = 3;
  float MyFloat = MyInteger;

  Debug.Log(MyInteger);
  Debug.Log(MyFloat);
  ```

  The output in the **Console** pane can be seen in the following screenshot:

  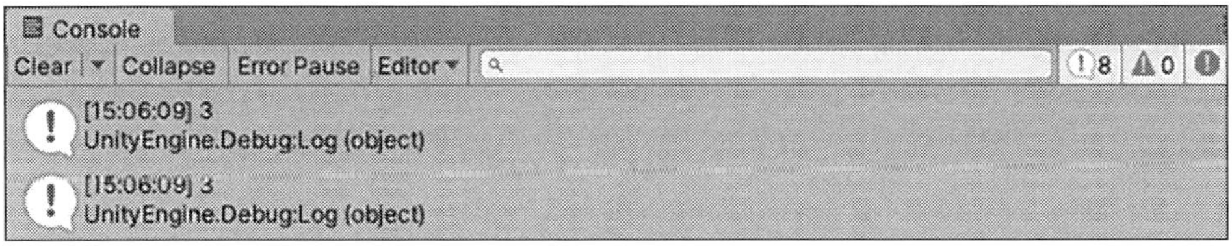
  

  Figure 3.7: Implicit type conversion debug log output

- **Explicit** conversions are needed when there is a risk of losing a variable's information during the conversion. For example, if we wanted to convert a `double` value into an `int` value, we would have to explicitly cast (convert) it by adding the destination type in parentheses before the value we want to convert.

- This tells the compiler that we are aware that data (or precision) might be lost:

```
int ExplicitConversion = (int)3.14;
```

  In this explicit conversion, `3.14` would be rounded down to `3`, losing the decimal values:

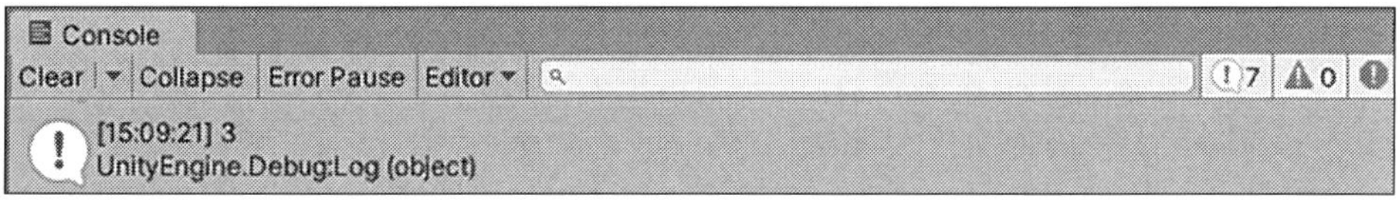


Figure 3.8: Explicit type conversion debug log output

> C# provides built-in methods for explicitly converting values to common types. For example, any type can be converted into a string value with the `ToString()` method, while the `Convert` class can handle more complicated conversions. You can find more info about these features under the *Methods* section at `https://docs.microsoft.com/en-us/dotnet/api/system.convert?view=netframework-4.7.2`.

So far, we've learned that types have rules regarding their interactions, operations, and conversion, but how do we handle a situation where we need to store a variable of an unknown type? This might sound crazy, but think about a data-download scenario—you know the information is coming into your game, but you're not sure what form it will take. We'll discuss how to handle this in the following section.

## Inferred declarations

Luckily, C# can *infer* a variable's type from its assigned value. For example, the `var` keyword can let the program know that the type of the data, `CurrentAge`, needs to be determined by its value of `32`, which is an integer:

```
var CurrentAge = 32;
```

> While this is handy in certain situations, don't be suckered into the lazy programming habit of using inferred variable declarations for everything. This adds a lot of guesswork to your code, where it should be crystal clear.

Before we wrap up our discussion on data types and conversion, we do need to briefly touch on the idea of creating custom types, which we'll do next.

## Custom types

When we're talking about data types, it's important to understand early on that numbers and words (referred to as *literal values*) are not the only kinds of values a variable can store. For instance, a class, struct, or enumeration can be stored as variables. We will introduce these topics in *Chapter 5*, *Working with Classes, Structs, and OOP*, and explore them in greater detail in *Chapter 10*, *Revisiting Types, Methods, and Classes*.

Types are complicated, and the only way to get comfortable with them is by using them. However, here are some important things to keep in mind:

- All variables need to have a specified type (be it explicit or inferred)
- Variables can only hold values of their assigned type (a `string` value can't be assigned an `int` variable)
- If a variable needs to be assigned or combined with a variable of a different type, a conversion needs to take place (either implicit or explicit)
- The C# compiler can infer a variable's type from its value using the `var` keyword, but should only be used when the type isn't known when it's created

That's a lot of nitty-gritty detail we've just jammed into a few sections, but we're not done yet. We still need to understand how naming conventions work in C#, as well as where the variables live in our scripts.

# Naming variables

Picking names for your variables might seem like an afterthought in light of everything we've learned about access modifiers and types, but it shouldn't be a straightforward choice. Clear and consistent naming conventions in your code will not only make it more readable but will also ensure that other developers on your team understand your intentions without having to ask.

The first rule when it comes to naming a variable is that the name you give it should be meaningful; the second rule is that you use Pascal case. Let's take a common example from games and declare a variable to store a player's health:

```
public int Health = 100;
```

If you find yourself declaring a variable like this, alarm bells should be going off in your head. Whose health? Is it storing the maximum or minimum value? What other code will be affected when this value changes? These are all questions that should be easily answered by a meaningful variable name; you don't want to find yourself confused by your code in a week or a month.

With that said, let's try to make this a bit better using a Pascal case name:

```
public int MaxPlayerHealth = 100;
```

> Remember, Pascal case starts each word in the variable name with an uppercase letter.

That's much better. With a little thought, we've updated the variable name with meaning and context. Since there is no technical limit in terms of how long a variable name can be, you might find yourself going overboard and writing out ridiculously descriptive names, which will give you problems just as much as a short, non-descriptive name would.

As a general rule, make a variable name as descriptive as it needs to be—no more, no less. Find your style and stick to it.

# Understanding variable scope

We're getting to the end of our dive into variables, but there's still one more important topic we need to cover: scope. Similar to access modifiers, which determine which outside classes can grab a variable's information, the variable scope is the term used to describe where a given variable exists and its access point within its containing class.

There are three main levels of variable scope in C#:

- **Global** scope refers to a variable that can be accessed by an entire program; in this case, a game. C# doesn't directly support global variables, but the concept is useful in certain cases, which we'll cover in *Chapter 10, Revisiting Types, Methods, and Classes.*
- **Class** or **member** scope refers to a variable that is accessible anywhere in its containing class.
- **Local** scope refers to a variable that is only accessible inside the specific block of code it's created in.

Take a look at the following screenshot. You don't need to put this into `LearningCurve` if you don't want to; it's only for visualization purposes at this point:

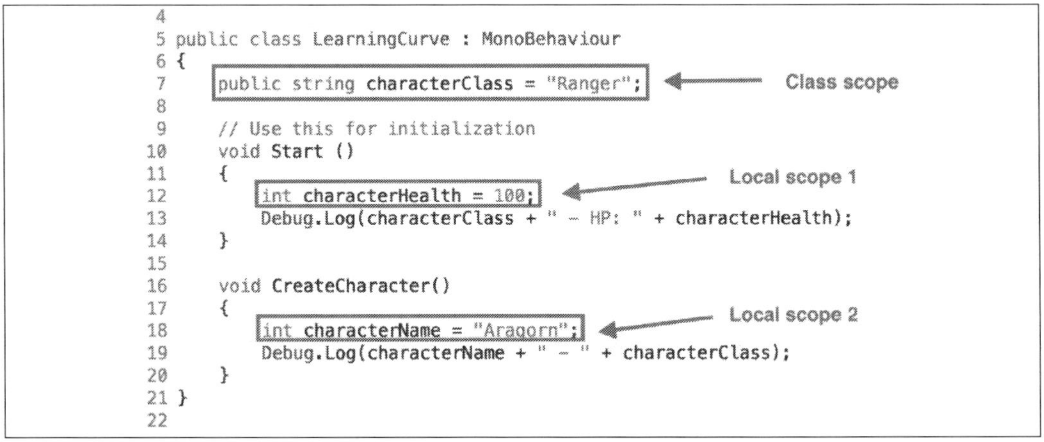


Figure 3.9: Diagram of different scopes in the LearningCurve script

> When we talk about code blocks, we're referring to the area inside any set of curly brackets. These brackets serve as a kind of visual hierarchy in programming; the farther right-indented they are, the deeper they are nested in the class.

Let's break down the class and local scope variables in the preceding screenshot:

- `CharacterClass` is declared at the very top of the class, which means we can reference it by name anywhere inside `LearningCurve`. You might hear this concept referred to as variable visibility, which is a good way of thinking about it.
- `CharacterHealth` is declared inside the `Start()` method, which means it is only visible inside that block of code. We can still access `CharacterClass` from `Start()` with no issue, but if we attempted to access `CharacterHealth` from anywhere but `Start()`, we would get an error.
- `CharacterName` is in the same boat as `CharacterHealth`; it can only be accessed from the `CreateCharacter()` method. This was just to illustrate that there can be multiple, even nested, local scopes in a single class.

If you spend enough time around programmers, you'll hear discussions (or arguments, depending on the time of day) about the best place to declare a variable. The answer is simpler than you might think: variables should be declared with their use in mind. If you have a variable that needs to be accessed throughout a class, make it a class variable. If you only need a variable in a specific section of code, declare it as a local variable.

Note that only class variables can be viewed in the Inspector window, which isn't an option for local or global variables.

With naming and scope in our toolbox, let's transport ourselves back to middle school math class and relearn how arithmetic operations work all over again!

# Introducing operators

Operator symbols in programming languages represent the *arithmetic*, *assignment*, *relational*, and *logical* functionality that types can perform. Arithmetic operators represent basic math functions, while assignment operators perform math and assignment functions together on a given value. Relational and logical operators evaluate conditions between multiple values, such as *greater than*, *less than*, and *equal to*.

C# also offers bitwise and miscellaneous operators, but these won't come into play for you until you're well on your way to creating more complex applications.

At this point, it only makes sense to cover arithmetic and assignment operators, but we'll get to relational and logical functionality when it becomes relevant in the next chapter.

## Arithmetic and assignments

You're already familiar with the arithmetic operator symbols from school:

- + for addition
- - for subtraction
- / for division
- * for multiplication

C# operators follow the conventional order of operations, that is, evaluating parentheses first, then exponents, then multiplication, then division, then addition, and finally subtraction. For instance, the following equations will provide different results, even though they contain the same values and operators:

```
5 + 4 - 3 / 2 * 1 = 8
5 + (4 - 3) / 2 * 1 = 5
```

Operators work the same when applied to variables as they do with literal values.

Assignment operators can be used as a shorthand replacement for any math operation by using any arithmetic and equals symbol together. For example, if we wanted to multiply a variable, you could use the following code:

```
int CurrentAge = 32;
CurrentAge = CurrentAge * 2;
```

The second, alternative, way to do this is shown here:

```
int CurrentAge = 32;
CurrentAge *= 2;
```

The equals symbol is also considered an assignment operator in C#. The other assignment symbols follow the same syntax pattern as our preceding multiplication example: `+=`, `-=`, and `/=` for add and assign, subtract and assign, and divide and assign, respectively.

Strings are a special case when it comes to operators as they can use the addition symbol to create patchwork text, as follows:

```
string FullName = "Harrison " + "Ferrone";
```

This will produce the following when logged in to the **Console** panel:

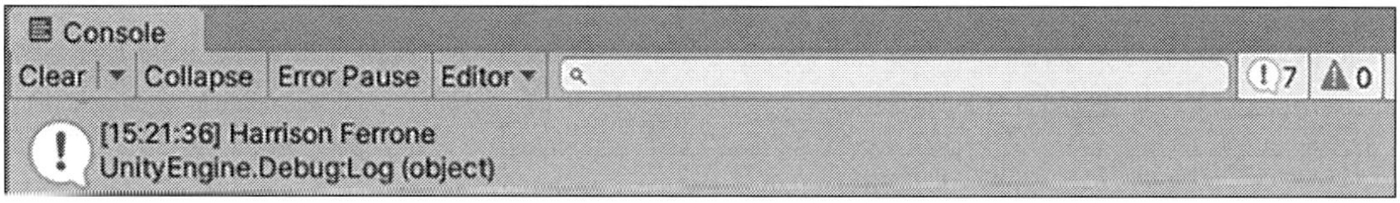


Figure 3.10: Using operators on strings

This approach tends to produce clunky code, making string interpolation the preferred method for putting together different bits of text in most cases.

Take note that arithmetic operators don't work on all data types. For example, the `*` and `/` operators don't work on string values, and none of these operators work on Booleans. Having learned that types have rules that govern what kind of operations and interactions they can have, let's give it a shot in practice in the next section.

Let's do a little experiment: we'll try to multiply our `string` and `float` variables together, as we did earlier with our numbers:

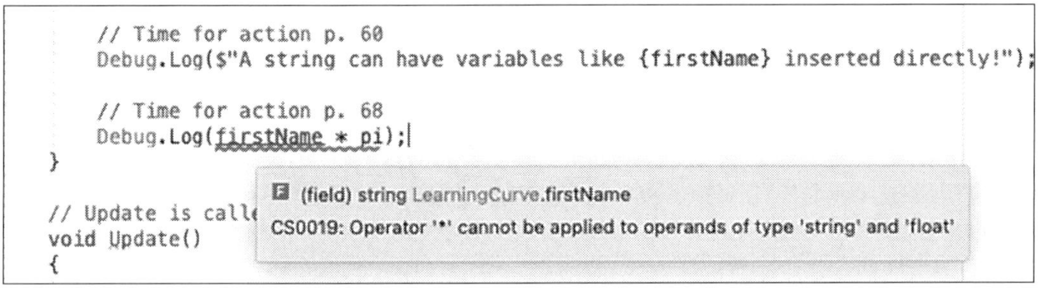


Figure 3.11: Visual Studio incorrect type operation error message

Look at Visual Studio and you'll see we've got an error message letting us know that a `string` type and a `float` type can't be multiplied. This error will also show up in the Unity **Console**, and won't let the project build.

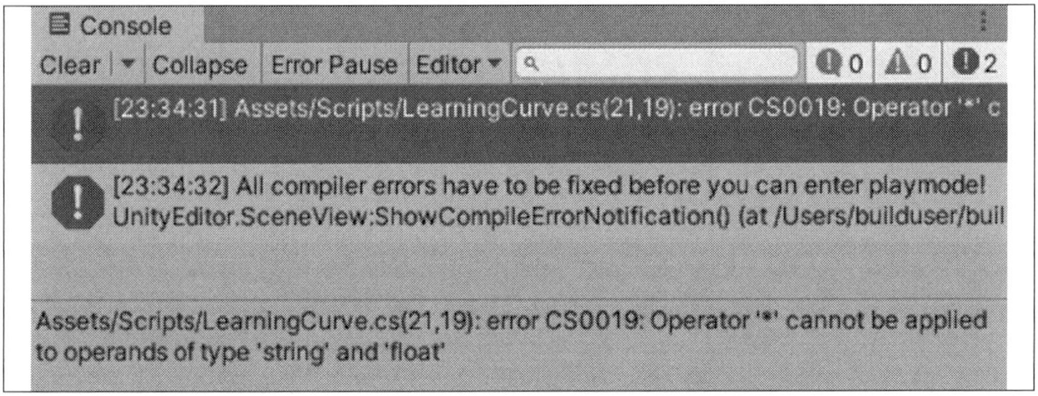


Figure 3.12: Console showing operator errors on incompatible data types

Whenever you see this type of error, go back and inspect your variable types for incompatibilities.

We must clean up this example, as the compiler won't allow us to run our game at this point. Choose between a pair of backslashes (`//`) at the beginning of the line `Debug.Log(FirstName*Pi)`, or delete it altogether.

That's as far as we need to go in terms of variables and types for the moment. Be sure to test yourself on this chapter's quiz before moving on!

# Defining methods

In the previous chapter, we briefly touched on the role methods play in our programs; namely, that they store and execute instructions, just like variables store values. Now, we need to understand the syntax of method declarations and how they drive action and behavior in our classes.

As with variables, method declarations have their basic requirements, which are as follows:

- The type of data that will be returned by the method
- A unique name, starting with a capital letter
- A pair of parentheses following the method name
- A pair of curly brackets marking the method body (where instructions are stored)

Putting all of these rules together, we get a simple method blueprint:

```
returnType UniqueName()
{
    method body
}
```

Let's break down the default `Start()` method in `LearningCurve` as a practical example:

```
void Start()
{

}
```

In the preceding output, we can see the following:

- The method starts with the `void` keyword, which is used as the method's return type if it doesn't return any data.
- The method has a unique name within the class. You can use the same name in different classes, but you should aim to always make your names unique no matter what.
- The method has a pair of parentheses after its name to hold any potential parameters.
- The method body is defined by a set of curly brackets.

> In general, if you have a method that has an empty method body, it's good practice to delete it from the class. You always want to be pruning your scripts of unused code.

Like variables, methods can also have security levels. However, they can also have input parameters, both of which we'll be discussing next!

# Declaring methods

Methods can also have the same four access modifiers that are available to variables, as well as input parameters. Parameters are variable placeholders that can be passed into methods and accessed inside them. The number of input parameters you can use isn't limited, but each one needs to be separated by a comma, show its data type, and have a unique name.

> Think of method parameters as variable placeholders whose values can be used inside the method body.

If we apply these options, our updated blueprint will look like this:

```
accessModifier returnType UniqueName(parameterType parameterName)
{
    method body
}
```

> If there is no explicit access modifier, the method defaults to private. A private method, like a private variable, cannot be called from other scripts.

To call a method (meaning to run or execute its instructions), we simply use its name, followed by a pair of parentheses, with or without parameters, and cap it off with a semicolon:

```
// Without parameters
UniqueName();

// With parameters
UniqueName(parameterVariable);
```

> Like variables, every method has a fingerprint that describes its access level, return type, and parameters. This is called its method signature. Essentially, a method's signature marks it as unique to the compiler so Visual Studio knows what to do with it.

Now that we understand how methods are structured, let's create one of our own.

The *Methods are placeholders too* section in the previous chapter had you blindly copy a method called `ComputeAge()` into `LearningCurve` without you knowing what you were getting into. This time, let's purposefully create a method:

1. Declare a `public` method with a void return type called `GenerateCharacter()`:

   ```
   public int GenerateCharacter()
   {

   }
   ```

2. Add a simple `Debug.Log()` inside the new method and print out a character name from your favorite game or movie:

   ```
   Debug.Log("Character: Spike");
   ```

3. Call `GenerateCharacter()` inside the `Start()` method and hit play:

   ```
   void Start()
   {
       GenerateCharacter();
   }
   ```

   When the game starts up, Unity automatically calls `Start()`, which, in turn, calls our `GenerateCharacter()` method and prints the result to the Console window.

> If you have read enough documentation, you'll see different terminology related to methods. Throughout the rest of this book, when a method is created or declared, I'll refer to this as **defining** a method. Similarly, I'll refer to running or executing a method as **calling** that method.

The power of naming is integral to the entirety of the programming landscape, so it shouldn't be a surprise that we're going to revisit naming conventions for methods before moving on.

# Naming conventions

Like variables, methods need unique, meaningful names to distinguish them in code. Methods drive actions, so it's a good practice to name them with that in mind. For example, `GenerateCharacter()` sounds like a command, which reads well when you call it in a script, whereas a name such as `Summary()` is bland and doesn't paint a very clear picture of what the method will accomplish. Like variables, method names are written in Pascal case.

# Methods as logic detours

We've seen that lines of code execute sequentially in the order they're written, but bringing methods into the picture introduces a unique situation. Calling a method tells the program to take a detour into the method instructions, run them one by one, and then resume sequential execution where the method was called.

Take a look at the following screenshot and see whether you can figure out in what order the debug logs will be printed out to the console:

```
13    // Use this for initialization
14    void Start ()
15    {
16        Debug.Log("Choose a character.");
17        GenerateCharacter();
18        Debug.Log("A fine choice.");
19    }
20
21    public void GenerateCharacter()
22    {
23        Debug.Log("Character: Spike");
24    }
```

Figure 3.13: Considering the order of debug logs

These are the steps that occur:

1. `Choose a character` prints out first because it's the first line of code.
2. When `GenerateCharacter()` is called, the program jumps to line 23, prints out `Character: Spike`, and then resumes execution at line 17.
3. `A fine choice` prints out last, after all the lines in `GenerateCharacter()` have finished running.

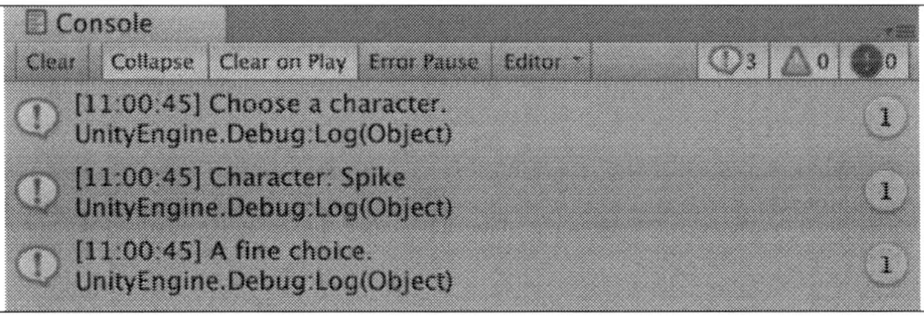


Figure 3.14: Console showing the output of character building code

Now, methods in themselves wouldn't be very useful beyond simple examples like these if we couldn't add parameter values to them, which is what we'll do next.

# Specifying parameters

Chances are your methods aren't always going to be as simple as `GenerateCharacter()`. To pass in additional information, we'll need to define parameters that our method can accept and work with. Every method parameter is an instruction and needs to have two things:

- An explicit type
- A unique name

Does this sound familiar? Method parameters are essentially stripped-down variable declarations and perform the same function. Each parameter acts like a local variable, only accessible inside their specific method.

> You can have as many parameters as you need. Whether you're writing custom methods or using built-in ones, the parameters that are defined are what the method requires to perform its specified task.

If parameters are the blueprint for the types of values a method can accept, then arguments are the values themselves. To break this down further, consider the following:

- The argument that's passed into a method needs to match the parameter type, just like a variable type and its value
- Arguments can be literal values (for instance, the number 2) or variables declared elsewhere in the class

> Argument names and parameter names don't need to match to compile.

Now, let's move on and add some method parameters to make `GenerateCharacter()` a bit more interesting.

Let's update `GenerateCharacter()` so that it can take in two parameters:

1. Add two method parameters: one for a character's name of the `string` type, and another for a character's level of the `int` type:

   ```
   public void GenerateCharacter(string name, int level)
   ```

2. Update `Debug.Log()` so that it uses these new parameters:

   ```
   Debug.LogFormat("Character: {0} - Level: {1}", name, level);
   ```

3. Update the `GenerateCharacter()` method call in `Start()` with your arguments, which can be either literal values or declared variables:

   ```
   int CharacterLevel = 32;
   GenerateCharacter("Spike", CharacterLevel);
   ```

   Your code should look like the following:

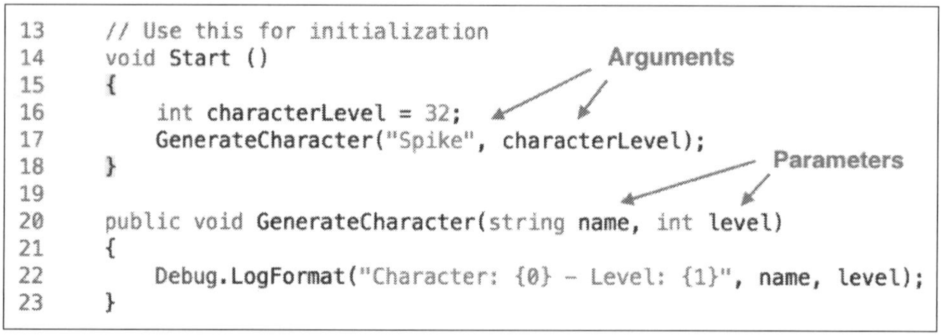


Figure 3.15: Updating the GenerateCharacter() method

Here, we defined two parameters, `name` (string) and `level` (int), and used them inside the `GenerateCharacter()` method, just like local variables. When we called the method inside `Start()`, we added argument values for each parameter with corresponding types. In the preceding screenshot, you can see that using the literal string value in quotations produced the same result as using `characterLevel`.

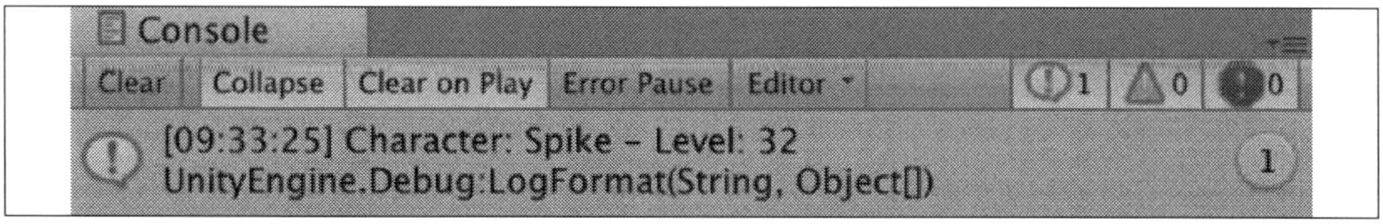


Figure 3.16: Console showing the output from method parameters

Going even further with methods, you might be wondering how we can pass values from inside the method and back out again. This brings us to our next section on return values.

# Specifying return values

Aside from accepting parameters, methods can return values of any C# type. All of our previous examples have used the `void` type, which doesn't return anything, but being able to write instructions and pass back computed results is where methods shine.

According to our blueprints, method return types are specified after the access modifier. In addition to the type, the method needs to contain the `return` keyword, followed by the return value. A return value can be a variable, a literal value, or even an expression, as long as it matches the declared return type.

> Methods that have a return type of `void` can still use the return keyword with no value or expression assigned. Once the line with the return keyword is reached, the method will stop executing. This is useful in cases where you want to avoid certain behaviors or guard against program crashes.

Next, add a return type to `GenerateCharacter()` and learn how to capture it in a variable. Let's update the `GenerateCharacter()` method so that it returns an integer:

1. Change the return type in the method declaration from `void` to `int`, and set the return value to `level += 5` using the `return` keyword.

```
public int GenerateCharacter(string name, int level)
{
        Debug.LogFormat("Character: {0} - Level: {1}", name,
level);

        return level += 5;
}
```

`GenerateCharacter()` will now return an integer. This is computed by adding `5` to the level argument. We haven't specified how, or if, we want to use this return value, which means that right now, the script won't do anything new.

Now, the question becomes: how do we capture and use the newly added return value? Well, we'll discuss that very topic in the following section.

# Using return values

When it comes to using return values, there are two approaches available:

- Create a local variable to capture (store) the returned value.
- Use the calling method itself as a stand-in for the returned value, using it just like a variable. The calling method is the actual line of code that fires the instructions, which, in our example, would be `GenerateCharacter("Spike", CharacterLevel)`. You can even pass a calling method into another method as an argument if need be.

> The first option is preferred in most programming circles for its readability. Throwing around method calls as variables can get messy fast, especially when we use them as arguments in other methods.

Let's give this a try in our code by capturing and debugging the return value that `GenerateCharacter()` returns.

We're going to use both ways of capturing and using return variables with two simple debug logs:

1. Create a new local variable in the `Start` method of the `int` type, called `NextSkillLevel`, and assign it to the return value of the `GenerateCharacter()` method call we already have in place:

   ```
   int NextSkillLevel = GenerateCharacter("Spike", CharacterLevel);
   ```

2. Add two debug logs, with the first printing out `NextSkillLevel` and the second printing out a new calling method with argument values of your choice:

   ```
   Debug.Log(NextSkillLevel);
   Debug.Log(GenerateCharacter("Faye", CharacterLevel));
   ```

3. Comment out the debug log inside `GenerateCharacter()` with two forward slashes (`//`) to make the console output less cluttered. Your code should look like the following:

```
// Start is called before the first frame update
void Start()
{
    int CharacterLevel = 32;
    int NextSkillLevel = GenerateCharacter("Spike",
CharacterLevel);

    Debug.Log(NextSkillLevel);
    Debug.Log(GenerateCharacter("Faye", CharacterLevel));
}

public int GenerateCharacter(string name, int level)
{
    // Debug.LogFormat("Character: {0} - Level: {1}", name,
level);
    return level += 5;
}
```

4. Save the file and hit play in Unity. To the compiler, the `NextSkillLevel` variable and the `GenerateCharacter()` method caller represent the same information, namely an integer, which is why both logs show the number `37`:

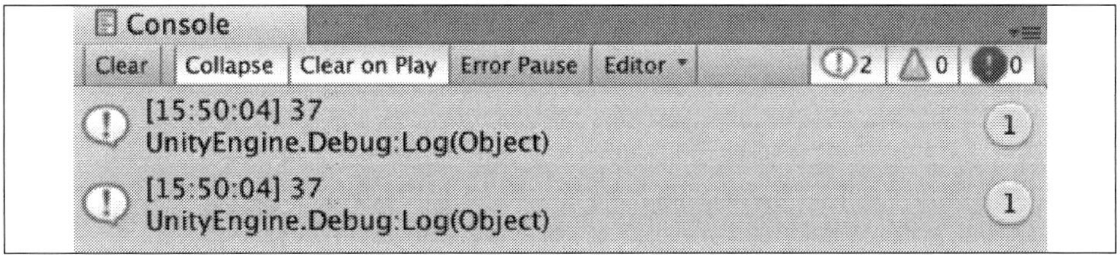


Figure 3.17: Console output from the character generation code

That was a lot to take in, especially given the exponential possibilities of methods with parameters and return values. However, we'll ease off the throttle here for a minute and consider some of Unity's most common methods to catch a little breathing room.

But first, see if you can handle a challenge in the next *Hero's trial*!

## Hero's trial – methods as arguments

If you're feeling brave, why not try creating a new method that takes in an `int` parameter and simply prints it out to the console? No return type is necessary. When you've got that, call the method in `Start`, pass in a `GenerateCharacter` method call as its argument, and take a look at the output.

# Dissecting common Unity methods

We're now at a point where we can realistically discuss the most common default methods that come with any new Unity C# script: `Start()` and `Update()`. Unlike the methods we define ourselves, methods belonging to the `MonoBehaviour` class are called automatically by the Unity engine according to their respective rules. In most cases, it's important to have at least one `MonoBehaviour` method in a script to kick off your code.

> You can find a complete list of all available MonoBehaviour methods and their descriptions at `https://docs.unity3d.com/ScriptReference/MonoBehaviour.html`. You can also find the order in which each method is executed at `https://docs.unity3d.com/Manual/ExecutionOrder.html`.

Just like stories, it's always a good idea to start at the beginning. So, naturally, we should take a look at every Unity script's first default method—`Start()`.

## The Start method

Unity calls the `Start()` method on the first frame where a script is enabled for the first time. Since `MonoBehaviour` scripts are almost always attached to *GameObjects* in a scene, their attached scripts are enabled at the same time they are loaded when you hit play. In our project, `LearningCurve` is attached to the **Main Camera** *GameObject*, which means that its `Start()` method runs when the main camera is loaded into the scene. `Start()` is primarily used to set up variables or perform logic that needs to happen before `Update()` runs for the first time.

> The examples we've worked on so far have all used `Start()`, even though they weren't performing setup actions, which isn't normally the way it would be used. However, it only fires once, making it an excellent tool to use for displaying one-time-only information on the console.

Other than `Start()`, there's one other major Unity method that you'll run into by default: `Update()`. Let's familiarize ourselves with how it works in the following section before we finish off this chapter.

## The Update method

If you spend enough time looking at the sample code in the Unity Scripting Reference (`https://docs.unity3d.com/ScriptReference/`), you'll notice that a vast majority of the code is executed using the `Update()` method. As your game runs, the Scene window is displayed many times per second, which is called the frame rate or **frames per second** (**FPS**).

After each frame is displayed, the `Update()` method is called by Unity, making it one of the most executed methods in your game. This makes it ideal for detecting mouse and keyboard input or running gameplay logic.

If you're curious about the FPS rating on your machine, hit play in Unity and click the **Stats** tab in the upper-right corner of the **Game** view:

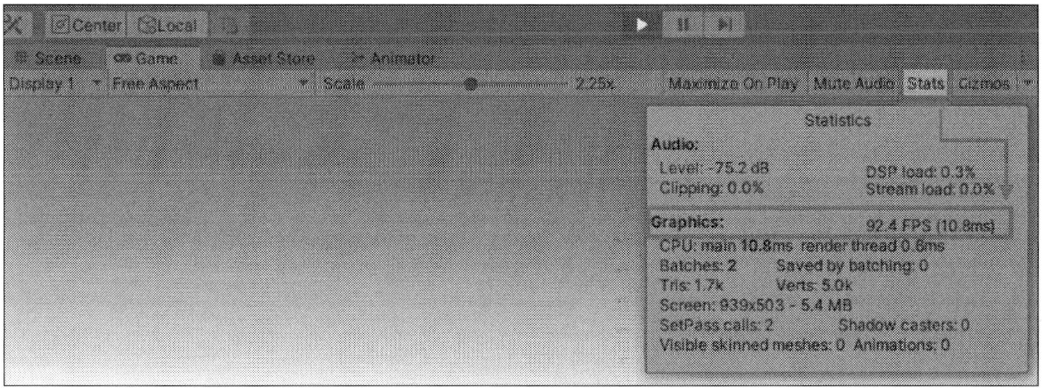


Figure 3.18: Unity editor showing the Stats panel with graphics FPS count

You'll be using the `Start()` and `Update()` methods in the lion's share of your initial C# scripts, so get acquainted with them. That being said, you've reached the end of this chapter with a pocketful of the most fundamental building blocks programming with C# has to offer.

# Summary

This chapter has been a fast descent from the basic theory of programming and its building blocks into the strata of real code and C# syntax. We've seen good and bad forms of code formatting, learned how to debug information in the Unity console, and created our first variables.

C# types, access modifiers, and variable scope weren't far behind, as we worked with member variables in the Inspector window and started venturing into the realm of methods and actions.

Methods helped us to understand written instructions in code, but more importantly, how to properly harness their power into useful behaviors. Input parameters, return types, and method signatures are all important topics, but the real gift they offer is the potential for new kinds of actions to be performed.

You're now armed with the two fundamental building blocks of programming; almost everything you'll do from now on will be an extension or application of these two concepts.

In the next chapter, we'll take a look at a special subset of C# types called collections, which can store groups of related data, and learn how to write decision-based code.

# Pop quiz – variables and methods

1. What is the proper way to write a variable name in C#?
2. How do you make a variable appear in Unity's Inspector window?
3. What are the four access modifiers available in C#?
4. When are explicit conversions needed between types?
5. What are the minimum requirements for defining a method?
6. What is the purpose of the parentheses at the end of the method name?
7. What does a return type of `void` mean in a method definition?
8. How often is the `Update()` method called by Unity?

# 4

# Control Flow and Collection Types

One of the central duties of a computer is to control what happens when predetermined conditions are met. When you click on a folder, you expect it to open; when you type on the keyboard, you expect the text to mirror your keystrokes. Writing code for applications or games is no different—they both need to behave in a certain way in one state, and in another when conditions change. In programming terms, this is called control flow, which is apt because it controls the flow of how code is executed in different scenarios.

In addition to working with control statements, we'll be taking a hands-on look at collection data types. Collections are a category of types that allow multiple values, and groupings of values, to be stored in a single variable. We'll break the chapter down into the following topics:

- Selection statements
- Working with array, dictionary, and list collections
- Iteration statements with `for`, `foreach`, and `while` loops
- Fixing infinite loops

## Selection statements

The most complex programming problems can often be boiled down to sets of simple choices that a game or program evaluates and acts on. Since Visual Studio and Unity can't make those choices by themselves, writing out those decisions is up to us.

The `if-else` and `switch` selection statements allow you to specify branching paths, based on one or more conditions, and the actions you want to be taken in each case. Traditionally, these conditions include the following:

- Detecting user input
- Evaluating expressions and Boolean logic
- Comparing variables or literal values

You're going to start with the simplest of these conditional statements, `if-else`, in the following section.

# The if-else statement

`if-else` statements are the most common way of making decisions in code. When stripped of all its syntax, the basic idea is, *If my condition is met, execute this block of code; if it's not, execute this other block of code*. Think of these statements as gates, or doors, with the conditions as their keys. To pass through, the key needs to be valid. Otherwise, entry will be denied and the code will be sent to the next possible gate. Let's take a look at the syntax for declaring one of these gates.

A valid `if-else` statement requires the following:

- The `if` keyword at the beginning of the line
- A pair of parentheses to hold the condition
- A statement body inside curly brackets

It looks like this:

```
if(condition is true)
{
    Execute code of code
}
```

Optionally, an `else` statement can be added to store the action you want to take when the `if` statement condition fails. The same rules apply for the `else` statement:

```
else
    Execute single line of code

// OR

else
{
```

```
    Execute multiple lines
    of code
}
```

In blueprint form, the syntax almost reads like a sentence, which is why this is the recommended approach:

```
if(condition is true)
{
    Execute this code
    block
}
else
{
    Execute this code
    block
}
```

Since these are great introductions to logical thinking, at least in programming, we'll break down the three different `if-else` variations in more detail:

1. A single `if` statement can exist by itself in cases where you don't care about what happens if the condition isn't met. In the following example, if `hasDungeonKey` is set to `true`, then a debug log will print out; if set to `false`, no code will execute:

```
public class LearningCurve: MonoBehaviour
{
    public bool hasDungeonKey = true;

    Void Start()
    {
        if(hasDungeonKey)
        {
            Debug.Log("You possess the sacred key - enter.");
        }
    }
}
```

> When referring to a condition as being met, I mean that it evaluates to true, which is often referred to as a passing condition.

2. Add an `else` statement in cases where an action needs to be taken whether the condition is true or false. If `hasDungeonKey` were `false`, the `if` statement would fail and the code execution would jump to the `else` statement:

```
public class LearningCurve: MonoBehaviour
{
    public bool hasDungeonKey = true;

    void Start()
    {
        if(hasDungeonKey)
        {
            Debug.Log("You possess the sacred key - enter.");
        }
        else
        {
            Debug.Log("You have not proved yourself yet.");
        }
    }
}
```

3. For cases where you need to have more than two possible outcomes, add an `else-if` statement with its parentheses, conditions, and curly brackets. This is best shown rather than explained, which we'll do next.

> Keep in mind that `if` statements can be used by themselves, but the other statements cannot exist on their own. You can also create more complex conditions with basic math operations, such as > (greater than), < (less than), >= (greater than or equal to), <= (less than or equal to), and == (equivalent). For example, a condition of (2 > 3) will return `false` and fail, while a condition of (2 < 3) will return `true` and pass.
>
> Don't worry too much about anything beyond this right now; you'll get your hands on this stuff soon enough.

Let's write out an `if-else` statement that checks the amount of money in a character's pocket, returning different debug logs for three different cases—greater than `50`, less than `15`, and anything else:

1. Open up `LearningCurve` and add a new public `int` variable, named `CurrentGold`. Set its value to between 1 and 100:

```
public int CurrentGold = 32;
```

2. Create a `public` method with no return value, called `Thievery`, and call it inside `Start`.
3. Inside the new function, add an `if` statement to check whether `CurrentGold` is greater than `50`, and print a message to the console if this is true:

```
if(CurrentGold > 50)
{
    Debug.Log("You're rolling in it!");
}
```

4. Add an `else-if` statement to check whether `CurrentGold` is less than `15` with a different debug log:

```
else if (CurrentGold < 15)
{
    Debug.Log("Not much there to steal...");
}
```

5. Add an `else` statement with no condition and a final default log:

```
else
{
    Debug.Log("Looks like your purse is in the sweet spot.");
}
```

6. Save the file, check that your method matches the code below, and click on play:

```
public void Thievery()
{
    if(CurrentGold > 50)
    {
        Debug.Log("You're rolling in it!");
    } else if (CurrentGold < 15)
    {
        Debug.Log("Not much there to steal...");
    } else
    {
        Debug.Log("Looks like your purse is in the sweet spot.");
    }
}
```

With `CurrentGold` set to `32` in my example, we can break down the code sequence as follows:

1. The `if` statement and debug log are skipped because `CurrentGold` is not greater than `50`.
2. The `else-if` statement and debug log are also skipped because `CurrentGold` is not less than `15`.
3. Since 32 is not less than 15 or greater than 50, neither of the previous conditions was met. The `else` statement executes and the third debug log is displayed:

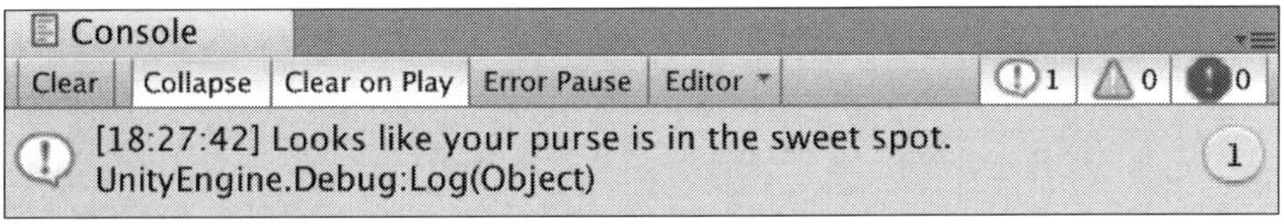


Figure 4.1: Screenshot of the console showing the debug output

After trying out some other values for `CurrentGold` on your own, let's discuss what happens if we want to test a failing condition.

## Using the NOT operator

Use cases won't always require checking for a positive, or `true`, condition, which is where the `NOT` operator comes in. Written with a single exclamation point, the `NOT` operator allows negative, or false, conditions to be met by `if` or `else-if` statements. This means that the following conditions are the same:

```
if(variable == false)

// AND

if(!variable)
```

As you already know, you can check for Boolean values, literal values, or expressions in an `if` condition. So, naturally, the `NOT` operator has to be adaptable.

Take a look at the following example of two different negative values, `hasDungeonKey` and `weaponType`, used in an `if` statement:

```
public class LearningCurve : MonoBehaviour
{
    public bool hasDungeonKey = false;
    public string weaponType = "Arcane Staff";
```

```
    void Start()
    {
        if(!hasDungeonKey)
        {
            Debug.Log("You may not enter without the sacred key.");
        }

        if(weaponType != "Longsword")
{
            Debug.Log("You don't appear to have the right type of
weapon...");
}
    }
}
```

We can evaluate each statement as follows:

- The first statement can be translated to, "If `hasDungeonKey` is `false`, the `if` statement evaluates to true and executes its code block."

> If you're asking yourself how a false value can evaluate to true, think of it this way: the `if` statement is not checking whether the value is true, but that the expression itself is true. `hasDungeonKey` might be set to false, but that's what we're checking for, so it's true in the context of the `if` condition.

- The second statement can be translated to, "If the string value of `weaponType` is `not equal` to `Longsword`, then execute this code block."

You can see the debug results in the following screenshot:

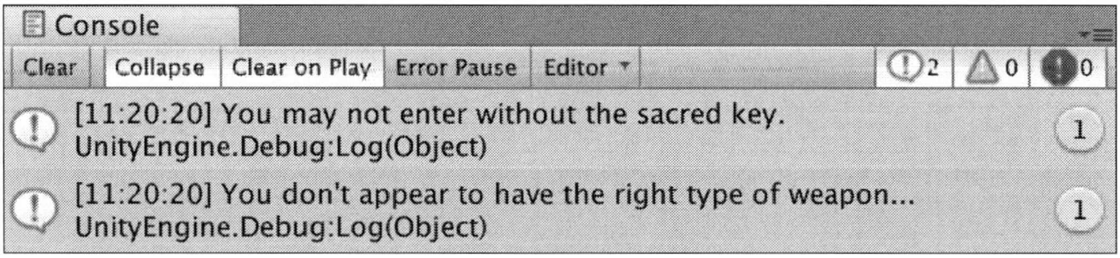


Figure 4.2: Screenshot of the console showing the NOT operator output

However, if you're still confused, copy the code we've looked at in this section into `LearningCurve` and play around with the variable values until it makes sense.

So far, our branching conditions have been fairly simple, but C# also allows conditional statements to be nested inside each other for more complex situations.

# Nesting statements

One of the most valuable functions of `if-else` statements is that they can be nested inside each other, creating complex logic routes through your code. In programming, we call them decision trees. Just like a real hallway, there can be doors behind other doors, creating a labyrinth of possibilities:

```
public class LearningCurve : MonoBehaviour
{
    public bool weaponEquipped = true;
    public string weaponType = "Longsword";

    void Start()
    {
        if(weaponEquipped)
        {
            if(weaponType == "Longsword")
            {
                Debug.Log("For the Queen!");
            }
        }
        else
        {
            Debug.Log("Fists aren't going to work against armor...");
        }
    }
}
```

Let's break down the preceding example:

- First, an `if` statement checks whether we have `weaponEquipped`. At this point, the code only cares whether it's `true`, not what type of weapon it is.
- The second `if` statement checks the `weaponType` and prints out the associated debug log.
- If the first `if` statement evaluates to `false`, the code would jump to the `else` statement and its debug log. If the second `if` statement evaluates to `false`, nothing is printed because there is no `else` statement.

> The responsibility of handling logic outcomes is 100% on the programmer. It's up to you to determine the possible branches or outcomes your code can take.

What you've learned so far will get you through simple use cases with no problem. However, you'll quickly find yourself in need of more complex statements, which is where evaluating multiple conditions comes into play.

# Evaluating multiple conditions

In addition to nesting statements, it's also possible to combine multiple condition checks into a single `if` or `else-if` statement with `AND OR` logic operators:

- `AND` is written with two ampersand characters, `&&`. Any condition using the `AND` operator means that all conditions need to evaluate to true for the `if` statement to execute.
- `OR` is written with two pipe characters, `||`. An `if` statement using the `OR` operator will execute if one or more of its conditions is true.
- Conditions are always evaluated from left to right.

In the following example, the `if` statement has been updated to check for both `weaponEquipped` and `weaponType`, both of which need to be true for the code block to execute:

```
if(weaponEquipped && weaponType == "Longsword")
{
    Debug.Log("For the Queen!");
}
```

> The `AND OR` operators can be combined to check multiple conditions in any order. There is also no limit on how many operators you can combine. Just be careful when using them together that you don't create logic conditions that will never execute.

It's time to put everything we've learned so far about `if` statements to the test. So, review this section if you need to, and then move on to the next section.

Let's cement this topic with a little treasure chest experiment:

1. Declare three variables at the top of `LearningCurve`: `PureOfHeart` is a `bool` and should be `true`, `HasSecretIncantation` is also a `bool` and should be `false`, and `RareItem` is a string and its value is up to you:

   ```
   public bool PureOfHeart = true;
   public bool HasSecretIncantation = false;
   public string RareItem = "Relic Stone";
   ```

2. Create a `public` method with no return value, called `OpenTreasureChamber`, and call it from inside `Start()`.
3. Inside `OpenTreasureChamber`, declare an `if-else` statement to check whether `PureOfHeart` is `true` *and* that `RareItem` matches the string value you assigned to it:

   ```
   if(PureOfHeart && RareItem == "Relic Stone")
   {
   }
   ```

4. Create a nested `if-else` statement inside the first, checking whether `HasSecretIncantation` is `false`:

   ```
   if(!HasSecretIncantation)
   {
       Debug.Log("You have the spirit, but not the knowledge.");
   }
   ```

5. Add debug logs for each `if-else` case.
6. Save, check that your code matches the code below, and click play:

   ```
   public class LearningCurve : MonoBehaviour
   {
       public bool PureOfHeart = true;
       public bool HasSecretIncantation  = false;
       public string RareItem = "Relic Stone";

       // Use this for initialization
       void Start()
       {
           OpenTreasureChamber();
       }

       public void OpenTreasureChamber()
       {
   ```

```
            if(PureOfHeart && RareItem == "Relic Stone")
            {
                if(!HasSecretIncantation)
                {
                    Debug.Log("You have the spirit, but not the
knowledge.");
                }
                else
                {
                    Debug.Log("The treasure is yours, worthy
hero!");
                }
            }
            else
            {
                Debug.Log("Come back when you have what it takes.");
            }
        }
    }
```

If you matched the variable values to the preceding screenshot, the nested `if` statement debug log will be printed out. This means that our code got past the first `if` statement checking for two conditions, but failed the third:

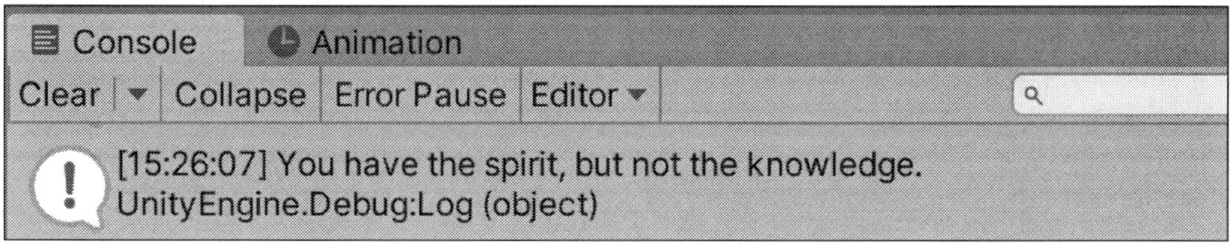


Figure 4.3: Screenshot of debut output in the console

Now, you could stop here and use even bigger `if-else` statements for all your conditional needs, but that's not going to be efficient in the long run. Good programming is about using the right tool for the right job, which is where the `switch` statement comes in.

# The switch statement

`if-else` statements are a great way to write decision logic. However, when you have more than three or four branching actions, they just aren't feasible. Before you know it, your code can end up looking like a tangled knot that's hard to follow, and a headache to update.

`switch` statements take in expressions and let us write out actions for each possible outcome, but in a much more concise format than `if-else`.

`switch` statements require the following elements:

- The `switch` keyword followed by a pair of parentheses holding its condition
- A pair of curly brackets
- A `case` statement for each possible path ending with a colon: individual lines of code or methods, followed by the `break` keyword and a semicolon
- A default `case` statement ending with a colon: individual lines of code or methods, followed by the `break` keyword and a semicolon

In blueprint form, it looks like this:

```
switch(matchExpression)
{
    case matchValue1:
        Executing code block
        break;
    case matchValue2:
        Executing code block
        break;
    default:
        Executing code block
        break;
}
```

The highlighted keywords in the preceding blueprint are the important bits. When a `case` statement is defined, anything between its colon and `break` keyword acts like the code block of an `if-else` statement. The `break` keyword just tells the program to exit the `switch` statement entirely after the selected `case` fires. Now, let's discuss how the statement determines which `case` gets executed, which is called pattern matching.

## Pattern matching

In `switch` statements, pattern matching refers to how a match expression is validated against multiple `case` statements. A match expression can be of any type that isn't null or nothing; all `case` statement values need to match the type of the match expression.

For example, if we had a `switch` statement that was evaluating an integer variable, each `case` statement would need to specify an integer value for it to check against.

The `case` statement with a value that matches the expression is the one that is executed. If no `case` is matched, the default `case` fires. Let's try this out for ourselves!

That was a lot of new syntax and information, but it helps to see it in action. Let's create a simple `switch` statement for different actions a character could take:

1. Create a new string variable (member or local), named `CharacterAction`, and set it to `Attack`:

   ```
   string CharacterAction = "Attack";
   ```

2. Create a `public` method with no return value called `PrintCharacterAction`, and call it inside `Start`.
3. Declare a `switch` statement and use `CharacterAction` as the match expression:

   ```
   switch(CharacterAction)
   {
   }
   ```

4. Create two `case` statements for `Heal` and `Attack` with different debug logs. Don't forget to include the `break` keyword at the end of each:

   ```
   case "Heal":
       Debug.Log("Potion sent.");
       break;
   case "Attack":
       Debug.Log("To arms!");
       break;
   ```

5. Add a default case with a debug log and `break`:

   ```
   default:
       Debug.Log("Shields up.");
       break;
   ```

6. Save the file, make sure your code matches the screenshot below, and click play:

   ```
   string CharacterAction = "Attack";

   // Start is called before the first frame update
   void Start()
   {
       PrintCharacterAction();
   }
   ```

```
public void PrintCharacterAction()
{
    switch(CharacterAction)
    {
        case "Heal":
            Debug.Log("Potion sent.");
            break;
        case "Attack":
            Debug.Log("To arms!");
            break;
        default:
            Debug.Log("Shields up.");
            break;
    }
}
```

Since `CharacterAction` is set to `Attack`, the `switch` statement executes the second case and prints out its debug log:

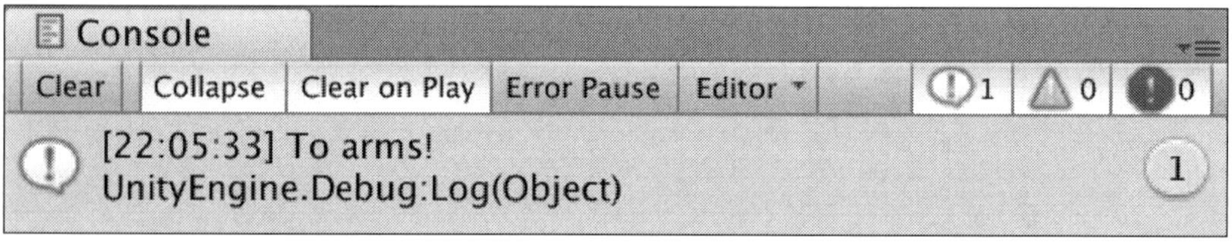


Figure 4.4: Screenshot of the switch statement output in the console

Change `CharacterAction` to either `Heal` or an undefined action to see the first and default cases in action.

There are going to be times where you need several, but not all, `switch` cases to perform the same action. These are called fall-through cases and are the subject of our next section.

# Fall-through cases

`switch` statements can execute the same action for multiple cases, similar to how we specified several conditions in a single `if` statement. The term for this is called fall-through or, sometimes, fall-through cases. Fall-through cases let you define a single set of actions for multiple cases. If a case block is left empty or has code without the `break` keyword, it will fall through to the case directly beneath it. This helps keep your switch code clean and efficient, without duplicated case blocks.

> Cases can be written in any order, so creating fall-through cases greatly increases code readability and efficiency.

Let's simulate a tabletop game scenario with a `switch` statement and fall-through case, where a dice roll determines the outcome of a specific action:

1. Create an `int` variable, named `DiceRoll`, and assign it a value of `7`:

   ```
   int DiceRoll = 7;
   ```

2. Create a `public` method with no return value, called `RollDice`, and call it inside `Start`.
3. Add a `switch` statement with `DiceRoll` as the match expression:

   ```
   switch(DiceRoll)
   {
   }
   ```

4. Add three cases for possible dice rolls at `7`, `15`, and `20`, with a default `case` statement at the end.
5. Cases `15` and `20` should have their own debug logs and `break` statements, while case `7` should fall through to case `15`:

   ```
   case 7:
   case 15:
       Debug.Log("Mediocre damage, not bad.");
       break;
   case 20:
       Debug.Log("Critical hit, the creature goes down!");
       break;
   default:
       Debug.Log("You completely missed and fell on your face.");
       break;
   ```

6. Save the file and run it in Unity.

> If you want to see the fall-through case in action, try adding a debug log to case 7, but without the `break` keyword.

With `DiceRoll` set to `7`, the `switch` statement will match with the first `case`, which will fall through and execute `case 15` because it lacks a code block and a `break` statement. If you change `DiceRoll` to `15` or `20`, the console will show their respective messages, and any other value will fire off the default case at the end of the statement:

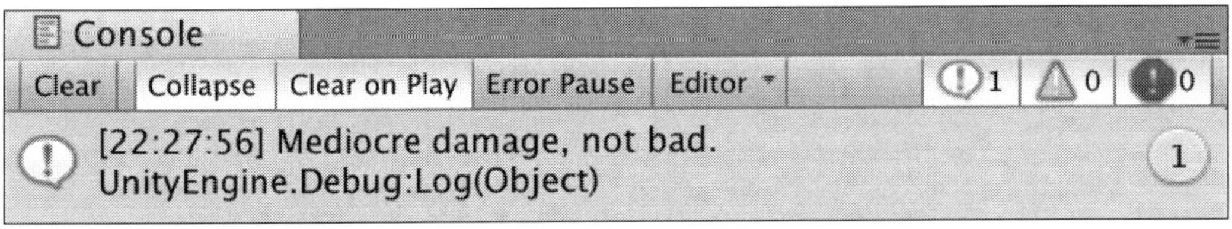


Figure 4.5: Screenshot of fall-through switch statement code

> `switch` statements are extremely powerful and can simplify even the most complex decision logic. If you want to dig deeper into switch pattern matching, refer to `https://docs.microsoft.com/en-us/dotnet/csharp/language-reference/keywords/switch`.

That's all we need to know about conditional logic for the moment. So, review this section if you need to, and then test yourself on the following quiz before moving on to collections!

# Pop quiz 1 – if, and, or but

Test your knowledge with the following questions:

1. What values are used to evaluate `if` statements?
2. Which operator can turn a true condition false or a false condition true?
3. If two conditions need to be true for an `if` statement's code to execute, what logical operator would you use to join the conditions?
4. If only one of two conditions needs to be true to execute an `if` statement's code, what logical operator would you use to join the two conditions?

With that done, you're ready to step into the world of collection data types. These types are going to open up a whole new subset of programming functionality for your games and C# programs!

# Collections at a glance

So far, we've only needed variables to store a single value, but there are many conditions where a group of values will be required. Collection types in C# include arrays, dictionaries, and lists—each has its strengths and weaknesses, which we'll discuss in the following sections.

# Arrays

**Arrays** are the most basic collection that C# offers. Think of them as containers for a group of values, called *elements* in programming terminology, each of which can be accessed or modified individually:

- Arrays can store any type of value; all the elements need to be of the same type.
- The length, or the number of elements an array can have, is set when it's created and can't be modified afterward.
- If no initial values are assigned when it's created, each element will be given a default value. Arrays storing number types default to zero, while any other type gets set to null or nothing.

Arrays are the least flexible collection type in C#. This is mainly because elements can't be added or removed after they have been created. However, they are particularly useful when storing information that isn't likely to change. That lack of flexibility makes them faster compared to other collection types.

Declaring an array is similar to other variable types we've worked with, but has a few modifications:

- Array variables require a specified element type, a pair of square brackets, and a unique name.
- The `new` keyword is used to create the array in memory, followed by the value type and another pair of square brackets. The reserved memory area is the exact size of the data you're intending to store in the new array.
- The number of elements the array will store goes inside the second pair of square brackets.

In blueprint form, it looks like this:

```
elementType[] name = new elementType[numberOfElements];
```

Let's take an example where we need to store the top three high scores in our game:

```
int[] topPlayerScores = new int[3];
```

Broken down, `topPlayerScores` is an array of integers that will store three integer elements. Since we didn't add any initial values, each of the three values in `topPlayerScores` is `0`. However, if you change the array size, the contents of the original array are lost, so be careful.

You can assign values directly to an array when it's created by adding them inside a pair of curly brackets at the end of the variable declaration. C# has a longhand and shorthand way of doing this, but both are equally valid:

```
// Longhand initializer
int[] topPlayerScores = new int[] {713, 549, 984};

// Shortcut initializer

int[] topPlayerScores = { 713, 549, 984 };
```

> Initializing arrays with the shorthand syntax is very common, so I'll be using it for the rest of the book. However, if you want to remind yourself of the details, feel free to use the explicit wording.

Now that the declaration syntax is no longer a mystery, let's talk about how array elements are stored and accessed.

## Indexing and subscripts

Each array element is stored in the order it's assigned, which is referred to as its index. Arrays are zero-indexed, meaning that the element order starts at zero instead of one. Think of an element's index as its reference, or location.

In `topPlayerScores`, the first integer, `452`, is located at index `0`, `713` at index `1`, and `984` at index `2`:

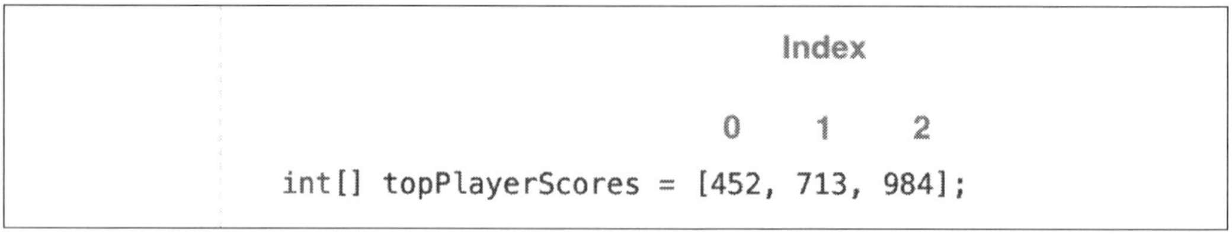


Figure 4.6: Array indexes mapped to their values

Individual values are located by their index using the subscript operator, which is a pair of square brackets that contains the index of the elements. For example, to retrieve and store the second array element in `topPlayerScores`, we would use the array name followed by subscript brackets and index `1`:

```
// The value of score is set to 713
int score = topPlayerScores[1];
```

The subscript operator can also be used to directly modify an array value just like any other variable, or even passed around as an expression by itself:

```
topPlayerScores[1] = 1001;
```

The values in `topPlayerScores` would then be `452`, `1001`, and `984`.

## Range exceptions

When arrays are created, the number of elements is set and unchangeable, which means we can't access an element that doesn't exist. In the `topPlayerScores` example, the array length is 3, so the range of valid indices is from `0` to `2`. Any index of `3` or higher is out of the array's range and will generate an aptly-named `IndexOutOfRangeException` error in the console:

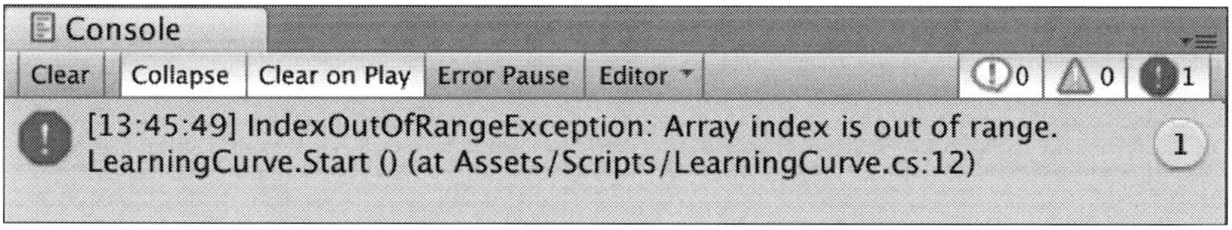


Figure 4.7: Screenshot of index out of range exception

> Good programming habits dictate that we avoid range exceptions by checking whether the value we want is within an array's index range, which we'll cover in the *Iteration statements* section.

You can always check the length of an array, that is, how many items it contains, with the `Length` property:

```
topPlayerScores.Length;
```

In our case, the length of `topPlayerScores` is 4.

Arrays aren't the only collection types C# has to offer. In the next section, we'll deal with lists, which are more flexible and more common in the programming landscape.

# Lists

**Lists** are closely related to arrays, collecting multiple values of the same type in a single variable. They're much easier to deal with when it comes to adding, removing, and updating elements, but their elements aren't stored sequentially. They are also mutable, meaning you can change the length or number of items you're storing, without overwriting the whole variable. This can, sometimes, lead to a higher performance cost over arrays.

> Performance cost refers to how much of a computer's time and energy a given operation takes up. Nowadays, computers are fast, but they can still get overloaded with big games or applications.

A list-type variable needs to meet the following requirements:

- The `List` keyword, its element type inside left and right arrow characters, and a unique name
- The `new` keyword to initialize the list in memory, with the `List` keyword and element type between arrow characters
- A pair of parentheses capped off by a semicolon

In blueprint form, it reads as follows:

```
List<elementType> name = new List<elementType>();
```

> List length can always be modified, so there is no need to specify how many elements it will eventually hold when created.

Like arrays, lists can be initialized in the variable declaration by adding element values inside a pair of curly brackets:

```
List<elementType> name = new List<elementType>() { value1, value2 };
```

Elements are stored in the order they are added (instead of the sequential order of the values themselves), are zero-indexed, and can be accessed using the subscript operator.

Let's start setting up a list of our own to test out the basic functionality this class has on offer.

Let's do a warm-up exercise by creating a list of party members in a fictional role-playing game:

1. Create a new `List` of the `string` type inside `Start` called `QuestPartyMembers`, and initialize it with the names of three characters:

   ```
   List<string> QuestPartyMembers = new List<string>()
       {
           "Grim the Barbarian",
           "Merlin the Wise",
           "Sterling the Knight"
       };
   ```

2. Add a debug log to print out the number of party members in the list using the `Count` method:

   ```
   Debug.LogFormat("Party Members: {0}", QuestPartyMembers.Count);
   ```

3. Save the file and play it in Unity.

We initialized a new list, called `QuestPartyMembers`, which now holds three string values, and used the `Count` method from the `List` class to print out the number of elements. Notice that you use `Count` for lists, but `Length` for arrays.

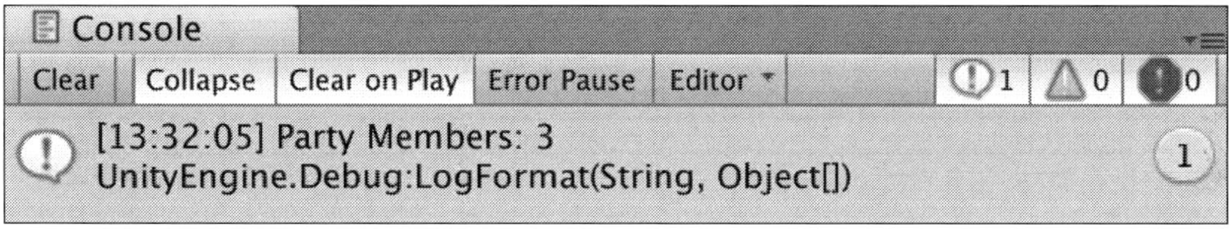


Figure 4.8: Screenshot of list item output in the console

Knowing how many elements are in a list is highly useful; however, in most cases, that information is not enough. We want to be able to modify our lists as needed, which we'll discuss next.

# Accessing and modifying lists

List elements can be accessed and modified like arrays with a subscript operator and index, as long as the index is within the `List` class's range. However, the `List` class has a variety of methods that extend its functionality, such as adding, inserting, and removing elements.

Sticking with the `QuestPartyMembers` list, let's add a new member to the team:

```
QuestPartyMembers.Add("Craven the Necromancer");
```

The `Add()` method appends the new element at the end of the list, which brings the `QuestPartyMembers` count to four and the element order to the following:

```
{ "Grim the Barbarian", "Merlin the Wise", "Sterling the Knight",
    "Craven the Necromancer"};
```

To add an element to a specific spot in a list, we can pass the index and the value that we want to add to the `Insert()` method:

```
QuestPartyMembers.Insert(1, "Tanis the Thief");
```

When an element is inserted at a previously occupied index, all the elements in the list have their indices increased by `1`. In our example, `"Tanis the Thief"` is now at index `1`, meaning that `"Merlin the Wise"` is now at index `2` instead of `1`, and so on:

```
{ "Grim the Barbarian", "Tanis the Thief", "Merlin the Wise", "Sterling
    the Knight", "Craven the Necromancer"};
```

Removing an element is just as simple; all we need is the index or the literal value, and the `List` class does the work:

```
// Both of these methods would remove the required element
QuestPartyMembers.RemoveAt(0);
QuestPartyMembers.Remove("Grim the Barbarian");
```

At the end of our edits, `QuestPartyMembers` now contains the following elements indexed from `0` to `3`:

```
{ "Tanis the Thief", "Merlin the Wise", "Sterling the Knight", "Craven
    the Necromancer"};
```

> There are many more `List` class methods that allow for value checks, finding and sorting elements, and working with ranges. A full method list, with descriptions, can be found here: `https://docs.microsoft.com/en-us/dotnet/api/system.collections.generic.list-1?view=netframework-4.7.2.`

While lists are great for single-value elements, there are cases where you'll need to store information or data containing more than one value. This is where dictionaries come into play.

# Dictionaries

The **Dictionary** type steps away from arrays and lists by storing value pairs in each element, instead of single values. These elements are referred to as key-value pairs: the key acts as the index, or lookup value, for its corresponding value. Unlike arrays and lists, dictionaries are unordered. However, they can be sorted and ordered in various configurations after they are created.

Declaring a dictionary is almost the same as declaring a list, but with one added detail—both the key and the value type need to be specified inside the arrow symbols:

```
Dictionary<keyType, valueType> name = new Dictionary<keyType,
  valueType>();
```

To initialize a dictionary with key-value pairs, do the following:

- Use a pair of curly brackets at the end of the declaration.
- Add each element within its pair of curly brackets, with the key and the value separated by a comma.
- Separate elements with a comma, except the last element where the comma is optional.

It looks like this:

```
Dictionary<keyType, valueType> name = new Dictionary<keyType,
  valueType>()
{
    {key1, value1},
    {key2, value2}
};
```

An important note to consider when picking key values is that each key must be unique, and they cannot be changed. If you need to update a key, then you need to change its value in the variable declaration or remove the entire key-value pair and add another in code, which we'll look at next.

> Just like with arrays and lists, dictionaries can be initialized on a single line with no problems from Visual Studio. However, writing out each key-value pair on its line, as in the preceding example, is a good habit to get into—both for readability and your sanity.

Let's create a dictionary to store items that a character might carry:

1. Declare a `Dictionary` with a `key` type of `string` and a `value` type of `int` called `ItemInventory` in the `Start` method.
2. Initialize it to `new Dictionary<string, int>()`, and add three key-value pairs of your choice. Make sure each element is in its pair of curly brackets:

```
Dictionary<string, int> ItemInventory = new Dictionary<string,
int>()
    {
        { "Potion", 5 },
        { "Antidote", 7 },
        { "Aspirin", 1 }
    };
```

3. Add a debug log to print out the `ItemInventory.Count` property so that we can see how items are stored:

```
Debug.LogFormat("Items: {0}", ItemInventory.Count);
```

4. Save the file and play.

Here, a new dictionary, called `ItemInventory`, was created and initialized with three key-value pairs. We specified the keys as strings, with corresponding values as integers, and printed out how many elements `ItemInventory` currently holds:

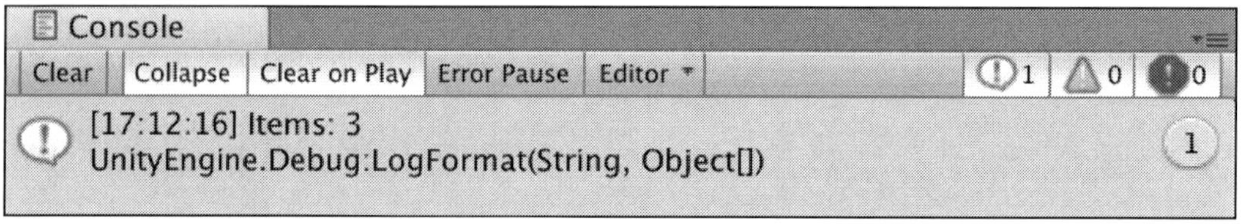


Figure 4.9: Screenshot of dictionary count in console

Like lists, we need to be able to do more than just print out the number of key-value pairs in a given dictionary. We'll explore adding, removing, and updating these values in the following section.

# Working with dictionary pairs

Key-value pairs can be added, removed, and accessed from dictionaries using both subscript and class methods. To retrieve an element's value, use the subscript operator with the element's key—in the following example, `numberOfPotions` would be assigned a value of `5`:

```
int numberOfPotions = ItemInventory["Potion"];
```

An element's value can be updated using the same method—the value associated with `"Potion"` would now be `10`:

```
ItemInventory["Potion"] = 10;
```

Elements can be added to dictionaries in two ways: with the `Add` method and with the subscript operator. The `Add` method takes in a key and a value and creates a new key-value element, as long as their types correspond to the dictionary declaration:

```
ItemInventory.Add("Throwing Knife", 3);
```

If the subscript operator is used to assign a value to a key that doesn't exist in a dictionary, the compiler will automatically add it as a new key-value pair. For example, if we wanted to add a new element for `"Bandage"`, we could do so with the following code:

```
ItemInventory["Bandage"] = 5;
```

This brings up a crucial point about referencing key-value pairs: it's better to be certain that an element exists before trying to access it, to avoid mistakenly adding new key-value pairs. Pairing the `ContainsKey` method with an `if` statement is the simple solution since `ContainsKey` returns a Boolean value based on whether the key exists. In the following example, we make sure that the `"Aspirin"` key exists using an `if` statement before modifying its value:

```
if(ItemInventory.ContainsKey("Aspirin"))
{
    ItemInventory["Aspirin"] = 3;
}
```

Finally, a key-value pair can be deleted from a dictionary using the `Remove()` method, which takes in a key parameter:

```
ItemInventory.Remove("Antidote");
```

> Like lists, dictionaries offer a variety of methods and functionality to make development easier, but we can't cover them all here. If you're curious, the official documentation can be found at `https://docs.microsoft.com/en-us/dotnet/api/system.collections.generic.dictionary-2?view=netframework-4.7.2`.

Collections are safely in our toolkit, so it's time for another quiz to make sure you're ready to move on to the next big topic: iteration statements.

# Pop quiz 2 – all about collections

- What is an element in an array or list?
- What is the index number of the first element in an array or list?
- Can a single array or list store different types of data?
- How can you add more elements to an array to make room for more data?

Since collections are groups or lists of items, they need to be accessible in an efficient manner. Luckily, C# has several iteration statements, which we'll talk about in the following section.

# Iteration statements

We've accessed individual collection elements through the subscript operator, along with collection type methods, but what do we do when we need to go through the entire collection element by element? In programming, this is called iteration, and C# provides several statement types that let us loop through (or iterate over, if you want to be technical) collection elements. Iteration statements are like methods, in that they store a block of code to be executed; unlike methods, they can repeatedly execute their code blocks as long as their conditions are met.

## for loops

The `for` loop is most commonly used when a block of code needs to be executed a certain number of times before the program continues. The statement itself takes in three expressions, each with a specific function to perform before the loop executes. Since `for` loops keep track of the current iteration, they are best suited to arrays and lists.

Take a look at the following looping statement blueprint:

```
for (initializer; condition; iterator)
{
    code block;
}
```

Let's break this down:

1. The `for` keyword starts the statement, followed by a pair of parentheses.

2. Inside the parentheses are the gatekeepers: the `initializer`, `condition`, and `iterator` expressions.
3. The loop starts with the `initializer` expression, which is a local variable created to keep track of how many times the loop has executed—this is usually set to 0 because collection types are zero-indexed.
4. Next, the `condition` expression is checked and, if true, proceeds to the iterator.
5. The `iterator` expression is used to either increase or decrease (increment or decrement) the initializer, meaning the next time the loop evaluates its condition, the initializer will be different.

> Increasing and decreasing a value by 1 is called incrementing and decrementing, respectively (`--` will decrease a value by 1, and `++` will increase it by 1).

That all sounds like a lot, so let's look at a practical example with the `QuestPartyMembers` list we created earlier:

```
List<string> QuestPartyMembers = new List<string>()
{ "Grim the Barbarian", "Merlin the Wise", "Sterling the Knight"};

for (int i = 0; i < QuestPartyMembers.Count; i++)
{
    Debug.LogFormat("Index: {0} - {1}", i, QuestPartyMembers[i]);
}
```

Let's go through the loop again and see how it works:

1. First, the `initializer` in the `for` loop is set as a local `int` variable named `i` with a starting value of `0`.
2. To ensure we never get an out-of-range exception, the `for` loop makes sure that the loop only runs another time if `i` is less than the number of elements in `QuestPartyMembers`:
    - With arrays, we use the `Length` property to determine how many items it has
    - With lists, we use the `Count` property
3. Finally, `i` is increased by 1 each time the loop runs with the `++` operator.

4. Inside the `for` loop, we've just printed out the index and the list element at that index using `i`.
5. Notice that `i` is in step with the index of the collection elements, since both start at 0:

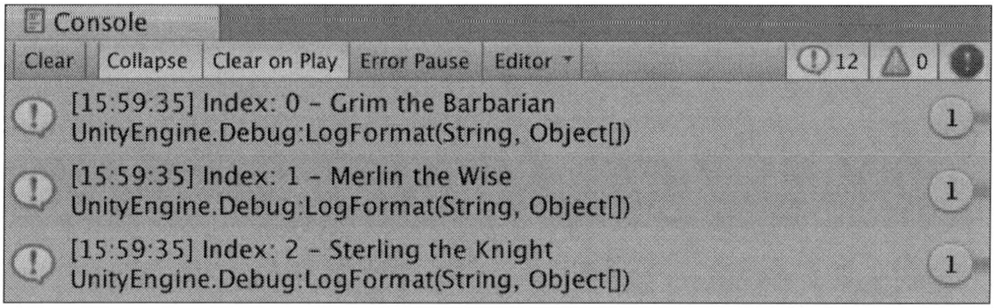


Figure 4.10: Screenshot of list values printed out with a for loop

> Traditionally, the letter `i` is typically used as the initializer variable name. If you happen to have nested `for` loops, the variable names used should be the letters j, k, l, and so on.

Let's try out our new iteration statements on one of our existing collections.

While we loop through `QuestPartyMembers`, let's see whether we can identify when a certain element is iterated over and add a special debug log just for that case:

1. Move the `QuestPartyMembers` list and `for` loop into a public function called `FindPartyMember` and call it in `Start`.
2. Add an `if` statement below the debug log in the `for` loop to check whether the current `questPartyMember` list matches `"Merlin the Wise"`:

```
if(QuestPartyMembers[i] == "Merlin the Wise")
{
    Debug.Log("Glad you're here Merlin!");
}
```

3. If it does, add a debug log of your choice, check that your code matches the screenshot below, and hit play:

```
// Start is called before the first frame update

void Start()
{
    FindPartyMember();
```

```
}

public void FindPartyMember()
{
    List<string> QuestPartyMembers = new List<string>()
    {
        "Grim the Barbarian",
        "Merlin the Wise",
        "Sterling the Knight"
    };
    Debug.LogFormat("Party Members: {0}", QuestPartyMembers.
Count);

    for(int i = 0; i < QuestPartyMembers.Count; i++)
    {
        Debug.LogFormat("Index: {0} - {1}", i,
QuestPartyMembers[i]);

        if(QuestPartyMembers[i] == "Merlin the Wise")
        {
            Debug.Log("Glad you're here Merlin!");
        }
    }
}
```

The console output should look almost the same, except that there is now an extra debug log—one that only printed once when it was Merlin's turn to go through the loop. More specifically, when `i` was equal to `1` on the second loop, the `if` statement fired and two logs were printed out instead of just one:

Figure 4.11: Screenshot of the for loop printing out list values and matching if statements

Using a standard `for` loop can be highly useful in the right situation, but there's seldom just one way to do things in programming, which is where the `foreach` statement comes into play.

# foreach loops

`foreach` loops take each element in a collection and store each one in a local variable, making it accessible inside the statement. The local variable type must match the collection element type to work properly. `foreach` loops can be used with arrays and lists, but they are especially useful with dictionaries, since dictionaries are key-value pairs instead of numeric indexes.

In blueprint form, a `foreach` loop looks like this:

```
foreach(elementType localName in collectionVariable)
{
    code block;
}
```

Let's stick with the `QuestPartyMembers` list example and do a roll call for each of its elements:

```
List<string> QuestPartyMembers = new List<string>()
{ "Grim the Barbarian", "Merlin the Wise", "Sterling the Knight"};

foreach(string partyMember in QuestPartyMembers)
{
    Debug.LogFormat("{0} - Here!", partyMember);
}
```

We can break this down as follows:

- The element type is declared as a `string`, which matches the values in `QuestPartyMembers`.
- A local variable, called `partyMember`, is created to hold each element as the loop repeats.

- The `in` keyword, followed by the collection we want to loop through, in this case, `QuestPartyMembers`, finishes things off:

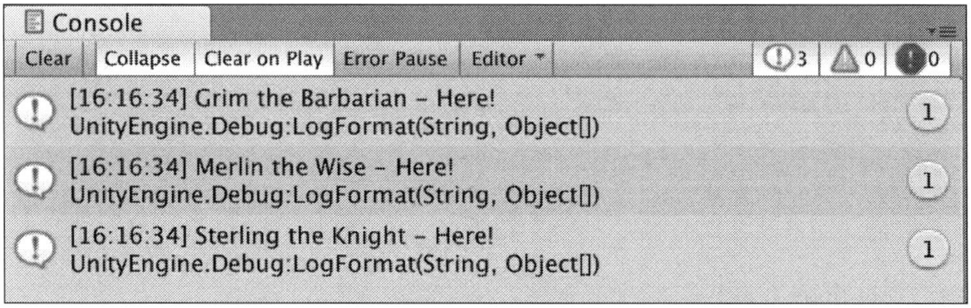


Figure 4.12: Screenshot of a foreach loop printing out list values

This is a good deal simpler than the `for` loop. However, when dealing with dictionaries, there are a few important differences we need to mention—namely how to deal with key-value pairs as local variables.

# Looping through key-value pairs

To capture a key-value pair in a local variable, we need to use the aptly named `KeyValuePair` type, assigning both the key and value types to match the dictionary's corresponding types. Since `KeyValuePair` is its type, it acts just like any other element type, as a local variable.

For example, let's loop through the `ItemInventory` dictionary we created earlier in the *Dictionaries* section and debug each key-value like a shop item description:

```
Dictionary<string, int> ItemInventory = new Dictionary<string, int>()
{
    { "Potion", 5},
    { "Antidote", 7},
    { "Aspirin", 1}
};

foreach(KeyValuePair<string, int> kvp in ItemInventory)
{
     Debug.LogFormat("Item: {0} - {1}g", kvp.Key, kvp.Value);
}
```

We've specified a local variable of `KeyValuePair`, called `kvp`, which is a common naming convention in programming, like calling the `for` loop initializer `i`, and setting the `key` and `value` types to `string` and `int` to match `ItemInventory`.

> To access the key and value of the local `kvp` variable, we use the `KeyValuePair` properties of `Key` and `Value`, respectively.

In this example, the keys are `strings` and the `values` are integers, which we can print out as the item name and item price:

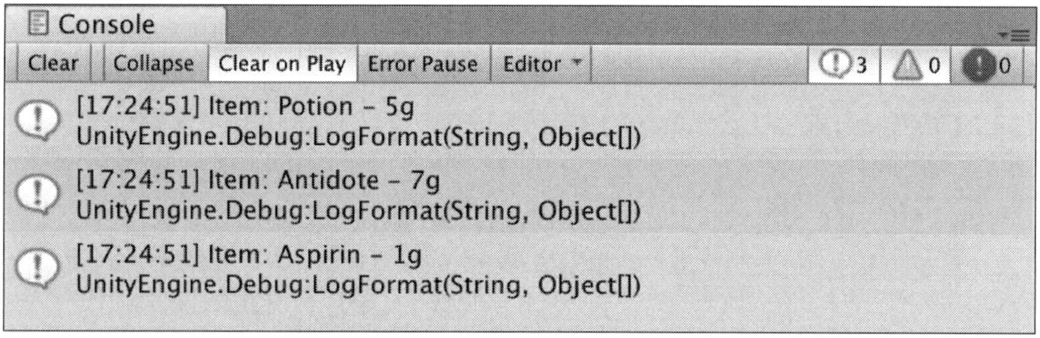


Figure 4.13: Screenshot of a foreach loop printing out dictionary key-value pairs

If you're feeling particularly adventurous, try out the following optional challenge to drive home what you've just learned.

## Hero's trial – finding affordable items

Using the preceding script, create a variable to store how much gold your fictional character has, and see whether you can add an `if` statement inside the `foreach` loop to check for items that you can afford.

> Hint: use `kvp.Value` to compare prices with what's in your wallet.

# while loops

`while` loops are similar to `if` statements in that they run as long as a single expression or condition is true.

Value comparisons and Boolean variables can be used as `while` conditions, and they can be modified with the `NOT` operator.

The `while` loop syntax says, *While my condition is true, keep running my code block indefinitely*:

```
Initializer
while (condition)
{
    code block;
    iterator;
}
```

With `while` loops, it's common to declare an initializer variable, as in a `for` loop, and manually increment or decrement it at the end of the loop's code block. We do this to avoid an infinite loop, which we will discuss at the end of the chapter. Depending on your situation, the initializer is usually part of the loop's condition.

> `while` loops are very useful when coding in C#, but they are not considered good practice in Unity because they can negatively impact performance and routinely need to be manually managed.

Let's take a common use case where we need to execute code while the player is alive, and then debug when that's no longer the case:

1. Create an initializer variable called `PlayerLives` of the `int` type, and set it to `3`:

   ```
   int PlayerLives = 3;
   ```

1. Create a new public function called `HealthStatus` and call it in `Start`.
2. Declare a `while` loop with the condition checking whether `PlayerLives` is greater than `0` (that is, the player is still alive):

   ```
   while(PlayerLives > 0)
   {
   }
   ```

3. Inside the `while` loop, debug something to let us know the character is still kicking, then decrement `PlayerLives` by 1 using the `--` operator:

   ```
   Debug.Log("Still alive!");
   PlayerLives--;
   ```

4. Add a debug log after the `while` loop curly brackets to print something when our lives run out:

```
Debug.Log("Player KO'd...");
```

Your code should look like the following:

```
int PlayerLives = 3;

// Start is called before the first frame update
void Start()
{
    HealthStatus();
}

public void HealthStatus()
{
    while(PlayerLives > 0)
    {
        Debug.Log("Still alive!");
        PlayerLives--;
    }

    Debug.Log("Player KO'd...");
}
```

With `PlayerLives` starting out at `3`, the `while` loop will execute three times. During each loop, the debug log, `"Still alive!"`, fires, and a life is subtracted from `PlayerLives`. When the `while` loop goes to run a fourth time, our condition fails because `PlayerLives` is `0`, so the code block is skipped and the final debug log prints out:

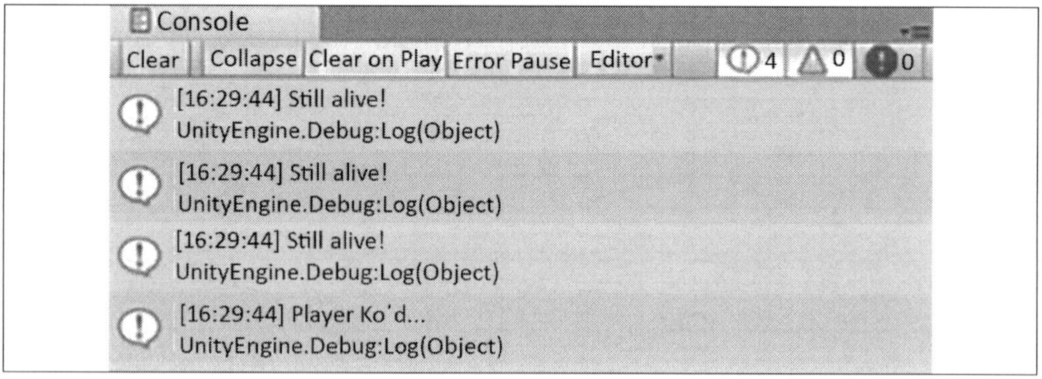


Figure 4.14: Screenshot of while-loop output in the console

If you're not seeing multiple "Still alive!" debug logs, make sure the **Collapse** button in the **Console** toolbar isn't selected.

The question now is what happens if a loop never stops executing? We'll discuss this issue in the following section.

# To infinity and beyond

Before finishing this chapter, we need to understand one extremely vital concept when it comes to iteration statements: *infinite loops*. These are exactly what they sound like: when a loop's conditions make it impossible for it to stop running and move on in the program. Infinite loops usually happen in `for` and `while` loops when the iterator is not increased or decreased; if the `PlayerLives` line of code was left out of the `while` loop example, Unity would freeze and/or crash, recognizing that `PlayerLives` would always be 3 and execute the loop forever.

Iterators are not the only culprits to be aware of; setting conditions in a `for` loop that will never fail, or evaluate to false, can also cause infinite loops. In the party members example, from the *Looping through key-value pairs* section, if we had set the `for` loop condition to `i < 0` instead of `i < QuestPartyMembers.Count`, `i` would always be less than `0`, looping until Unity crashed.

# Summary

As we bring the chapter to a close, we should reflect on how much we've accomplished and what we can build with that new knowledge. We know how to use simple `if-else` checks and more complex `switch` statements, allowing decision making in code. We can create variables that hold collections of values with arrays and lists or key-value pairs with dictionaries. This allows complex and grouped data to be stored efficiently. We can even choose the right looping statement for each collection type, while carefully avoiding infinite-loop crashes.

If you're feeling overloaded, that's perfectly OK—logical, sequential thinking is all part of exercising your programming brain.

The next chapter will complete the basics of C# programming with a look at classes, structs, and **object-oriented programming** (**OOP**). We'll be putting everything we've learned so far into these topics, preparing for our first real dive into understanding and controlling objects in the Unity engine.

# 5

# Working with Classes, Structs, and OOP

For obvious reasons, the goal of this book isn't to give you a splitting headache from information overload. However, these next topics will take you out of the beginner's cubicle and into the open air of **object-oriented programming** (**OOP**). Up to this point, we've been relying exclusively on predefined variable types that are part of the C# language: under-the-hood strings, lists, and dictionaries that are classes, which is why we can create them and use their properties through dot notation. However, relying on built-in types has one glaring weakness—the inability to deviate from the blueprints that C# has already set.

Creating your classes gives you the freedom to define and configure blueprints of your design, capturing information and driving action that is specific to your game or application. In essence, custom classes and OOP are the keys to the programming kingdom; without them, unique programs will be few and far between.

In this chapter, you'll get hands-on experience creating classes from scratch and discuss the inner workings of class variables, constructors, and methods. You'll also be introduced to the differences between reference and value type objects, and how these concepts can be applied inside Unity. The following topics will be discussed in more detail as you move along:

- Introducing OOP
- Defining classes
- Declaring structs
- Understanding reference and value types

- Integrating the object-oriented mindset
- Applying OOP in Unity

# Introducing OOP

OOP is the main programming paradigm that you'll use when coding in C#. If class and struct instances are the blueprints of our programs, then OOP is the architecture that holds everything together. When we refer to OOP as a programming paradigm, we are saying that it has specific principles for how the overall program should work and communicate.

Essentially, OOP focuses on objects rather than pure sequential logic—the data they hold, how they drive action, and, most importantly, how they communicate with each other.

# Defining classes

Back in *Chapter 2, The Building Blocks of Programming*, we briefly talked about how classes are blueprints for objects and mentioned that they can be treated as custom variable types. We also learned that the `LearningCurve` script is a class, but a special one that Unity can attach to objects in the scene. The main thing to remember with classes is that they are *reference types*—that is, when they are assigned or passed to another variable, the original object is referenced, not a new copy. We'll get into this after we discuss structs. However, before any of that, we need to understand the basics of creating classes.

For now, we're going to set aside how classes and scripts work in Unity and focus on how they are created and used in C#. Classes are created using the `class` keyword, as follows:

```
accessModifier class UniqueName
{
    Variables
    Constructors
    Methods
}
```

Any variables or methods declared inside a class belong to that class and are accessed through its unique class name.

To make the examples as cohesive as possible throughout this chapter, we'll be creating and modifying a simple `Character` class that a typical game would have. We'll also be moving away from code screenshots to get you accustomed to reading and interpreting code as you would see it "in the wild." However, the first thing we need is a custom class of our own, so let's create one.

We'll need a class to practice with before we can understand their inner workings, so let's create a new C# script and start from scratch:

1. Right-click on the `Scripts` folder that you created in *Chapter 1, Getting to Know Your Environment*, and choose **Create | C# Script**.
2. Name the script `Character`, open it up in Visual Studio, and delete all the generated code.
3. Declare a public class called `Character` followed by a set of curly braces, and then save the file. Your class code should exactly match the following code:

```
using System.Collections;
using System.Collections.Generic;
using UnityEngine;

public class Character
{

}
```

4. We deleted the generated code because we won't need to attach this script to a Unity GameObject.

`Character` is now registered as a public class blueprint. This means that any class in the project can use it to create characters. However, these are just the instructions—to create a character takes an additional step. This creational step is called *instantiation* and is the subject of the next section.

# Instantiating class objects

Instantiation is the act of creating an object from a specific set of instructions, which is called an instance. If classes are blueprints, instances are the houses built from their instructions; every new instance of `Character` is its object, just like two houses built from the same instructions are still two different physical structures. What happens to one doesn't have any repercussions on the other.

In *Chapter 4, Control Flow and Collection Types*, we created lists and dictionaries, which are default classes that come with C#, using their types and the `new` keyword. We can do the same thing for custom classes such as `Character`, which you'll do next.

We declared the `Character` class as public, which means that a `Character` instance can be created in any other class. Since we have `LearningCurve` working already, let's declare a new character in the `Start()` method.

Open `LearningCurve` and declare a new `Character` type variable, called `hero`, in the `Start()` method:

```
Character hero = new Character();
```

Let's break this down one step at a time:

1. The variable type is specified as `Character`, meaning that the variable is an instance of that class.
2. The variable is named `hero`, and it is created using the `new` keyword, followed by the `Character` class name and two parentheses. This is where the actual instance is created in the program's memory, even if the class is empty right now.
3. We can use the `hero` variable just like any other object we've worked with so far. When the `Character` class gets variables and methods of its own, we can access them from `hero` using dot notation.

> You could just as easily have used an inferred declaration when creating the `hero` variable, like so:
>
> ```
> var hero = new Character();
> ```

Now our character class can't do much without any class fields to work with. You'll be adding class fields, and more, in the next few sections.

# Adding class fields

Adding variables, or fields, to a custom class is no different than what we've already been doing with `LearningCurve`. The same concepts apply, including access modifiers, variable scope, and value assignments. However, any variables belonging to a class are created with the class instance, meaning that if there are no values assigned, they will default to zero or null. In general, choosing to set initial values comes down to what information they will store:

- If a variable needs to have the same starting value whenever a class instance is created, setting an initial value is a solid idea. This would be useful for something like experience points or the starting score.
- If a variable needs to be customized in every class instance, like `CharacterName`, leave its value unassigned and use a class constructor (a topic that we'll get to in the *Using constructors* section).

Every character class is going to need a few basic fields; it's your job to add them in the following section.

Let's incorporate two variables to hold the character's name and the number of starting experience points:

1. Add two `public` variables inside the `Character` class's curly braces—a `string` variable for the name, and an `integer` variable for the experience points.
2. Leave the `name` value empty, but set the experience points to `0` so that every character starts from the bottom:

```
public class Character
{
    public string name;
    public int exp = 0;
}
```

3. Add a debug log in `LearningCurve` right after the `Character` instance was initialized. Use it to print out the new character's `name` and `exp` variables using dot notation:

```
Character hero = new Character();
Debug.LogFormat("Hero: {0} - {1} EXP", hero.name, hero.exp);
```

4. When `hero` is initialized, `name` is assigned a null value that shows up as an empty space in the debug log, while `exp` prints out `0`. Notice that we didn't have to attach the `Character` script to any GameObjects in the scene; we just referenced them in `LearningCurve` and Unity did the rest. The console will now debug out our character information, which is referenced as follows:

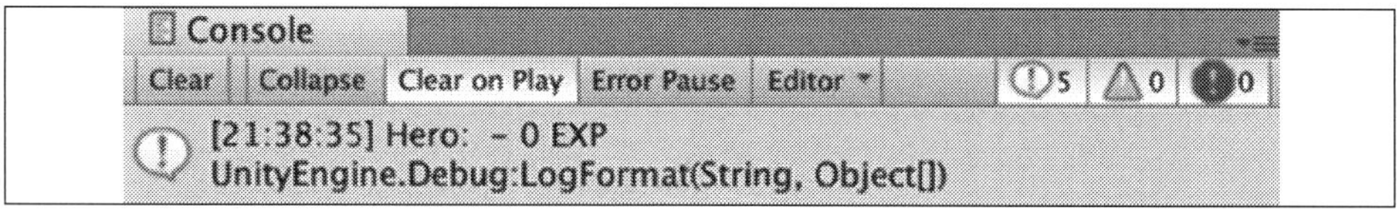


Figure 5.1: Screenshot of custom class properties printed in the console

At this point, our class is working, but it's not very practical with these empty values. You'll need to fix that with what's called a class constructor.

# Using constructors

Class constructors are special methods that fire automatically when a class instance is created, which is similar to how the `Start` method runs in `LearningCurve`. Constructors build the class according to its blueprint:

- If a constructor is not specified, C# generates a default one. The default constructor sets any variables to their default type values—numeric values are set to zero, Booleans to false, and reference types (classes) to null.
- Custom constructors can be defined with parameters, just like any other method, and are used to set class variable values at initialization.
- A class can have multiple constructors.

Constructors are written like regular methods but with a few differences; for instance, they need to be public, have no return type, and the method name is always the class name. As an example, let's add a basic constructor with no parameters to the `Character` class and set the name field to something other than null.

Add this new code directly underneath the class variables, as follows:

```
public string name;
public int exp = 0;

public Character()
{
    name = "Not assigned";
}
```

Run the project in Unity and you'll see the `hero` instance using this new constructor. The debug log will show the hero's name as **Not assigned** instead of a null value:

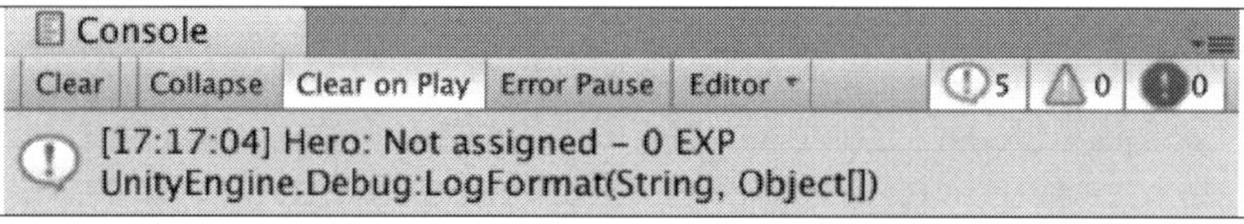


Figure 5.2: Screenshot of unassigned custom class variables printed to the console

This is good progress, but we need the class constructor to be more flexible. This means that we need to be able to pass in values so that they can be used as starting values, which you'll do next.

Now, the `Character` class is starting to behave more like a real object, but we can make this even better by adding a second constructor to take in a name at initialization and set it to the `name` field:

1. Add another constructor to `Character` that takes in a `string` parameter, called `name`.
2. Assign the parameter to the class's `name` variable using the `this` keyword. This is called *constructor overloading*:

```
public Character(string name)
{
    this.name = name;
}
```

> For convenience, constructors will often have parameters that share a name with a class variable. In these cases, use the `this` keyword to specify which variable belongs to the class. In the example here, `this.name` refers to the class's name variable, while `name` is the parameter; without the `this` keyword, the compiler will throw a warning because it won't be able to tell them apart.

3. Create a new `Character` instance in `LearningCurve`, called `heroine`. Use the custom constructor to pass in a name when it's initialized and print out the details in the console:

```
Character heroine = new Character("Agatha");
Debug.LogFormat("Hero: {0} - {1} EXP", heroine.name,
        heroine.exp);
```

When a class has multiple constructors or a method has multiple variations, Visual Studio will show a set of arrows in the autocomplete popup that can be scrolled through using the arrow keys:

Figure 5.3: Screenshot of multiple method constructors in Visual Studio

4. We can now choose between the basic and custom constructor when we initialize a new `Character` class. The `Character` class itself is now far more flexible when it comes to configuring different instances for different situations:

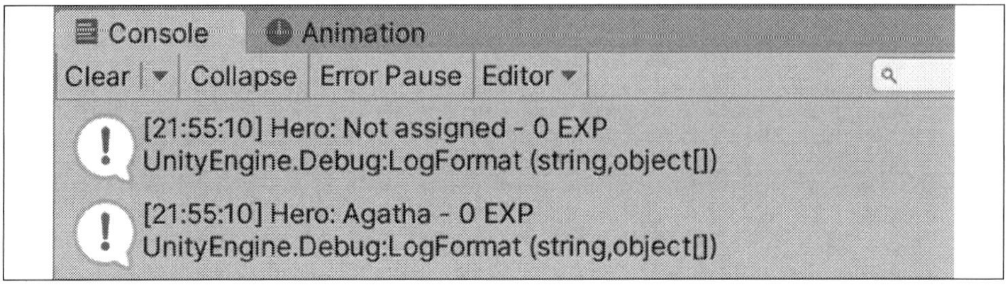


Figure 5.4: Screenshot of multiple custom class instances printed in the console

Now the real work starts; our class needs methods to be able to do anything useful besides acting as a storage facility for variables. Your next task is to put this into practice.

# Declaring class methods

Adding methods to custom classes is no different from adding them to `LearningCurve`. However, this is a good opportunity to talk about a staple of good programming—**Don't Repeat Yourself** (**DRY**). DRY is a benchmark of all well-written code. Essentially, if you find yourself writing the same line, or lines, over and over, it's time to rethink and reorganize. This usually takes the form of a new method to hold the repeated code, making it easier to modify and call that functionality elsewhere in the current script or even from other scripts.

> In programming terms, you'll see this referred to as **abstracting** out a method or feature.

We have a fair bit of repeated code already, so let's take a look and see where we can increase the legibility and efficiency of our scripts.

Our repeated debug logs are a perfect opportunity to abstract out some code directly into the `Character` class:

1. Add a new `public` method with a `void` return type, called `PrintStatsInfo`, to the `Character` class.

2. Copy and paste the debug log from `LearningCurve` into the method body.
3. Change the variables to `name` and `exp`, since they can now be referenced from the class directly:

```
public void PrintStatsInfo()
{
    Debug.LogFormat("Hero: {0} - {1} EXP", name, exp);
}
```

4. Replace the character debug log that we previously added to `LearningCurve` with method calls to `PrintStatsInfo`, and click on play:

```
Character hero = new Character();
hero.PrintStatsInfo();

Character heroine = new Character("Agatha");
heroine.PrintStatsInfo();
```

5. Now that the `Character` class has a method, any instance can freely access it using dot notation. Since `hero` and `heroine` are both separate objects, `PrintStatsInfo` debugs their respective `name` and `exp` values to the console.

> This behavior is better than having the debug logs directly in `LearningCurve`. It's always a good idea to group functionality into a class and drive action through methods. This makes the code more readable—as our `Character` objects are giving a command when printing out the debug logs, instead of repeating code.

The entire `Character` class should look like the following code:

```
using System.Collections;
using System.Collections.Generic;
using UnityEngine;

public class Character
{
    public string name;
    public int exp = 0;

    public Character()
    {
        name = "Not assigned";
    }
```

```
        public Character(string name)
        {
            this.name = name;
        }

        public void PrintStatsInfo()
        {
            Debug.LogFormat("Hero: {0} - {1} EXP", name, exp);
        }
    }
```

With classes covered, you're well on your way to writing modularized code that's readable, lightweight, and reusable. Now it's time to tackle the class's cousin object —the struct!

# Declaring structs

**Structs** are similar to classes in that they are also blueprints for objects you want to create in your programs. The main difference is that they are *value types*, meaning they are passed by value instead of reference, like classes are. When structs are assigned or passed to another variable, a new copy of the struct is created, so the original isn't referenced at all. We'll go into this in more detail in the next section. First, we need to understand how structs work and the specific rules that apply when creating them.

Structs are declared in the same way as classes, and can hold fields, methods, and constructors:

```
accessModifier struct UniqueName
{
    Variables
    Constructors
    Methods
}
```

Like classes, any variables and methods belong exclusively to the struct and are accessed by its unique name.

However, structs have a few limitations:

- Variables cannot be initialized with values inside the struct declaration unless they're marked with the `static` or `const` modifier—you can read more about this in *Chapter 10, Revisiting Types, Methods, and Classes*.

- Constructors without parameters aren't permitted.
- Structs come with a default constructor that will automatically set all variables to their default values according to their type.

Every character requires a good weapon, and these weapons are the perfect fit for a struct object over a class. We'll discuss why that is in the *Understanding reference and value types* section of this chapter. However, first, you're going to create one to play around with.

Our characters are going to need good weapons to see them through quests, which are good candidates for a simple struct:

1. Right-click on the `Scripts` folder, choose **Create**, and select **C# Script**.
2. Name it `Weapon`, open it up in Visual Studio, and delete all the generated code after `using UnityEngine`.
3. Declare a public struct called `Weapon`, followed by a set of curly braces, and then save the file.
4. Add a field for `name` of type `string` and another field for `damage` of type `int`:

> You can have classes and structs nested within each other, but this is generally frowned upon because it clutters up the code.

```
public struct Weapon
{
    public string name;
    public int damage;
}
```

5. Declare a constructor with the `name` and `damage` parameters, and set the struct fields using the `this` keyword:

```
public Weapon(string name, int damage)
{
    this.name = name;
    this.damage = damage;
}
```

6. Add a debug method below the constructor to print out the weapon information:

```
public void PrintWeaponStats()
```

```
{
    Debug.LogFormat("Weapon: {0} - {1} DMG", name, damage);
}
```

7. In `LearningCurve`, create a new `Weapon` struct using the custom constructor and the `new` keyword:

   ```
   Weapon huntingBow = new Weapon("Hunting Bow", 105);
   ```

8. Our new `huntingBow` object uses the custom constructor and provides values for both fields on initialization.

> It's a good idea to limit scripts to a single class, but it's fairly common to see structs that are used exclusively by a class included in the file.

Now that we have an example of both reference (class) and value (struct) objects, it's time to get acquainted with each of their finer points. More specifically, you'll need to understand how each of these objects is passed and stored in memory.

# Understanding reference and value types

Other than keywords and initial field values, we haven't seen much difference between classes and structs so far. Classes are best suited for grouping together complex actions and data that will change throughout a program; structs are a better choice for simple objects and data that will remain constant for the most part. Besides their uses, they are fundamentally different in one key area—that is, how they are passed or assigned between variables. Classes are *reference types*, meaning that they are passed by reference; structs are *value types*, meaning that they are passed by value.

## Reference types

When the instances of our `Character` class are initialized, the `hero` and `heroine` variables don't hold their class information—instead, they hold a reference to where the object is located in the program's memory. If we assigned `hero` or `heroine` to another variable in the same class, the memory reference is assigned, not the character data. This has several implications, the most important being that if we have multiple variables storing the same memory reference, a change to one affects them all.

Topics like this are better demonstrated than explained; it's up to you to try this out in a practical example, next.

It's time to test that the `Character` class is a reference type:

1. Declare a new `Character` variable in `LearningCurve` called `hero2`. Assign `hero2` to the `hero` variable and use the `PrintStatsInfo` method to print out both sets of information.
2. Click play and take a look at the two debug logs that show up in the console:

```
Character hero = new Character();
Character hero2 = hero;

hero.PrintStatsInfo();
hero2.PrintStatsInfo();
```

3. The two debug logs will be identical because `hero2` was assigned to `hero` when it was created. At this point, both `hero2` and `hero` point to where `hero` is located in memory:

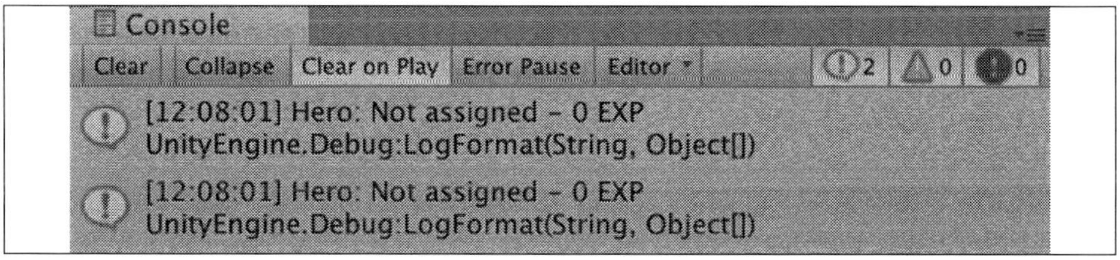


Figure 5.5: Screenshot of the struct stats printed to the console

4. Now, change the name of `hero2` to something fun and click play again:

```
Character hero2 = hero;
hero2.name = "Sir Krane the Brave";
```

5. You'll see that both `hero` and `hero2` now have the same name, even though only one of our characters' data was changed:

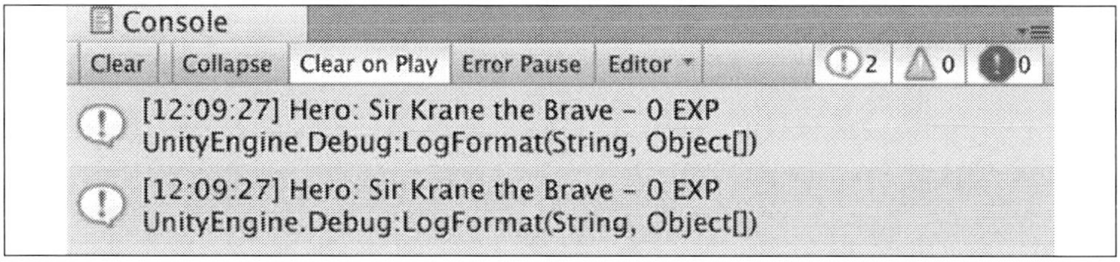


Figure 5.6: Screenshot of class instance properties printed to the console

The lesson here is that reference types need to be treated carefully and not copied when assigned to new variables. Any change to one reference trickles through all other variables holding the same reference.

If you're trying to copy a class, either create a new, separate instance or reconsider whether a struct might be a better choice for your object blueprint. You'll get a better glimpse of value types in the following section.

# Value types

When a struct object is created, all of its data is stored in its corresponding variable with no references or connections to its memory location. This makes structs useful for creating objects that need to be copied quickly and efficiently, while still retaining their separate identities. Try this out with our `Weapon` struct in the following exercise.

Let's create a new weapon object by copying `huntingBow` into a new variable and updating its data to see whether the changes affect both structs:

1. Declare a new `Weapon` struct in `LearningCurve`, and assign `huntingBow` as its initial value:

```
Weapon huntingBow = new Weapon("Hunting Bow", 105);
Weapon warBow = huntingBow;
```

2. Print out each weapon's data using the debug method:

```
huntingBow.PrintWeaponStats();
warBow.PrintWeaponStats();
```

3. The way they're set up now, both `huntingBow` and `warBow` will have the same debug logs, just like our two characters did before we changed any data:

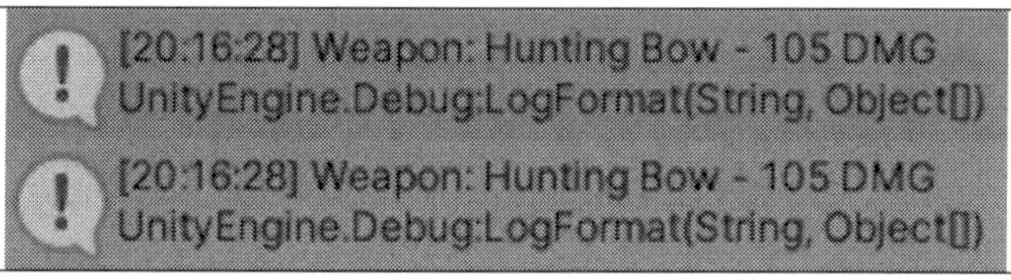


Figure 5.7: Screenshot of the struct instances printed to the console

4. Change the `warBow.name` and `warBow.damage` fields to values of your choice and click on play again:

```
Weapon warBow = huntingBow;
warBow.name = "War Bow";
warBow.damage = 155;
```

5. The console will show that only the data relating to `warBow` was changed, and that `huntingBow` retains its original data.

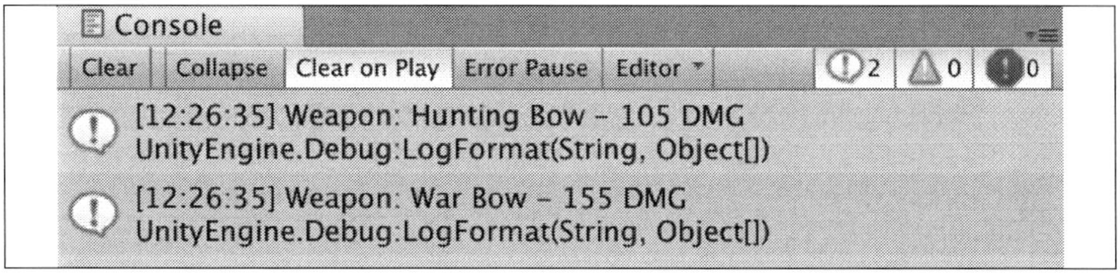


Figure 5.8: Screenshot of updated struct properties printed to console

The takeaway from this example is that structs are easily copied and modified as their separate objects, unlike classes, which retain references to an original object. Now that we understand a little more about how structs and classes work under the hood, and confirmed how reference and value types behave in their natural habitat, we're in a good place to start talking about one of the most important coding topics, OOP, and how it fits into the programming landscape.

# Integrating the object-oriented mindset

Things in the physical world operate on a similar level to OOP; when you want to buy a soft drink, you grab a can of soda, not the liquid itself. The can is an object, grouping related information and actions together in a self-contained package. However, there are rules when dealing with objects, both in programming and the grocery store —for instance, who can access them. Different variations and generic actions all play into the nature of the objects all around us.

In programming terms, these rules are the main tenets of OOP: *encapsulation*, *inheritance*, and *polymorphism*.

# Encapsulation

One of the best things about OOP is that it supports encapsulation—defining how accessible an object's variables and methods are to outside code (this is sometimes referred to as *calling code*). Take our soda can as an example—in a vending machine, the possible interactions are limited. Since the machine is locked, not just anyone can come up and grab one; if you happen to have the right change, you'll be allowed provisional access to it, but in a specified quantity. If the machine itself is locked inside a room, only someone with the door key will even know the soda can exists.

The question you're asking yourself now is, how do we set these limitations? The simple answer is that we've been using encapsulation this entire time by specifying access modifiers for our object variables and methods.

If you need a refresher, go back and visit the *Access modifiers* section in *Chapter 3, Diving into Variables, Types, and Methods*.

Let's try out a simple encapsulation example to understand how this works in practice. Our `Character` class is public, as are its fields and methods. However, what if we wanted a method that can reset a character's data to its initial values? This could come in handy, but could prove disastrous if it was accidentally called, making it a perfect candidate for a private object member:

1. Create a `private` method called `Reset`, with no return value inside the `Character` class. Set the `name` and `exp` variables back to `"Not assigned"` and `0`, respectively:

```
private void Reset()
{
    this.name = "Not assigned";
    this.exp = 0;
}
```

2. Try and call `Reset()` from `LearningCurve` after printing out the `hero2` data:

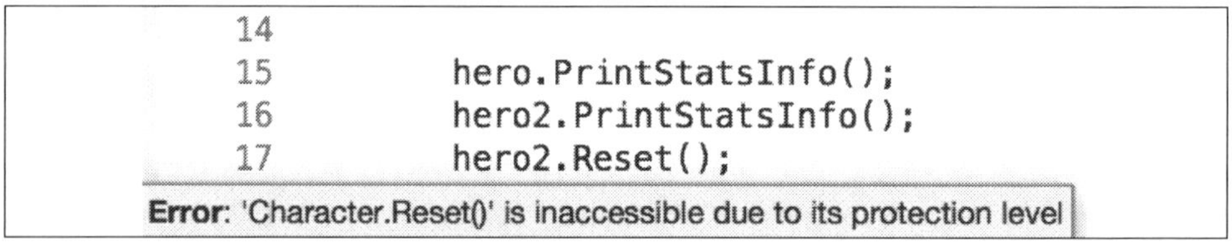


Figure 5.9: Screenshot of an inaccessible method in the Character class

If you're wondering whether Visual Studio is broken, it's not. Marking a method or variable as private will make it inaccessible inside this class or struct using dot notation; if you manually type it in and hover over `Reset()`, you'll see an error message regarding the method being protected.

To actually call this private method, we could add a reset command inside the class constructor:

```
public Character()
{
    Reset();
}
```

> Encapsulation does allow more complex accessibility setups with objects; however, for now, we're going to stick with `public` and `private` members. As we begin to flesh out our game prototype in the next chapter, we'll add in different modifiers as needed.

Now, let's talk about inheritance, which is going to be your best friend when creating class hierarchies in your future games.

# Inheritance

A C# class can be created in the image of another class, sharing its member variables and methods, but able to define its unique data. In OOP, we refer to this as *inheritance*, and it's a powerful way of creating related classes without having to repeat code. Take the soda example again—there are generic sodas on the market that have all the same basic properties, and then there are special sodas. The special sodas share the same basic properties but have different branding, or packaging, that sets them apart. When you look at both side by side, it's obvious that they're both cans of soda—but they're also obviously not the same.

The original class is usually called the base or parent class, while the inheriting class is called the derived or child class. Any base class members marked with the `public`, `protected`, or `internal` access modifiers are automatically part of the derived class—except for constructors. Class constructors always belong to their containing class, but they can be used from derived classes to keep repeated code to a minimum. Don't worry too much about the different base class scenarios right now. Instead, let's try out a simple game example.

Most games have more than one type of character, so let's create a new class called `Paladin` that inherits from the `Character` class. You can add this new class to the `Character` script or create a new one. If you're adding the new class to the `Character` script, make sure it's outside the `Character` class's curly brackets:

```
public class Paladin: Character
{

}
```

Just as `LearningCurve` inherits from `MonoBehavior`, all we need to do is add a colon and the base class we want to inherit from, and C# does the rest. Now, any `Paladin` instances will have access to a `name` property and an `exp` property along with a `PrintStatsInfo` method.

> It's generally considered best practice to create a new script for different classes instead of adding them to existing ones. This separates your scripts and avoids having too many lines of code in any single file (called a bloated file).

This is great, but how do inherited classes handle their construction? You can find out in the following section.

## Base constructors

When a class inherits from another class, they form a pyramid of sorts with member variables flowing down from the parent class to any of its derived children. The parent class isn't aware of any of its children, but all children are aware of their parent. However, parent class constructors can be called directly from child constructors with a simple syntax modification:

```
public class ChildClass: ParentClass
{
    public ChildClass(): base()
    {

    }
}
```

The `base` keyword stands in for the parent constructor—in this case, the default constructor. However, since `base` is standing in for a constructor, and a constructor is a method, a child class can pass parameters up the pyramid to its parent constructor.

Since we want all `Paladin` objects to have a name, and `Character` already has a constructor that handles this, we can call the `base` constructor directly from the `Paladin` class and save ourselves the trouble of rewriting a constructor:

1. Add a constructor to the `Paladin` class that takes in a `string` parameter, called `name`. Use a `colon` and the `base` keyword to call the parent constructor, passing in `name`:

```
public class Paladin: Character
{
    public Paladin(string name): base(name)
    {

    }
}
```

2. In `LearningCurve`, create a new `Paladin` instance called `knight`. Use the base constructor to assign a value. Call `PrintStatsInfo` from `knight` and take a look at the console:

```
Paladin knight = new Paladin("Sir Arthur");
knight.PrintStatsInfo();
```

3. The debug log will be the same as our other `Character` instances, but with the name that we assigned to the `Paladin` constructor:

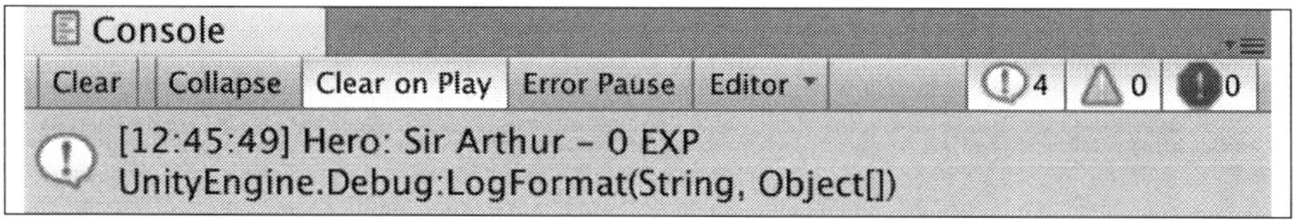


Figure 5.10: Screenshot of base character constructor properties

When the `Paladin` constructor fires, it passes the `name` parameter to the `Character` constructor, which sets the `name` value. Essentially, we used the `Character` constructor to do the initialization work for the `Paladin` class, making the `Paladin` constructor only responsible for initializing its unique properties, which it doesn't have at this point.

Aside from inheritance, there will be times when you want to make new objects out of a combination of other existing objects. Think of Lego; you don't start building from nothing—you already have blocks of different colors and structures to work with. In programming terms, this is called *composition*, which we'll discuss in the following section.

# Composition

Aside from inheritance, classes can be composed of other classes. Take our `Weapon` struct, for example. `Paladin` can easily contain a `Weapon` variable inside itself and have access to all its properties and methods. Let's do that by updating `Paladin` to take in a starting weapon and assign its value in the constructor:

```
public class Paladin: Character
{
    public Weapon;

    public Paladin(string name, Weapon weapon): base(name)
    {
        this.weapon = weapon;
    }
}
```

Since `weapon` is unique to `Paladin` and not `Character`, we need to set its initial value in the constructor. We also need to update the `knight` instance to include a `Weapon` variable. So, let's use `huntingBow`:

```
Paladin knight = new Paladin("Sir Arthur", huntingBow);
```

If you run the game now, you won't see anything different because we're using the `PrintStatsInfo` method from the `Character` class, which doesn't know about the `Paladin` class's `weapon` property. To tackle this problem, we need to talk about polymorphism.

# Polymorphism

Polymorphism is the Greek word for *many-shaped* and applies to OOP in two distinct ways:

- Derived class objects are treated the same as parent class objects. For example, an array of `Character` objects could also store `Paladin` objects, as they derive from `Character`.
- Parent classes can mark methods as `virtual`, meaning that their instructions can be modified by derived classes using the `override` keyword. In the case of `Character` and `Paladin`, it would be useful if we could debug different messages from `PrintStatsInfo` for each one.

Polymorphism allows derived classes to keep the structure of their parent class while also having the freedom to tailor actions to fit their specific needs. Any method you mark as `virtual` will give you the freedom of object polymorphism. Let's take this new knowledge and apply it to our character debug method.

Let's modify `Character` and `Paladin` to print out different debug logs using `PrintStatsInfo`:

1. Change `PrintStatsInfo` in the `Character` class by adding the `virtual` keyword between `public` and `void`:

   ```
   public virtual void PrintStatsInfo()
   {
       Debug.LogFormat("Hero: {0} - {1} EXP", name, exp);
   }
   ```

2. Declare the `PrintStatsInfo` method in the `Paladin` class using the `override` keyword. Add a debug log to print out the `Paladin` properties in whatever way you like:

   ```
   public override void PrintStatsInfo()
   {
       Debug.LogFormat("Hail {0} - take up your {1}!", name,
                weapon.name);
   }
   ```

This might look like repeated code, which we already said is bad form, but this is a special case. What we've done by marking `PrintStatsInfo` as `virtual` in the `Character` class is to tell the compiler that this method can have many shapes according to the calling class.

3. When we declared the overridden version of `PrintStatsInfo` in `Paladin`, we added the custom behavior that only applies to that class. Thanks to polymorphism, we don't have to choose which version of `PrintStatsInfo` we want to call from a `Character` or `Paladin` object—the compiler already knows:

Figure 5.11: Screenshot of polymorphic character properties

This was a lot to take in, I know. So, let's review some of the main points of OOP as we approach the finish line:

- OOP is all about grouping related data and actions into objects—objects that can communicate and act independently from each other.
- Access to class members can be set using access modifiers, just like variables.
- Classes can inherit from other classes, creating trickle-down hierarchies of parent/child relationships.
- Classes can have members of other class or struct types.
- Classes can override any parent methods marked as `virtual`, allowing them to perform custom actions while retaining the same blueprint.

> OOP is not the only programming paradigm that can be used with C#—you can find practical explanations of the other main approaches here: `http://cs.lmu.edu/~ray/notes/paradigms`.

All the OOP you've learned in this chapter is directly applicable to the C# world. However, we still need to put this into perspective with Unity, which is what you'll spend the rest of the chapter focusing on.

# Applying OOP in Unity

If you're around OOP languages enough, you'll eventually hear the phrase *everything is an object* whispered like a secret prayer between developers. Following OOP principles, everything in a program should be an object, but GameObjects in Unity can represent your classes and structs. However, that's not to say all objects in Unity have to be in the physical scene, so we can still use our newfound programmed classes behind the scenes.

## Objects are a class act

Back in *Chapter 2, The Building Blocks of Programming*, we discussed how a script is transformed into a component when it's added to a GameObject in Unity. Think of this in terms of the OOP principle of composition—GameObjects are the parent containers, and they can be made up of multiple components. This might sound contradictory to the idea of one C# class per script but, in truth, that's more of a guideline for better readability than an actual requirement. Classes can be nested inside one another—it just gets messy fast. However, having multiple script components attached to a single GameObject can be very useful, especially when dealing with manager classes or behaviors.

> Always try to boil down objects to their most basic elements, and then use composition to build bigger, more complex objects out of those smaller classes. It's easier to modify a GameObject made out of small, interchangeable components than one large, clunky one.

Let's take a look at **Main Camera** to see this in action:

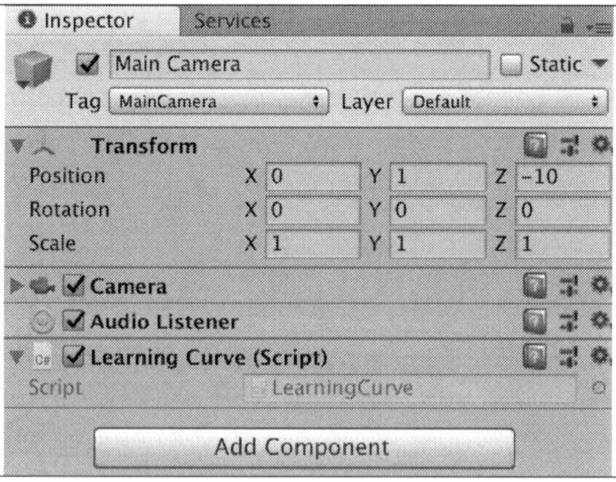


Figure 5.12: Screenshot of the Main Camera object in the Inspector

Each component in the preceding screenshot (**Transform**, **Camera**, **Audio Listener**, and the **Learning Curve** script) started as a class in Unity. Like instances of `Character` or `Weapon`, these components become objects in computer memory when we click on play, complete with their member variables and methods.

If we were to attach `LearningCurve` (or any script or component) to 1,000 GameObjects and click on play, 1,000 separate instances of `LearningCurve` would be created and stored in memory.

We can even create our instances of these components using their component name as the data type. Like classes, Unity component classes are reference types and can be created like any other variable. However, finding and assigning these Unity components is slightly different than what you've seen so far. For that, you'll need to understand a little more about how GameObjects work in the following section.

# Accessing components

Now that we know how components act on GameObjects, how do we go about accessing their specific instances? Lucky for us, all GameObjects in Unity inherit from the `GameObject` class, which means we can use their member methods to find anything we need in a scene. There are two ways to assign or retrieve GameObjects that are active in the current scene:

1. Through the `GetComponent()` or `Find()` methods in the `GameObject` class, which work with public and private variables.
2. By dragging and dropping the GameObjects themselves from the `Project` panel directly into variable slots in the **Inspector** tab. This option only works with public variables in C#, since they are the only ones that will appear in the Inspector. If you decide you need a private variable displayed in the Inspector, you can mark it with the `SerializeField` attribute.

> You can learn more about attributes and `SerializeField` in the Unity documentation: `https://docs.unity3d.com/ScriptReference/SerializeField.html`.

Let's take a look at the syntax of the first option.

## Accessing components in code

Using `GetComponent` is fairly simple, but its method signature is slightly different from other methods that we've seen so far:

```
GameObject.GetComponent<ComponentType>();
```

All we need is the component type that we're looking for, and the `GameObject` class will return the component if it exists and null if it doesn't. There are other variations of the `GetComponent` method, but this one is the simplest because we don't need to know specifics about the `GameObject` class that we're looking for. This is called a `generic` method, which we'll discuss further in *Chapter 13, Exploring Generics, Delegates, and Beyond*. However, for now, let's just work with the camera's transform.

Since `LearningCurve` is already attached to the **Main Camera** object, let's grab the camera's `Transform` component and store it in a public variable. The `Transform` component controls an object's position, rotation, and scale in Unity, so it's a handy example:

1. Add a new public `Transform` type variable, called `CamTransform`, to `LearningCurve`:

```
public Transform CamTransform;
```

2. Initialize `CamTransform` in `Start` using the `GetComponent` method from the `GameObject` class. Use the `this` keyword, since `LearningCurve` is attached to the same `GameObject` component as the `Transform` component.
3. Access and debug the `localPosition` property of `CamTransform` using dot notation:

```
void Start()
{
    CamTransform = this.GetComponent<Transform>();
    Debug.Log(CamTransform.localPosition);
}
```

4. We've added an uninitialized `public Transform` variable at the top of `LearningCurve` and initialized it using the `GetComponent` method inside `Start`. `GetComponent` finds the `Transform` component attached to this `GameObject` component and returns it to `CamTransform`. With `CamTransform` now storing a `Transform` object, we have access to all its class properties and methods—including `localPosition` in the following screenshot:

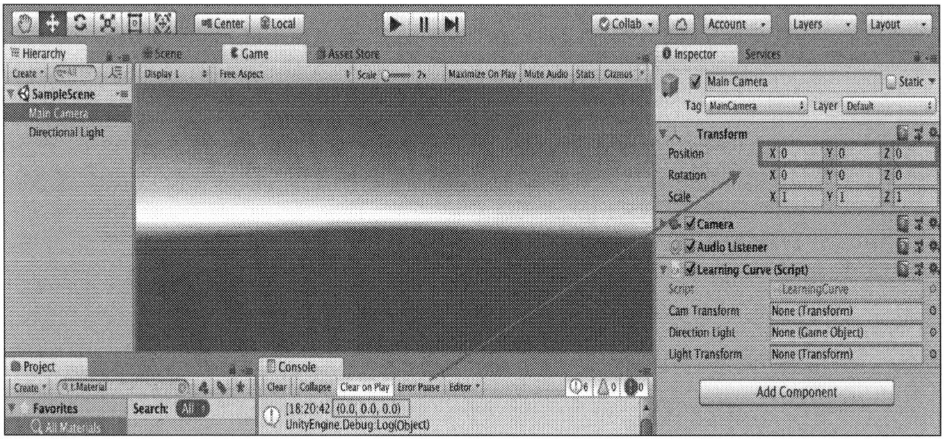

Figure 5.13: Screenshot of the Transform position printed to the console

The `GetComponent` method is fantastic for quickly retrieving components, but it only has access to components on the GameObject that the calling script is attached to. For instance, if we use `GetComponent` from the `LearningCurve` script attached to the **Main Camera**, we'll only be able to access the **Transform**, **Camera**, and **Audio Listener** components.

If we want to reference a component on a separate GameObject, such as **Directional Light**, we would need to get a reference to the object first using the `Find` method. All it takes is the name of a GameObject, and Unity will kick back the appropriate GameObject for us to store or manipulate.

For reference, the name of each GameObject can be found at the top of the **Inspector** tab with the object selected:

Figure 5.14: Screenshot of the Directional Light object in the Inspector

Finding objects in your game scenes is crucial in Unity, so you'll need to practice. Let's take the objects we have to work with and practice finding and assigning their components.

Let's take the `Find` method out for a spin and retrieve the **Directional Light** object from `LearningCurve`:

1. Add two variables to `LearningCurve` underneath `CamTransform`—one of type `GameObject` and one of type `Transform`:

    ```
    public GameObject DirectionLight;
    public Transform LightTransform;
    ```

2. Find the `Directional Light` component by name, and use it to initialize `DirectionLight` inside the `Start()` method:

    ```
    void Start()
    {
        DirectionLight = GameObject.Find("Directional Light");
    }
    ```

3. Set the value of `LightTransform` to the `Transform` component attached to `DirectionLight`, and debug its `localPosition`. Since `DirectionLight` is its `GameObject` now, `GetComponent` works perfectly:

    ```
    LightTransform = DirectionLight.GetComponent<Transform>();
    Debug.Log(LightTransform.localPosition);
    ```

4. Before running the game, it's important to understand that method calls can be chained together to cut down the number of code steps. For instance, we could initialize `LightTransform` in a single line by combining `Find` and `GetComponent` without having to go through `DirectionLight`:

    ```
    GameObject.Find("Directional Light").GetComponent<Transform>();
    ```

> A word of warning—long lines of chained code can lead to poor readability and confusion when working on complex applications. It's a good rule of thumb to avoid lines longer than this example.

While finding objects in code always works, you can also simply drag and drop the objects themselves into the **Inspector** tab. Let's demonstrate how to do that in the following section.

# Drag and drop

Now that we've covered the code-intensive way of doing things, let's take a quick look at Unity's drag and drop functionality. Although dragging and dropping is much faster than using the `GameObject` class in code, Unity sometimes loses the connections between objects and variables made this way when saving or exporting projects, or when Unity updates.

> When you need to assign a few variables quickly, then, by all means, take advantage of this feature. For most cases, I'd advise sticking with code.

Let's change `LearningCurve` to show how to assign a `GameObject` component using drag and drop:

1. Comment out the following line of code, where we used `GameObject.Find()` to retrieve and assign the `Directional Light` object to the `DirectionLight` variable:

```
//DirectionLight = GameObject.Find("Directional Light");
```

2. Select the **Main Camera** GameObject, drag **Directional Light** to the `Direction Light` field in the **Learning Curve** component, and click on play:

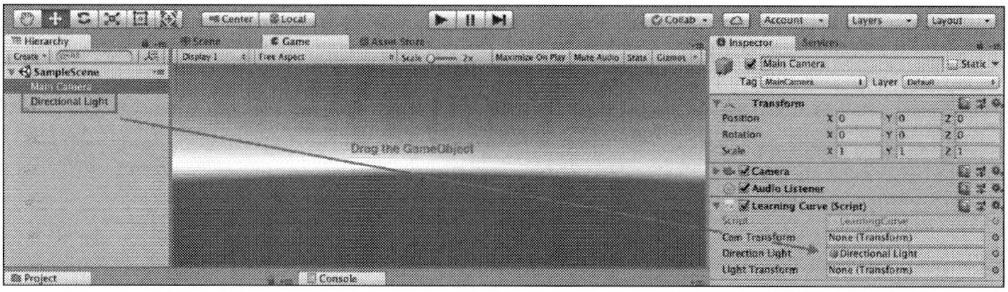


Figure 5.15: Screenshot of dragging Directional Light to the script property

3. The **Directional Light** GameObject is now assigned to the `DirectionLight` variable. No code was involved because Unity assigned the variable internally, with no change to the `LearningCurve` class.

> It is important to understand a few things when deciding whether to assign variables using drag and drop or `GameObject.Find()`. First, the `Find()` method is marginally slower, leaving your game open to performance issues if you are calling the method multiple times in multiple scripts. Second, you need to be sure your GameObjects all have unique names in the scene hierarchy; if they don't, it may lead to some nasty bugs in situations where you have several objects of the same name or change the object names themselves.

# Summary

Our journey into classes, structs, and OOP marks the end of the first section on the fundamentals of C#. You've learned how to declare your classes and structs, which is the scaffolding for every application or game you'll ever make. You've also identified the differences in how these two objects are passed and accessed and how they relate to OOP. Finally, you got hands-on with the tenets of OOP—creating classes using inheritance, composition, and polymorphism.

Identifying related data and actions, creating blueprints to give them shape, and using instances to build interactions are a strong foundation for approaching any program or game. Add the ability to access components to the mix, and you've got the makings of a Unity developer.

The next chapter will segue into the basics of game development and scripting object behavior directly in Unity. We'll start by fleshing out the requirements of a simple open-world adventure game, work with GameObjects in the scene, and finish off with a white-boxed environment ready for our characters.

# Pop quiz – all things OOP

1. What method handles the initialization logic inside a class?
2. Being value types, how are structs passed?
3. What are the main tenets of OOP?
4. Which `GameObject` class method would you use to find a component on the same object as the calling class?

# 6

# Getting Your Hands Dirty with Unity

Creating a game involves much more than just simulating actions in code. Design, story, environment, lighting, and animation all play an important part in setting the stage for your players. A game is, first and foremost, an experience, which code alone can't deliver.

Unity has placed itself at the forefront of game development over the past decade by bringing advanced tools to programmers and non-programmers alike. Animation and effects, audio, environment design, and much more are all available directly from the Unity Editor without a single line of code. We'll discuss these topics as we define the requirements, environment, and game mechanics of our game. However, first, we need a topical introduction to game design.

Game design theory is a big area of study and learning all its secrets can consume an entire career. However, we'll only be getting hands-on with the basics; everything else is up to you to explore! This chapter will set us up for the rest of the book and will cover the following topics:

- A game design primer
- Building a level
- Lighting basics
- Animating in Unity

# A game design primer

Before jumping into any game project, it's important to have a blueprint of what you want to build. Sometimes, ideas will start crystal clear in your mind, but the minute you start creating character classes or environments, things seem to drift away from your original intention. This is where the game's design allows you to plan out the following touchpoints:

- **Concept**: The big-picture idea and design of a game, including its genre and play style.
- **Core mechanics**: The playable features or interactions that a character can take in-game. Common gameplay mechanics include jumping, shooting, puzzle-solving, or driving.
- **Control schemes**: A map of the buttons and/or keys that give players control over their character, environment interactions, and other executable actions.
- **Story**: The underlying narrative that fuels a game, creating empathy and a connection between players and the game world they play in.
- **Art style**: The game's overarching look and feel, consistent across everything from characters and menu art to the levels and environment.
- **Win and lose conditions**: The rules that govern how the game is won or lost, usually consisting of objectives or goals that carry the weight of potential failure.

These topics are by no means an exhaustive list of what goes into designing a game. However, they're a good place to start fleshing out something called a game design document, which is your next task!

# Game design documents

Googling game design documents will result in a flood of templates, formatting rules, and content guidelines that can leave a new programmer ready to give it all up. The truth is, design documents are tailored to the team or company that creates them, making them much easier to draft than the internet would have you think.

In general, there are three types of design documentation, as follows:

- **Game Design Document** (**GDD**): The GDD houses everything from how the game is played to its atmosphere, story, and the experience it's trying to create. Depending on the game, this document can be a few pages long or several hundred.

- **Technical Design Document** (**TDD**): This document focuses on all the technical aspects of the game, from the hardware it will run on to how the classes and program architecture need to be built out. Like a GDD, the length will vary based on the project.
- **One-page**: Usually used for marketing or promotional situations, a one-page is essentially a snapshot of your game. As the name suggests, it should only take up a single page.

> There's no right or wrong way to format a GDD, so it's a good place to let your brand of creativity thrive. Throw in pictures of reference material that inspires you; get creative with the layout—this is your place to define your vision.

The game we'll be working on throughout the rest of this book is fairly simple and won't require anything as detailed as a GDD or TDD. Instead, we'll create a one-page to keep track of our project objectives and some background information.

# The Hero Born one-page

To keep us on track going forward, I've put together a simple document that lays out the basics of the game prototype. Read through it before moving on, and try to start imagining some of the programming concepts that we've learned so far being put into practice:

**Concept**

Game prototype focused on stealthily avoiding enemies and collecting health items - with a little FPS on the side.

**Gameplay**

Main mechanic centers around using line-of-sight to stay one step ahead of patrolling enemies and collecting required items.

Combat will consist of shooting projectiles at enemies, which will automatically trigger an attack response.

**Interface**

Control scheme for movement will be the WASD or arrow keys using the mouse for camera control. Shooting mechanic will use the Space bar, and item collection will work off of object collisions.

Simple HUD will show items collected and remaining ammo, as well as a standard health bar.

**Art Style**

Level and character art style will be all primitive GameObjects for fast and efficient, no-frills development. These can be swapped out at a later date with 3D models or terrain environments if needed.

Figure 6.1: Hero Born one-page document

Now that you have a high-level view of the bones of our game, you're ready to start building a prototype level to house the game experience.

# Building a level

When building your game levels, it's always a good idea to try to see things from the perspective of your players. How do you want them to see the environment, interact with it, and feel while walking around in it? You're literally building the world your game exists in, so be consistent.

With Unity, you have the option of creating outdoor environments using the Terrain tool, blocking out something set indoors with basic shapes and geometry, or a mixture of the two. You can even import 3D models from other programs, such as Blender, to use as objects in your scenes.

> Unity has a great introduction to the Terrain tool at `https://docs.unity3d.com/Manual/script-Terrain.html`. If you're going down that route, there's also a wonderful free asset on the Unity Asset Store called Terrain Toolkit 2017, available at `https://assetstore.unity.com/packages/tools/terrain/terrain-toolkit-2017-83490`. You can also use tools like Blender to create your game assets, which you can find at `https://www.blender.org/features/modeling/`.

For *Hero Born*, we'll stick with a simple indoor arena-like setting that's easy to get around, but with a few corners to hide in. You'll cobble all this together using **primitives**—base object shapes provided in Unity—because of how easy they are to create, scale, and position in a scene.

# Creating primitives

Looking at games you might play regularly, you're probably wondering how you'll ever create models and objects that look so realistic that it seems you could reach through the screen and grab them. Fortunately, Unity has a set of primitive GameObjects that you can select from to prototype faster. These won't be super fancy or high-definition, but they are a lifesaver when you're learning the ropes or don't have a 3D artist on your development team.

If you open up Unity, you can go into the **Hierarchy** panel and click on **+ | 3D Object**, and you'll see all the available options, but only about half of these are primitives or common shapes, indicated in the following screenshot by a red highlight:

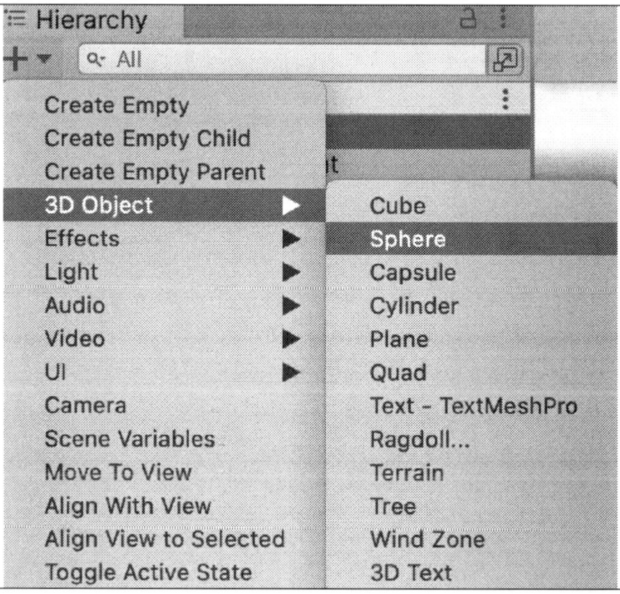


Figure 6.2: Unity Hierarchy window with the Create option selected

Other 3D object options, such as **Terrain**, **Wind Zone**, and **Tree**, are a bit too advanced for what we need, but feel free to experiment with them if you're interested.

> You can find out more about building Unity environments at `https://docs.unity3d.com/Manual/CreatingEnvironments.html`.

Before we jump too far ahead, it's usually easier to walk around when you've got a floor underneath you, so let's start by creating a ground plane for our arena using the following steps:

1. In the **Hierarchy** panel, click on **+ | 3D Object | Plane**
2. Ensuring the new object is selected in the **Hierarchy** tab, rename the GameObject to `Ground` in the **Inspector** tab

3. In the **Transform** dropdown, change **Scale** to 3 in the **X**, **Y**, and **Z** axes:

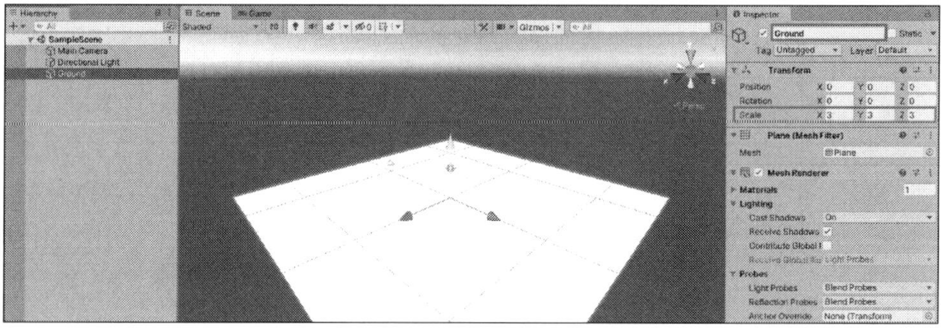


Figure 6.3: Unity Editor with a ground plane

4. If the lighting in your scene looks dimmer or different from the preceding screenshot, select **Directional Light** in the **Hierarchy** panel, and set the **Intensity** value of the **Directional Light** component to 1:

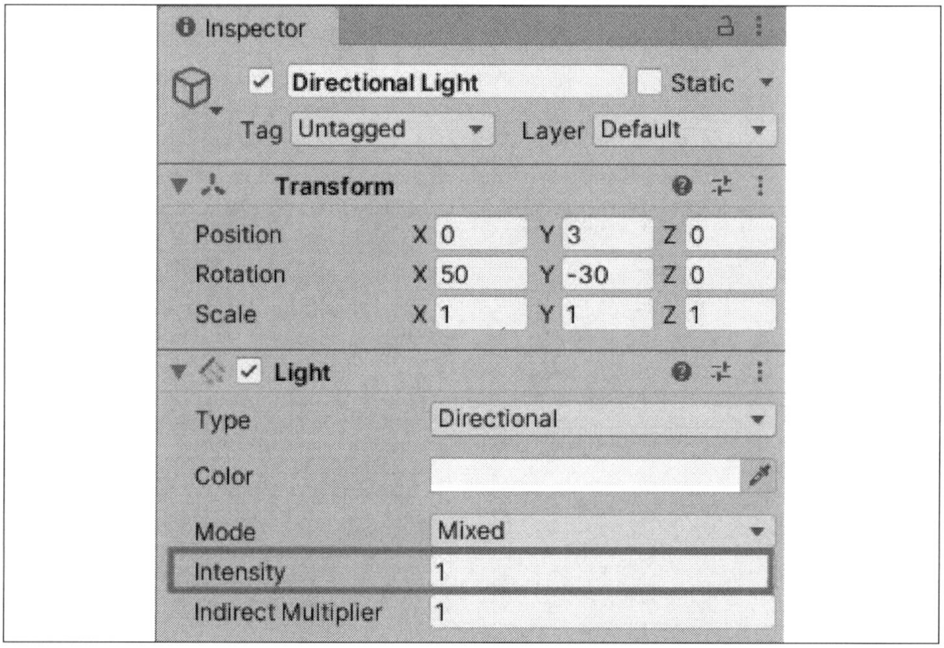


Figure 6.4: Directional Light object selected in the Inspector pane

We created a plane GameObject and increased its size to make more room for our future character to walk around. This plane will act like a 3D object bound by real-life physics, meaning other objects can't just fall through. We'll talk more about the Unity physics system and how it works in *Chapter 7, Movement, Camera Controls, and Collisions*. Right now, we need to start thinking in 3D.

# Thinking in 3D

Now that we have our first object in the scene, we can talk about 3D space—specifically, how an object's position, rotation, and scale behave in three dimensions. If you think back to high school geometry, a graph with an *x* and *y* coordinate system should be familiar. To put a point on the graph, you had to have an *x* value and a *y* value.

Unity supports both 2D and 3D game development, and if we were making a 2D game, we could leave our explanation there. However, when dealing with 3D space in the Unity Editor, we have an extra axis, called the *z* axis. The *z* axis maps depth, or perspective, giving our space and the objects in it their 3D quality.

This might be confusing at first, but Unity has some nice visual aids to help you get your head on straight. In the top right of the **Scene** panel, you'll see a geometric-looking icon with the *x*, *y*, and *z* axes marked in red, green, and blue, respectively. All GameObjects in the scene will show their axis arrows when they're selected in the **Hierarchy** window:

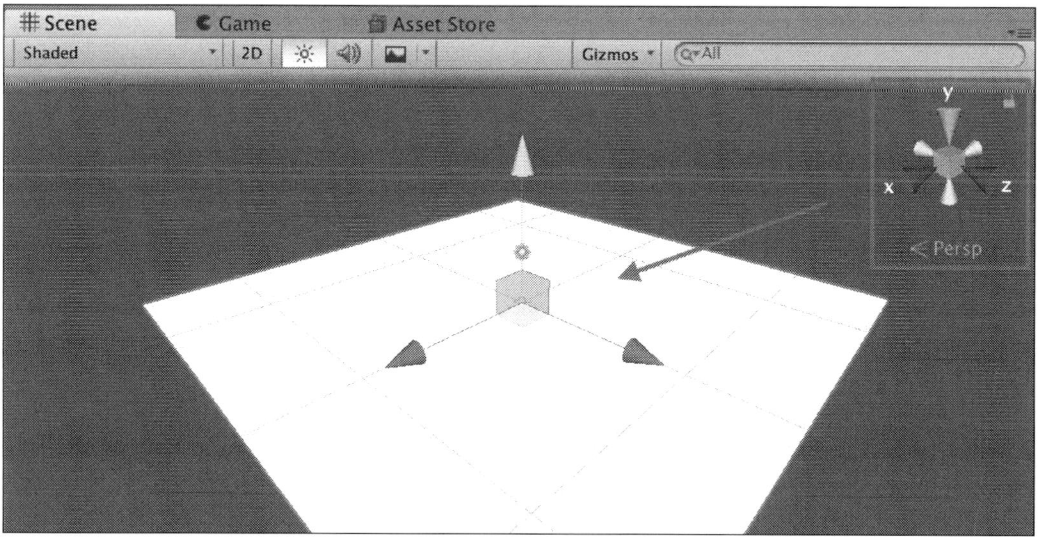


Figure 6.5: Scene view with the orientation gizmo highlighted

This will always show the current orientation of the scene and the objects placed inside it. Clicking on any of these colored axes will switch the scene orientation to the selected axis. Give this a go by yourself to get comfortable with switching perspectives.

If you take a look at the **Ground** object's **Transform** component in the **Inspector** pane, you'll see that the position, rotation, and scale are all determined by these three axes.

The position determines where the object is placed in the scene, its rotation governs how it's angled, and its scale takes care of its size. These values can be changed at any time in the **Inspector** pane or in a C# script:

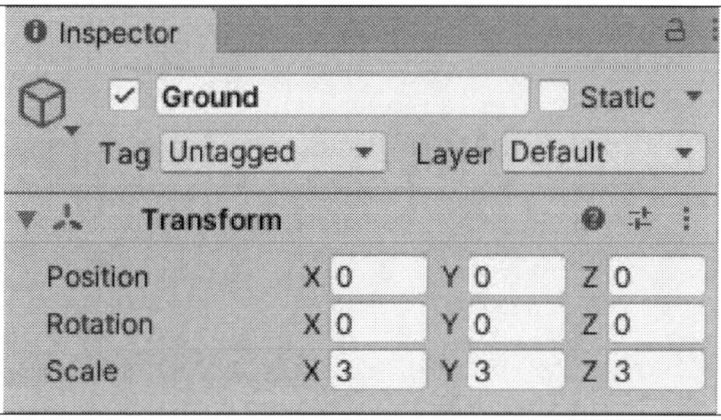


Figure 6.6: Ground object selected in Hierarchy

Right now, the ground is looking a little boring. Let's change that with a material.

# Materials

Our ground plane isn't very interesting right now, but we can use **materials** to breathe a little life into the level. Materials control how GameObjects are rendered in the scene, which is determined by the material's Shader. Think of **Shaders** as being responsible for combining lighting and texture data into a representation of how the material looks.

Each GameObject starts with a default **Material** and **Shader** (pictured here from the **Inspector** pane), setting its color to a standard white:

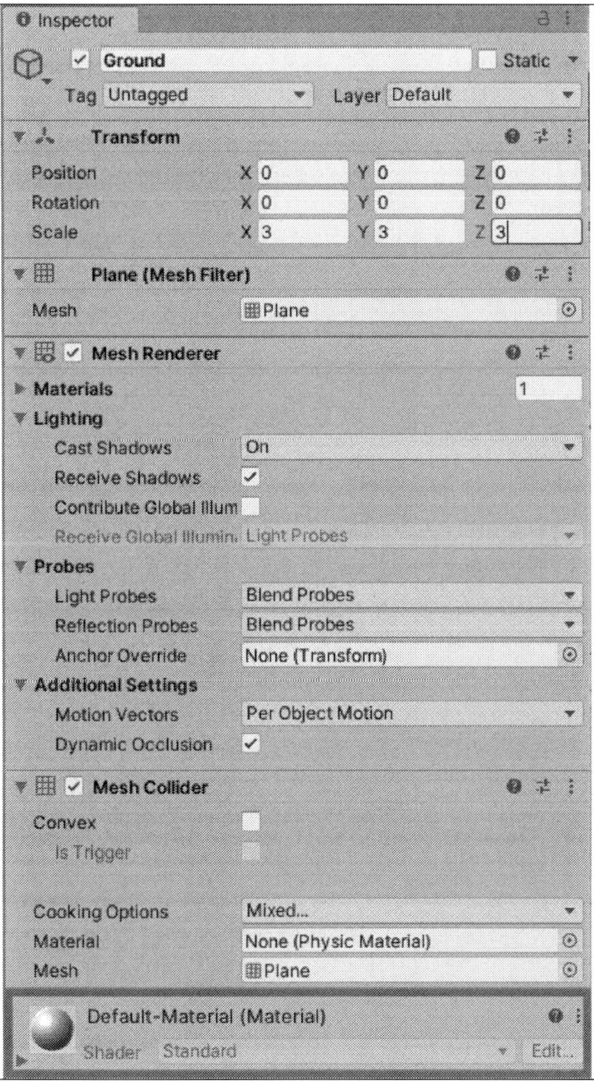


Figure 6.7: Default material on an object

To change an object's color, we need to create a material and drag it to the object that we want to modify. Remember, everything is an object in Unity—materials are no different. Materials can be reused on as many GameObjects as needed, but any change to a material will also carry through to any objects the material is attached to. If we had several enemy objects in the scene with a material that set them all to red, and we changed that base material color to blue, all our enemies would then be blue.

Blue is eye-catching; let's change the color of the ground plane to match, and create a new material to turn the ground plane from a dull white to a dark and vibrant blue:

1. Create a new folder in the **Project** panel and name it `Materials`.
2. Inside the **Materials** folder, right-click **+ | Material**, and name it `Ground_Mat`.
3. Click on the color box next to the **Albedo** property, select your color from the color picker window that pops up, and then close it.
4. Drag the `Ground_Mat` object from the **Project** pane, and drop it onto the `Ground` GameObject in the **Hierarchy** panel:

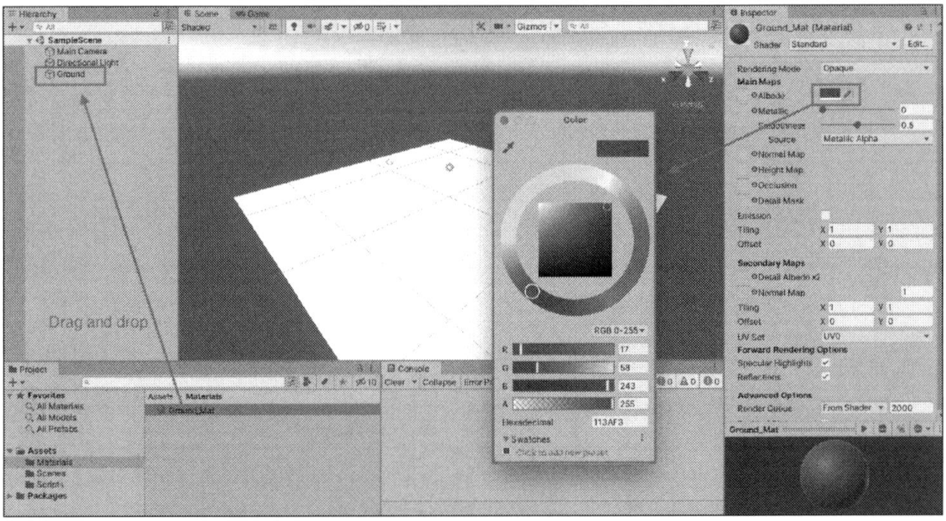


Figure 6.8: Material color picker

The new material you created is now a project asset. Dragging and dropping `Ground_Mat` into the `Ground` GameObject changed the color of the plane, which means any changes to `Ground_Mat` will be reflected in the `Ground`:

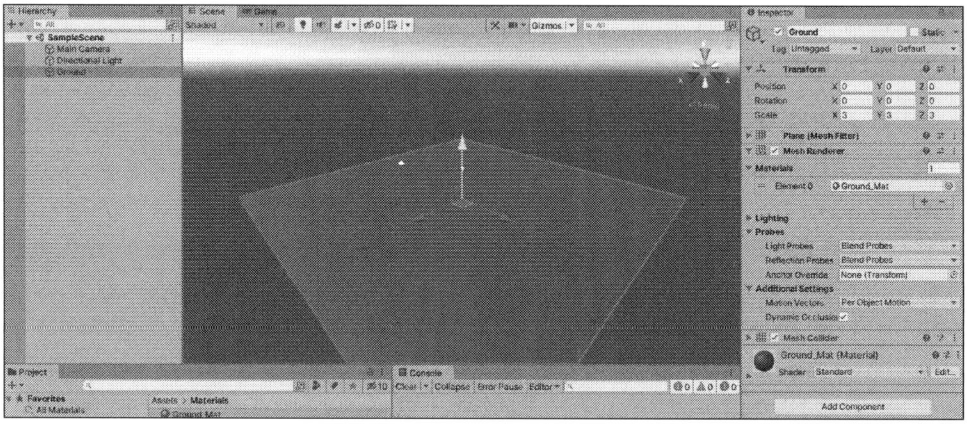


Figure 6.9: Ground plane with the updated color material

The ground is our canvas; however, in 3D space, it can support other 3D objects on its surface. It'll be up to you to populate it with fun and interesting obstacles for your future players.

# White-boxing

White-boxing is a design term for laying out ideas using placeholders, usually with the intent of replacing them with finished assets at a later date. In level design, the practice of white-boxing is to block out an environment with primitive GameObjects to get a sense of how you want it to look. This is a great way to start things off, especially during the prototyping stages of your game.

Before diving into Unity, I'd like to start with a simple sketch of the basic layout and position of my level. This gives us a bit of direction and will help to get our environment laid out quicker.

In the following drawing, you'll be able to see the arena I have in mind, with a raised platform in the middle that is accessible by ramps, complete with small turrets in each corner:

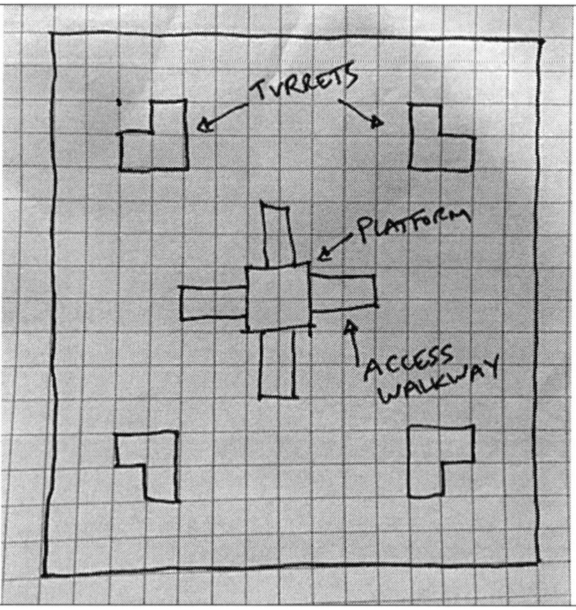


Figure 6.10: Sketch of the Hero Born level arena

> Don't worry if you're not an artist—neither am I. The important thing is to get your ideas down on paper to solidify them in your mind and work out any kinks before getting busy in Unity.

Before you go ahead full steam and put this sketch into production, you'll need to familiarize yourself with a few Unity Editor shortcuts to make white-boxing easier.

# Editor tools

When we discussed the Unity interface in *Chapter 1*, *Getting to Know Your Environment*, we skimmed over some of the Toolbar functionality, which we need to revisit so that we know how to efficiently manipulate GameObjects. You can find these in the upper-left corner of the Unity Editor:

Figure 6.11: Unity Editor toolbar

Let's break down the different tools that are available to us from the toolbar in the preceding screenshot:

1. **Hand**: This allows you to pan and change your position in the scene by clicking and dragging your mouse.
2. **Move**: This lets you move objects along the *x*, *y*, and *z* axes by dragging their respective arrows.
3. **Rotate**: This lets you adjust an object's rotation by turning or dragging its respective markers.
4. **Scale**: This lets you modify an object's scale by dragging it to specific axes.
5. **Rect Transform**: This combines the move, rotate, and scale tool functionality into one package.
6. **Transform**: This gives you access to the position, rotation, and scale of an object all at once.
7. **Custom Editor Tools**: This allows you to access any custom tools you've built for the editor. Don't worry about this one, as it's way beyond our scope. If you want to know more, please refer to the documentation at `https://docs.unity3d.com/2020.1/Documentation/ScriptReference/EditorTools.EditorTool.html`.

> You can find more information about navigating and positioning GameObjects in the **Scene** panel at `https://docs.unity3d.com/Manual/PositioningGameObjects.html`. It's also worth noting that you can move, position, and scale objects using the **Transform** component, as we discussed earlier in the chapter.

Panning and navigating the Scene can be done with similar tools, although not from the Unity Editor itself:

- To look around, hold down the right mouse button and drag it to pan the camera around.
- To move around while using the camera, continue to hold the right mouse button and use the *W*, *A*, *S*, and *D* keys to move forward, back, left, and right, respectively.
- Hit the *F* key to zoom in and focus on a GameObject that has been selected in the **Hierarchy** panel.

> This kind of scene navigation is more commonly known as fly-through mode, so when I ask you to focus on or navigate to a particular object or viewpoint, use a combination of these features.
>
> Getting around the Scene view can be a task in itself sometimes, but it all comes down to repeated practice. For a more detailed list of scene navigation features, visit `https://docs.unity3d.com/Manual/SceneViewNavigation.html`.

Even though the ground plane won't allow our character to fall through it, we could still walk off the edge at this point. Your job is to wall in the arena so that the player has a confined locomotion area.

# Hero's trial – putting up drywall

Using primitive cubes and the toolbar, position four walls around the level using the **Move**, **Rotate**, and **Scale** tools to section off the main arena:

1. In the **Hierarchy** panel, select **+** | **3D Object** | **Cube** to create the first wall and name it `Wall_01`.
2. Set its scale value to 30 for the *x* axis, 1.5 for the *y* axis, and 0.2 for the *z* axis.

> Note that planes operate on a scale 10 times larger than objects—so our plane with a length of 3 is the same length as an object of length 30.

3. With the `Wall_01` object selected in the **Hierarchy** panel, switch to the position tool in the upper-left corner and use the red, green, and blue arrows to position the wall at the edge of the ground plane.
4. Repeat *steps 1-3* until you have four walls surrounding your area:

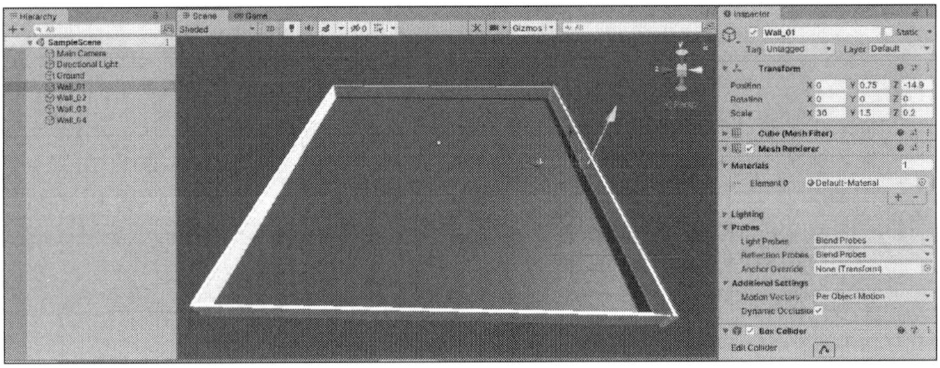

Figure 6.12: Level arena with four walls and a ground plane

> From this chapter onward, I'll be giving some basic values for wall position, rotation, and scale, but feel free to be adventurous and use your own creativity. I want you to experiment with the Unity Editor tools so you get comfortable faster.

That was a bit of construction, but the arena is starting to take shape! Before we move on to adding in obstacles and platforms, you'll want to get into the habit of cleaning up your object hierarchy. We'll talk about how that works in the following section.

## Keeping the hierarchy clean

Normally, I would put this sort of advice in a blurb at the end of a section, but making sure your project hierarchy is as organized as possible is so important that it needs its own subsection. Ideally, you'll want all related GameObjects to be under a single **parent object**. Right now, it's not a risk because we only have a few objects in the scene; however, when that gets into the hundreds on a big project, you'll be struggling.

The easiest way to keep your hierarchy clean is to store related objects in a parent object, just as you would with files inside a folder on your desktop. Our level has a few objects that could use some organization, and Unity makes this easy by letting us create empty GameObjects. An empty object is a perfect container (or folder) for holding related groups of objects because it doesn't come with any components attached—it's a shell.

Let's take our ground plane and four walls and group them all under a common empty GameObject:

1. Select **+** | **Create Empty** in the **Hierarchy** panel and name the new object `Environment`
2. Drag and drop the ground plane and the four walls into **Environment**, making them child objects

3. Select the **Environment** empty object and check that its **X**, **Y**, and **Z** positions are all set to 0:

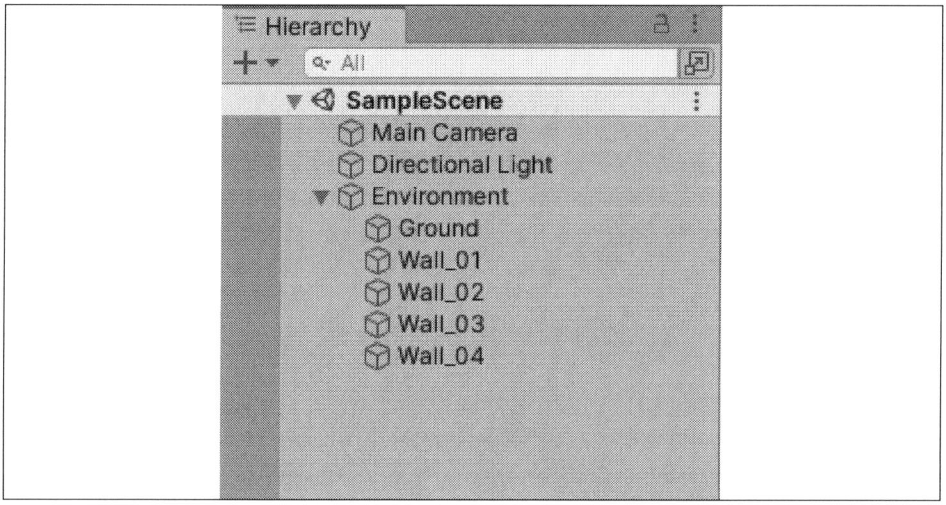


Figure 6.13: Hierarchy panel showing the empty GameObject parent

The environment exists in the **Hierarchy** tab as a parent object, with the arena objects as its children. Now we're able to expand or close the **Environment** object drop-down list with the arrow icon, making the **Hierarchy** panel less cluttered.

It's important to set the **Environment** object's **X**, **Y**, and **Z** positions to 0 because the child object positions are now relative to the parent position. This leads to an interesting question: what are the origin points of these positions, rotations, and scales that we're setting? The answer is that they depend on what relative space we're using, which, in Unity, is either **World** or **Local**:

- **World space** uses a set origin point in the scene as a constant reference for all GameObjects. In Unity, this origin point is (0, 0, 0), or 0 on the *x*, *y*, and *z* axes.
- **Local space** uses the object's parent `Transform` component as its origin, essentially changing the perspective of the scene. Unity also sets this local origin to (0, 0, 0). Think of this as the parent transform being the center of the universe, with everything else orbiting in relation to it.

Both of these orientations are useful in different situations, but right now, resetting it at this point starts everyone on an even playing field.

## Working with Prefabs

Prefabs are one of the most powerful components you'll come across in Unity. They come in handy not only in level building but in scripting as well. Think of Prefabs as GameObjects that can be saved and reused with every child object, component, C# script, and property setting intact. Once created, a Prefab is like a class blueprint; each copy used in a scene is a separate instance of that Prefab. Consequently, any change to the base Prefab will also change all of the active instances in the scene.

The arena looks a little too simple and completely wide open, making it a perfect place to test out creating and editing Prefabs. Since we want four identical turrets in each corner of the arena, they're a perfect case for a Prefab, which we can create with the following steps:

> Again, I haven't included any precise barrier position, rotation, or scale values because I want you to get up close and personal with the Unity Editor tools.
>
> Going forward, when you see a task ahead of you that doesn't include specific position, rotation, or scale values, I'm expecting you to learn by doing.

1. Create an empty parent object inside the **Environment** parent object by selecting **+** | **Create Empty** and naming it `Barrier_01`.
2. Create two cubes by selecting **+** | **3D Object** | **Cube** and position and scale them as a v-shaped base.
3. Create two more cube primitives and place them on the ends of the turret base:

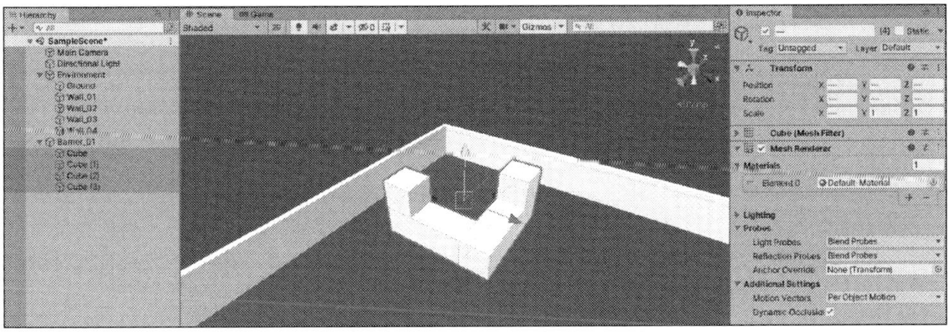

Figure 6.14: Screenshot of the turret composed of cubes

4. Create a new folder in the **Project** panel under **Assets** and name it `Prefabs`. Then, drag the **Barrier_01** GameObject from the **Hierarchy** panel to the **Prefabs** folder in the project view:

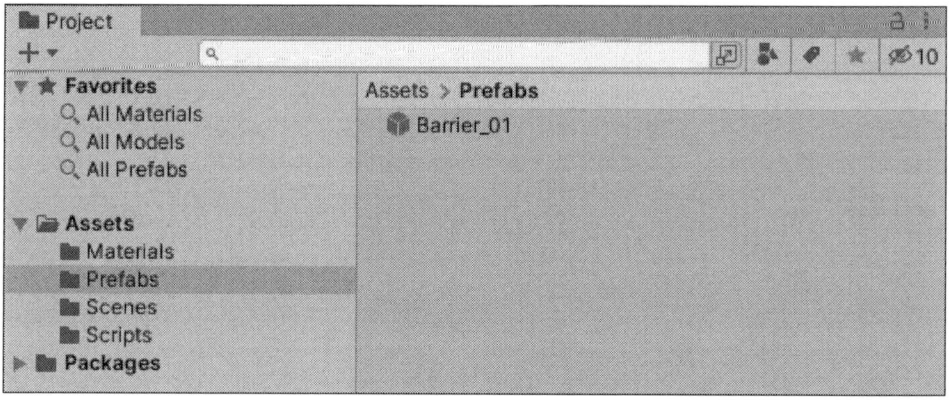


Figure 6.15: Barrier Prefab in the Prefabs folder

**Barrier_01**, and all its child objects, are now Prefabs, meaning that we can reuse it by dragging copies from the `Prefabs` folder or duplicating the one in the scene. **Barrier_01** turned blue in the **Hierarchy** tab to signify its status change, and also added a row of Prefab function buttons in the **Inspector** tab underneath its name:

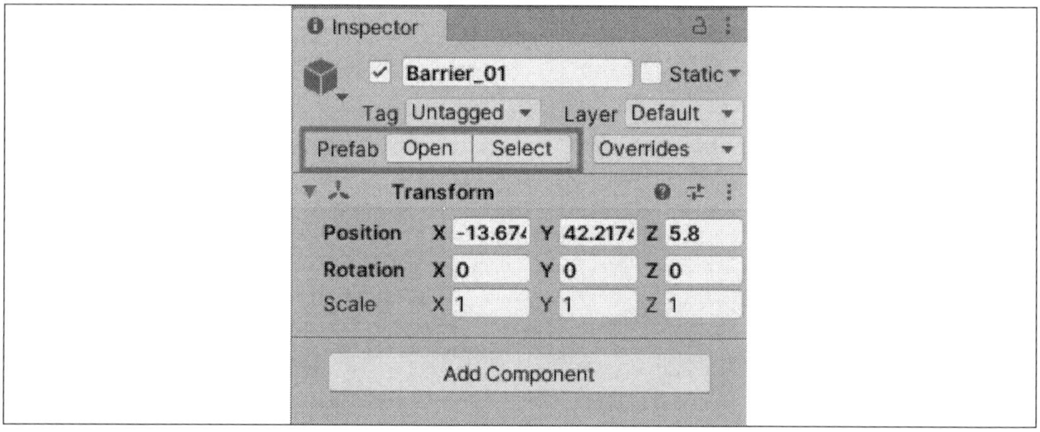


Figure 6.16: Barrier_01 Prefab highlighted in the Inspector pane

Any edits to the original Prefab object, **Barrier_01**, will now affect any copies in the Scene. Since we need a fifth cube to complete the barrier, let's update and save the Prefab to see this in action.

Now our turret has a huge gap in the middle, which isn't ideal for covering our character, so let's update the **Barrier_01** Prefab by adding another cube and applying the change:

1. Create a **Cube** primitive and place it at the intersection of the turret base.
2. The new **Cube** primitive will be marked as gray with a little + icon next to its name in the **Hierarchy** tab. This means it's not officially part of the Prefab yet:

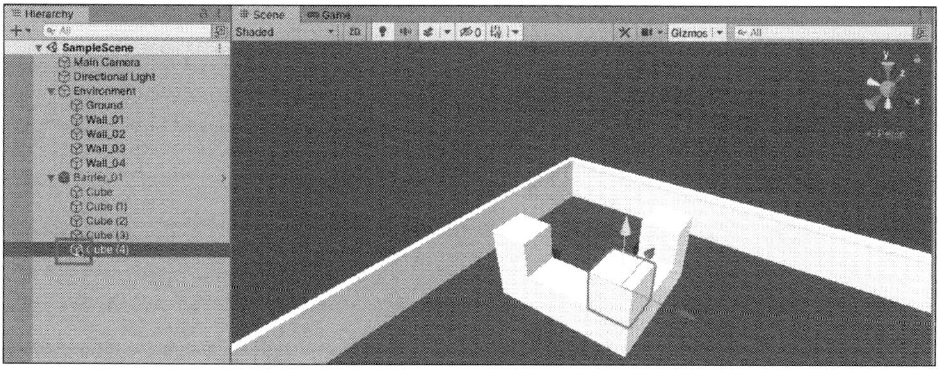


Figure 6.17: New Prefab update marked in the Hierarchy window

3. Right-click on the new Cube primitive in the **Hierarchy** panel and select **Added GameObject | Apply to Prefab 'Barrier_01'**:

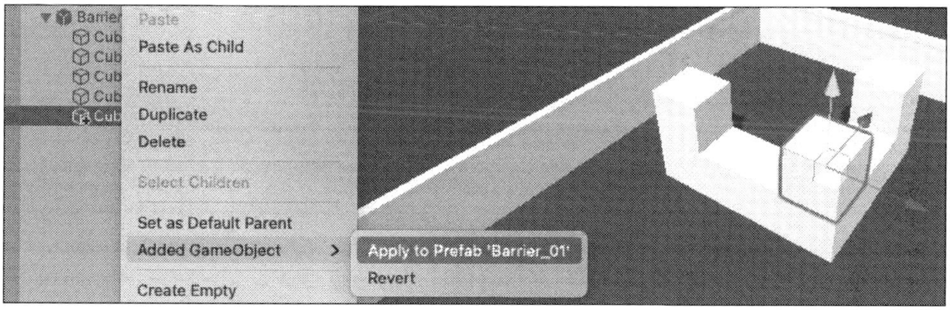


Figure 6.18: Option to apply Prefab changes to the base Prefab

The **Barrier_01** Prefab is now updated to include the new cube, and the entire Prefab hierarchy should be blue again. You now have a turret Prefab that looks like the preceding screenshot or, if you're feeling adventurous, something more creative. However, we want these to be in every corner of the arena. It's going to be your job to add them!

Now that we've got a reusable barrier Prefab, let's build out the rest of the level to match the rough sketch that we had at the beginning of the section:

1. Duplicate the **Barrier_01** Prefab three times and place each one in a different corner of the arena. You can do this by dragging multiple **Barrier_01** objects from the **Prefabs** folder into the scene, or right-clicking on **Barrier_01** in the **Hierarchy** and selecting duplicate.

2. Create a new empty GameObject inside the **Environment** parent object and name it `Raised_Platform`.
3. Create a **Cube** and scale it to form a platform as shown in *Figure 6.19* below.
4. Create a **Plane** and scale it into a ramp:
    - Hint: Rotate the plane around the *x* or *y* axis to create an angled plane
    - Then, position it so that it connects the platform to the ground
5. Duplicate the ramp object by using *Cmd* + *D* on a Mac, or *Ctrl* + *D* on Windows. Then, repeat the rotation and positioning steps.
6. Repeat the previous step twice more, until you have four ramps in total leading to the platform:

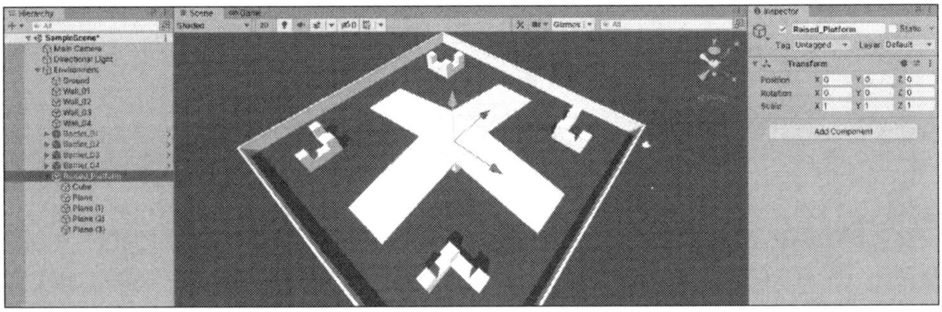

Figure 6.19: Raised platform parent GameObject

You've now successfully white-boxed your first game level! Don't get too caught up in it yet, though—we're just getting started. All good games have items that players can pick up or interact with. In the following challenge, it's your job to create a health item and make it a Prefab.

## Hero's trial – creating a health pickup

Putting together everything we've learned so far in this chapter might take you a few minutes, but it's well worth the time. Create the pickup item as follows:

1. Create a **Capsule** GameObject by selecting **+** | **3D Object** | **Capsule** and name it `Health_Pickup`.
2. Set the scale to 0.3 for the *x*, *y*, and *z* axes, and then switch to the **Move** tool and position it near one of your barriers.
3. Create and attach a new yellow-colored **Material** to the **Health_Pickup** object.
4. Drag the **Health_Pickup** object from the **Hierarchy** pane into the **Prefab** folder.

Refer to the following screenshot for an example of what the finished product should look like:

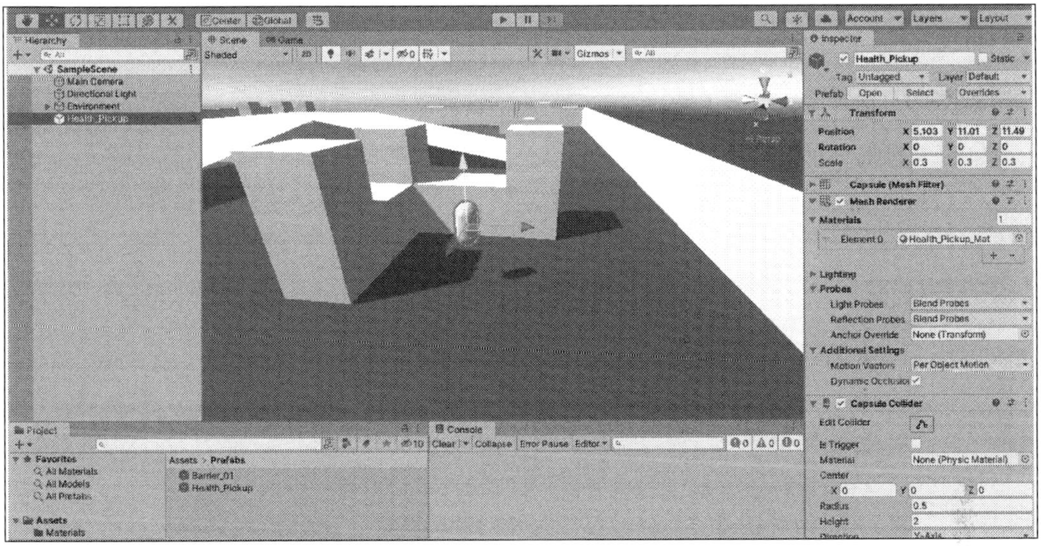

Figure 6.20: Pickup item and barrier Prefab in Scene

That wraps up our work with level design and layout for now. Next up, you're going to get a crash course in lighting with Unity, and we'll learn about animating our item later on in the chapter.

# Lighting basics

Lighting in Unity is a broad topic, but it can be boiled down into two categories: real-time and precomputed. Both types of lights take into account properties such as the color and intensity of the light, as well as the direction it is facing in the scene, which can all be configured in the **Inspector** pane. The difference is how the Unity engine computes how the lights act.

*Real-time lighting* is computed every frame, meaning that any object that passes in its path will cast realistic shadows and generally behave like a real-world light source. However, this can significantly slow down your game and cost an exponential amount of computing power, depending on the number of lights in your Scene. *Precomputed lighting*, on the other hand, stores the Scene's lighting in a texture called a **lightmap**, which is then applied, or baked, into the scene. While this saves computing power, baked lighting is static. This means that it doesn't react realistically or change when objects move in the scene.

There is also a mixed type of lighting called Precomputed Realtime Global Illumination, which bridges the gap between real-time and precomputed processes. This is an advanced Unity-specific topic, so we won't cover it in this book, but feel free to view the documentation at `https://docs.unity3d.com/Manual/GIIntro.html`.

Let's now take a look at how to create light objects in the Unity Scene itself.

# Creating lights

By default, every Scene comes with a directional light component to act as a main source of illumination, but lights can be created in the hierarchy like any other GameObject. Even though the idea of controlling light sources might be new to you, they are objects in Unity, which means they can be positioned, scaled, and rotated to fit your needs:

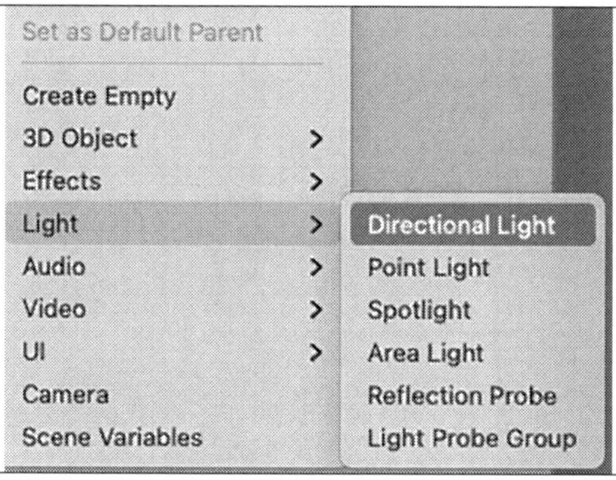


Figure 6.21: Lighting creation menu option

Let's take a look at some examples of real-time light objects and their performance:

- **Directional lights** are great for simulating natural light, such as sunshine. They don't have an actual position in the scene, but their light hits everything as if it's always pointed in the same direction.
- **Point lights** are essentially floating globes, sending light rays out from a central point in all directions. These have defined positions and intensities in the scene.
- **Spotlights** send light out in a given direction, but they are locked in by their angle and focused on a specific area of the scene. Think of these as spotlights or floodlights in the real world.

- **Area lights** are shaped like rectangles, sending out light from their surface from a single side of the rectangle.

> **Reflection Probes** and **Light Probe Groups** are beyond what we need for *Hero Born*; however, if you're interested, you can find out more at `https://docs.unity3d.com/Manual/ReflectionProbes.html` and `https://docs.unity3d.com/Manual/LightProbes.html`.

Like all GameObjects in Unity, lights have properties that can be adjusted to give a Scene a specific ambiance or theme.

# Light component properties

The following screenshot shows the **Light** component on the directional light in our Scene. All of these properties can be configured to create immersive environments, but the basic ones we need to be aware of are **Color**, **Mode**, and **Intensity**. These properties govern the light's tint, real-time or computed effects, and general strength:

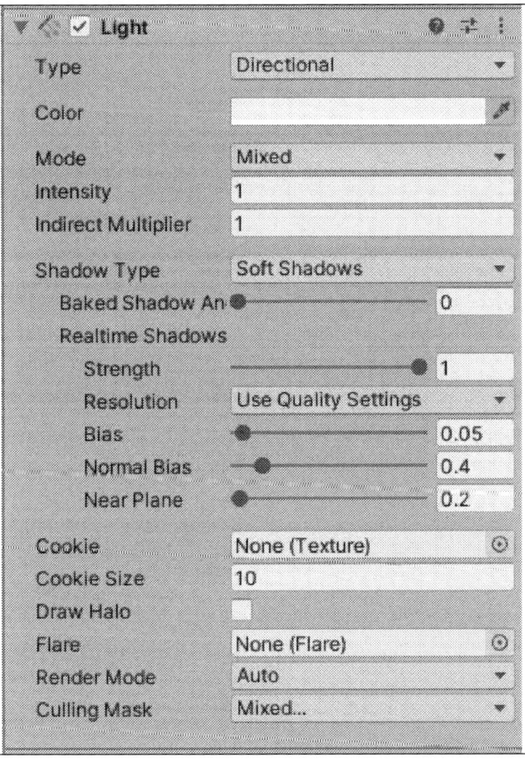


Figure 6.22: Light component in the Inspector window

> Like other Unity components, these properties can be accessed through scripts and the `Light` class, which can be found at `https://docs.unity3d.com/ScriptReference/Light.html`.

Try this out for yourself by selecting **+** | **Light** | **Point Light** and seeing how it affects the area lighting. After you've played around with the settings, delete the point light by right-clicking on it in the **Hierarchy** panel and choosing **Delete**.

Now that we know a little more about what goes into lighting up a game scene, let's turn our attention to adding some animations!

# Animating in Unity

Animating objects in Unity can range from a simple rotation effect to complex character movements and actions. You can create animations in code or with the Animation and Animator windows:

- The **Animation** window is where animation segments, called clips, are created and managed using a timeline. Object properties are recorded along this timeline and are then played back to create an animated effect.
- The **Animator** window manages these clips and their transitions using objects called animation controllers.

> You can find more information about the Animator window and its controllers at `https://docs.unity3d.com/Manual/AnimatorControllers.html`.

Creating and manipulating your target objects in clips will have your game moving in no time. For our short trip into Unity animations, we'll create the same rotation effect in code and using the Animator.

## Creating animations in code

To start, we're going to create an animation in code to rotate our health item pickup. Since all GameObjects have a `Transform` component, we can grab our item's `Transform` component and rotate it indefinitely.

To create an animation in code, you need to perform the following steps:

1. Create a new script inside the `Scripts` folder, name it `ItemRotation`, and open it in Visual Studio Code.
2. At the top of the new script and inside the class, add in an `int` variable containing the value `100` called `RotationSpeed`, and a `Transform` variable called `ItemTransform`:

```
public int RotationSpeed = 100;
Transform ItemTransform;
```

3. Inside the `Start()` method body, grab the GameObject's `Transform` component and assign it to `ItemTransform`:

```
ItemTransform = this.GetComponent<Transform>();
```

4. Inside the `Update()` method body, call `ItemTransform.Rotate`. This `Transform` class method takes in three axes, one for the *X*, *Y*, and *Z* rotations you want to execute. Since we want the item to rotate end over end, we'll use the *x* axis and leave the others set to 0:

```
ItemTransform.Rotate(RotationSpeed * Time.deltaTime, 0, 0);
```

> You'll notice that we're multiplying our `RotationSpeed` by something called `Time.deltaTime`. This is the standard way of normalizing movement effects in Unity so that they look smooth no matter how fast or slow the player's computer is running. In general, you should always multiply your movement or rotation speeds by `Time.deltaTime`.

5. Back in Unity, select the `Health_Pickup` object in the `Prefabs` folder in the **Projects** pane and scroll down to the bottom of the **Inspector** window. Click **Add Component**, search for the `ItemRotation` script, and then press *Enter*:

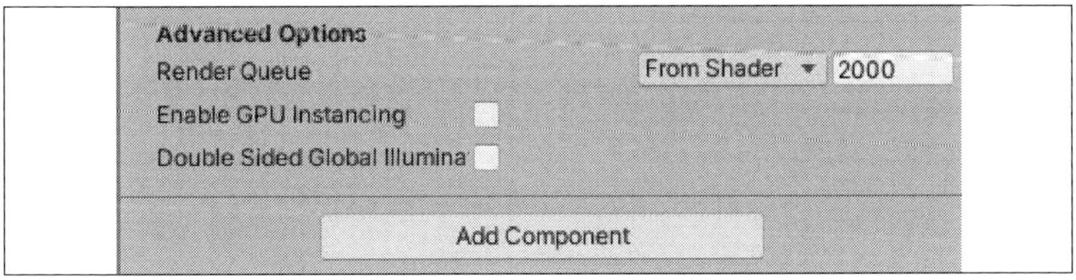


Figure 6.23: Add Component button in the Inspector panel

6. Now that our Prefab is updated, move the **Main Camera** so that you can see the `Health_Pickup` object and click on play!

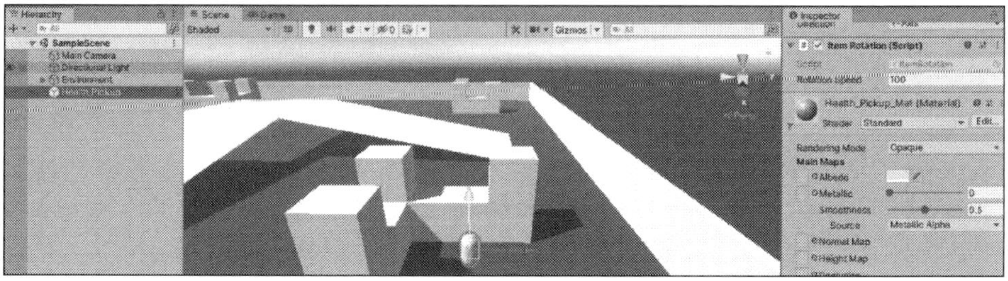

Figure 6.24: Screenshot of the camera focused on the health item

As you can see, the health pickup now spins around its $x$ axis in a continuous and smooth animation! Now that you've animated the item in code, we'll duplicate our animation using Unity's built-in animation system.

# Creating animations in the Unity Animation window

Any GameObject that you want to apply an animation clip to needs to be attached to an Animator component with an **Animation Controller** set. If there is no controller in the project when a new clip is created, Unity will create one and save it in the project panel, which you can then use to manage your clips. Your next challenge is to create a new animation clip for the pickup item.

We're going to start animating the `Health_Pickup` Prefab by creating a new animation clip, which will spin the object around in an infinite loop. To create a new animation clip, we need to perform the following steps:

1. Navigate to **Window** | **Animation** | **Animation** to open up the **Animation** panel and drag and drop the **Animation** tab next to the **Console**.
2. Make sure the `Health_Pickup` item is selected in **Hierarchy** and then click on **Create** in the **Animation** panel:

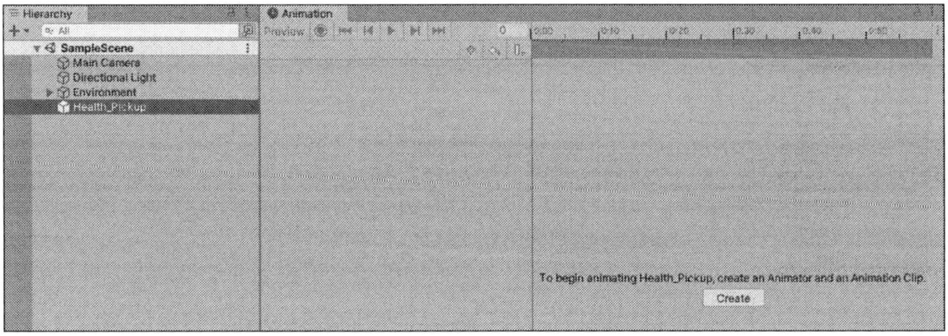


Figure 6.25: Screenshot of the Unity Animation window

3. Create a new folder from the following drop-down list, name it `Animations`, and then name the new clip `Pickup_Spin`:

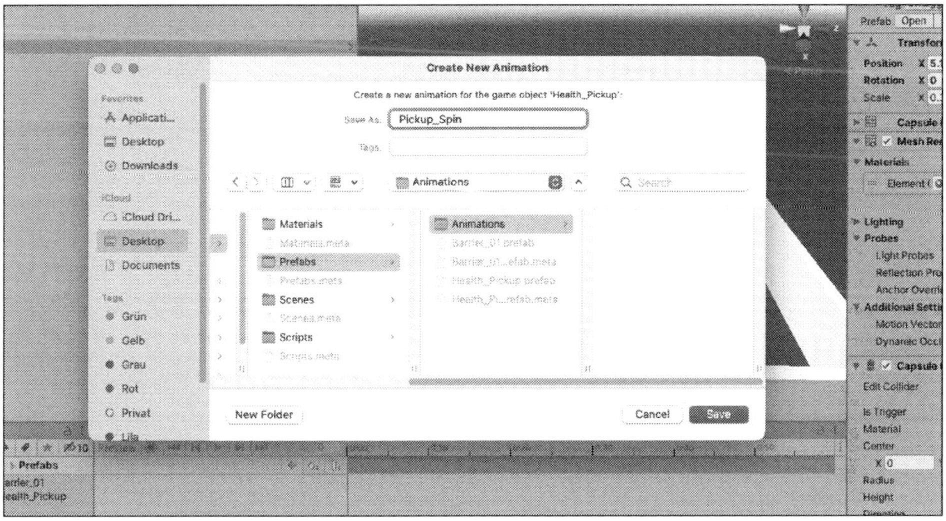


Figure 6.26: Screenshot of the Create New Animation window

4. Make sure the new clip shows up in the **Animation** panel:

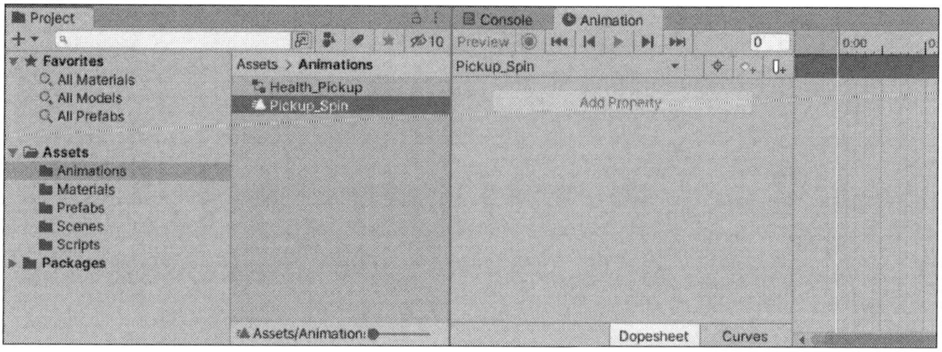


Figure 6.27: Screenshot of the Animation window with a clip selected

5. Since we didn't have any **Animator** controllers, Unity created one for us in the `Animation` folder called **Health_Pickup**. With **Health_Pickup** selected, note in the **Inspector** pane that when we created the clip, an **Animator** component was also added to the Prefab for us but hasn't been officially saved to the Prefab yet with the **Health_Pickup** controller set.
6. Notice that the **+** icon is showing in the top left of the **Animator** component, meaning it's not yet part of the **Health_Pickup** Prefab:

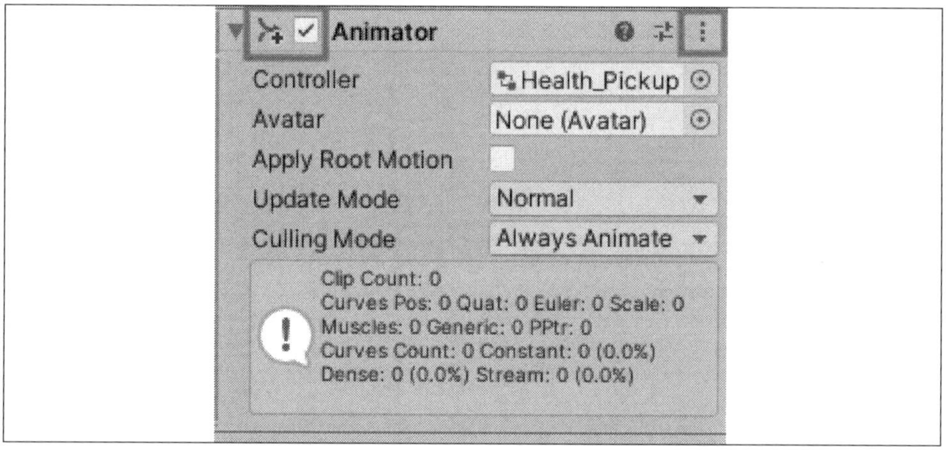


Figure 6.28: Animator component in the Inspector panel

7. Select the three-vertical-dots icon at the top right and choose **Added Component | Apply to Prefab 'Health_Pickup'**:

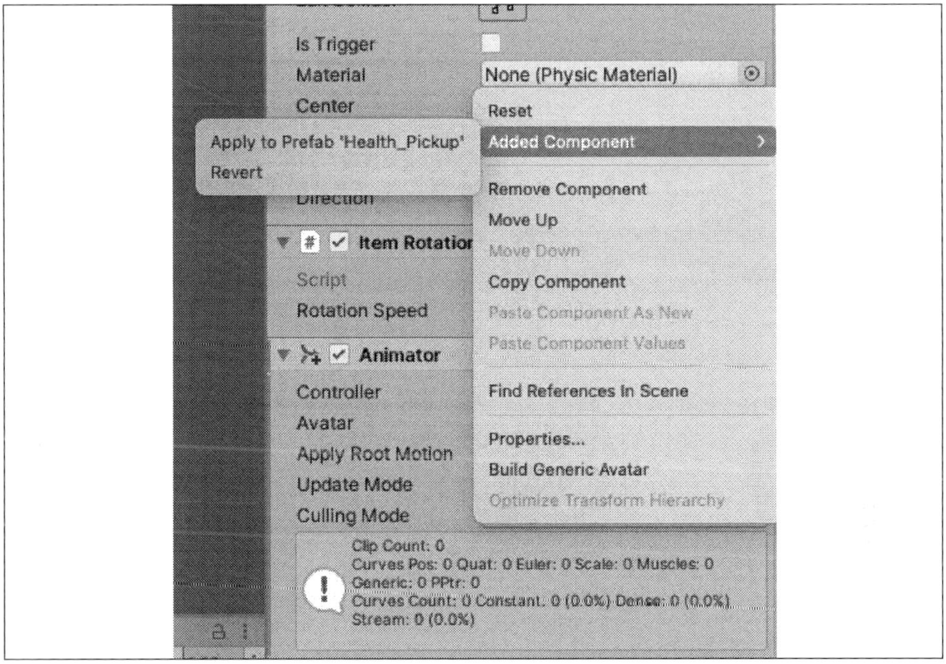


Figure 6.29: Screenshot of a new component being applied to the Prefab

Now that you've created and added an Animator component to the **Health_Pickup** Prefab, it's time to start recording some animation frames. When you think of motion clips, as in movies, you may think of frames. As the clip moves through its frames, the animation advances, giving the effect of movement. It's no different in Unity; we need to record our target object in different positions throughout different frames so that Unity can play the clip.

# Recording keyframes

Now that we have a clip to work with, you'll see a blank timeline in the **Animation** window. Essentially, when we modify our **Health_Pickup** Prefab's *z* rotation, or any other property that can be animated, the timeline will record those changes as keyframes. Unity then assembles those keyframes into your complete animation, similar to how individual frames on analog film play together into a moving picture.

Take a look at the following screenshot and remember the locations of the record button and the timeline:

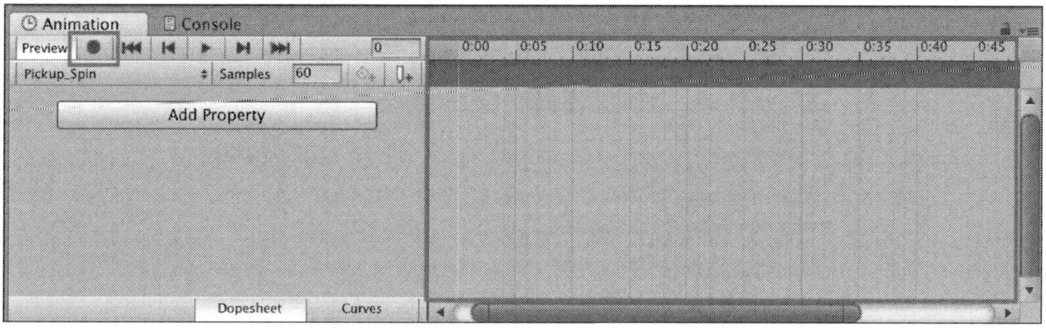


Figure 6.30: Screenshot of the Animation window and keyframe timeline

Now, let's get our item spinning. For the spinning animation, we want the **Health_ Pickup** Prefab to make a complete 360-degree rotation on its *z* axis every second, which can be done by setting three keyframes and letting Unity take care of the rest:

1. Select the **Health_Pickup** object in the **Hierarchy** window, choose **Add Property** | **Transform**, and then click on the **+** sign next to **Rotation**:

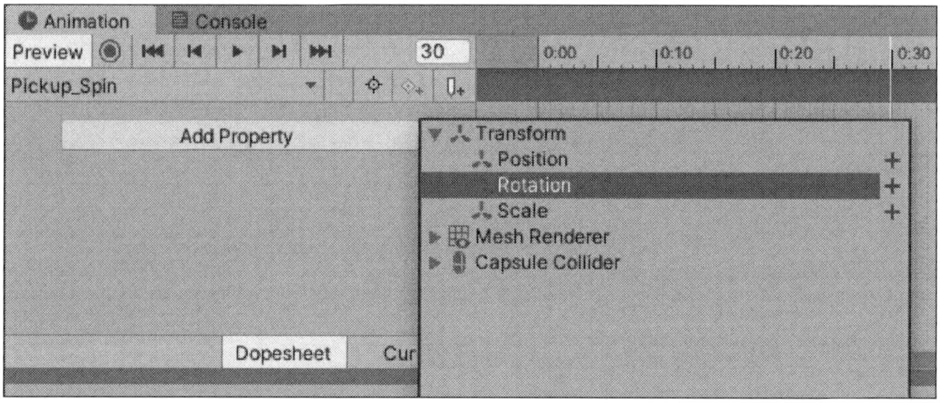


Figure 6.31: Screenshot of adding a Transform property for animation

2. Click on the record button to start the animation:
   - Place your cursor at **0:00** on the timeline but leave the **Health_Pickup** Prefab's *z* rotation at 0
   - Place your cursor at **0:30** on the timeline and set the *z* rotation to **180**
   - Place your cursor at **1:00** on the timeline and set the *z* rotation to **360**

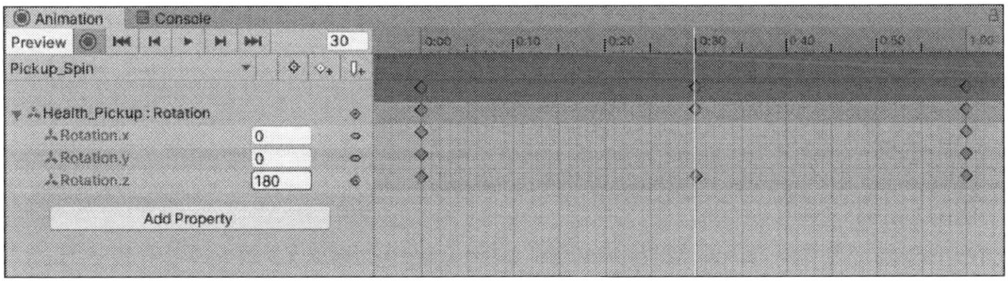


Figure 6.32: Screenshot of Animation keyframes being recorded

3. Click on the record button to finish the animation
4. Click on the play button to the right of the record button to see the animation loop

You'll notice that our **Animator** animation overrides the one we wrote in code earlier. Don't worry; this is expected behavior. You can click the small checkbox to the right of any component in the **Inspector** panel to activate or deactivate it. If you deactivate the **Animator** component, **Health_Pickup** will rotate around the *x* axis again using our code.

The **Health_Pickup** object now rotates on the *z* axis between 0, 180, and 360 degrees every second, creating the looping spin animation. If you play the game now, the animation will run indefinitely until the game is stopped:

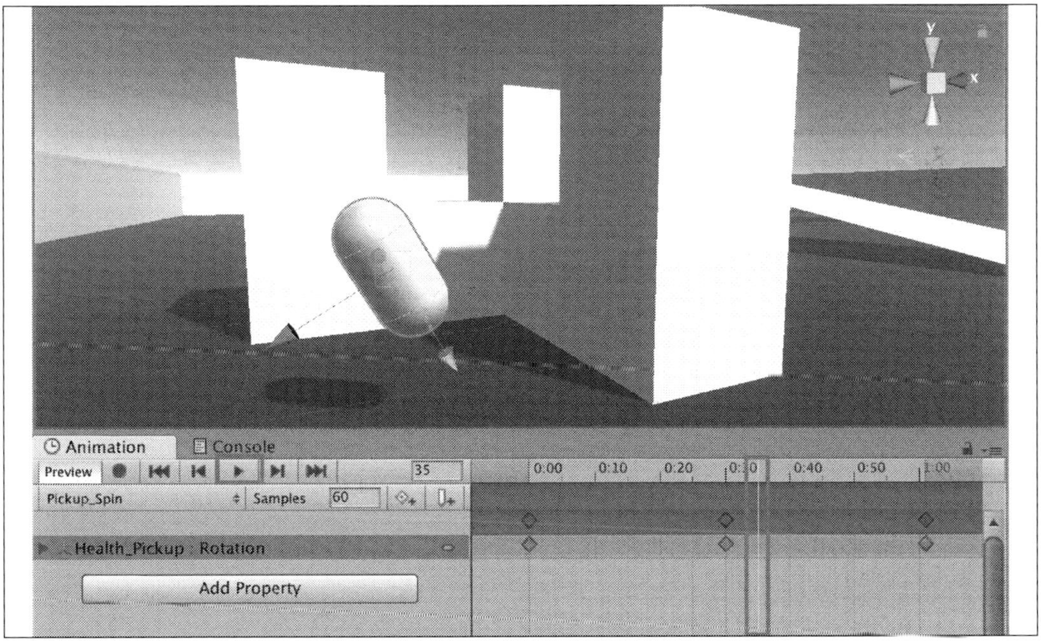


Figure 6.33: Screenshot of an animation playing in the Animation window

All animations have curves, which determine specific properties of how an animation executes. We won't be doing too much with these, but it's important to understand the basics. We'll get into them in the following section.

# Curves and tangents

In addition to animating an object property, Unity lets us manage how the animation plays out over time with animation curves. So far, we've been in **Dopesheet** mode, which you can change at the bottom of the Animation window. If you click on the **Curves** view (pictured in the following screenshot), you'll see a different graph with accent points in place of our recorded keyframes.

We want the spinning animation to be smooth—what we call linear—so we'll leave everything as is. However, speeding up, slowing down, or altering the animation at any point in its run can be done by dragging or adjusting the points on the curve graph in any direction:

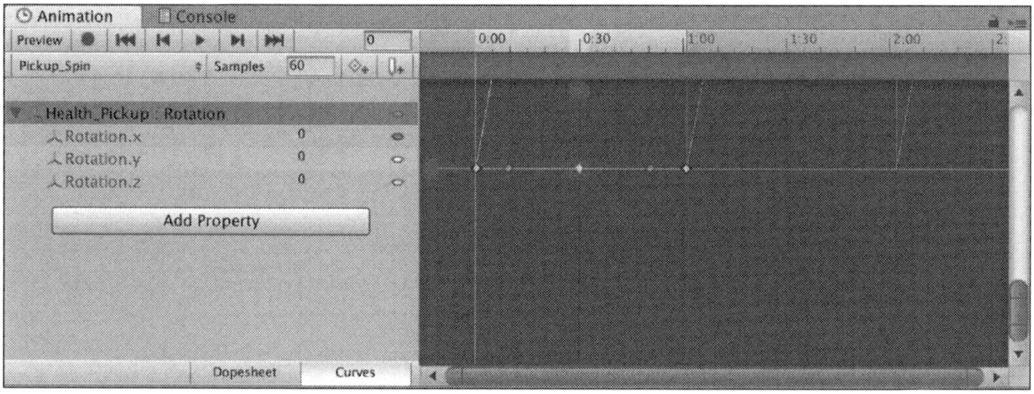


Figure 6.34: Screenshot of the Curves timeline in the Animation window

With animation curves handling how properties act over time, we still need a way to fix the stutter that occurs every time the **Health_Pickup** animation repeats. For that, we need to change the animation's tangent, which manages how keyframes blend from one into another.

These options can be accessed by right-clicking on any keyframe on the timeline in **Dopesheet** mode, which you can see here:

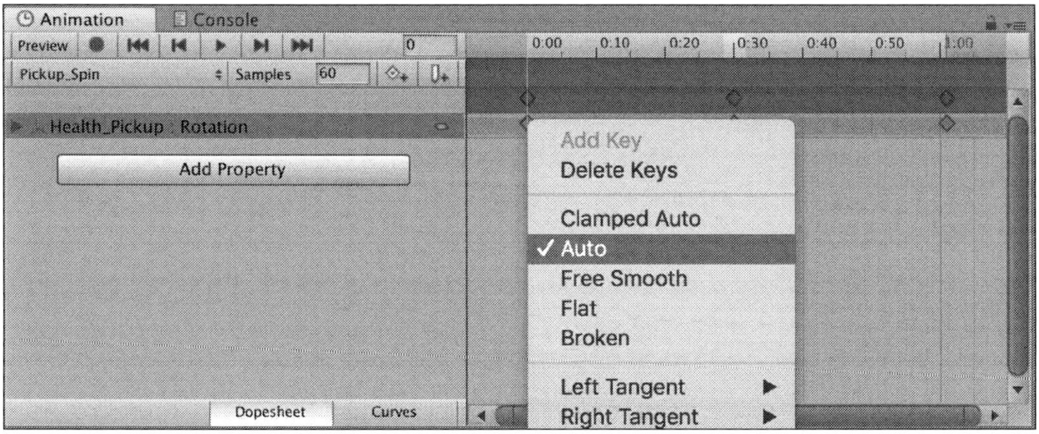


Figure 6.35: Screenshot of keyframe smoothing options

> Both curves and tangents are intermediate/advanced, so we won't be delving too deeply into them. If you're interested, you can take a look at the documentation on animation curves and tangent options at `https://docs.unity3d.com/Manual/animeditor-AnimationCurves.html`.

If you play the spinning animation as it is now, there's a slight pause between when the item completes its full rotation and starts a new one. Your job is to smooth that out, which is the subject of the next challenge.

Let's adjust the tangents on the first and last frames of the animation so that the spinning animation blends seamlessly together when it repeats:

1. Right-click on the first and last keyframes' diamond icons on the animation timeline and select **Auto**:

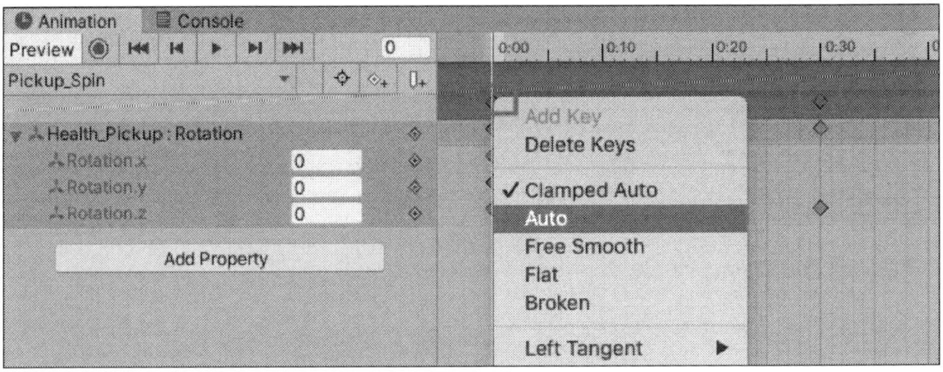


Figure 6.36: Changing keyframe smoothing options

2. If you haven't already done so, move the **Main Camera** so that you can see the `Health_Pickup` object and click on play:

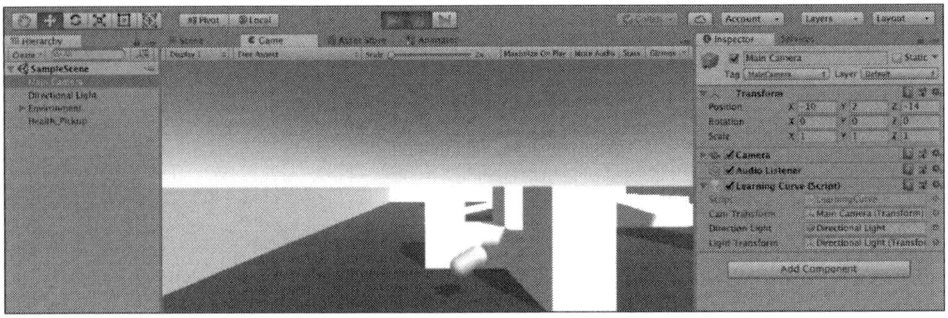


Figure 6.37: Screenshot of the final smoothed animation playing

Changing the first and last keyframe tangents to **Auto** tells Unity to make their transitions smooth, which eliminates the jerky stop/start motion when the animation loops.

That's all the animation you'll need for this book, but I'd encourage you to check out the full toolbox that Unity offers in this area. Your games will be more engaging and your players will thank you!

# Summary

We made it to the end of another chapter that had a lot of moving parts, which might especially be a lot for those of you who are new to Unity.

Even though this book is focused on the C# language and its implementation in Unity, we still need to take time to get an overview of game development, documentation, and the non-scripting features of the engine. While we didn't have time for in-depth coverage of the lighting and animation, it's worth getting to know them if you're thinking about continuing to create Unity projects.

In the next chapter, we'll be switching our focus back to programming *Hero Born*'s core mechanics, starting with setting up a moveable player object, controlling the camera, and understanding how Unity's physics system governs the game world.

# Pop quiz – basic Unity features

1. Cubes, capsules, and spheres are examples of what kind of GameObject?
2. What axis does Unity use to represent depth, which gives scenes their 3D appearance?
3. How do you turn a GameObject into a reusable Prefab?
4. What unit of measurement does the Unity animation system use to record object animations?

# 7

# Movement, Camera Controls, and Collisions

One of the first things a player does when starting a new game is to try out character movement (if, of course, the game has a moveable character) and camera controls. Not only is this exciting, but it lets your player know what kind of gameplay they can expect. The character in *Hero Born* will be a capsule object that can be moved and rotated using the *W*, *A*, *S*, *D*, or arrow keys, respectively.

We'll start by learning how to manipulate the player object's `Transform` component and then replicate the same player control scheme using applied force. This produces a more realistic movement effect. When we move the player, the camera will follow along from a position that is slightly behind and above the player, making aiming easier when we implement the shooting mechanic. Finally, we'll explore how collisions and physical interactions are handled by Unity's physics system by working with our item pickup Prefab.

All of this will come together at a playable level, albeit without any shooting mechanics just yet. It's also going to give us our first taste of C# being used to program game features by tying together the following topics:

- Managing player movement
- Moving the player with the `Transform` component
- Scripting camera behavior
- Working with the Unity physics system

# Managing player movement

When you're deciding on how best to move your player character around your virtual world, consider what's going to look the most realistic and not run your game into the ground with expensive computations. This is somewhat of a trade-off in most cases, and Unity is no different.

The three most common ways of moving a `GameObject` and their results are as follows:

- **Option A**: Use a `GameObject`'s `Transform` component for movement and rotation. This is the easiest solution and the one we'll be working with first.
- **Option B**: Use real-world physics by attaching a **Rigidbody** component to a `GameObject` and apply force in code. `Rigidbody` components add simulated real-world physics to any `GameObject` they are attached to. This solution relies on Unity's physics system to do the heavy lifting, delivering a far more realistic effect. We'll update our code to use this approach later on in this chapter to get a feel for both methods.

> Unity suggests sticking to a consistent approach when moving or rotating a `GameObject`; either manipulate an object's `Transform` or `Rigidbody` component, but never both at the same time.

- **Option C**: Attach a ready-made Unity component or Prefab, such as Character Controller or First Person Controller. This cuts out the boilerplate code and still delivers a realistic effect while speeding up the prototyping time.

> You can find more information on the Character Controller component and its uses at `https://docs.unity3d.com/ScriptReference/CharacterController.html`.
>
> The First Person Controller Prefab is available from the Standard Assets package, which you can download from `https://assetstore.unity.com/packages/essentials/asset-packs/standard-assets-32351`.

Since you're just getting started with player movement in Unity, you'll start off using the player Transform component in the next section, and then move on to `Rigidbody` physics later in the chapter.

# Moving the player with the Transform component

We want a third-person adventure setup for *Hero Born*, so we'll start with a capsule that can be controlled with keyboard input and a camera to follow the capsule as it moves. Even though these two GameObjects will work together in the game, we'll keep them and their scripts separate for better control.

Before we can do any scripting, you'll need to add a player capsule to the scene, which is your next task.

We can create a nice player capsule in just a few steps:

1. Click on **+** | **3D Object** | **Capsule** from the **Hierarchy** panel and name it `Player`.
2. Select the `Player` GameObject and click on **Add Component** at the bottom of the **Inspector** tab. Search for **Rigidbody** and hit *Enter* to add it. We won't use this component until later, but it's good to set things up properly at the beginning.
3. Expand the **Constraints** property at the bottom of the **Rigidbody** component:
    - Check the boxes for **Freeze Rotation** on the **X**, **Y**, and **Z** axes so the player can't be rotated in any way other than through the code we'll write later on:

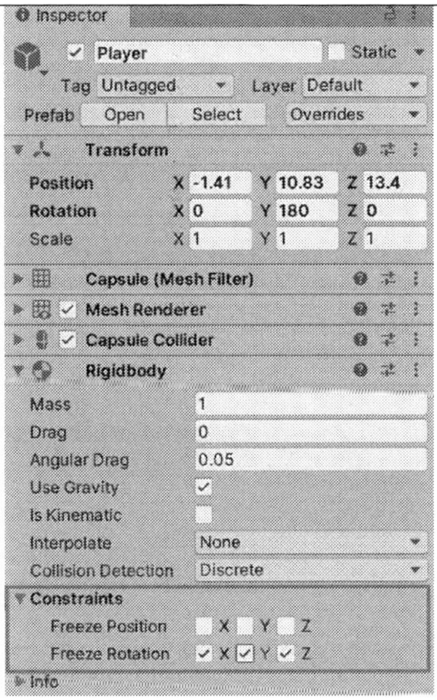


Figure 7.1: Rigidbody component

4. Select the `Materials` folder in the **Project** panel and click on **Create | Material**. Name it `Player_Mat`.
5. Select `Player_Mat` in the **Hierarchy**, then change the **Albedo** property in the **Inspector** to a bright green and drag the material to the **Player** object in the **Hierarchy** panel:

Figure 7.2: Player material attached to capsule

You've created the **Player** object out of a capsule primitive, a Rigidbody component, and a new bright green material. Don't worry about what the Rigidbody component is just yet—all you need to know right now is that it allows our capsule to interact with the physics system. We'll go into more detail at the end of this chapter when we discuss how Unity's physics system works. Before we get to that, we need to talk about a very important subject in 3D space: vectors.

# Understanding vectors

Now that we have a player capsule and camera set up, we can start looking at how to move and rotate a GameObject using its `Transform` component. The `Translate` and `Rotate` methods are part of the `Transform` class that Unity provides, and each needs a vector parameter to perform its given function.

In Unity, vectors are used to hold position and direction data in 2D and 3D spaces, which is why they come in two varieties—`Vector2` and `Vector3`. These can be used like any other variable type we've seen; they just hold different information. Since our game is in 3D, we'll be using `Vector3` objects, which means we'll need to construct them using *x*, *y*, and *z* values.

For 2D vectors, only the *x* and *y* positions are required. Remember, the most up-to-date orientation in your 3D scene will be displayed in the upper-right graphic that we discussed in the previous chapter, *Chapter 6, Getting Your Hands Dirty with Unity*:

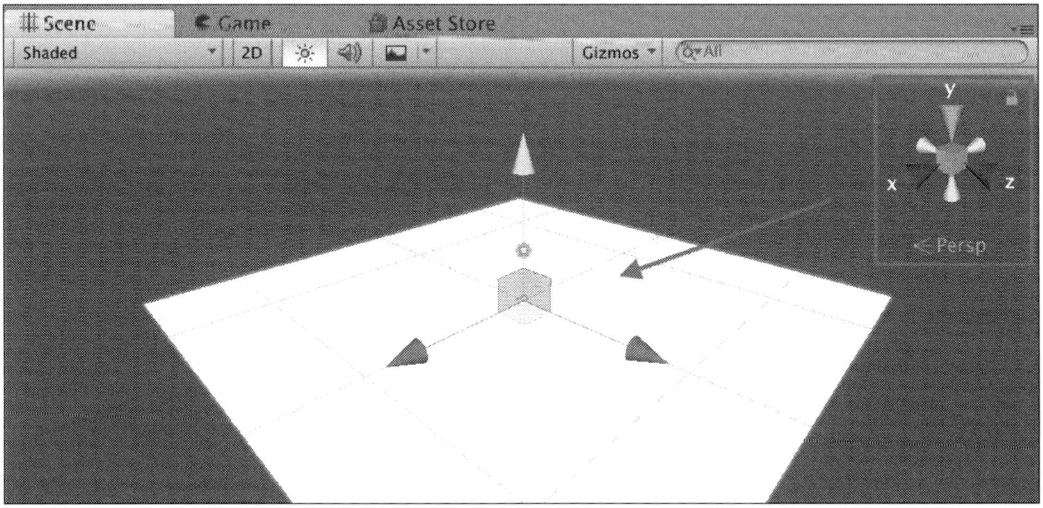


Figure 7.3: Vector gizmos in Unity editor

> If you would like more information about vectors in Unity, refer to the documentation and scripting reference at `https://docs.unity3d.com/ScriptReference/Vector3.html`.

For instance, if we wanted to create a new vector to hold the origin position of our scene, we could use the following code:

```
Vector3 Origin = new Vector(0f, 0f, 0f);
```

All we've done here is created a new `Vector3` variable and initialized it with a `0` for the *x* position, `0` for the *y* position, and `0` for the *z* position, in that order. This spawns the player at the origin of the game arena. `Float` values can be written with or without a decimal, but they always need to end with a lowercase `f`.

We can also create directional vectors by using the `Vector2` or `Vector3` class properties:

```
Vector3 ForwardDirection = Vector3.forward;
```

Instead of holding a position, `ForwardDirection` references the forward direction in our scene along the *z* axis in the 3D space. The neat thing about using the Vector3 direction is that no matter which way we make the player  look, our code will always know which way is forward. We'll look at using vectors later in this chapter, but for now just get used to thinking about 3D movement in terms of *x*, *y*, and *z* positions and directions.

> Don't worry if the concept of vectors is new to you—it's a complicated topic. Unity's vector cookbook is a great place to start: `https://docs.unity3d.com/Manual/VectorCookbook.html`.

Now that you understand vectors a bit more, you can start implementing the basics of moving the player capsule. For that, you'll need to gather player input from the keyboard, which is the topic of the following section.

# Getting player input

Positions and directions are useful in themselves, but they can't generate movement without input from the player. This is where the `Input` class comes in, which handles everything from keystrokes and mouse position to acceleration and gyroscopic data.

We're going to be using the *W*, *A*, *S*, *D*, and arrow keys for movement in *Hero Born*, coupled with a script that allows the camera to follow where the player points the mouse. To do that, we'll need to understand how input axes work.

First, go to **Edit** | **Project Settings** | **Input Manager** to open up the **Input Manager** tab shown in the following screenshot:

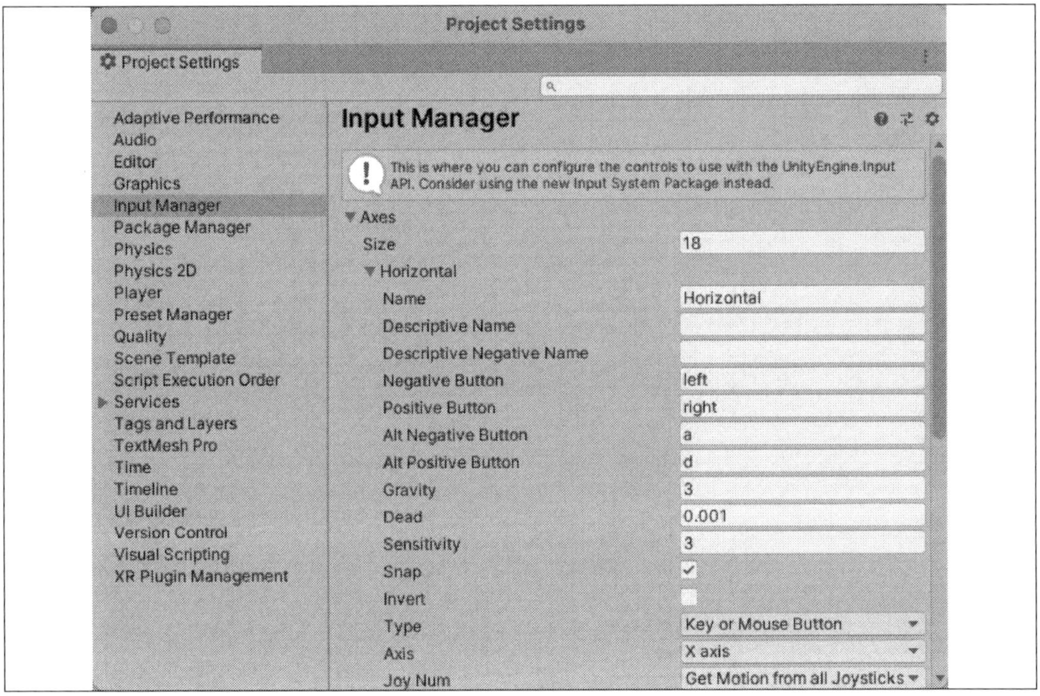


Figure 7.4: Input Manager window

> Unity 2021 has a new input system that removes a lot of the coding work, making it easier to set up inputs as actions in the editor. Since this is a programming book, we're going to do things from scratch. However, if you want to see how the new input system works, check out this great tutorial: `https://learn.unity.com/project/using-the-input-system-in-unity`.

You'll see a long list of Unity's default inputs already configured, but let's take the **Horizontal** axis as an example. You can see that the **Horizontal** input axis has the **Positive** and **Negative** buttons set to `left` and `right`, and the **Alt Negative** and **Alt Positive** buttons set to the `a` and `d` keys.

Whenever an input axis is queried from the code, its value will be between -1 and 1. For example, when the left arrow or *A* key is pushed down, the horizontal axis registers a -1 value. When those keys are released, the value returns to 0. Likewise, when the right arrow or *D* keys are used, the horizontal axis registers a value of 1. This allows us to capture four different inputs for a single axis with only one line of code, as opposed to writing out a long `if-else` statement chain for each.

Capturing input axes is as simple as calling `Input.GetAxis()` and specifying the axis we want by name, which is what we'll do with the `Horizontal` and `Vertical` inputs in the following sections. As a side benefit, Unity applies a smoothing filter, which makes the input frame rate independent.

> Default inputs can be modified in any way you need, but you can also create custom axes by increasing the `Size` property in the input manager and renaming the copy that's been created for you. You have to increase the `Size` property in order to add a custom input.

Let's start getting our player moving using Unity's input system and a custom locomotion script of our own.

# Moving the player

Before you get the player moving, you'll need to attach a script to the player capsule:

1. Create a new C# script in the `Scripts` folder, name it `PlayerBehavior`, and drag it onto the **Player** capsule in the **Hierarchy** panel.
2. Add the following code and save:

```
using System.Collections;
using System.Collections.Generic;
```

```
using UnityEngine;

public class PlayerBehavior : MonoBehaviour
{
    // 1
    public float MoveSpeed = 10f;
    public float RotateSpeed = 75f;

    // 2
    private float _vInput;
    private float _hInput;

    void Update()
    {
        // 3
        _vInput = Input.GetAxis("Vertical") * MoveSpeed;

        // 4
        _hInput = Input.GetAxis("Horizontal") * RotateSpeed;

        // 5
        this.transform.Translate(Vector3.forward * _vInput *
        Time.deltaTime);

        // 6
        this.transform.Rotate(Vector3.up * _hInput *
        Time.deltaTime);
    }
}
```

> Using the `this` keyword is optional. Visual Studio 2019 may suggest that you remove it to simplify the code, but I prefer leaving it in for clarity. When you have empty methods, such as `Start`, in this case, it's common to delete them for clarity.

Here's a breakdown of the preceding code:

1. Declares two public variables to be used as multipliers:
    - `MoveSpeed` for how fast we want the Player to go forward and backward
    - `RotateSpeed` for how fast we want the Player to rotate left and right

2. Declares two private variables to hold inputs from the player; initially set with no value:
    - `_vInput` will store the vertical axis input.
    - `_hInput` will store the horizontal axis input.
3. `Input.GetAxis("Vertical")` detects when the up arrow, down arrow, *W*, or *S* keys are pressed and multiplies that value by `MoveSpeed`:
    - The up arrow and *W* keys return a value of 1, which will move the player in the forward (positive) direction.
    - The down arrow and *S* keys return -1, which moves the player backward in the negative direction.
4. `Input.GetAxis("Horizontal")` detects when the left arrow, right arrow, *A*, and *D* keys are pressed and multiplies that value by `RotateSpeed`:
    - The right arrow and *D* keys return a value of 1, which will rotate the capsule to the right.
    - The left arrow and *A* keys return -1, rotating the capsule to the left.

> If you're wondering whether it's possible to do all the movement calculations on one line, the simple answer is yes. However, it's better to have your code broken down, even if you're the only one reading it.

5. Uses the `Translate` method, which takes in a `Vector3` parameter, to move the capsule's Transform component:
    - Remember that the `this` keyword specifies the GameObject the current script is attached to, which, in this case, is the player capsule.
    - `Vector3.forward` multiplied by `_vInput` and `Time.deltaTime` supplies the direction and speed the capsule needs to move forward or back along the *z* axis at the speed we've calculated.
    - `Time.deltaTime` will always return the value in seconds since the last frame of the game was executed. It's commonly used to smooth values that are captured or run in the `Update` method instead of letting it be determined by a device's frame rate.
6. Uses the `Rotate` method to rotate the capsule's Transform component relative to the vector we pass in as a parameter:
    - `Vector3.up` multiplied by `_hInput` and `Time.deltaTime` gives us the left/right rotation axis we want.
    - We use the `this` keyword and `Time.deltaTime` here for the same reasons.

> As we discussed earlier, using direction vectors in the `Translate` and `Rotate` functions is only one way to go about this. We could have created new Vector3 variables from our axis inputs and used them as parameters just as easily.

When you click play, you'll be able to move the capsule forward and backward using the up/down arrow keys and the *W*/*S* keys, while rotating or turning with the left/right arrow keys and the *A*/*D* keys.

With these few lines of code, you've set up two separate controls that are frame rate independent and easily modified. However, our camera doesn't follow the capsule as it moves around, so let's fix that in the following section.

# Scripting camera behavior

The easiest way to get one GameObject to follow another is to make one of them a child of the other. When an object is a child of another, the child object's position and rotation are relative to the parent. This means that any child object will move and rotate with the parent object.

However, this approach means that any kind of movement or rotation that happens to the player capsule also affects the camera, which is something we don't necessarily want. We always want the camera to be positioned a set distance behind our player and always rotate to look at it, no matter what. Luckily, we can easily set the position and rotation of the camera relative to the capsule with methods from the `Transform` class. It's your task to script out the camera logic in the next challenge.

Since we want the camera behavior to be entirely separate from how the player moves, we'll be controlling where the camera is positioned relative to a target we can set from the **Inspector** tab:

1. Create a new C# script in the `Scripts` folder, name it `CameraBehavior`, and drag it into **Main Camera** in the **Hierarchy** panel.
2. Add the following code and save it:

```
using System.Collections;
using System.Collections.Generic;
using UnityEngine;

public class CameraBehavior : MonoBehaviour
{
    // 1
```

```
    public Vector3 CamOffset= new Vector3(0f, 1.2f, -2.6f);

    // 2
    private Transform _target;

    void Start()
    {
        // 3
        _target = GameObject.Find("Player").transform;
    }

    // 4
    void LateUpdate()
    {
        // 5
        this.transform.position = _target.
TransformPoint(CamOffset);

        // 6
        this.transform.LookAt(_target);
    }
}
```

Here's a breakdown of the preceding code:

1. Declares a `Vector3` variable to store the distance we want between the **Main Camera** and the **Player** capsule:
    - We'll be able to manually set the *x*, *y*, and *z* positions of the camera offset in the **Inspector** because it's `public`.
    - These default values are what I think looks best, but feel free to experiment.
2. Creates a variable to hold the player capsule's Transform information:
    - This will give us access to its position, rotation, and scale.
    - We don't want any other script to be able to change the camera's target, which is why it's `private`.
3. Uses `GameObject.Find` to locate the capsule by name and retrieve its Transform property from the scene:
    - This means the capsule's *x*, *y*, and *z* positions are updated and stored in the `_target` variable every frame.

- Finding objects in the scene is a computationally expensive task, so it's good practice to only do it once in the `Start` method and store the reference. Never use `GameObject.Find` in the `Update` method, as that will try to continually find the object you're looking for and potentially crash the game.

4. `LateUpdate` is a `MonoBehavior` method, like `Start` or `Update`, that executes after `Update`:
   - Since our `PlayerBehavior` script moves the capsule in its `Update` method, we want the code in `CameraBehavior` to run after the movement happens; this guarantees that `_target` has the most up-to-date position to reference.
5. Sets the camera's position to `_target.TransformPoint(CamOffset)` for every frame, which creates the following effect:
   - The `TransformPoint` method calculates and returns a relative position in the world space.
   - In this case, it returns the position of the `target` (our capsule) offset by `0` in the *x* axis, `1.2` in *the* y axis (putting the camera above the capsule), and `-2.6` in the *z* axis (putting the camera slightly behind the capsule).
6. The `LookAt` method updates the capsule's rotation every frame, focusing on the Transform parameter we pass in, which, in this case, is `_target`:

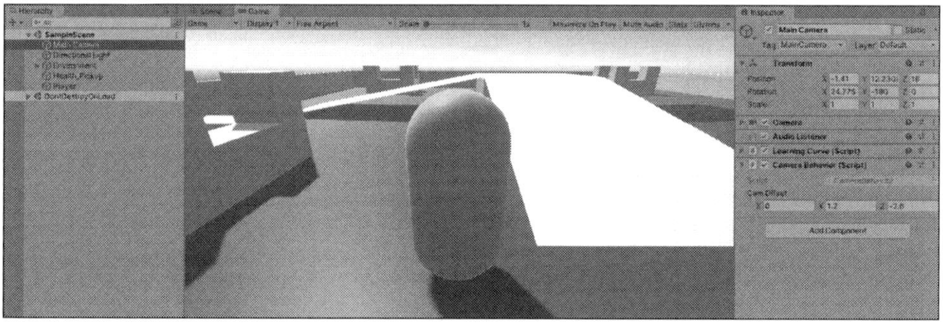

Figure 7.5: Capsule and following camera in Play mode

This was a lot to take in, but it's easier to process if you break it down into its chronological steps:

1. We created an offset position for the camera.
2. We found and stored the player capsule's position.

3. We manually updated its position and rotation every frame so that it's always following at a set distance and looking at the player.

> When using class methods that deliver platform-specific functionality, always remember to break things down to their most basic steps. This will help you to stay above water in new programming environments.

While the code you've written to manage player movement is perfectly functional, you might have noticed that it's a little jerky in places. To create a smoother, more realistic movement effect, you'll need to understand the basics of the Unity physics system, which you'll dive into next.

# Working with the Unity physics system

Up to this point, we haven't talked about how the Unity engine works, or how it manages to create lifelike interactions and movement in a virtual space. We'll spend the rest of this chapter learning the basics of Unity's physics system.

The two main components that power Unity's NVIDIA PhysX engine are as follows:

- **Rigidbody** components, which allow GameObjects to be affected by gravity and add properties such as **Mass** and **Drag**. Rigidbody components can also be affected by an applied force if they have a Collider component attached, which generates more realistic movement:

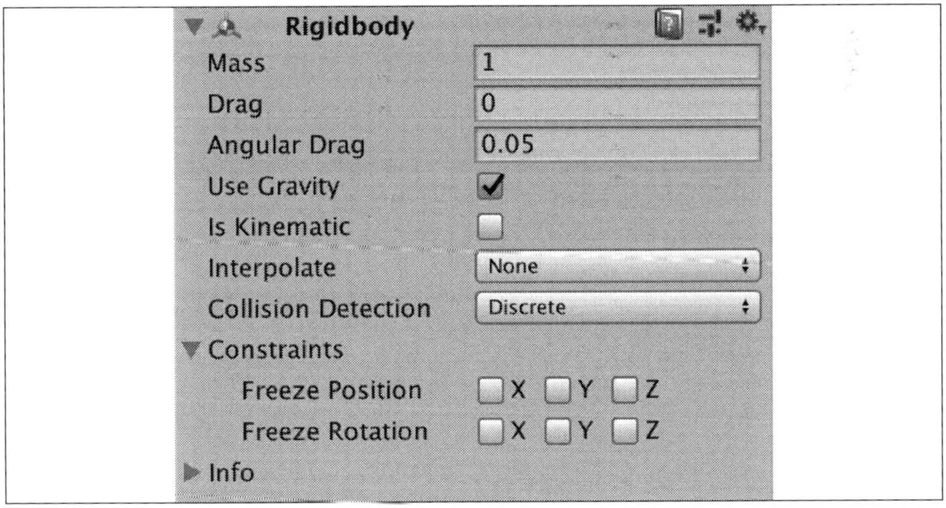


Figure 7.6: Rigidbody component in the Inspector pane

- **Collider** components, which determine how and when GameObjects enter and exit each other's physical space or simply collide and bounce away. While there should only be one Rigidbody component attached to a given GameObject, there can be several Collider components if you need different shapes or interactions. This is commonly referred to as a compound Collider setup:

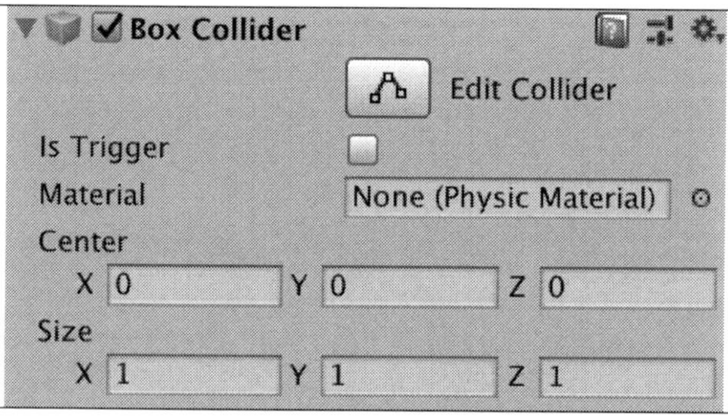


Figure 7.7: Box collider component in the Inspector pane

When two Collider components interact with each other, the Rigidbody properties determine the resulting interaction. For example, if one GameObject's mass is higher than the other, the lighter GameObject will bounce away with more force, just like in real life. These two components are responsible for all physical interactions and simulated movement in Unity.

There are some caveats to using these components, which are best understood in terms of the types of movement Unity allows:

- *Kinematic* movement happens when a Rigidbody component is attached to a GameObject, but it doesn't register to the physics system in the scene. In other words, kinematic objects have physics interactions but don't react to them, like a wall in real life. This is only used in certain cases and can be enabled by checking the **Is Kinematic** property of a Rigidbody component. Since we want our capsule to interact with the physics system, we won't be using this kind of motion.
- *Non-kinematic* movement is when a Rigidbody component is moved or rotated by applying force rather than manually changing a GameObject's Transform properties. Our goal for this section is to update the `PlayerBehavior` script to implement this type of motion.

> The setup we have now, that is, manipulating the capsule's Transform component while using a Rigidbody component to interact with the physics system, was meant to get you thinking about movement and rotation in a 3D space. However, it's not meant for production and Unity suggests avoiding a mix of kinematic and non-kinematic movement in your code.

Your next task is to use applied force to convert the current movement system into a more realistic locomotion experience.

# Rigidbody components in motion

Since our player has a Rigidbody component attached, we should let the physics engine control our movement instead of manually translating and rotating the Transform. There are two options when it comes to applying force:

- You can do it directly by using Rigidbody class methods such as `AddForce` and `AddTorque` to move and rotate an object, respectively. This approach has its drawbacks and often requires additional code to compensate for unexpected physics behavior such as unwanted torque or applied force during collisions.
- Alternatively, you can use other Rigidbody class methods such as `MovePosition` and `MoveRotation`, which still use applied force.

> We'll take the second route in the next section so that Unity takes care of the applied physics for us, but if you're curious about manually applying force and torque to your GameObjects, then start here: `https://docs.unity3d.com/ScriptReference/Rigidbody.AddForce.html`.

Either of these will give the player a more lifelike feel and allow us to add in jumping and dashing mechanics in *Chapter 8, Scripting Game Mechanics*.

> If you're curious about what happens when a moving object without a Rigidbody component interacts with pieces of the environment that have them equipped, remove the component from the Player and run around the arena. Congratulations – you're a ghost and can walk through walls! Don't forget to add the Rigidbody component back, though!

The player capsule already has a Rigidbody component attached, which means that you can access and modify its properties. First, though, you'll need to find and store the component, which is your next challenge.

You'll need to access and store the Rigidbody component on our player capsule before modifying it. Update `PlayerBehavior` with the following changes:

```
using System.Collections;
using System.Collections.Generic;
using UnityEngine;

public class PlayerBehavior : MonoBehaviour
{
    public float MoveSpeed = 10f;
    public float RotateSpeed = 75f;

    private float _vInput;
    private float _hInput;

    // 1
    private Rigidbody _rb;

    // 2
    void Start()
    {
        // 3
        _rb = GetComponent<Rigidbody>();
    }

    void Update()
    {
      _vInput = Input.GetAxis("Vertical") * MoveSpeed;
      _hInput = Input.GetAxis("Horizontal") * RotateSpeed;


      /*
      this.transform.Translate(Vector3.forward * _vInput *
      Time.deltaTime);
      this.transform.Rotate(Vector3.up * _hInput * Time.deltaTime);
      */
    }
}
```

Here's a breakdown of the preceding code:

1. Adds a private variable of type `Rigidbody` that will contain a reference to the capsule's Rigidbody component.
2. The `Start` method fires when a script is initialized in a scene, which happens when you click on play, and should be used any time variables need to be set at the beginning of a class.
3. The `GetComponent` method checks whether the component type we're looking for, in this case, `Rigidbody`, exists on the GameObject the script is attached to and returns it:
   - If the component isn't attached to the GameObject, the method will return `null`, but since we know there's one on the player, we won't worry about error checking right now.
4. Comments out the `Transform` and `Rotate` method calls in the `Update` function so that we won't be running two different kinds of player controls:
   - We want to keep our code that captures player input so that we can still use it later on.

You've initialized and stored the Rigidbody component on the player capsule and commented out the obsolete `Transform` code to set the stage for physics-based movement. The character is now ready for the next challenge, which is to add force.

Use the following steps to move and rotate the Rigidbody component. Add in the following code to `PlayerBehavior` underneath the `Update` method, and then save the file:

```
// 1
void FixedUpdate()
{
    // 2
    Vector3 rotation = Vector3.up * _hInput;

    // 3
    Quaternion angleRot = Quaternion.Euler(rotation *
        Time.fixedDeltaTime);

    // 4
    _rb.MovePosition(this.transform.position +
        this.transform.forward * _vInput * Time.fixedDeltaTime);

    // 5
    _rb.MoveRotation(_rb.rotation * angleRot);
}
```

Here's a breakdown of the preceding code:

1. Any physics- or Rigidbody-related code always goes inside the `FixedUpdate` method, rather than `Update` or the other `MonoBehavior` methods:
    - `FixedUpdate` is frame rate independent and is used for all physics code.
2. Creates a new `Vector3` variable to store our left and right rotation:
    - `Vector3.up * _hInput` is the same rotation vector we used with the `Rotate` method in the previous example.
3. `Quaternion.Euler` takes a `Vector3` parameter and returns a rotation value in Euler angles:
    - We need a `Quaternion` value instead of a `Vector3` parameter to use the `MoveRotation` method. This is just a conversion to the rotation type that Unity prefers.
    - We multiply by `Time.fixedDeltaTime` for the same reason we used `Time.deltaTime` in `Update`.
4. Calls `MovePosition` on our `_rb` component, which takes in a `Vector3` parameter and applies force accordingly:
    - The vector that's used can be broken down as follows: the capsule's `Transform` position in the forward direction, multiplied by the vertical inputs and `Time.fixedDeltaTime`.
    - The Rigidbody component takes care of applying movement force to satisfy our vector parameter.
5. Calls the `MoveRotation` method on the `_rb` component, which also takes in a `Vector3` parameter and applies the corresponding forces under the hood:
    - `angleRot` already has the horizontal inputs from the keyboard, so all we need to do is multiply the current Rigidbody rotation by `angleRot` to get the same left and right rotation.

> Be aware that `MovePosition` and `MoveRotation` work differently for non-kinematic game objects. You can find more information in the Rigidbody scripting reference at `https://docs.unity3d.com/ScriptReference/Rigidbody.html`.

If you click on play now, you'll be able to move forward and backward in the direction you're looking, as well as rotate around the *y* axis.

Applied force produces stronger effects than translating and rotating a Transform component, so you may need to fine-tune the `MoveSpeed` and `RotateSpeed` variables in the **Inspector** pane. You've now recreated the same type of movement scheme as before, just with more realistic physics.

If you run up a ramp or drop off the central platform, you might see the player launch into the air, or slowly drop to the ground. Even though the Rigidbody component is set to use gravity, it's fairly weak. We'll tackle applying our gravity to the player in the next chapter when we implement the jump mechanic. For now, your job is to get comfortable with how Collider components handle collisions in Unity.

# Colliders and collisions

Collider components not only allow GameObjects to be recognized by Unity's physics system, but they also make interactions and collisions possible. Think of colliders as invisible force fields that surround GameObjects; they can be passed through or bumped into depending on their settings, and they come with a host of methods that execute during different interactions.

> Unity's physics system works differently for 2D and 3D games, so we will only be covering the 3D topics in this book. If you're interested in making 2D games, refer to the `Rigidbody2D` component at `https://docs.unity3d.com/Manual/class-Rigidbody2D.html` and the list of available 2D colliders at `https://docs.unity3d.com/Manual/Collider2D.html`.

Take a look at the following screenshot of the **Capsule** in the **Health_Pickup** object. If you want to see the **Capsule Collider** a little better, increase the **Radius** property:

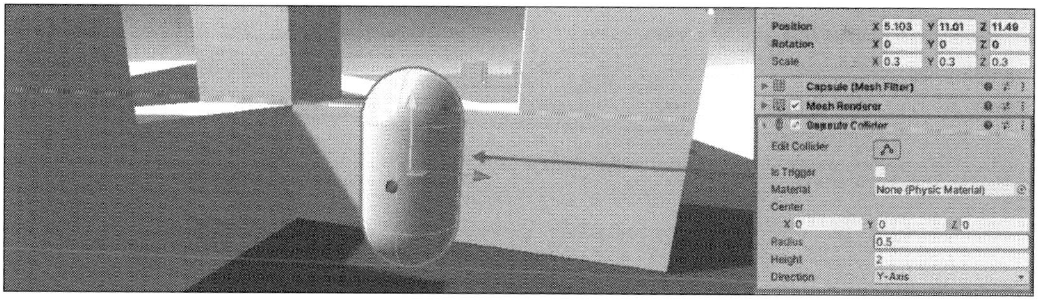


Figure 7.8: Capsule collider component attached to pickup item

The green shape around the object is the **Capsule Collider**, which can be moved and scaled using the **Center**, **Radius**, and **Height** properties.

When a primitive is created, the Collider matches the primitive's shape by default; since we created a capsule primitive, it comes with a Capsule Collider.

> Colliders also come in **Box**, **Sphere**, and **Mesh** shapes and can be manually added from the **Component** | **Physics** menu or from the **Add Component** button in the **Inspector**.

When a Collider comes into contact with other components, it sends out what's called a message, or broadcast. Any script that adds one or more of those methods will receive a notification when the Collider sends out a message. This is called an *event*, which is a topic that we'll cover in more detail in *Chapter 14, The Journey Continues*.

For example, when two GameObjects with colliders come into contact, both objects register an `OnCollisionEnter` event, complete with a reference to the object they ran into. Think of an event like a message being sent out - if you choose to listen for it you'll get notified when a collision happens in this case. This information can be used to track a variety of interactive events, but the simplest one is picking up an item. For cases where you want objects to be able to pass through others, you can use collision triggers, which we'll talk about in the next section.

> A complete list of Collider notifications can be found here underneath the **Messages** header at `https://docs.unity3d.com/ScriptReference/Collider.html`.
>
> Collision and trigger events are only sent out when the colliding objects belong to a specific combination of Collider, Trigger, and RigidBody components and kinematic or non-kinematic motion. You can find details under the **Collision action matrix** section at `https://docs.unity3d.com/Manual/CollidersOverview.html`.

The health item you previously created is a perfect place to test out how collisions work. You'll tackle that in the next challenge.

## Picking up an item

To update the `Health_Pickup` object using collision logic, you need to do the following:

1. Create a new C# script in the `Scripts` folder, name it `ItemBehavior`, and then drag it onto the `Health_Pickup` object in the **Hierarchy** panel:

- Any script that uses collision detection *must* be attached to a GameObject with a Collider component, even if it's the child of a Prefab.

2. Select `Health_Pickup` in the **Hierarchy panel**, click the three vertical dots icon in the **Inspector** to the right of the **Item Behavior (Script)** component, and choose **Added Component** | **Apply to Prefab 'Health_Pickup'**:

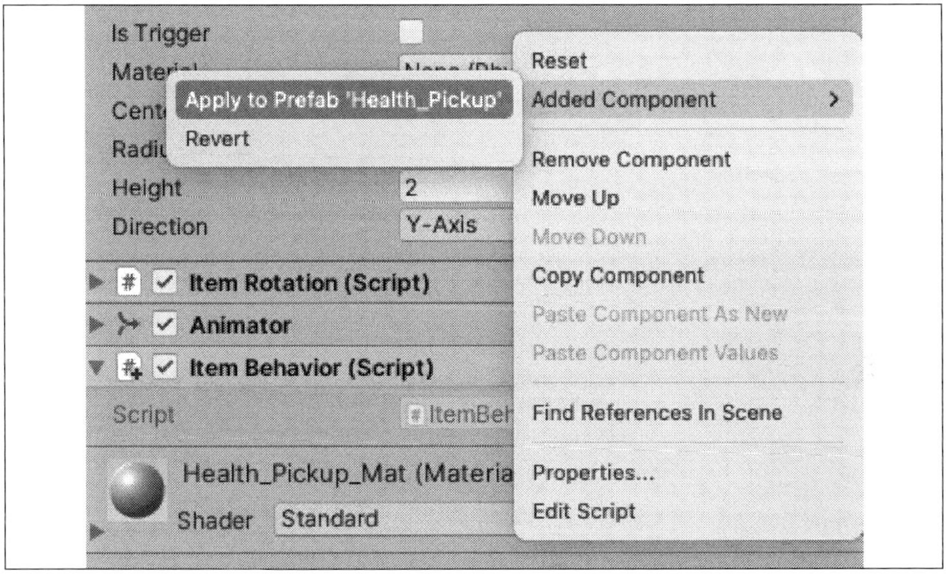


Figure 7.9: Applying Prefab changes to pickup item

3. Replace the default code in `ItemBehavior` with the following, and then save it:

```
using System.Collections;
using System.Collections.Generic;
using UnityEngine;

public class ItemBehavior : MonoBehaviour
{
    // 1
    void OnCollisionEnter(Collision collision)
    {
        // 2
        if(collision.gameObject.name == "Player")
        {
            // 3
            Destroy(this.transform.gameObject);
```

```
                // 4
                Debug.Log("Item collected!");
            }
        }
    }
```

4. Click on play and move the player over the capsule to pick it up!

Here's a breakdown of the preceding code:

1. When another object runs into the `Item` Prefab, Unity automatically calls the `OnCollisionEnter` method:
    - `OnCollisionEnter` comes with a parameter that stores a reference to the Collider that ran into it.
    - Notice that the collision is of type `Collision`, not `Collider`.
2. The `Collision` class has a property, called `gameObject`, which holds a reference to the colliding GameObject's Collider:
    - We can use this property to get the GameObject's name and use an `if` statement to check whether the colliding object is the player.
3. If the colliding object is the player, we'll call the `Destroy()` method, which takes in a GameObject parameter and removes the object from the scene.
4. It then prints out a simple log to the console that we have collected an item:

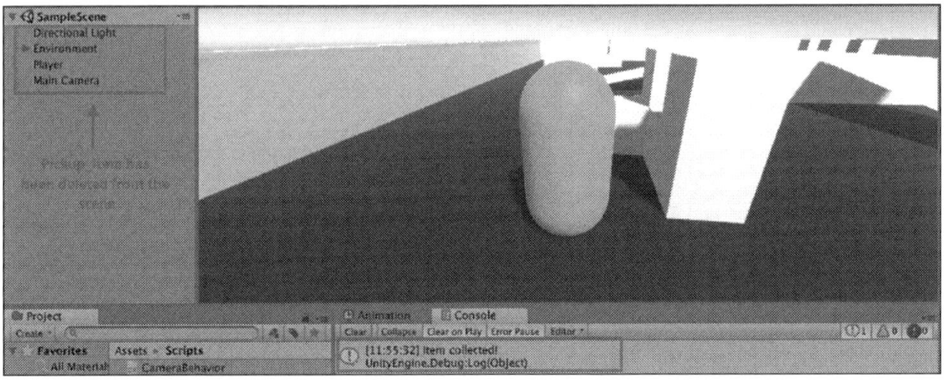


Figure 7.10: Example of game objects being deleted from a scene

We've set up `ItemBehavior` to essentially listen for any collisions with the `Health_Pickup` object Prefab. Whenever a collision occurs, `ItemBehavior` uses `OnCollisionEnter()` and checks whether the colliding object is the player and, if so, destroys (or collects) the item.

If you're feeling lost, think of the collision code we wrote as a receiver for notifications from the `Health_Pickup`; any time it's hit, the code fires.

It's also important to understand that we could have created a similar script with an `OnCollisionEnter()` method, attached it to the player, and then checked whether the colliding object was a `Health_Pickup` Prefab. Collision logic depends on the perspective of the object being collided with.

Now the question is, how would you set up a collision without stopping the colliding objects from moving through each other? We'll tackle that in the next section.

# Using Collider triggers

By default, Colliders are set with the `isTrigger` property unchecked, meaning that the physics system treats them as solid objects and will raise a Collision event on impact. However, in some cases, you'll want to be able to pass through a Collider component without it stopping your GameObject. This is where triggers come in. With `isTrigger` checked, a GameObject can pass through it, but the Collider will send out the `OnTriggerEnter`, `OnTriggerExit`, and `OnTriggerStay` notifications instead.

Triggers are most useful when you need to detect when a GameObject enters a certain area or passes a certain point. We'll use this to set up the areas around our enemies; if the player walks into the trigger zone, the enemies will be alerted, and, later on, attack the player. For now, you're going to focus just on the enemy logic in the following challenge.

## Creating an enemy

Use the following steps to create an enemy:

1. Create a new primitive using **+** | **3D Object** | **Capsule** in the **Hierarchy** panel and name it `Enemy`.
2. Inside the `Materials` folder, use **+** | **Material**, name it `Enemy_Mat`, and set its **Albedo** property to a bright red:
    - Drag and drop `Enemy_Mat` into the `Enemy` GameObject.
3. With `Enemy` selected, click on **Add Component**, search for **Sphere Collider**, and hit *Enter* to add it:

- Check the **isTrigger** property box and change the **Radius** to `8`:

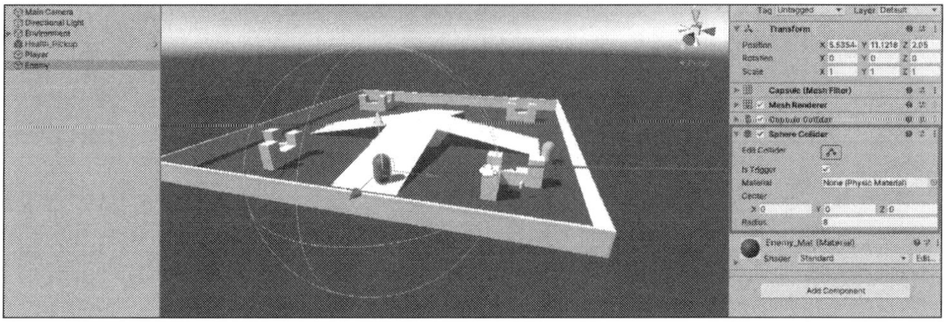

Figure 7.11: Sphere collider component attached to an enemy object

Our new **Enemy** primitive is now surrounded by an 8-unit trigger radius shaped like a sphere. Any time another object enters, stays inside, or exits that area, Unity will send out notifications that we can capture, just like we did with collisions. Your next challenge will be to capture that notification and act on it in code.

To capture trigger events, you'll need to create a new script by following these steps:

1. Create a new C# script in the `Scripts` folder, name it `EnemyBehavior`, and then drag it into **Enemy**.
2. Add the following code and save the file:

```
using System.Collections;
using System.Collections.Generic;
using UnityEngine;

public class EnemyBehavior : MonoBehaviour
{
    // 1
    void OnTriggerEnter(Collider other)
    {
        //2
        if(other.name == "Player")
        {
            Debug.Log("Player detected - attack!");
        }
    }

    // 3
    void OnTriggerExit(Collider other)
    {
        // 4
```

```
            if(other.name == "Player")
            {
                Debug.Log("Player out of range, resume patrol");
            }
        }
    }
```

3. Click play and walk over to the Enemy to set off the first notification, then walk away from the Enemy to set off the second notification.

Here's a breakdown of the preceding code:

1. `OnTriggerEnter()` is fired whenever an object enters the Enemy Sphere Collider radius:
    - Similar to `OnCollisionEnter()`, `OnTriggerEnter()` stores a reference to the trespassing object's Collider component.
    - Note that `other` is of type `Collider`, not `Collision`.
2. We can use `other` to access the name of the colliding GameObject, and check whether it's the `Player` with an `if` statement. If it is, the console prints out a log that the `Player` is in the danger zone.

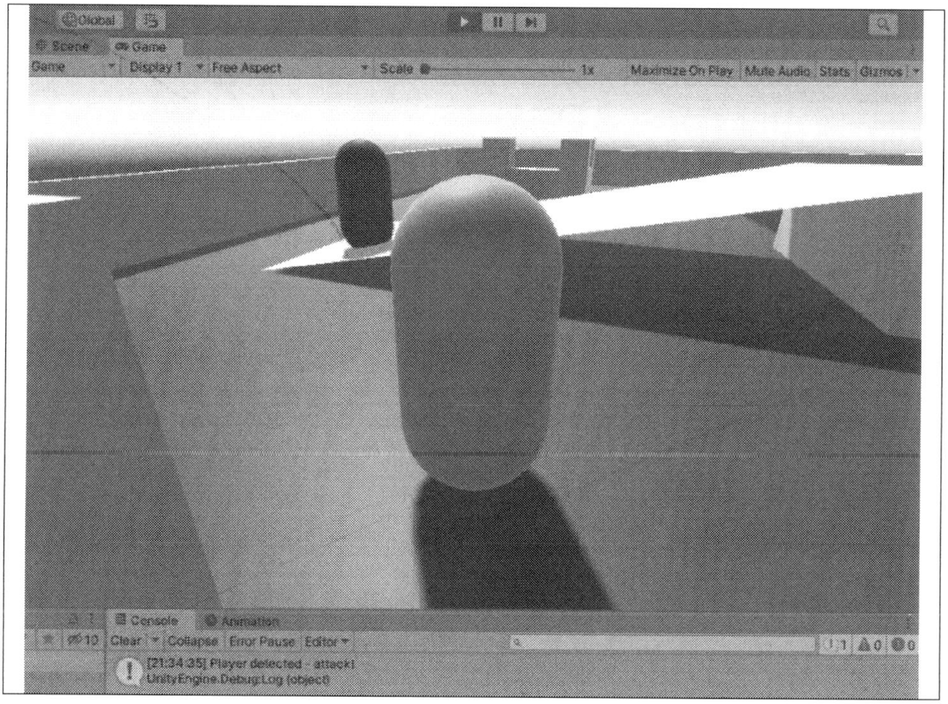


Figure 7.12: Collision detection between player and enemy objects

3. `OnTriggerExit()` is fired when an object leaves the Enemy Sphere Collider radius:
    - This method also has a reference to the colliding object's Collider component:
4. We check the object leaving the Sphere Collider radius by name using another `if` statement:
    - If it's `Player`, we print out another log to the console saying that they're safe:

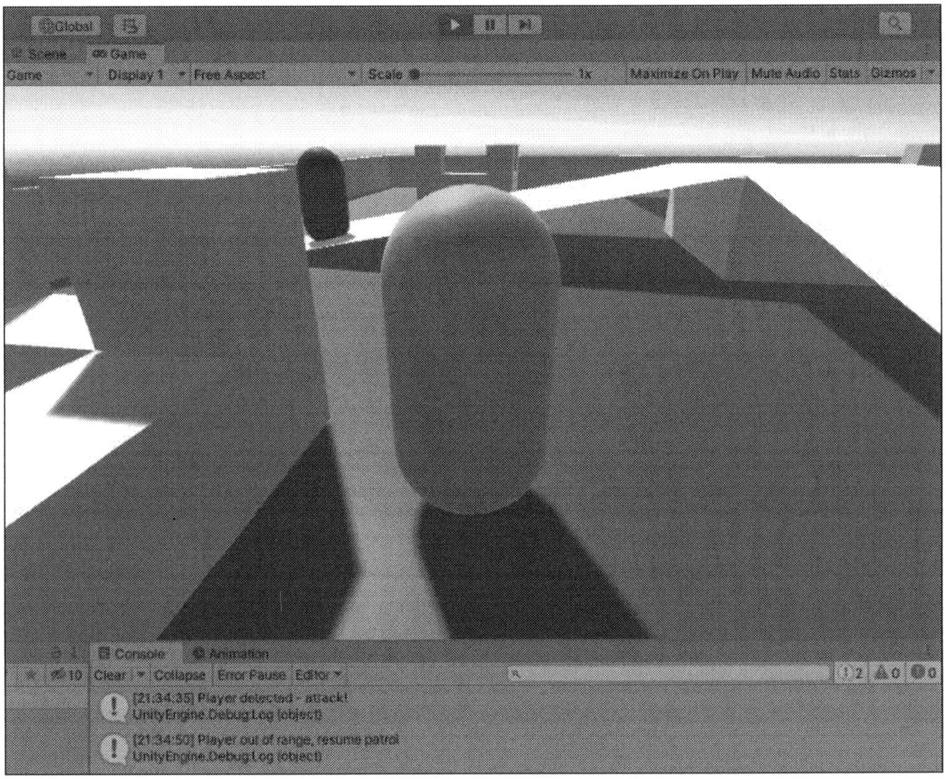


Figure 7.13: Example of collision triggers

The Sphere Collider on our Enemy sends out notifications when its area is invaded, and the `EnemyBehavior` script captures two of those events. Whenever the player enters or exits the collision radius, a debug log appears in the console to let us know that the code is working. We'll continue to build on this in *Chapter 9, Basic AI and Enemy Behavior*.

> Unity makes use of something called the Component design pattern. Without going into too much detail, that's a fancy way of saying objects (and, by extension, their classes) should be responsible for their behavior as opposed to having all the code in one huge file. This is why we put separate collision scripts on the pickup item and enemy instead of having a single class handle everything. We'll discuss this further in *Chapter 14, The Journey Continues*.

Since this book is all about instilling as many good programming habits as possible, your last task for the chapter is to make sure all your core objects are converted into Prefabs.

## Hero's trial – all the Prefabs!

To get the project ready for the next chapter, go ahead and drag the `Player` and `Enemy` objects into the **Prefabs** folder. Remember, from now on you always need to right-click on the Prefab in the **Hierarchy** panel and choose **Added Component | Apply to Prefab** to solidify any changes you make to these GameObjects.

With that done, continue to the *Physics roundup* section and make sure that you've internalized all the major topics we've covered before moving on.

# Physics roundup

Before we wrap up the chapter, here are a few high-level concepts to cement what we've learned so far:

- Rigidbody components add simulated real-world physics to GameObjects they are attached to.
- Collider components interact with each other, as well as objects, using Rigidbody components:
    - If a Collider component is not a trigger, it acts as a solid object.
    - If a Collider component is a trigger, it can be walked through.
- An object is *kinematic* if it uses a Rigidbody component and has **Is Kinematic** checked, telling the physics system to ignore it.
- An object is *non-kinematic* if it uses a Rigidbody component and applied force or torque to power its movement and rotation.

- Colliders send out notifications based on their interactions. These notifications depend on whether the Collider component is set to be triggered or not. Notifications can be received from either colliding party, and they come with reference variables that hold an object's collision information.

Remember, a topic as broad and complex as the Unity physics system isn't learned in a day. Use what you've learned here as a springboard to launch yourself into more intricate topics!

# Summary

This wraps up your first experience of creating independent gameplay behaviors and tying them all together into a cohesive, albeit simple, game prototype. You've used vectors and basic vector math to determine positions and angles in a 3D space, and you're familiar with player input and the two main methods of moving and rotating GameObjects. You've even gone down into the bowels of the Unity physics system to get comfortable with Rigidbody physics, collisions, triggers, and event notifications. All in all, *Hero Born* is off to a great start.

In the next chapter, we'll start tackling more game mechanics, including jumping, dashing, shooting projectiles, and interacting with parts of the environment. This will give you more hands-on experience of using force with Rigidbody components, gathering player input, and executing logic based on the desired scenario.

# Pop quiz – player controls and physics

1. What data type would you use to store 3D movement and rotation information?
2. What built-in Unity component allows you to track and modify player controls?
3. Which component adds real-world physics to a GameObject?
4. What method does Unity suggest using to execute physics-related code on GameObjects?

# 8

# Scripting Game Mechanics

In the last chapter, we focused on using code to move the player and camera, with a trip into Unity physics on the side. However, controlling a playable character isn't enough to make a compelling game; in fact, it's probably the one area that remains fairly constant across different titles.

A game's unique spark comes from its core mechanics, and the feeling of power and agency those mechanics give to the players. Without fun and engrossing ways to affect the virtual environment you've created, your game doesn't stand a chance of repeat play, to say nothing of fun. As we venture into implementing the game's mechanics, we'll also be upgrading our knowledge of C# and its intermediate-level features.

This chapter will build on the *Hero Born* prototype by focusing on individually implemented game mechanics, as well as the basics of system design and **user interfaces** (**UIs**). You'll be diving into the following topics:

- Adding jumps
- Shooting projectiles
- Creating a game manager
- Creating a GUI

## Adding jumps

Remember from the last chapter that Rigidbody components add simulated real-world physics to GameObjects, and Collider components interact with each other using Rigidbody objects.

Another great thing that we didn't discuss in the previous chapter about using a Rigidbody component to control player movement is that we can easily add in different mechanics that rely on applied force, such as jumping. In this section, we'll get our player jumping and write our first utility function.

> A utility function is a class method that performs some kind of grunt work so that we don't clutter up gameplay code—for instance, wanting to check whether the player capsule is touching the ground to jump.

Before that, you'll need to get acquainted with a new data type called enumerations, which you'll do in the following section.

# Introducing enumerations

By definition, an enumeration type is a set, or collection, of named constants that belong to the same variable. These are useful when you want a collection of different values, but with the added benefit of them all being of the same parent type.

It's easier to show rather than tell with enumerations, so let's take a look at their syntax in the following code snippet:

```
enum PlayerAction { Attack, Defend, Flee };
```

Let's break down how this works, as follows:

- The `enum` keyword declares the type followed by the variable name.
- The different values an enum can have are written inside curly brackets, separated by a comma (except for the last item).
- The `enum` has to end with a semicolon, just like all other data types we've worked with.

In this case, we're declaring a variable called `PlayerAction`, of type `enum`, which can be set to one of three values—`Attack`, `Defend`, or `Flee`.

To declare an enumeration variable, we use the following syntax:

```
PlayerAction CurrentAction = PlayerAction.Defend;
```

Again, we can break this down, as follows:

- The type is set as `PlayerAction`, since our enumeration is just like any other type, like a string or integer.

- The variable is named `currentAction` and set equal to a `PlayerAction` value.
- Each enum constant can be accessed using dot notation.

Our `currentAction` variable is now set to `Defend`, but it can be changed to `Attack` or `Flee` at any time.

Enumerations may look simple at first glance, but they are extremely powerful in the right situations. One of their most useful features is the ability to store underlying types, which is the next subject you'll be jumping into.

# Underlying types

Enums come with an *underlying type*, meaning that each constant inside the curly brackets has an associated value. The default underlying type is `int` and starts at 0, just like arrays, with each sequential constant getting the next highest number.

> Not all types are created equal—underlying types for enumerations are limited to `byte`, `sbyte`, `short`, `ushort`, `int`, `uint`, `long`, and `ulong`. These are called integral types, which are used to specify the size of numeric values that a variable can store.
>
> This is a bit advanced for this book, but you'll be using `int` in most cases. More information on these types can be found here: `https://docs.microsoft.com/en-us/dotnet/csharp/language-reference/keywords/enum`.

For example, our `PlayerAction` enumeration values right now are listed as follows, even though they aren't explicitly written out:

```
enum PlayerAction { Attack = 0, Defend = 1, Flee = 2 };
```

There's no rule that says underlying values need to start at `0`; in fact, all you have to do is specify the first value and then C# increments the rest of the values for us, as illustrated in the following code snippet:

```
enum PlayerAction { Attack = 5, Defend, Flee };
```

In the preceding example, `Defend` equals `6`, and `Flee` equals `7` automatically. However, if we wanted the `PlayerAction` enum to hold non-sequential values, we could explicitly add them in, like this:

```
enum PlayerAction { Attack = 10, Defend = 5, Flee = 0};
```

We can even change the underlying type of `PlayerAction` to any of the approved types by adding a colon after the enum name, as follows:

```
enum PlayerAction :  byte { Attack, Defend, Flee };
```

Retrieving an enum's underlying type takes an explicit conversion, but we've already covered those, so the following syntax shouldn't be a surprise:

```
enum PlayerAction { Attack = 10, Defend = 5, Flee = 0};

PlayerAction CurrentAction = PlayerAction.Attack;
int ActionCost = (int)CurrentAction;
```

Since `CurrentAction` is set to `Attack`, `ActionCost` would be `10` in the above example code.

Enumerations are extremely powerful tools in your programming arsenal. Your next challenge is to use your knowledge of enumerations to gather more specific user input from the keyboard.

Now that we have a basic grasp of enumeration types, we can capture keyboard input using the `KeyCode` enum. Update the `PlayerBehavior` script with the following highlighted code, save it, and hit play:

```
public class PlayerBehavior : MonoBehaviour
{
    // ... No other variable changes needed ...

    // 1
    public float JumpVelocity = 5f;
    private bool _isJumping;

    void Start()
    {
        _rb = GetComponent<Rigidbody>();
    }

    void Update()
    {
        // 2
        _isJumping |= Input.GetKeyDown(KeyCode.Space);

        // ... No other changes needed ...
    }
```

```
    void FixedUpdate()
    {
        // 3
        if(_isJumping)
        {
            // 4
            _rb.AddForce(Vector3.up * JumpVelocity, ForceMode.Impulse);
        }

        // 5
        _isJumping = false;

        // ... No other changes needed ...
    }
}
```

Let's break down this code, as follows:

1. First, we create two new variables—a public variable to hold the amount of applied jump force we want and a private boolean to check if our player should be jumping.
2. We set the value of `_isJumping` to the `Input.GetKeyDown()` method, which returns a `bool` value depending on whether a specified key is pressed.
   - We use the |= operator to set `_isJumping`, which is the logical `or` condition. This operator makes sure that we don't have consecutive input checks override each other when the player is jumping.
   - The method accepts a key parameter as either a `string` or a `KeyCode`, which is an enumeration type. We specify that we want to check for `KeyCode.Space`.

> Checking for inputs in `FixedUpdate` can sometimes lead to input loss or even double inputs because it doesn't run once per frame. This is why we're checking for inputs in `Update` and then applying force or setting the velocity in `FixedUpdate`.

3. We use an `if` statement to check if `_isJumping` is true, and trigger the jump mechanic if it is.
4. Since we already have the Rigidbody component stored, we can pass the `Vector3` and `ForceMode` parameters to `RigidBody.AddForce()` and make the player jump.

- We specify that the vector (or applied force) should be in the `up` direction, multiplied by `JumpVelocity`.
- The `ForceMode` parameter determines how the force is applied and is also an enumeration type. `Impulse` delivers an instant force to an object while taking its mass into account, which is perfect for a jump mechanic.

> Other `ForceMode` choices can be useful in different situations, all of which are detailed here: `https://docs.unity3d.com/ScriptReference/ForceMode.html`.

5. At the end of every `FixedUpdate` frame, we reset `_isJumping` to false so the input check knows a complete jump and the landing cycle has been completed.

If you play the game now, you'll be able to move around and jump when you hit the spacebar. However, the mechanic allows you to keep jumping indefinitely, which isn't what we want. We'll work on limiting our jump mechanic to one at a time in the next section, using something called a layer mask.

# Working with layer masks

Think of layer masks as invisible groups that a GameObject can belong to, used by the physics system to determine anything from navigation to intersecting collider components. While more advanced uses of layer masks are outside the scope of this book, we'll create and use one to perform a simple check—whether the player capsule is touching the ground, in order to limit the player to one jump at a time.

Before we can check that the player capsule is touching the ground, we need to add all the environment objects in our level to a custom layer mask. This will let us perform the actual collision calculation with the Capsule Collider component that's already attached to the player. Proceed as follows:

1. Select any environment GameObject in the **Hierarchy** and in the corresponding **Inspector** pane, click on **Layer** | **Add Layer...**, as illustrated in the following screenshot:

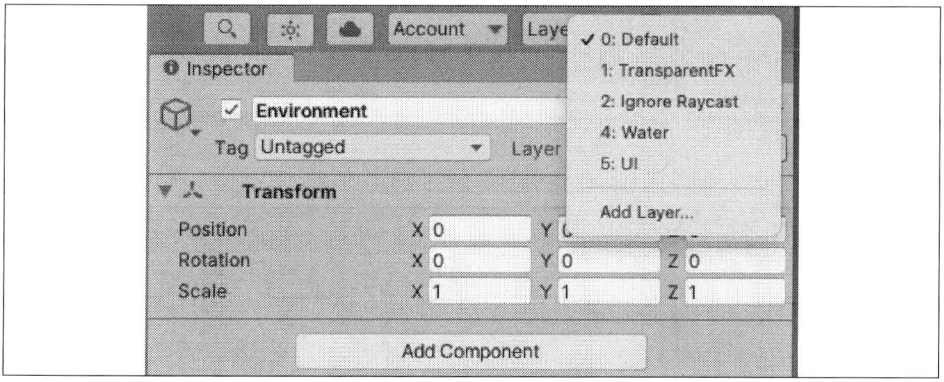


Figure 8.1: Selecting layers in the Inspector pane

2. Add a new layer called `Ground` by typing the name into the first available slot, which is Layer 6. Layers 0-5 are reserved for Unity's default layers, even though Layer 3 is empty, as illustrated in the following screenshot:

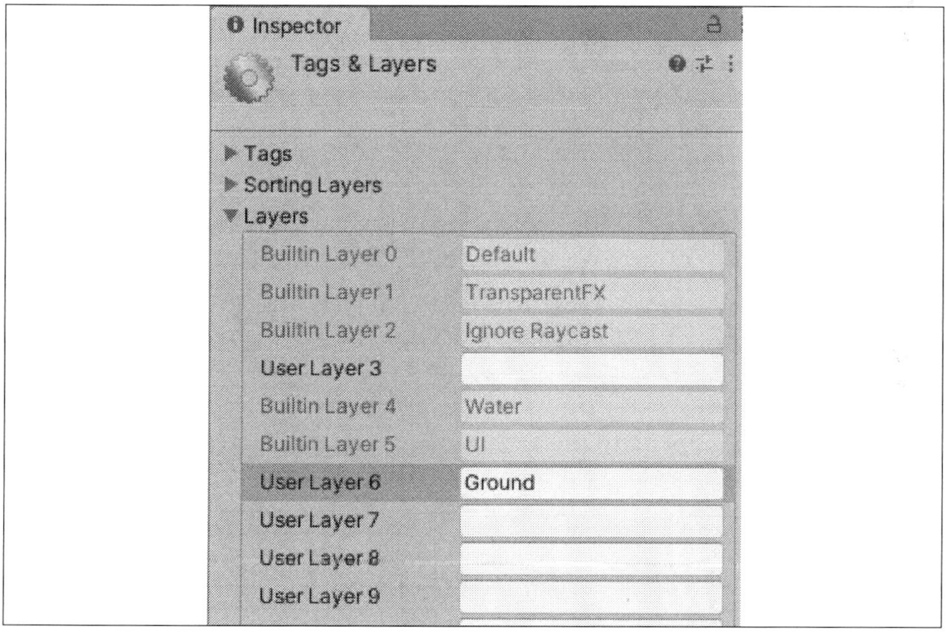


Figure 8.2: Adding layers in the Inspector pane

3. Select the **Environment** parent GameObject in the **Hierarchy**, click on the **Layer** dropdown, and select **Ground**.

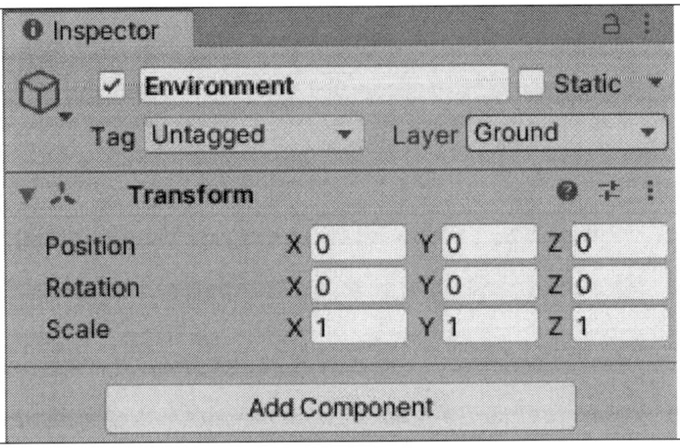


Figure 8.3: Setting a custom layer

After you have selected the **Ground** option shown in the following screenshot, click **Yes, change children** when a dialog appears asking you if you want to change all child objects. Here, you've defined a new layer called **Ground** and assigned every child object of **Environment** to that layer.

Going forward, all the objects on the **Ground** layer can be checked to see if they intersect with a specific object. You'll use this in the following challenge to make sure the player can perform a jump if it's on the ground; no unlimited jump hacks here.

Since we don't want code cluttering up the `Update()` method, we'll do our layer mask calculations in a utility function and return a `true` or `false` value based on the outcome. To do so, proceed as follows:

1. Add the following highlighted code to `PlayerBehavior` and play the scene again:

```
public class PlayerBehavior : MonoBehaviour
{
    // 1
    public float DistanceToGround = 0.1f;

    // 2
    public LayerMask GroundLayer;

    // 3
    private CapsuleCollider _col;
```

```
    // ... No other variable changes needed ...

    void Start()
    {
        _rb = GetComponent<Rigidbody>();

        // 4
        _col = GetComponent<CapsuleCollider>();
    }

    void Update()
    {
        // ... No changes needed ...
    }

    void FixedUpdate()
    {
        // 5
        if(IsGrounded() && _isJumping)
        {
            _rb.AddForce(Vector3.up * JumpVelocity,
                 ForceMode.Impulse);
         }

         // ... No other changes needed ...
    }

    // 6
    private bool IsGrounded()
    {
        // 7
        Vector3 capsuleBottom = new Vector3(_col.bounds.center.x,
             _col.bounds.min.y, _col.bounds.center.z);

        // 8
        bool grounded = Physics.CheckCapsule(_col.bounds.center,
            capsuleBottom, DistanceToGround, GroundLayer,
               QueryTriggerInteraction.Ignore);

        // 9
        return grounded;
    }
}
```

2. With the `PlayerBehavior` script selected, set **Ground Layer** in the **Inspector** pane to **Ground** from the **Ground Layer** dropdown, as illustrated in the following screenshot:

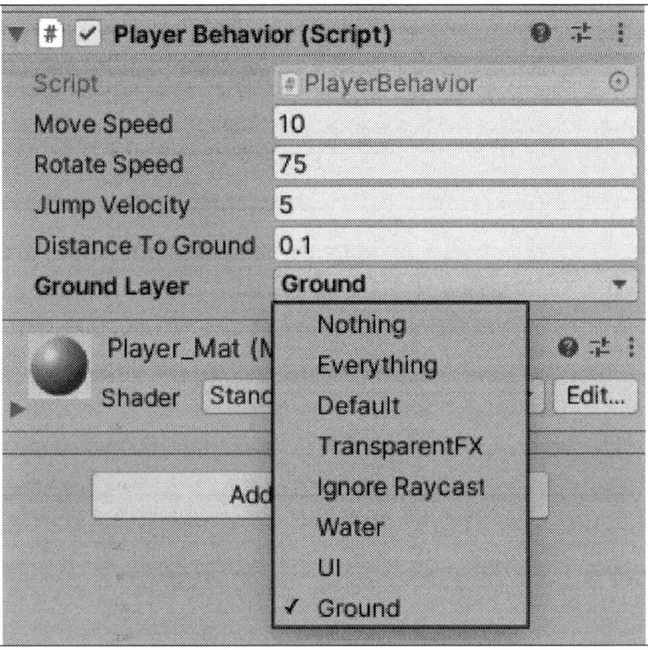


Figure 8.4: Setting the Ground Layer

Let's break down the preceding code, as follows:

1. We create a new variable for the distance we'll check between the player Capsule Collider and any **Ground Layer** object.
2. We create a `LayerMask` variable that we can set in the **Inspector** and use for the collider detection.
3. We create a variable to store the player's Capsule Collider component.
4. We use `GetComponent()` to find and return the Capsule Collider attached to the player.
5. We update the `if` statement to check whether `IsGrounded` returns `true` and the spacebar is pressed before executing the jump code.
6. We declare the `IsGrounded()` method with a `bool` return type.
7. We create a local `Vector3` variable to store the position at the bottom of the player's Capsule Collider, which we'll use to check for collisions with any objects on the **Ground** layer.

- All Collider components have a `bounds` property, which gives us access to the min, max, and center positions of its *x*, *y*, and *z* axes.
- The bottom of the collider is the 3D point at center *x*, min *y*, and center *z*.

8. We create a local `bool` to store the result of the `CheckCapsule()` method that we call from the `Physics` class, which takes in the following five arguments:
   - The start of the capsule, which we set to the middle of the Capsule Collider since we only care about checking whether the bottom touches the ground.
   - The end of the capsule, which is the `capsuleBottom` position we've already calculated.
   - The radius of the capsule, which is the `DistanceToGround` already set.
   - The layer mask we want to check collisions on, set to `GroundLayer` in the **Inspector**.
   - The query trigger interaction, which determines whether the method should ignore colliders that are set as triggers. Since we want to ignore all triggers, we used the `QueryTriggerInteraction.Ignore` enum.

> We could also use the `Distance` method from the `Vector3` class to determine how far we are from the ground since we know the height of the player capsule. However, we're going to stick with using the `Physics` class since that's the focus of this chapter.

9. We return the value stored in `grounded` at the end of the calculation.

> We could have done the collision calculation manually, but that would require more complex 3D math than we have time to cover here. However, it's always a good idea to use built-in methods when available.

That was an involved piece of code that we just added into `PlayerBehavior`, but when you break it down, the only new thing we did was use a method from the `Physics` class. In plain English, we supplied `CheckCapsule()` with a start and endpoint, a collision radius, and a layer mask. If the endpoint gets closer than the collision radius to an object on the layer mask, the method returns `true`—meaning the player is touching the ground. If the player is in a mid-jump position, `CheckCapsule()` returns `false`.

Since we're checking `IsGround` in the `if` statement every frame in `Update()`, our player's jump skills are only allowed when touching the ground.

That's all you're going to do with the jump mechanic, but the player still needs a way to interact and defend themself against the hordes of enemies that will eventually populate the arena. In the following section, you'll fix that gap by implementing a simple shooting mechanic.

# Shooting projectiles

Shooting mechanics are so common that it's hard to think of a first-person game without some variation present, and *Hero Born* is no different. In this section, we'll talk about how to instantiate GameObjects from Prefabs while the game is running, and use the skills we've learned to propel them forward using Unity physics.

## Instantiating objects

The concept of instantiating a GameObject in the game is similar to instantiating an instance of a class—both require starting values so that C# knows what kind of object we want to create and where it needs to be created. To create objects in the scene at runtime, we use the `Instantiate()` method and provide a Prefab object, a starting position, and a starting rotation.

Essentially, we can tell Unity to create a given object with all its components and scripts at this spot, looking in this direction, and then manipulate it as needed once it's born in the 3D space. Before we instantiate an object, you'll need to create the object Prefab itself, which is your next task.

Before we can shoot any projectiles, we'll need a Prefab to use as a reference, so let's create that now, as follows:

1. Select **+** | **3D Object** | **Sphere** in the **Hierarchy** panel and name it `Bullet`.
    - Change its **Scale** to 0.15 in the *x*, *y*, and *z* axes in the **Transform** component.
2. Select the **Bullet** in the **Inspector** and use the **Add Component** button at the bottom to search for and add a **Rigidbody** component, leaving all default properties as they are.

3. Create a new material in the `Materials` folder using **Create** | **Material**, and name it `Bullet_Mat`:
    - Change the **Albedo** property to a deep yellow.
    - Drag and drop the material from the **Materials** folder onto the `Bullet` GameObject in the **Hierarchy** pane.

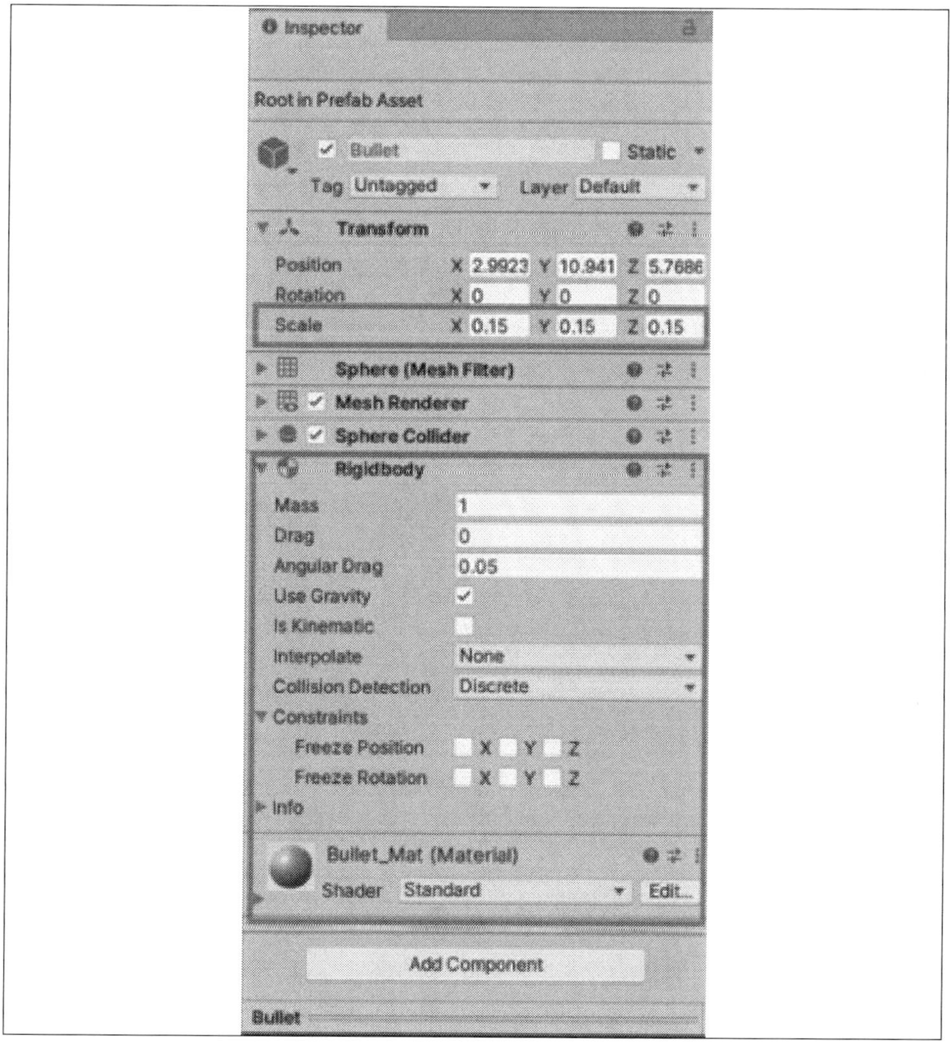


Figure 8.5: Setting projectile properties

4. Select the **Bullet** in the **Hierarchy** panel and drag it into the `Prefabs` folder in the **Project** panel. Then, delete it from the **Hierarchy** to clean up the scene:

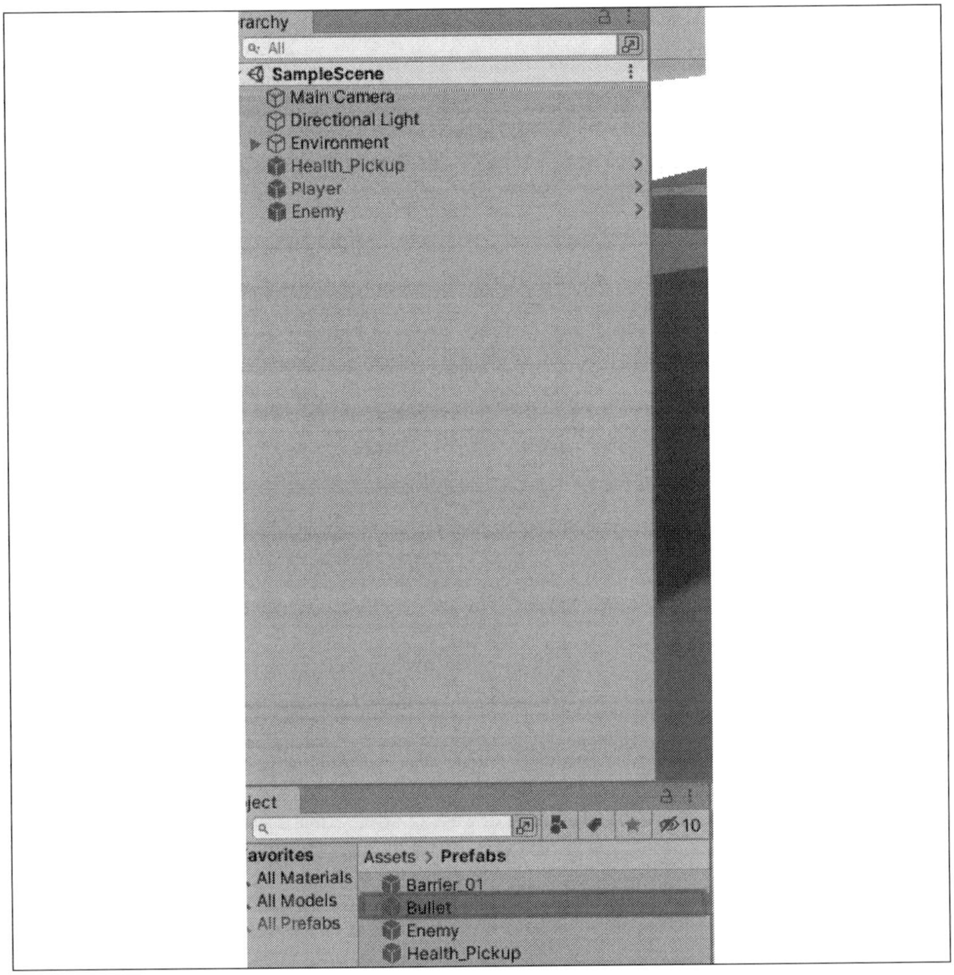


Figure 8.6: Creating a projectile Prefab

You created and configured a **Bullet** Prefab GameObject that can be instantiated as many times as we need in the game and updated as needed. This means you're ready for the next challenge—shooting projectiles.

# Adding the shooting mechanic

Now that we have a Prefab object to work with, we can instantiate and move copies of the Prefab whenever we hit the left mouse button to create a shooting mechanic, as follows:

1. Update the `PlayerBehavior` script with the following code:

```
public class PlayerBehavior : MonoBehaviour
{
    // 1
    public GameObject Bullet;
    public float BulletSpeed = 100f;

    // 2
    private bool _isShooting;

    // ... No other variable changes needed ...

    void Start()
    {
        // ... No changes needed ...
    }

    void Update()
    {
        // 3
        _isShooting |= Input.GetMouseButtonDown(0);

        // ... No other changes needed ...
    }

    void FixedUpdate()
    {
        // ... No other changes needed ...

        // 4
        if (_isShooting)
        {
            // 5
            GameObject newBullet = Instantiate(Bullet,
                this.transform.position + new Vector3(1, 0, 0),
                   this.transform.rotation);

            // 6
            Rigidbody BulletRB =
                 newBullet.GetComponent<Rigidbody>();

            // 7
```

```
            BulletRB.velocity = this.transform.forward *
                                                BulletSpeed;
        }

        // 8
        _isShooting = false;
    }

    private bool IsGrounded()
    {
        // ... No changes needed ...
    }
}
```

2. In the **Inspector**, drag the **Bullet** Prefab from the **Project** panel into the **Bullet** property of `PlayerBehavior`, as illustrated in the following screenshot:

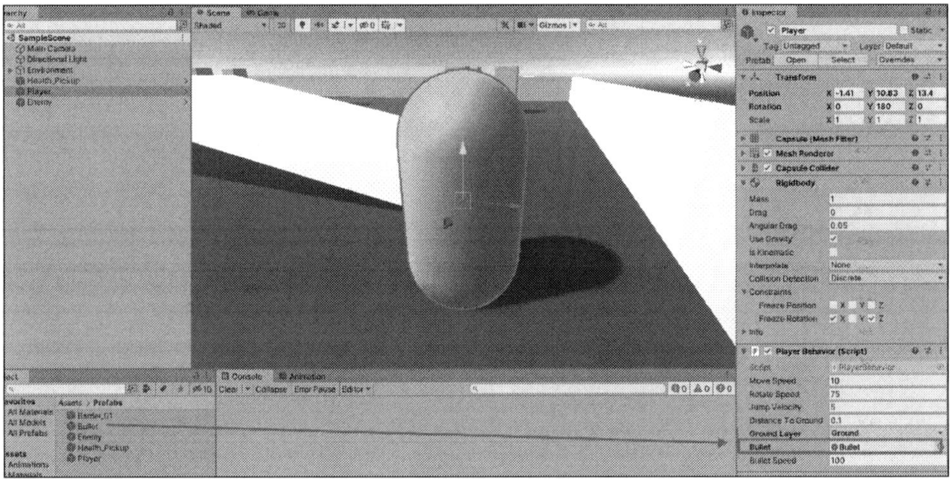

Figure 8.7: Setting the Bullet Prefab

3. Play the game and use the left mouse button to fire projectiles in the direction the player is facing!

Let's break down the code, as follows:

1. We create two variables: one to store the Bullet Prefab, the other to hold the Bullet speed.
2. Like our jumping mechanic, we use a boolean in the `Update` method to check if our player should be shooting.

3. We set the value of `_isShooting` using the `or` logical operator and `Input.GetMouseButtonDown()`, which returns `true` if we're pushing the specified button, just like with `Input.GetKeyDown()`.
    - `GetMouseButtonDown()` takes an `int` parameter to determine which mouse button we want to check for; `0` is the left button, `1` is the right button, and `2` is the middle button or scroll wheel.
4. Then we check if our player is supposed to be shooting using the `_isShooting` input check variable.
5. We create a local GameObject variable every time the left mouse button is pressed:
    - We use the `Instantiate()` method to assign a GameObject to `newBullet` by passing in the `Bullet` Prefab. We also use the player capsule's position to place the new `Bullet` Prefab in front of the player to avoid any collisions.
    - We append it as a `GameObject` to explicitly cast the returned object to the same type as `newBullet`, which in this case is a GameObject.
6. We call `GetComponent()` to return and store the Rigidbody component on `newBullet`.
7. We set the `velocity` property of the Rigidbody component to the player's `transform.forward` direction multiplied by `BulletSpeed`:
    - Changing the `velocity` instead of using `AddForce()` ensures that gravity doesn't pull our bullets down in an arc when fired.
8. Finally, we set the `_isShooting` value to `false` so our shooting input is reset for the next input event.

Again, you've significantly upgraded the logic the player script is using. You should now be able to use the mouse to shoot projectiles that fly straight out from the player's position.

However, the problem now is that your game scene, and hierarchy, are flooded with spent Bullet objects. Your next task is to clean those objects up once they've been fired, to avoid any performance issues.

# Managing object build-up

Whether you're writing a completely code-based application or a 3D game, it's important to make sure that unused objects are regularly deleted to avoid overloading the program. Our bullets don't exactly play an important role after they are shot; they sort of just keep existing on the floor near whatever wall or object they collided with.

With a mechanic such as shooting, this could result in hundreds, if not thousands, of bullets down the line, which is something we don't want. Your next challenge is to destroy each bullet after a set delay time.

For this task, we can take the skills we've already learned and make the bullets responsible for their self-destructive behavior, as follows:

1. Create a new C# script in the `Scripts` folder and name it `BulletBehavior`.
2. Drag and drop the `BulletBehavior` script onto the `Bullet` Prefab in the `Prefabs` folder and add the following code:

```
using System.Collections;
using System.Collections.Generic;
using UnityEngine;

public class BulletBehavior : MonoBehaviour
{
    // 1
    public float OnscreenDelay = 3f;

    void Start ()
    {
        // 2
        Destroy(this.gameObject, OnscreenDelay);
    }
}
```

Let's break down this code, as follows:

1. We declare a `float` variable to store how long we want the Bullet Prefabs to remain in the scene after they are instantiated.
2. We use the `Destroy()` method to delete the GameObject.
    - `Destroy()` always needs an object as a parameter. In this case, we use the `this` keyword to specify the object that the script is attached to.
    - `Destroy()` can optionally take an additional `float` parameter as a delay, which we use to keep the bullets on screen for a short amount of time.

Play the game again, shoot some bullets, and watch as they are deleted from the **Hierarchy** by themselves in the scene after a specific delay. This means that the bullet executes its defined behavior, without another script having to tell it what to do, which is an ideal application of the *Component* design pattern.

Now that our housekeeping is done, you're going to learn about a key component of any well-designed and organized project—the manager class.

# Creating a game manager

A common misconception when learning to program is that all variables should automatically be made public, but in general, this is not a good idea. In my experience, variables should be thought of as protected and private from the start, and only made public if necessary. One way you'll see experienced programmers protect their data is through manager classes, and since we want to build good habits, we'll be following suit. Think of manager classes as a funnel where important variables and methods can be accessed safely.

When I say safely, I mean just that, which might seem unfamiliar in a programming context. However, when you have different classes communicating and updating data with each other, things can get messy. That's why having a single contact point, such as a manager class, can keep this to a minimum. We'll get into how to do that effectively in the following section.

## Tracking player properties

*Hero Born* is a simple game, so the only two data points we need to keep track of are how many items the player has collected and how much health they have left. We want these variables to be private so that they can only be modified from the manager class, giving us control and safety. Your next challenge is to create a game manager for *Hero Born* and populate it with helpful functionality.

Game manager classes will be a constant facet of any project you develop in the future, so let's learn how to properly create one, as follows:

1. Create a new C# script in the `Scripts` folder and name it `GameBehavior`.

> Usually, this script would be named `GameManager`, but Unity reserves that name for its own scripts. If you ever create a script and a cogwheel icon shows up next to its name instead of the C# file icon, that tells you it's restricted.

2. Create a new empty game object in the **Hierarchy** by using **+** | **Create Empty**, and name it `Game_Manager`.

3. Drag and drop the `GameBehavior.cs` script from the **Scripts** folder onto the `Game_Manager` object, as illustrated in the following screenshot:

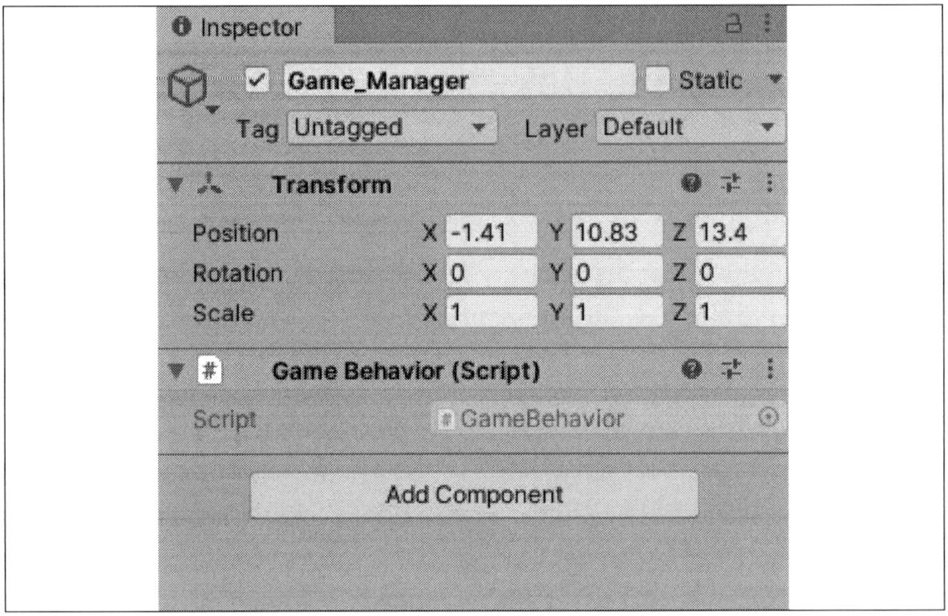


Figure 8.8: Attaching the game manager script

> Manager scripts, and other non-game files, are set up on empty objects to put them in the scene, even though they don't interact with the actual 3D space.

4. Add the following code to `GameBehavior.cs`:

```
public class GameBehavior : MonoBehaviour
{
    private int _itemsCollected = 0;
    private int _playerHP = 10;
}
```

Let's break down this code. We added two new `private` variables to hold the number of items picked up and how many lives the player has left; these are `private` because they should only be modifiable in this class. If they were made `public`, other classes could change them at will, which could lead to the variables storing incorrect or concurrent data.

Having these variables declared as `private` means that you are responsible for how they are accessed. The following topic on `get` and `set` properties will introduce you to a standard, safe way to accomplish this task going forward.

# The get and set properties

We've got our manager script and private variables set up, but how do we access them from other classes if they're private? While we could write separate public methods in `GameBehavior` to handle passing new values to the private variables, let's see whether there is a better way of doing things.

In this case, C# provides all variables with `get` and `set` properties, which are perfectly suited to our task. Think of these as methods that are automatically fired by the C# compiler whether we explicitly call them or not, similar to how `Start()` and `Update()` are executed by Unity when a scene starts.

`get` and `set` properties can be added to any variable, with or without an initial value, as illustrated in the following code snippet:

```
public string FirstName { get; set; };

// OR

public string LastName { get; set; } = "Smith";
```

However, using them like this doesn't add any additional benefits; for that, you need to include a code block for each property, as illustrated in the following code snippet:

```
public string FirstName
{
    get {
        // Code block executes when variable is accessed
    }

    set {
        // Code block executes when variable is updated
    }
}
```

Now, the `get` and `set` properties are set up to execute additional logic, depending on where it's needed. We're not done yet though, as we still need to handle the new logic.

Every get code block needs to return a value, while every set block needs to

assign a value; this is where having a combination of a private variable, called a backing variable, and a public variable with get and set properties comes into play. The private variable remains protected, while the public variable allows controlled access from other classes, as shown in the following code snippet:

```
private string _firstName
public string FirstName {
    get {
        return _firstName;
    }

    set {
        _firstName = value;
    }
}
```

Let's break this down, as follows:

- We can return the value stored in the private variable from the get property anytime another class needs it, without actually giving that outside class direct access.
- We can update the private variable any time an outside class assigns a new value to the public variable, keeping them in sync.
- The value keyword is a stand-in for whatever new value is assigned.

This can seem a little esoteric without an actual application, so let's update GameBehavior with public variables with getter and setter properties to go along with our existing private variables.

Now that we understand the syntax of the get and set property accessors, we can implement them in our manager class for greater efficiency and code readability.

Update the code in GameBehavior, as follows:

```
public class GameBehavior : MonoBehaviour
{
    private int _itemsCollected = 0;
    private int _playerHP = 10;

    // 1
    public int Items
```

```
    {
        // 2
        get { return _itemsCollected; }

        // 3
        set {
                _itemsCollected = value;
                Debug.LogFormat("Items: {0}", _itemsCollected);
        }
    }

    // 4
    public int HP
    {
        get { return _playerHP; }
        set {
                _playerHP = value;
                Debug.LogFormat("Lives: {0}", _playerHP);
         }
    }
}
```

Let's break down the code, as follows:

1. We declare a new `public` variable called `Items` with `get` and `set` properties.
2. We use the `get` property to `return` the value stored in `_itemsCollected` whenever `Items` are accessed from an outside class.
3. We use the `set` property to assign `_itemsCollected` to the new `value` of `Items` whenever it's updated, with an added `Debug.LogFormat()` call to print out the modified value of `_itemsCollected`.
4. We set up a `public` variable called `HP` with `get` and `set` properties to complement the private `_playerHP` backing variable.

Both private variables are now readable, but only through their public counterparts; they can only be changed in `GameBehavior`. With this setup, we ensure that our private data can only be accessed and modified from specific contact points. This makes it easier to communicate with `GameBehavior` from our other mechanical scripts, as well as to display the real-time data in the simple UI we'll create at the end of the chapter.

Let's test this out by updating the `Items` property when we successfully interact with an item pickup in the arena.

# Updating item collection

Now that we have our variables set up in `GameBehavior`, we can update `Items` every time we collect an `Item` in the scene, as follows:

1. Add the following highlighted code to the `ItemBehavior` script:

```
public class ItemBehavior : MonoBehaviour
{
    // 1
    public GameBehavior GameManager;

    void Start()
    {
        // 2
        GameManager = GameObject.Find("Game_Manager").
GetComponent<GameBehavior>();
    }

    void OnCollisionEnter(Collision collision)
    {
        if (collision.gameObject.name == "Player")
        {
            Destroy(this.transform.parent.gameObject);
            Debug.Log("Item collected!");

            // 3
            GameManager.Items += 1;
        }
    }
}
```

2. Hit play and collect the pickup item to see the new console log print out from the manager script, as illustrated in the following screenshot:

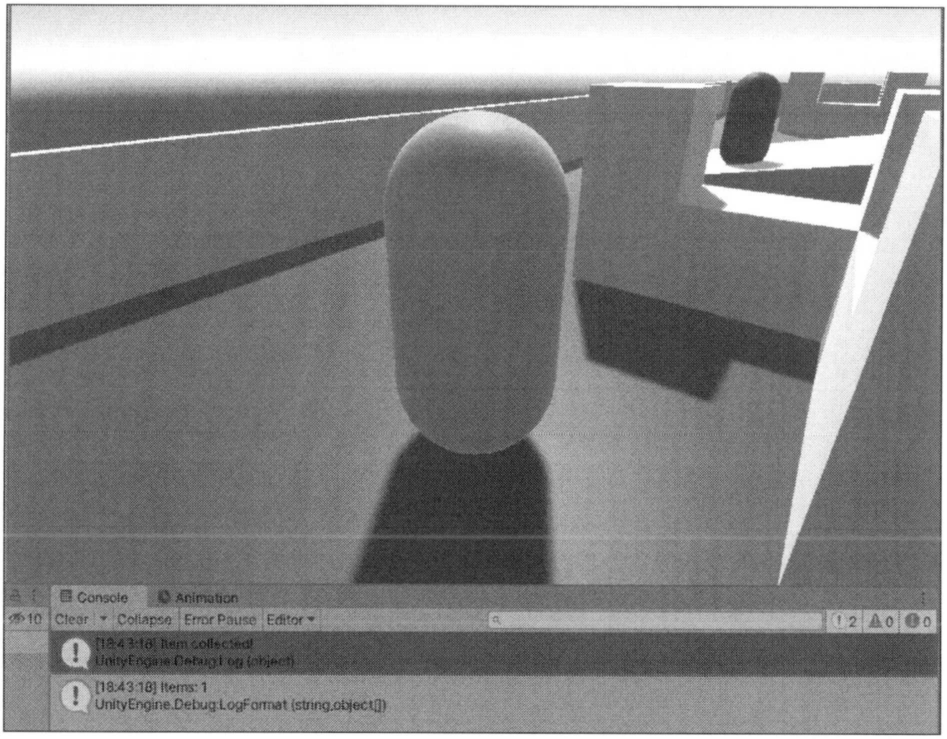


Figure 8.9: Collecting a pickup item

Let's break down the code, as follows:

1. We create a new variable of the `GameBehavior` type to store a reference to the attached script.
2. We use `Start()` to initialize `GameManager` by looking it up in the scene with `Find()` and adding a call to `GetComponent()`.

> You'll see this kind of code done in a single line quite often in Unity documentation and community projects. This is done for simplicity, but if you feel more comfortable writing out the `Find()` and `GetComponent()` calls separately, go right ahead; there's nothing wrong with clear, explicit formatting.

3. We increment the `Items` property in the `GameManager` class in `OnCollisionEnter()` after the Item Prefab is destroyed.

Since we already set up `ItemBehavior` to take care of collision logic, it's easy to modify `OnCollisionEnter()` to communicate with our manager class when an item is picked up by the player. Keep in mind that separating functionality like this is what makes the code more flexible and less likely to break as you make changes during development.

The last piece *Hero Born* is missing is some kind of interface that displays game data to the player. In programming and game development, this is called a UI. Your final task in this chapter is to familiarize yourself with how Unity creates and handles the UI code.

# Creating a GUI

At this point, we have several scripts working together to give players access to movement, jumping, collecting, and shooting mechanics. However, we're still missing any kind of display or visual cue that shows our player's stats, as well as a way to win and lose the game. We'll focus on these two topics as we close out this last section.

## Displaying player stats

UIs are the visual components of any computer system. The mouse cursor, folder icons, and programs on your laptop are all UI elements. For our game, we want a simple display to let our players know how many items they've collected, their current health, and a textbox to give them updates when certain events happen.

UI elements in Unity can be added in the following two ways:

- Directly from the **+** menu in the **Hierarchy** panel, like with any other GameObject
- Using the built-in GUI class in code

We're going to stick with the first option, since the built-in GUI classes are part of the Unity legacy UI system, and we want to stay current, right? This isn't to say that you can't do everything programmatically, but for our prototype, the newer UI systems are a better fit.

> If you're curious about programmatic UI in Unity, take a look at the documentation yourself: `https://docs.unity3d.com/ScriptReference/GUI.html`.

Your next task is to add a simple UI to the game scene that displays the items collected, player health, and progress information variables that are stored in `GameBehavior.cs`.

First, let's create three text objects in our scene. User interfaces in Unity work off of a canvas, which is exactly what it sounds like. Think of the canvas as a blank painting that you can draw on that Unity will render on top of the game world for you. Whenever you create your first UI element in the **Hierarchy** panel, a **Canvas** parent object is created along with it.

1. Right-click in the **Hierarchy** panel and select **UI** | **Text** and name the new object **Health**. This will create a **Canvas** parent object and the new **Text** object all at once:

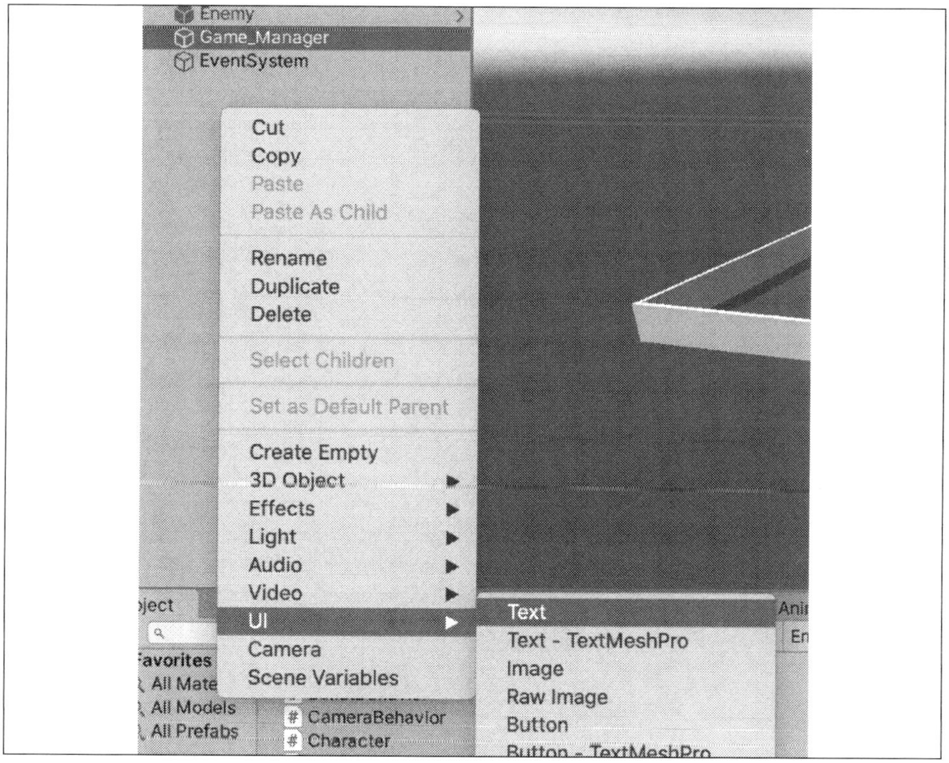


Figure 8.10: Creating a Text element

2. To see the canvas correctly, select **2D** mode at the top of the **Scene** tab. From this view, our entire level is that tiny white line in the lower-left hand corner.
    - Even though the **Canvas** and level don't overlap in the scene, when the game plays Unity will automatically overlay them correctly.

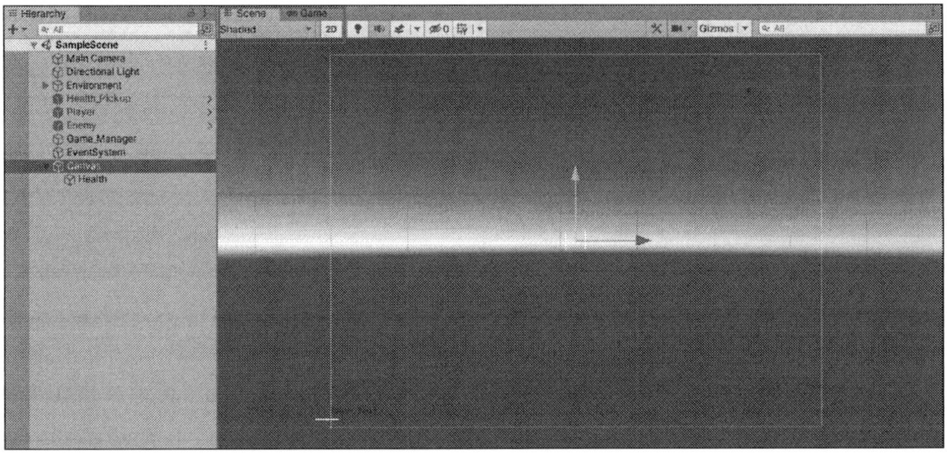


Figure 8.11: Canvas in the Unity editor

3. If you select the **Health** object in the **Hierarchy**, you'll see that the new text object was created in the lower-left corner of the canvas by default, and it has a whole list of customizable properties, like text and color, in the **Inspector** pane:

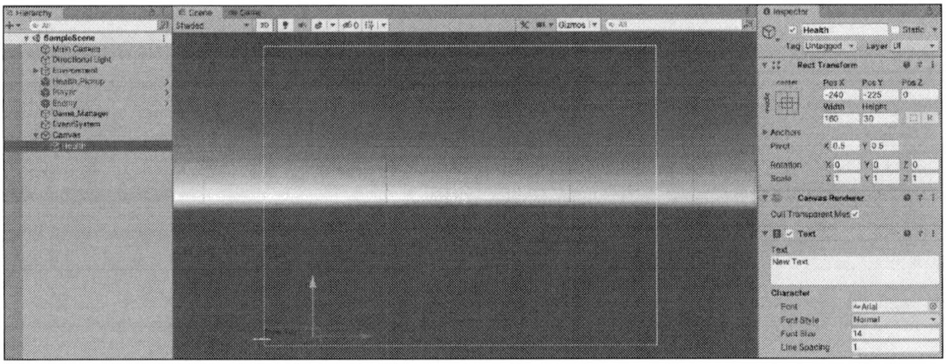

Figure 8.12: Text element on the Unity Canvas

4. With the **Health** object selected in the **Hierarchy** pane, click on the **Anchor** presets in the **Rect Transform** component of the **Inspector** and choose **Top Left**.
    - Anchors set a UI element's point of reference on the canvas, meaning that whatever the size of the device screen, our health points will always be anchored to the top left of the screen:

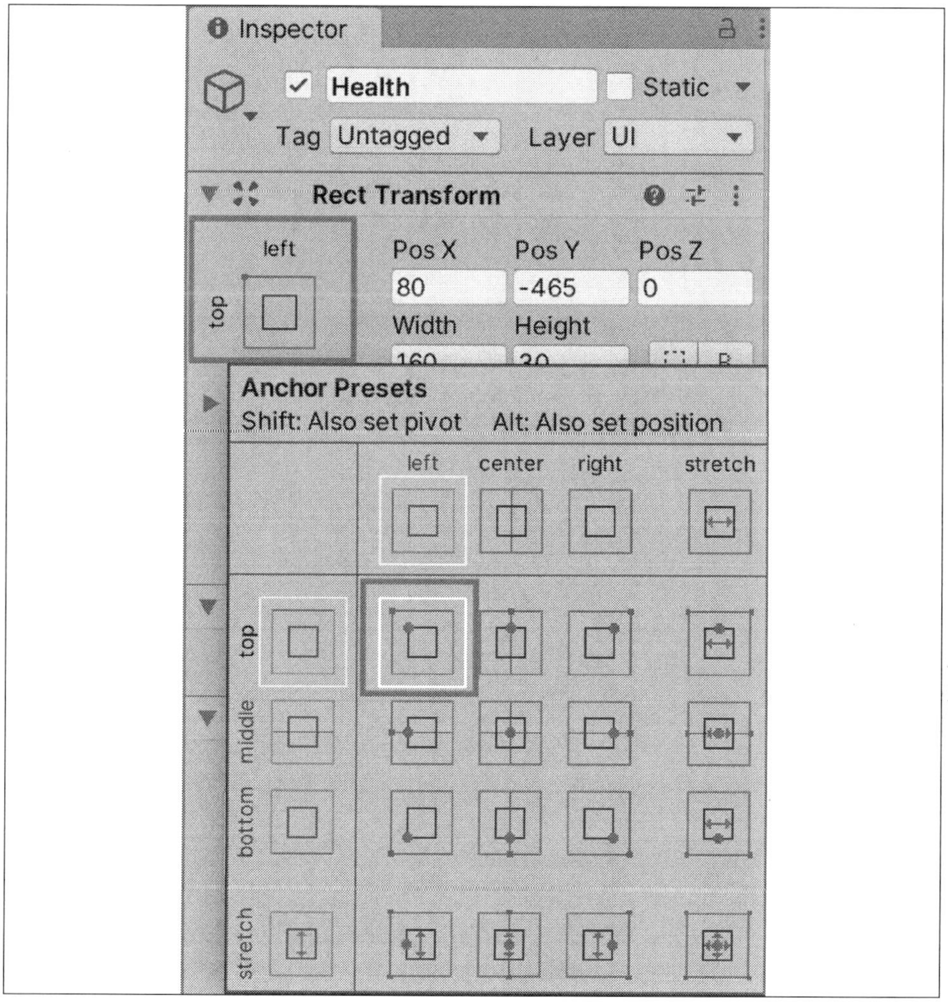


Figure 8.13: Setting anchor presets

5. In the **Inspector** pane, change the **Rect Transform** position to **100** on the **X** axis and **-30** on the **Y** axis to position the text in the upper-right corner. Also change the **Text** property to say **Player Health:**. We'll be setting the actual value in code in a later step:

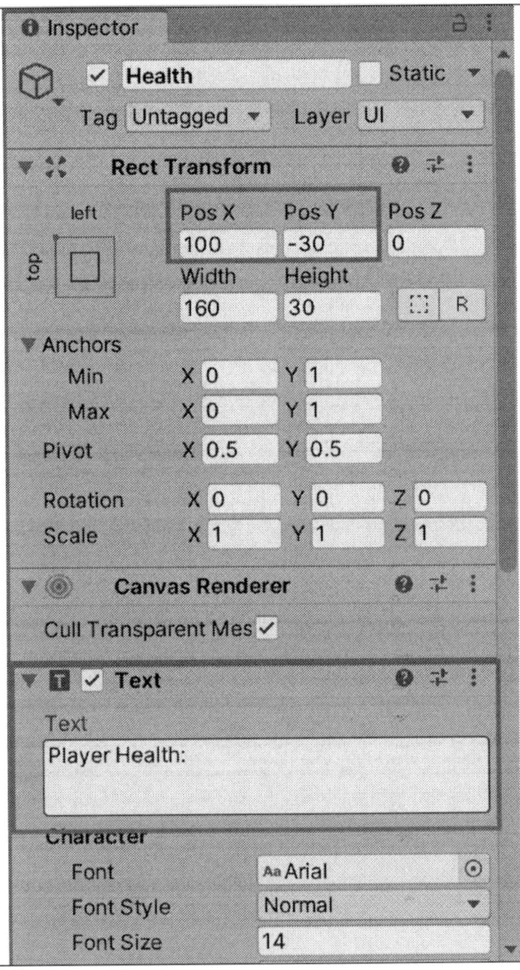


Figure 8.14: Setting text properties

6. Repeat steps 1-5 to create a new UI **Text** object and name it **Items**:
   - Set the anchor presets to **Top Left**, the **Pos X** to **100**, and the **Pos Y** to **-60**

- Set **Text** to **Items Collected:**

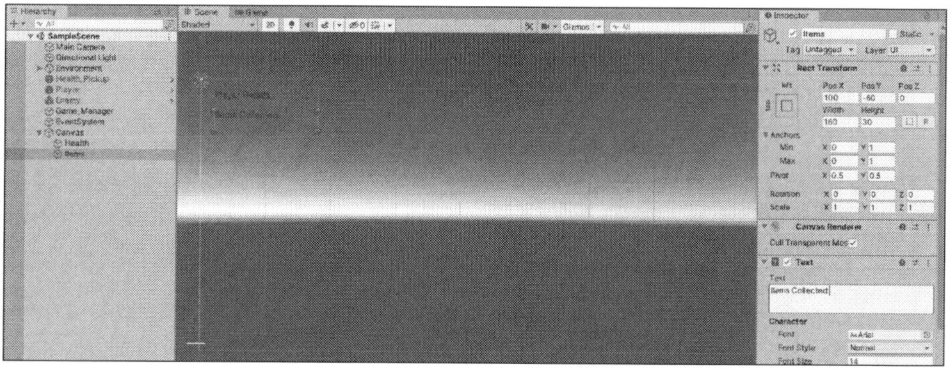

Figure 8.15: Creating another Text element

7. Repeat *steps 1-5* to create a new UI **Text** object and name it **Progress**:
    - Set the anchor presets to **Bottom Center**, the **Pos X** to **0**, the **Pos Y** to **15**, and the **Width** to **280**
    - Set **Text** to **Collect all the items and win your freedom!**

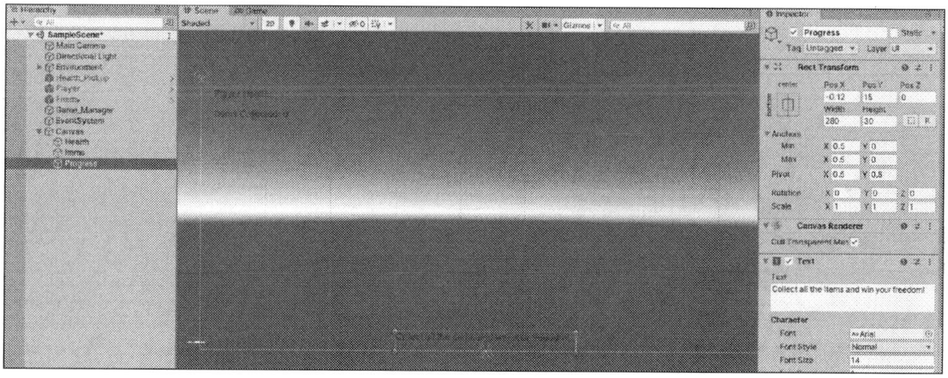

Figure 8.16: Creating a progress text element

Now that we have our UI set up, let's connect the variables we already have in our game manager script. Proceed as follows:

1. Update `GameBehavior` with the following code to collect an item and display on-screen text when items are collected:

```
// 1
using UnityEngine.UI;

public class GameBehavior : MonoBehaviour
{
```

```
    // 2
    public int MaxItems = 4;

    // 3
    public Text HealthText;
    public Text ItemText;
    public Text ProgressText;

    // 4
    void Start()
    {
        ItemText.text += _itemsCollected;
        HealthText.text += _playerHP;
    }

    private int _itemsCollected = 0;
    public int Items
    {
        get { return _itemsCollected; }
        set {
            _itemsCollected = value;

            // 5
            ItemText.text = "Items Collected: " + Items;

            // 6
            if(_itemsCollected >= MaxItems)
            {
                ProgressText.text = "You've found all the items!";
            }
            else
            {
                ProgressText.text = "Item found, only " +
(MaxItems - _itemsCollected) + " more to go!";
            }
        }
    }

    private int _playerHP = 10;
    public int HP
    {
        get { return _playerHP; }
        set {
```

```
                _playerHP = value;

                // 7
                HealthText.text = "Player Health: " + HP;
                Debug.LogFormat("Lives: {0}", _playerHP);
            }
        }
    }
```

2. Select **Game_Manager** in the **Hierarchy** and drag over our three text objects one by one into their corresponding `GameBehavior` script fields in the **Inspector**:

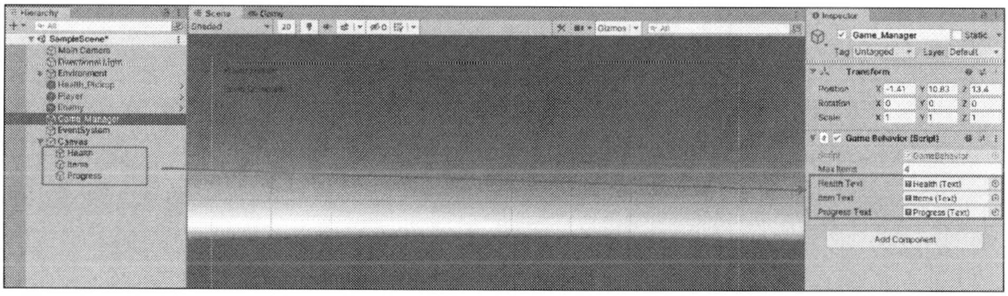

Figure 8.17: Dragging text elements to script components

3. Run the game and take a look at our new onscreen GUI boxes, shown in the following screenshot:

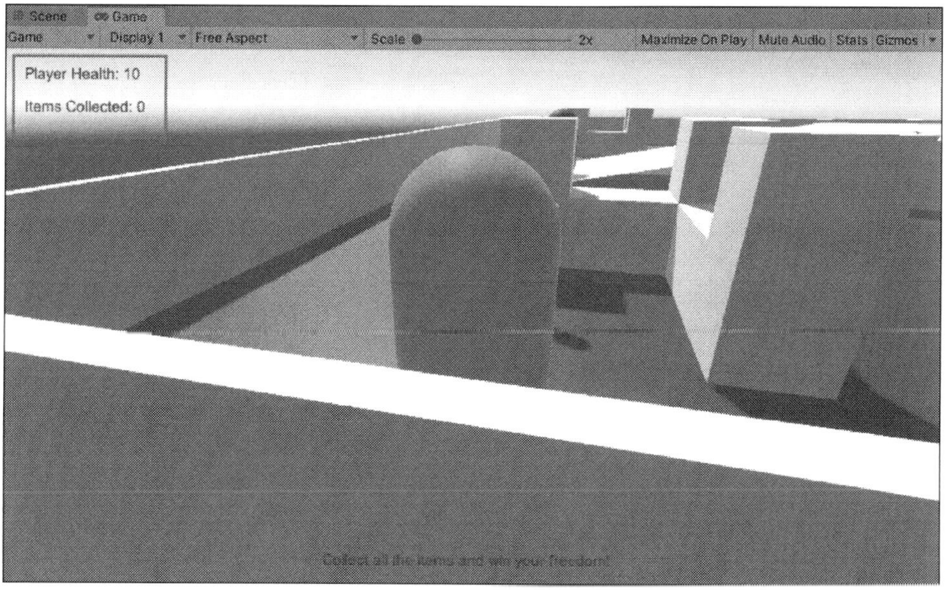


Figure 8.18: Testing UI elements in play mode

Let's break down the code, as follows:

1. We add the `UnityEngine.UI` namespace so we have access to the **Text** variable type.
2. We create a new public variable for the max number of items in the level.
3. We create three new **Text** variables, which we connect in the **Inspector** panel.
4. Then, we use the `Start` method to set the initial values of our health and items text using the += operator.
5. Every time an item is collected, we update the `text` property of **ItemText** to show the updated `items` count.
6. We declare an `if` statement in the set property of `_itemsCollected`.
    - If the player has gathered more than or equal to `MaxItems`, they've won, and `ProgressText.text` is updated.
    - Otherwise, `ProgressText.text` shows how many items are still left to collect.
7. Every time the player's health is damaged, which we'll cover in the next chapter, we update the `text` property of `HealthText` with the new value.

When we play the game now, our three UI elements show up with the correct values; when an Item is collected, the `ProgressText` and `_itemsCollected` counts update, as illustrated in the following screenshot:

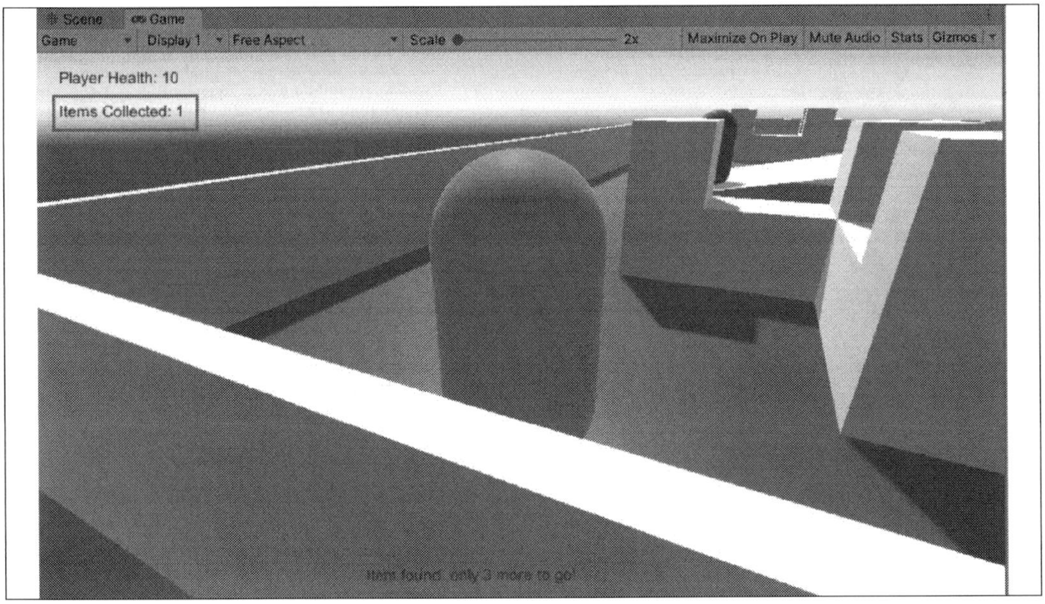


Figure 8.19: Updating the UI text

Every game can either be won or lost. In the last section of this chapter, your task is to implement those conditions and the UI that goes along with them.

# Win and loss conditions

We've implemented our core game mechanics and a simple UI, but *Hero Born* is still missing an important game design element: its win and loss conditions. These conditions will manage how the player wins or loses the game and execute different code depending on the situation.

Back in the game document from *Chapter 6, Getting Your Hands Dirty with Unity*, we set out our win and loss conditions as follows:

- Collecting all items in the level with at least 1 health point remaining to win
- Taking damage from enemies until health points are at 0 to lose

These conditions are going to affect both our UI and game mechanics, but we've already set up `GameBehavior` to handle this efficiently. Our `get` and `set` properties will handle any game-related logic and changes to the UI when a player wins or loses.

We're going to implement the win condition logic in this section because we have the pickup system already in place. When we get to the enemy AI behavior in the next chapter, we'll add in the loss condition logic. Your next task is to determine when the game is won in code.

We always want to give players clear and immediate feedback, so we'll start by adding in the logic for a win condition, as follows:

1. Update `GameBehavior` to match the following code:

```
public class GameBehavior : MonoBehaviour
{
    // 1
    public Button WinButton;

    private int _itemsCollected = 0;
    public int Items
    {
        get { return _itemsCollected; }
        set
        {
            _itemsCollected - value;
            ItemText.text = "Items Collected: " + Items;
```

```
            if (_itemsCollected >= MaxItems)
            {
                ProgressText.text = "You've found all the items!";

                // 2
                WinButton.gameObject.SetActive(true);
            }
            else
            {
                ProgressText.text = "Item found, only " +
(MaxItems - _itemsCollected) + " more to go!";
            }
        }
    }
}
```

2. Right-click in the **Hierarchy** and select **UI** | **Button**, then name it **Win Condition**:
    - Select **Win Condition** and set the **Pos X** and **Pos Y** to **0**, its **Width** to **225**, and its **Height** to **115**.

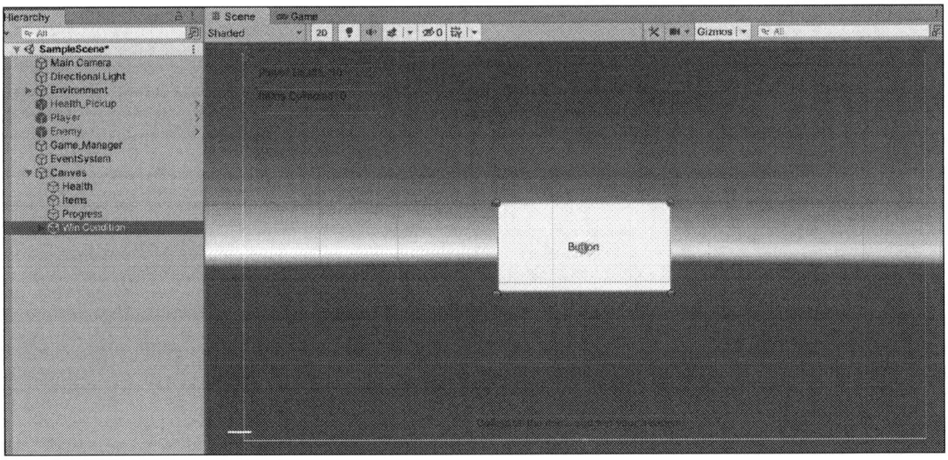


Figure 8.20: Creating a UI button

3. Click on the arrow to the right of the **Win Condition** button to expand its text child object, then change the text to say **You won!**:

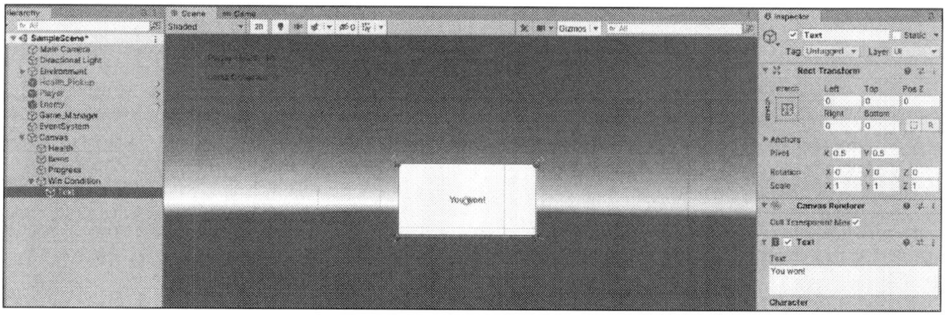

Figure 8.21: Updating button text

4. Select the **Win Condition** parent object again and click the checkmark icon in the upper right of the **Inspector**.

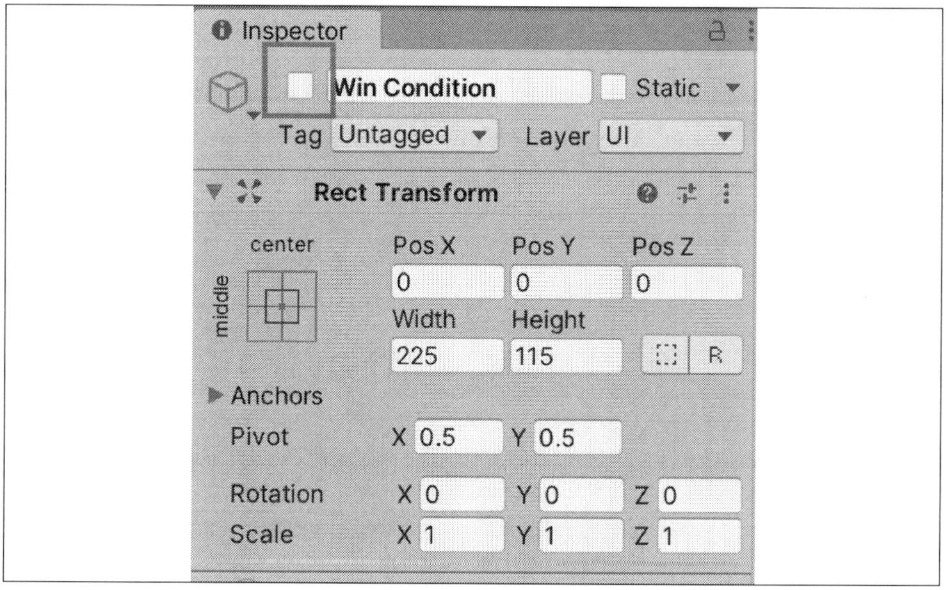


Figure 8.22: Deactivating the game object

This will hide the button until we've won the game:

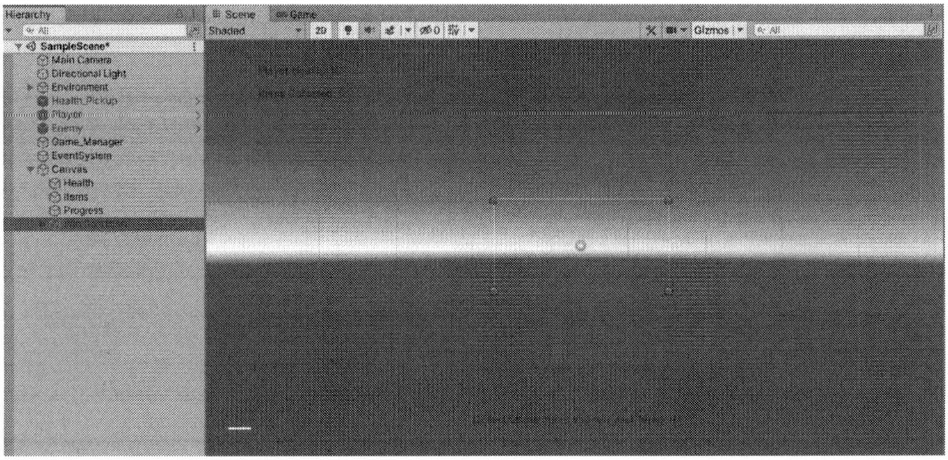


Figure 8.23: Testing the hidden UI button

5. Select **Game_Manager** in the **Hierarchy** and drag the **Win Condition** button from the **Hierarchy** to the **Game Behavior (Script)** in the **Inspector**, just like we did with the text objects:

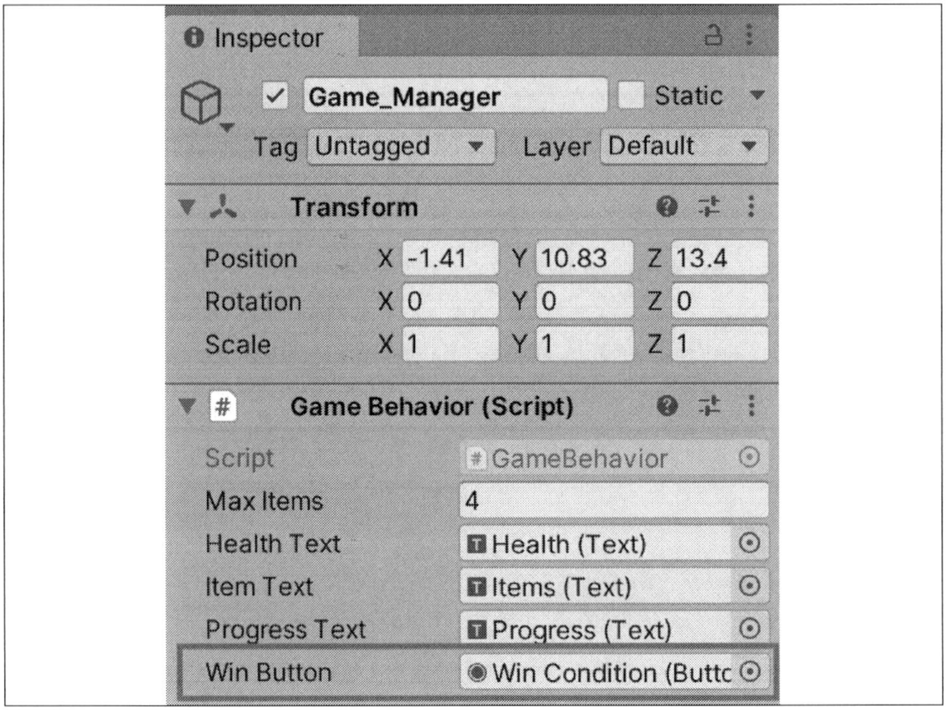


Figure 8.24: Dragging the UI button onto the script component

6. Change **Max Items** to `1` in the **Inspector** to test out the new screen, as illustrated in the following screenshot:

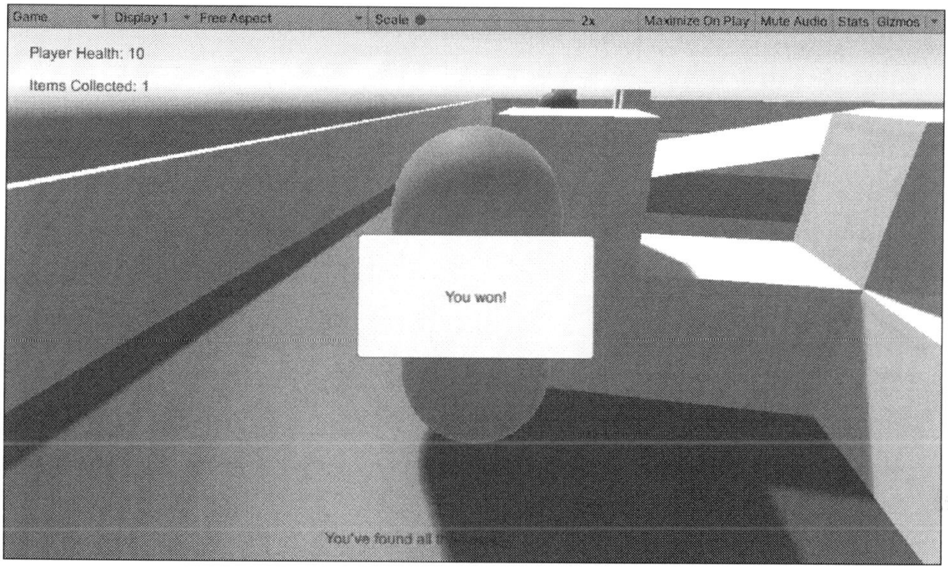


Figure 8.25: Showing the win screen

Let's break down the code, as follows:

1. We created a UI button variable to connect to our Win Condition button in the **Hierarchy**.
2. Since we set the Win Condition button as **Hidden** when the game starts, we reactivate it when the game is won.

With **Max Items** set to `1`, the **Win** button will show up on collecting the only `Pickup_Item` in the scene. Clicking the button doesn't do anything right now, but we'll address that in the following section.

# Pausing and restarting the game with using directives and namespaces

Right now, our win condition works as expected, but the player still has control over the capsule and doesn't have a way of restarting the game once it's over. Unity provides a property in the `Time` class called `timeScale`, which when set to `0` freezes the game scene. However, to restart the game, we need access to a **namespace** called `SceneManagement` that isn't accessible from our classes by default.

A namespace collects and groups a set of classes under a specific name to organize large projects and avoid conflicts between scripts that may share the same names. A `using` directive needs to be added to a class to access a namespace's classes.

All C# scripts created from Unity come with three default `using` directives, shown in the following code snippet:

```
using System.Collections;
using System.Collections.Generic;
using UnityEngine;
```

These allow access to common namespaces, but Unity and C# offer plenty more that can be added with the `using` keyword followed by the name of the namespace.

Since our game will need to be paused and restarted when a player wins or loses, this is a good time to use a namespace that isn't included in new C# scripts by default.

1. Add the following code to `GameBehavior` and play:

```
using System.Collections;
using System.Collections.Generic;
using UnityEngine;
using UnityEngine.UI;

// 1
using UnityEngine.SceneManagement;

public class GameBehavior : MonoBehaviour
{
    // ... No changes needed ...

    private int _itemsCollected = 0;
    public int Items
    {
        get { return _itemsCollected; }
        set {
            _itemsCollected = value;
```

```
            if (_itemsCollected >= MaxItems)
            {
                ProgressText.text = "You've found all the items!";
                WinButton.gameObject.SetActive(true);

                // 2
                Time.timeScale = 0f;
            }
            else
            {
                ProgressText.text= "Item found, only " +
(MaxItems - _itemsCollected) + " more to go!";
            }
        }
    }

    public void RestartScene()
    {
        // 3
        SceneManager.LoadScene(0);

        // 4
        Time.timeScale = 1f;
    }

    // ... No other changes needed ...

}
```

2. Select **Win Condition** from the **Hierarchy**, scroll down in the **Inspector** to the **OnClick** section of the **Button** component, and hit the plus icon:
    - Every UI button has an **OnClick** event, which means you can assign a method from a script to execute when the button is pushed.

- You can have multiple methods fire when a button is clicked, but we only need one in this case:

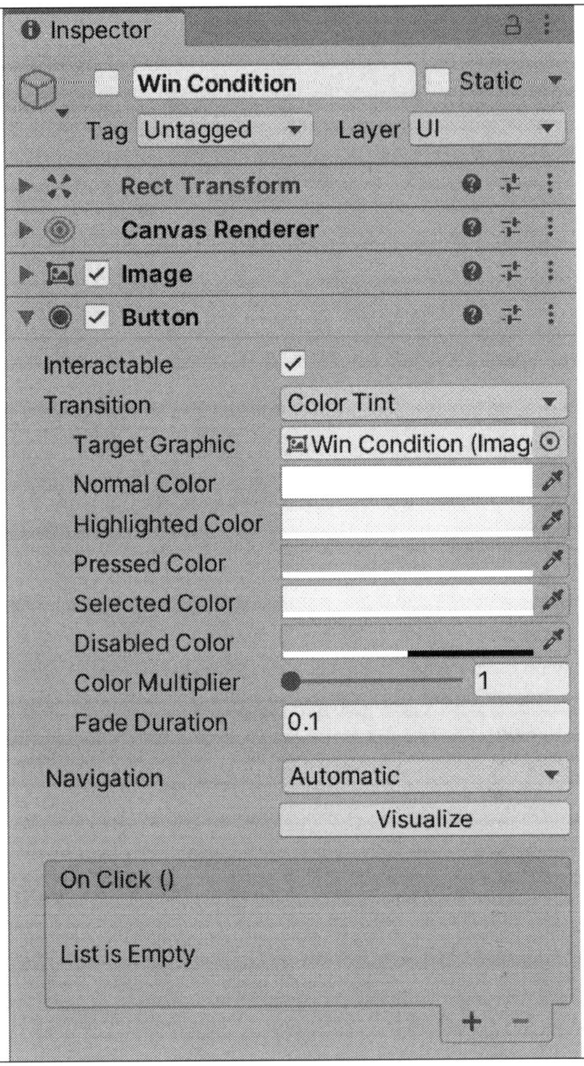


Figure 8.26: OnClick section of the button

3. From the **Hierarchy**, drag the **Game_Manager** into the slot underneath **Runtime** to tell the button we want to choose a method from our manager script to fire when the button is pushed:

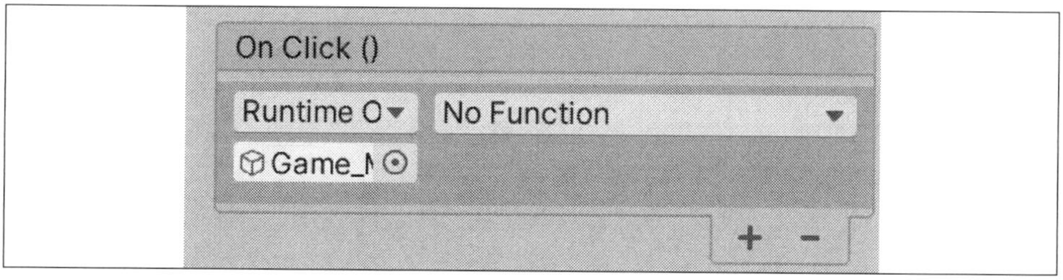


Figure 8.27: Setting the game manager object in On Click

4. Select the **No Function** dropdown and choose **GameBehavior** | **RestartScene ()** to set the method we want the button to execute:

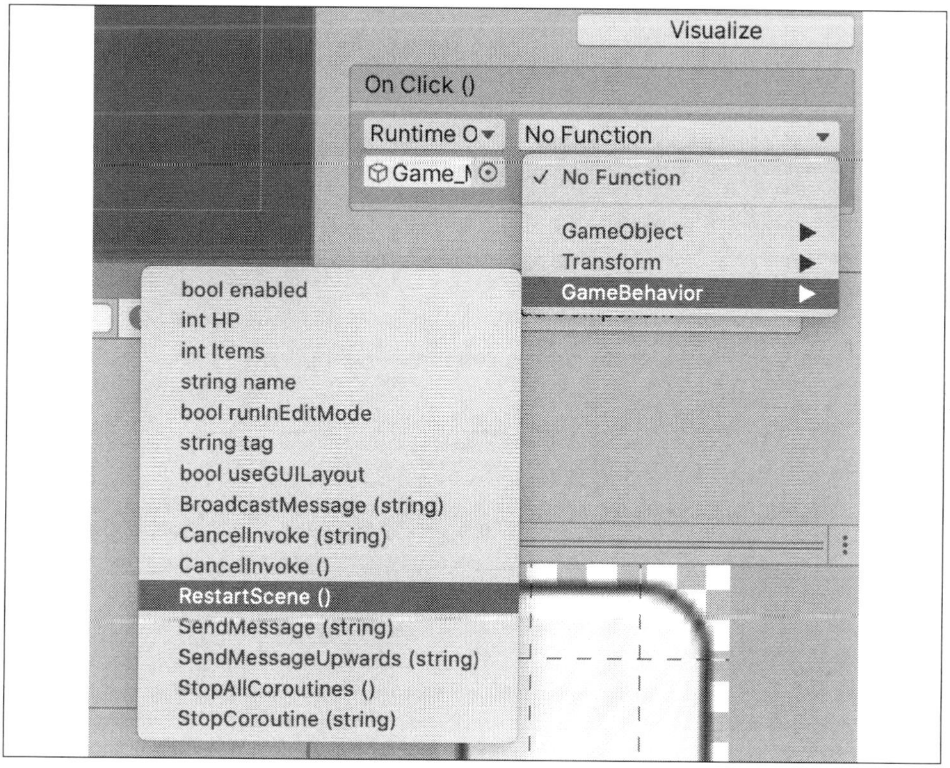


Figure 8.28: Choosing the restart method for the button click

5. Go to **Window** | **Rendering** | **Lighting** and select **Generate Lighting** at the bottom. Make sure **Auto Generate** is not selected:

> This step is necessary to address a Unity issue that reloads scenes without any lighting.

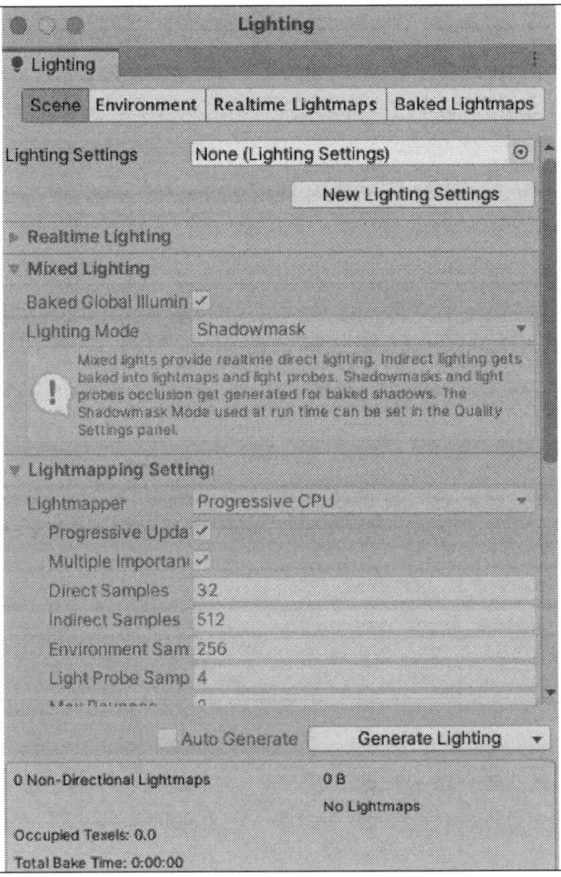


Figure 8.29: Lighting panel in the Unity editor

Let's break down the code, as follows:

1. We add the `SceneManagement` namespace with the `using` keyword, which handles all scene-related logic like creating loading scenes.
2. We set `Time.timeScale` to `0` to pause the game when the win screen is displayed, which disables any input or movement.

3. We create a new method called `RestartScene` and call `LoadScene()` when the win screen button is clicked:
    - `LoadScene()` takes in a scene index as an `int` parameter.
    - Because there is only one scene in our project, we use index `0` to restart the game from the beginning.
4. We reset `Time.timeScale` to the default value of `1` so that when the scene restarts, all controls and behaviors will be able to execute again.

Now, when you collect an item and click on the win screen button, the level restarts, with all scripts and components restored to their original values and set up for another round!

# Summary

Congratulations! *Hero Born* is now a playable prototype. We implemented jumping and shooting mechanics, managed physics collisions and spawning objects, and added in a few basic UI elements to display feedback. We even got as far as resetting the level when the player wins.

A lot of new topics were introduced in this chapter, and it's important to go back and make sure you understand what went into the code we wrote. Pay special attention to our discussions on enumerations, `get` and `set` properties, and namespaces. From here on in, the code is only going to get more complex as we dive further into the possibilities of the C# language.

In the next chapter, we'll start working on getting our enemy GameObjects to take notice of our player when we get too close, resulting in a follow-and-shoot protocol that will up the stakes for our player.

# Pop quiz – working with mechanics

1. What type of data do enumerations store?
2. How would you create a copy of a Prefab GameObject in an active scene?
3. Which variable properties allow you to add functionality when their value is referenced or modified?
4. Which Unity method displays all UI objects in the scene?

# 9

# Basic AI and Enemy Behavior

Virtual scenarios need conflicts, consequences, and potential rewards to feel real. Without these three things, there's no incentive for the player to care about what happens to their in-game character, much less continue to play the game. And while there are plenty of game mechanics that deliver on one or more of these conditions, nothing beats an enemy that will seek you out and try to end your session.

Programming an intelligent enemy is no easy task, and often goes hand in hand with long working hours and frustration. However, Unity has built-in features, components, and classes we can use to design and implement AI systems in a more user-friendly way. These tools will push the first playable iteration of *Hero Born* over the finish line and provide a springboard for more advanced C# topics.

In this chapter, we'll focus on the following topics:

- The Unity navigation system
- Static objects and navigation meshes
- Navigation agents
- Procedural programming and logic
- Taking and dealing damage
- Adding a loss condition
- Refactoring and keeping it DRY

Let's get started!

# Navigating 3D space in Unity

When we talk about navigation in real life, it's usually a conversation about how to get from point A to point B. Navigating around virtual 3D space is largely the same, but how do we account for the experiential knowledge we humans have accumulated since the day we first started crawling? Everything from walking on a flat surface to climbing stairs and jumping off of curbs is a skill we learned by doing; how can we possibly program all that into a game without going insane?

Before you can answer any of these questions, you'll need to know what navigation components Unity has to offer.

# Navigation components

The short answer is that Unity has spent a lot of time perfecting its navigation system and delivering components that we can use to govern how playable and non-playable characters can get around. Each of the following components comes as standard with Unity and has complex features already built in:

- A **NavMesh** is essentially a map of the walkable surfaces in a given level; the NavMesh component itself is created from the level geometry in a process called baking. Baking a NavMesh into your level creates a unique project asset that holds the navigation data.
- If a **NavMesh** is the level map, then a **NavMeshAgent** is the moving piece on the board. Any object with a NavMeshAgent component attached will automatically avoid other agents or obstacles it comes into contact with.
- The navigation system needs to be aware of any moving or stationary objects in the level that could cause a NavMeshAgent to alter their route. Adding NavMeshObstacle components to those objects lets the system know that they need to be avoided.

While this description of the Unity navigation system is far from complete, it's enough for us to move forward with our enemy behavior. For this chapter, we'll be focusing on adding a NavMesh to our level, setting up the Enemy Prefab as a NavMeshAgent, and getting the Enemy Prefab to move along a predefined route in a seemingly intelligent way.

> We'll only be using the NavMesh and NavMeshAgent components in this chapter, but if you want to spice up your level, take a look at how to create obstacles here: `https://docs.unity3d.com/Manual/nav-CreateNavMeshObstacle.html`.

Your first task in setting up an "intelligent" enemy is to create a NavMesh over the arena's walkable areas. Let's set up and configure our level's NavMesh:

1. Select the **Environment** GameObject, click on the arrow icon next to **Static** in the **Inspector** window, and choose **Navigation Static**:

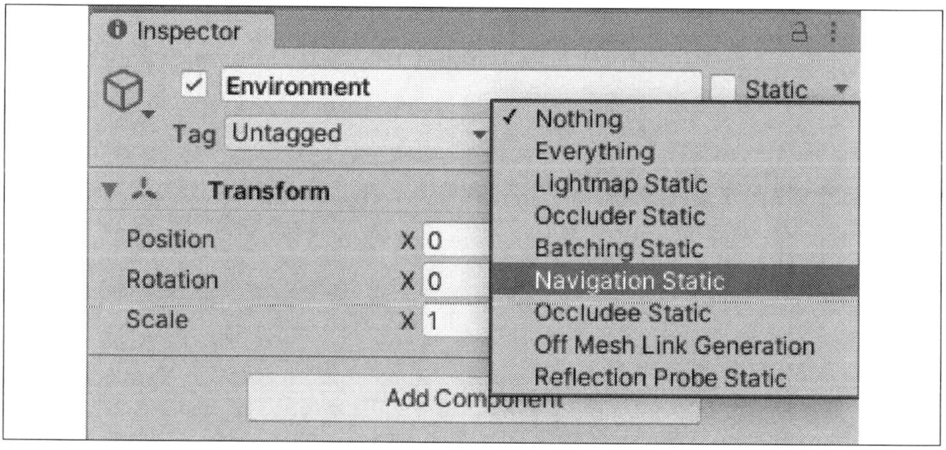


Figure 9.1: Setting objects to Navigation Static

2. Click **Yes, change children** when the dialog window pops up to set all the **Environment** child objects to **Navigation Static**:

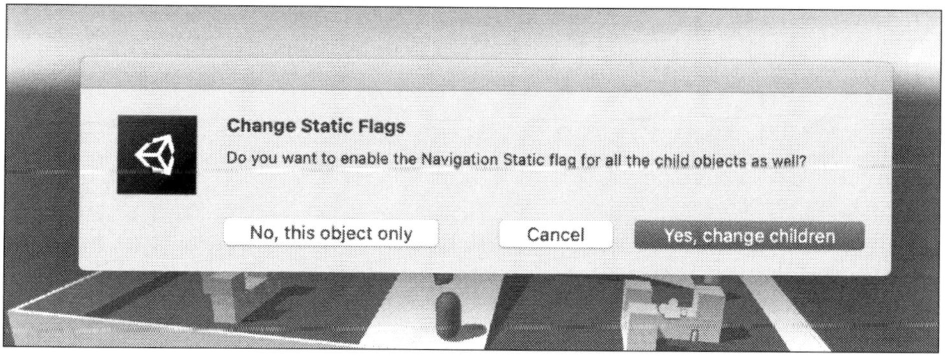


Figure 9.2: Changing all child objects

3. Go to **Window** | **AI** | **Navigation** and select the **Bake** tab. Leave everything set to their default values and click **Bake**. Once baking is finished, you'll see a new folder inside the **Scenes** folder with lighting, navigation mesh, and reflection probe data:

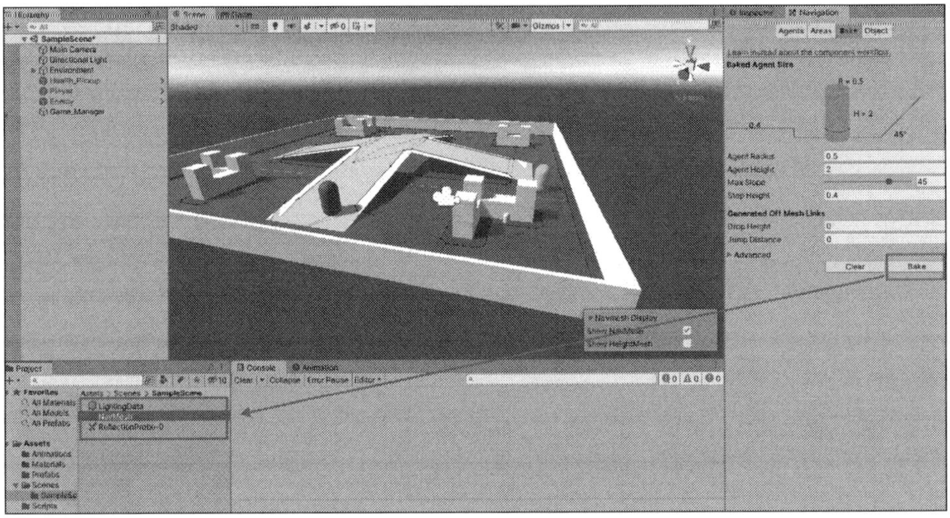

Figure 9.3: Baking navigation mesh

Every object in our level is now marked as **Navigation Static**, which means that our newly baked NavMesh has evaluated their accessibility based on its default NavMeshAgent settings. Everywhere you can see a light blue overlay in the preceding screenshot is a walkable surface for any object with a NavMeshAgent component attached, which is your next task.

# Setting up enemy agents

Let's register the Enemy Prefab as a NavMeshAgent:

1. Select the Enemy Prefab in the **Prefabs** folder, click **Add Component** in the **Inspector** window, and search for **NavMesh Agent**:

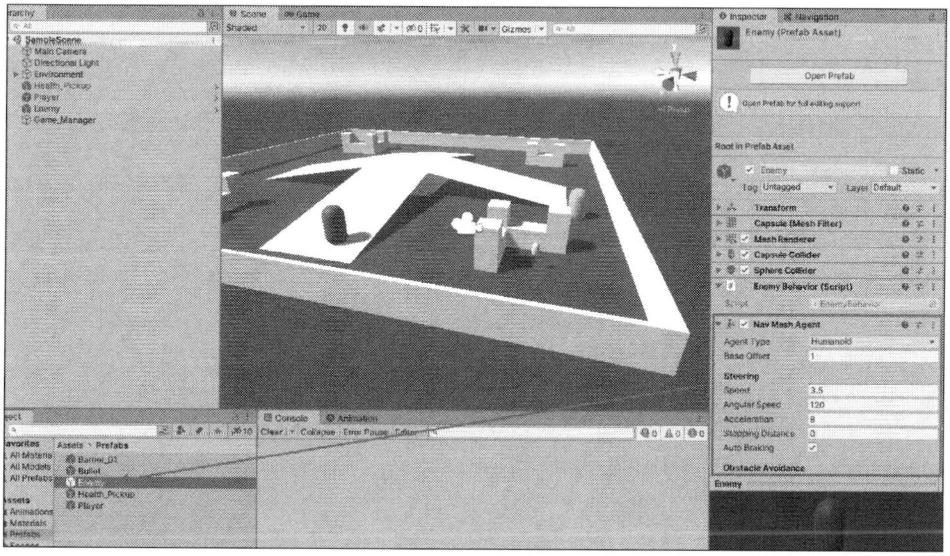


Figure 9.4: Adding a NavMeshAgent component

2. Click **+ | Create Empty** from the **Hierarchy** window and name the GameObject `Patrol_Route`:
    - Select `Patrol_Route`, click **+ | Create Empty** to add a child GameObject, and name it `Location_1`. Position `Location_1` in one of the corners of the level:

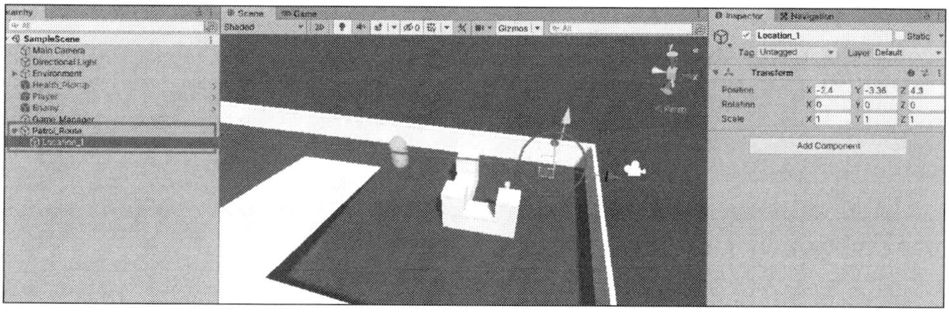


Figure 9.5: Creating an empty patrol route object

3. Create three more empty child objects in `Patrol_Route`, name them `Location_2`, `Location_3`, and `Location_4`, respectively, and position them in the remaining corners of the level to form a square:

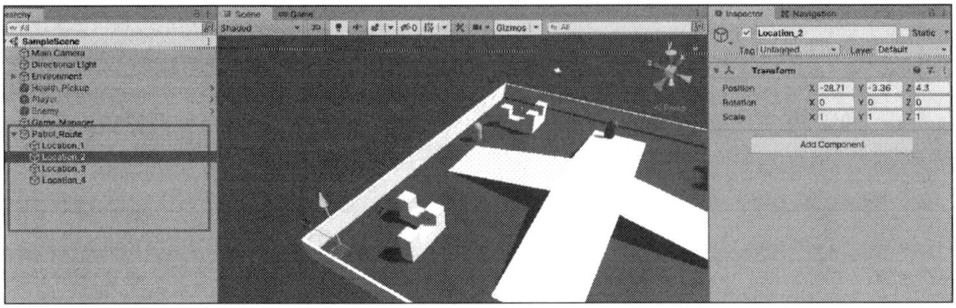

Figure 9.6: Creating all empty patrol route objects

Adding a NavMeshAgent component to the Enemy tells the NavMesh component to take notice and register it as an object that has access to its autonomous navigation features. Creating the four empty game objects in each corner of the level lays out the simple route we want our enemies to eventually patrol; grouping them in an empty parent object makes it easier to reference them in code and makes for a more organized Hierarchy window. All that's left is the code to make the enemy walk the patrol route, which you'll add in the next section.

# Moving enemy agents

Our patrol locations are set and the Enemy Prefab has a NavMeshAgent component, but now we need to figure out how to reference those locations and get the enemy moving on its own. To do that, we'll first need to talk about an important concept in the world of software development: procedural programming.

# Procedural programming

Even though it's in the name, the idea behind procedural programming can be elusive until you get your head around it; once you do, you'll never see a code challenge the same way.

Any task that executes the same logic on one or more sequential objects is the perfect candidate for procedural programming. You already did a little procedural programming when you debugged arrays, lists, and dictionaries with `for` and `foreach` loops. Each time those looping statements were executed, you performed the same call to `Debug.Log()`, iterating over each item sequentially. The idea now is to use that skill to get a more useful outcome.

One of the most common uses of procedural programming is adding items from one collection to another, often modifying them along the way. This works great for our purposes since we want to reference each child object in the `Patrol_Route` parent and store them in a list.

# Referencing the patrol locations

Now that we understand the basics of procedural programming, it's time to get a reference to our patrol locations and assign them to a usable list:

1. Add the following code to `EnemyBehavior`:

```
public class EnemyBehavior : MonoBehaviour
{
    // 1
    public Transform PatrolRoute;

    // 2
    public List<Transform> Locations;

    void Start()
    {
        // 3
        InitializePatrolRoute();
    }

        // 4
    void InitializePatrolRoute()
    {
        // 5
        foreach(Transform child in PatrolRoute)
        {
            // 6
            Locations.Add(child);
        }
    }

    void OnTriggerEnter(Collider other)
    {
        // ... No changes needed ...
    }

    void OnTriggerExit(Collider other)
    {
```

```
            // ... No changes needed ...
        }
    }
```

2. Select `Enemy` and drag the `Patrol_Route` object from the **Hierarchy** window onto the **Patrol Route** variable in `EnemyBehavior`:

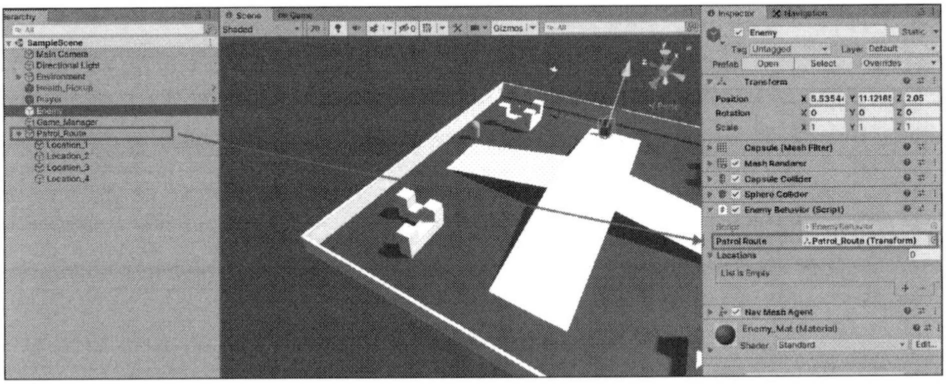

Figure 9.7: Dragging Patrol_Route to the enemy script

3. Hit the arrow icon next to the **Locations** variable in the **Inspector** window and run the game to see the list populate:

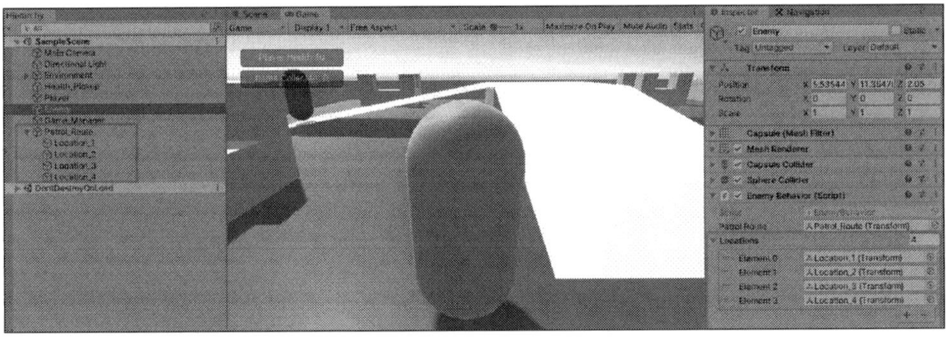

Figure 9.8: Testing procedural programming

Let's break down the code:

1. First, it declares a variable for storing the `PatrolRoute` empty parent GameObject.
2. Then, it declares a `List` variable to hold all the child `Transform` components in `PatrolRoute`.
3. After that, it uses `Start()` to call the `InitializePatrolRoute()` method when the game begins.

4. Next, it creates `InitializePatrolRoute()` as a private utility method to procedurally fill `Locations` with `Transform` values:
    - Remember that not including an access modifier makes variables and methods `private` by default.
5. Then, we use a `foreach` statement to loop through each child GameObject in `PatrolRoute` and reference its Transform component:
    - Each Transform component is captured in the local `child` variable declared in the `foreach` loop.
6. Finally, we add each sequential `child` `Transform` component to the list of locations using the `Add()` method as we loop through the child objects in `PatrolRoute`:
    - This way, no matter what changes we make in the **Hierarchy** window, `Locations` will always be filled in with all the `child` objects under the `PatrolRoute` parent.

While we could have assigned each location GameObject to `Locations` by dragging and dropping them directly from the **Hierarchy** window into the **Inspector** window, it's easy to lose or break these connections; making changes to the location object names, object additions or deletions, or project updates can all throw a wrench into a class's initialization. It's much safer, and more readable, to procedurally fill GameObject lists or arrays in the `Start()` method.

> Due to that reasoning, I also tend to use `GetComponent()` in the `Start()` method to find and store component references attached to a given class instead of assigning them in the **Inspector** window.

Now, we need the enemy object to follow the patrol route we laid out, which is your next task.

# Moving the enemy

With a list of patrol locations initialized on `Start()`, we can grab the enemy NavMeshAgent component and set its first destination.

Update `EnemyBehavior` with the following code and hit play:

```
// 1
using UnityEngine.AI;
```

```
public class EnemyBehavior : MonoBehaviour
{
    public Transform PatrolRoute;
    public List<Transform> Locations;
    // 2
    private int _locationIndex = 0;

    // 3
    private NavMeshAgent _agent;

    void Start()
    {
        // 4
        _agent = GetComponent<NavMeshAgent>();

        InitializePatrolRoute();

        // 5
        MoveToNextPatrolLocation();
    }

    void InitializePatrolRoute()
    {
         // ... No changes needed ...
    }

    void MoveToNextPatrolLocation()
    {
        // 6
        _agent.destination = Locations[_locationIndex].position;
    }

    void OnTriggerEnter(Collider other)
    {
        // ... No changes needed ...
    }

    void OnTriggerExit(Collider other)
    {
        // ... No changes needed ...
    }
}
```

Let's break down the code:

1. First, it adds the `UnityEngine.AI` `using` directive so that `EnemyBehavior` has access to Unity's navigation classes, in this case, `NavMeshAgent`.
2. Then, it declares a variable to keep track of which patrol location the enemy is currently walking toward. Since `List` items are zero-indexed, we can have the Enemy Prefab move between patrol points in the order they are stored in `Locations`.
3. Next, it declares a variable to store the NavMeshAgent component attached to the Enemy GameObject. This is `private` because no other classes should be able to access or modify it.
4. After that, it uses `GetComponent()` to find and return the attached NavMeshAgent component to the agent.
5. Then, it calls the `MoveToNextPatrolLocation()` method on `Start()`.
6. Finally, it declares `MoveToNextPatrolLocation()` as a private method and sets `_agent.destination`:
    - `destination` is a `Vector3` position in 3D space.
    - `Locations[_locationIndex]` grabs the Transform item in `Locations` at a given index.
    - Adding `.position` references the Transform component's `Vector3` position.

Now, when our scene starts, locations are filled with patrol points and `MoveToNextPatrolLocation()` is called to set the destination position of the NavMeshAgent component to the first item at `_locationIndex 0` in the list of locations. The next step is to have the enemy object move from the first patrol location to all the other locations in sequence.

Our enemy moves to the first patrol point just fine, but then it stops. What we want is for it to continually move between each sequential location, which will require additional logic in `Update()` and `MoveToNextPatrolLocation()`. Let's create this behavior.

Add the following code to `EnemyBehavior` and hit play:

```
public class EnemyBehavior : MonoBehaviour
{
    // ... No changes needed ...

    void Update()
    {
        // 1
```

```
        if(_agent.remainingDistance < 0.2f && !_agent.pathPending)
        {
            // 2
            MoveToNextPatrolLocation();
        }
    }

    void MoveToNextPatrolLocation()
    {
        // 3
        if (Locations.Count == 0)
            return;

        _agent.destination = Locations[_locationIndex].position;

        // 4
        _locationIndex = (_locationIndex + 1) % Locations.Count;
    }

    // ... No other changes needed ...
}
```

Let's break down the code:

1. First, it declares the `Update()` method and adds an `if` statement to check whether two different conditions are true:
    - `remainingDistance` returns how far the NavMeshAgent component currently is from its set destination, so we're checking if that is less than 0.2.
    - `pathPending` returns a `true` or `false` Boolean, depending on whether Unity is computing a path for the NavMeshAgent component.
2. If `_agent` is very close to its destination, and no other path is being computed, the `if` statement returns `true` and calls `MoveToNextPatrolLocation()`.
3. Here, we added an `if` statement to make sure that `Locations` isn't empty before the rest of the code in `MoveToNextPatrolLocation()` is executed:
    - If `Locations` is empty, we use the `return` keyword to exit the method without continuing.

> This is referred to as defensive programming, and, coupled with refactoring, it is an essential skill to have in your arsenal as you move toward more intermediate C# topics. We will consider refactoring at the end of the chapter.

4. Then, we set `_locationIndex` to its current value, `+1`, followed by the modulo (`%`) of `Locations.Count`:
   - This will increment the index from 0 to 4 and then restart it at 0 so that our Enemy Prefab moves in a continuous path.
   - The modulo operator returns the remainder of two values being divided—2 divided by 4 has a remainder of 2 when the result is an integer, so 2 % 4 = 2. Likewise, 4 divided by 4 has no remainder, so 4 % 4 = 0.

> Dividing an index by the maximum number of items in a collection is a quick way to always find the next item. If you're rusty on the modulo operator, revisit *Chapter 2, The Building Blocks of Programming*.

We now need to check that the enemy is moving toward its set patrol location every frame in `Update()`; when it gets close, `MoveToNextPatrolLocation()` is fired, which increments `_locationIndex` and sets the next patrol point as the destination.

If you drag the **Scene** view down next to the **Console** window, as shown in the following screenshot, and hit play, you can watch the Enemy Prefab walk around the corners of the level in a continuous loop:

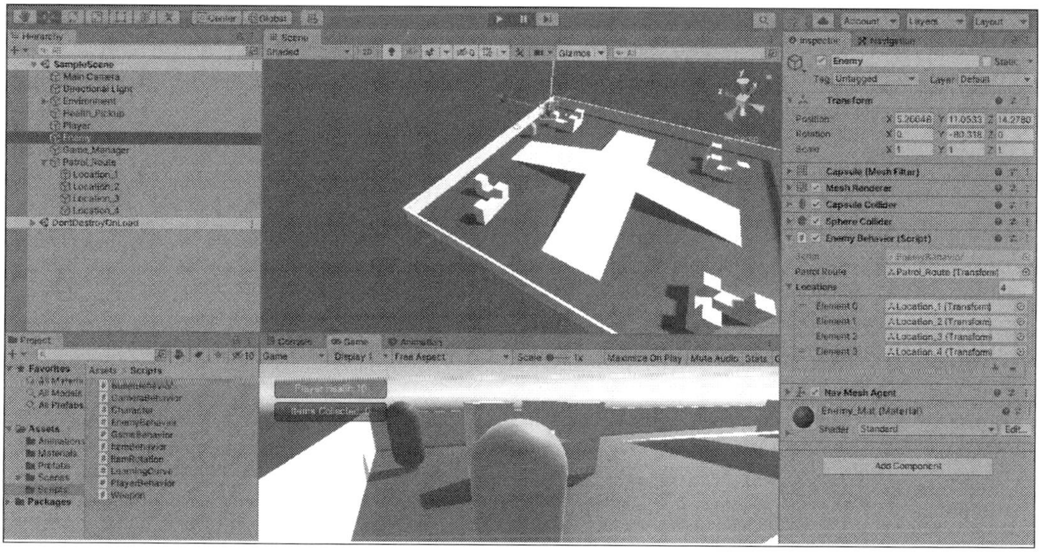

Figure 9.9: Testing the enemy patrol route

The enemy now follows the patrol route around the outside of the map, but it doesn't seek out the player and attack when it's within a preset range. You'll use the NavAgent component to do just that in the next section.

# Enemy game mechanics

Now that our enemy is on a continuous patrol circuit, it's time to give it some interaction mechanics of its own; there wouldn't be much risk or reward if we left it walking around with no way to act against us.

## Seek and destroy: changing the agent's destination

In this section, we'll be focusing on switching the target of the enemies' NavMeshAgent component when the player gets too close and dealing damage if a collision occurs. When the enemy successfully lowers the player's health, it will return to its patrol route until its next run-in with the player.

However, we're not going to leave our player helpless; we'll also add in code to track enemy health, detect when an enemy is successfully hit with one of the player's bullets, and when an enemy needs to be destroyed.

Now that the Enemy Prefab is moving around on patrol, we need to get a reference to the player's position and change the destination of NavMeshAgent if it gets too close.

1. Add the following code to `EnemyBehavior`:

```
public class EnemyBehavior : MonoBehaviour
{
    // 1
    public Transform Player;

    public Transform PatrolRoute;
    public List<Transform> Locations;

    private int _locationIndex = 0;
    private NavMeshAgent _agent;

    void Start()
    {
        _agent = GetComponent<NavMeshAgent>();
```

```
        // 2
        Player = GameObject.Find("Player").transform;

        // ... No other changes needed ...
    }

    /* ... No changes to Update,
           InitializePatrolRoute, or
           MoveToNextPatrolLocation ... */

    void OnTriggerEnter(Collider other)
    {
        if(other.name == "Player")
        {
            // 3
            _agent.destination = Player.position;

            Debug.Log("Enemy detected!");
        }
    }

    void OnTriggerExit(Collider other)
    {
        // .... No changes needed ...
    }
}
```

Let's break down the code:

1. First, it declares a `public` variable to hold the `Player` capsule's `Transform` value.
2. Then, we use `GameObject.Find("Player")` to return a reference to the player object in the scene:
   - Adding `.transform` directly references the object's `Transform` value in the same line.
3. Finally, we set `_agent.destination` to the player's `Vector3` position in `OnTriggerEnter()` whenever the player enters the enemies' attack zone that we set up earlier with a Collider component.

If you play the game now and get too close to the patrolling enemy, you'll see that it breaks from its path and comes straight for you. Once it reaches the player, the code in the `Update()` method takes over again and the Enemy Prefab resumes its patrol.

We still need the enemy to be able to hurt the player in some way, which we'll learn how to do in the next section.

# Lowering player health

While our enemy mechanic has come a long way, it's still anti-climactic to have nothing happen when the Enemy Prefab collides with the player Prefab. To fix this, we'll tie in the new enemy mechanics with the game manager.

Update `PlayerBehavior` with the following code and hit play:

```
public class PlayerBehavior : MonoBehaviour
{
    // ... No changes to public variables needed ...

    // 1
    private GameBehavior _gameManager;

    void Start()
    {
        _rb = GetComponent<Rigidbody>();
        _col = GetComponent<CapsuleCollider>();

        // 2
        _gameManager = GameObject.Find("Game_Manager").
GetComponent<GameBehavior>();
    }

    /* ... No changes to Update,
           FixedUpdate, or
           IsGrounded ... */

    // 3
    void OnCollisionEnter(Collision collision)
    {
        // 4
        if(collision.gameObject.name == "Enemy")
        {
            // 5
            _gameManager.HP -= 1;
```

```
        }
    }
}
```

Let's break down the code:

1. First, it declares a `private` variable to hold the reference to the instance of `GameBehavior` we have in the scene.
2. Then, it finds and returns the `GameBehavior` script that's attached to the `Game Manager` object in the scene:
    - Using `GetComponent()` on the same line as `GameObject.Find()` is a common way to cut down on unnecessary lines of code.
3. Since our player is the object being collided with, it makes sense to declare `OnCollisionEnter()` in `PlayerBehavior`.
4. Next, we check for the name of the colliding object; if it's the Enemy Prefab, we execute the body of the `if` statement.
5. Finally, we subtract `1` from the public `HP` variable using the `_gameManager` instance.

Whenever the enemy now tracks and collides with the player, the game manager will fire the set property on HP. The UI will update with a new value for player health, which means we have an opportunity to put in some additional logic for the loss condition later on.

# Detecting bullet collisions

Now that we have our loss condition, it's time to add in a way for our player to fight back and survive enemy attacks.

Open up `EnemyBehavior` and modify it with the following code:

```
public class EnemyBehavior : MonoBehaviour
{
    //... No other variable changes needed ...

    // 1
    private int _lives = 3;
    public int EnemyLives
    {
        // 2
        get { return _lives; }
```

```
        // 3
        private set
        {
            _lives = value;

            // 4
            if (_lives <= 0)
            {
                Destroy(this.gameObject);
                Debug.Log("Enemy down.");
            }
        }
    }

    /* ... No changes to Start,
           Update,
           InitializePatrolRoute,
           MoveToNextPatrolLocation,
           OnTriggerEnter, or
           OnTriggerExit ... */

    void OnCollisionEnter(Collision collision)
    {
        // 5
        if(collision.gameObject.name == "Bullet(Clone)")
        {
            // 6
            EnemyLives -= 1;
            Debug.Log("Critical hit!");
        }
    }
}
```

Let's break down the code:

1. First, it declares a `private int` variable called `_lives` with a `public` backing variable called `EnemyLives`. This will let us control how `EnemyLives` is referenced and set, just like in `GameBehavior`.
2. Then, we set the `get` property to always return `_lives`.
3. Next, we use `private set` to assign the new value of `EnemyLives` to `_lives` to keep them both in sync.

> We haven't seen `private get` or `set` before, but they can have their access modifiers, just like any other executable code. Declaring `get` or `set` as `private` means that only the parent class has access to their functionality.

4. Then, we add an `if` statement to check whether `_lives` is less than or equal to 0, meaning that the enemy should be dead:
    - When that's the case, we destroy the `Enemy` GameObject and print out a message to the console.
5. Because `Enemy` is the object getting hit with bullets, it's sensible to include a check for those collisions in `EnemyBehavior` with `OnCollisionEnter()`.
6. Finally, if the name of the colliding object matches a bullet clone object, we decrement `EnemyLives` by `1` and print out another message.

> Notice that the name we're checking for is `Bullet(Clone)`, even though our bullet Prefab is named `Bullet`. This is because Unity adds the `(Clone)` suffix to any object created with the `Instantiate()` method, which is how we made them in our shooting logic.
>
> You can also check for the GameObjects' tag, but since that's a Unity-specific feature, we're going to leave the code as-is and do things with pure C#.

Now, the player can fight back when the enemy tries to take one of its lives by shooting it three times and destroying it. Again, our use of the `get` and `set` properties to handle additional logic proves to be a flexible and scalable solution. With that done, your final task is to update the game manager with a loss condition.

# Updating the game manager

To fully implement the loss condition, we need to update the manager class:

1. Open up `GameBehavior` and add the following code:

```
public class GameBehavior : MonoBehaviour
{
    // ... No other variable changes...
```

```
    // 1
    public Button LossButton;

    private int _itemsCollected = 0;
    public int Items
    {
        // ... No changes needed ...
    }

    private int _playerHP = 10;
    public int HP
    {
        get { return _playerHP; }
        set {
            _playerHP = value;
                HealthText.text = "Player Health: " + HP;

            // 2
            if(_playerHP <= 0)
            {
                ProgressText.text= "You want another life with
that?";
    LossButton.gameObject.SetActive(true);
                Time.timeScale = 0;
            }
            else
            {
                ProgressText.text = "Ouch... that's got hurt.";
            }
        }
    }
}
```

2. In the **Hierarchy** window, right-click on **Win Condition**, choose **Duplicate**, and name it **Loss Condition**:
    - Click the arrow to the left of **Loss Condition** to expand it, select the **Text** object, and change the text to **You lose...**

3. Select **Game_Manager** in the **Hierarchy** window and drag **Loss Condition** into the **Loss Button** slot in the **Game Behavior (Script)** component:

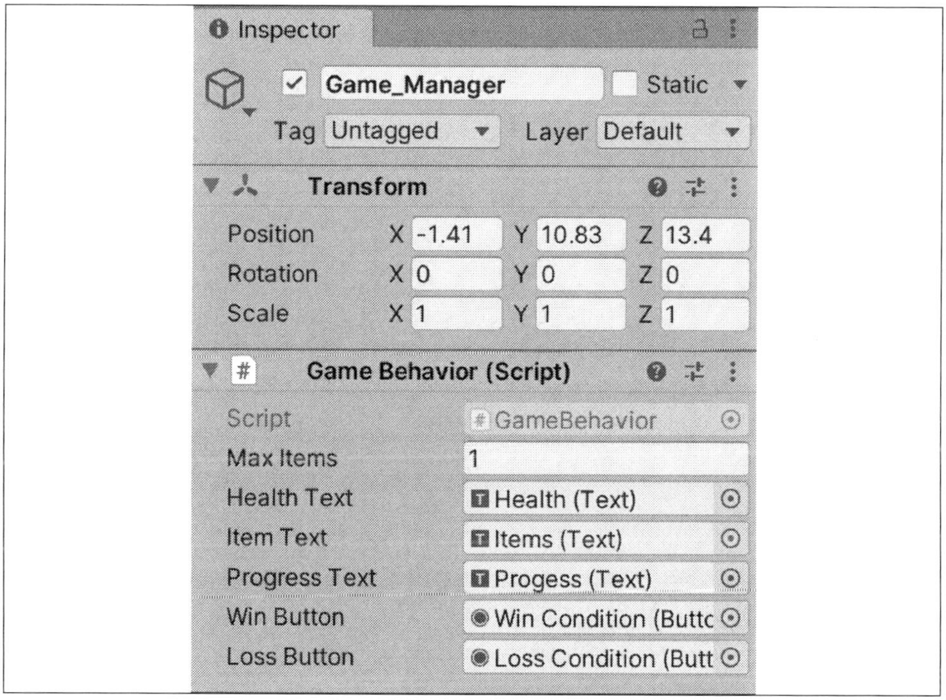


Figure 9.10: Game behavior script with text and button variables completed in the Inspector pane

Let's break down the code:

1. First, we declare a new button that we want to show when the player loses the game.
2. Then, we add in an `if` statement to check when `_playerHP` drops below `0`:
   - If it's `true`, `ProgessText` and `Time.timeScale` are updated and the loss button is activated.
   - If the player is still alive following an enemy collision, `ProgessText` shows a different message: "Ouch... that's got to hurt.".

Now, change `_playerHP` to 1 in `GameBehavior.cs` and get the Enemy Prefab to collide with you and observe what happens.

That's a wrap! You've successfully added a "smart" enemy that can damage the player and be damaged right back, as well as a loss screen through the game manager. Before we finish this chapter, there's one more important topic that we need to discuss, and that's how to avoid repeating code.

Repeated code is the bane of all programmers, so it makes sense that you learn how to keep it out of your projects early on!

# Refactoring and keeping it DRY

The **Don't Repeat Yourself** (**DRY**) acronym is the software developer's conscience: it tells you when you're in danger of making a bad or questionable decision, and gives you a feeling of satisfaction after a job well done.

In practice, repeated code is part of programming life. Trying to avoid it by constantly thinking ahead will put up so many roadblocks in your project that it won't seem worthwhile carrying on. A more efficient—and sane—approach to dealing with repeating code is to quickly identify it when and where it occurs and then look for the best way to remove it. This task is called refactoring, and our `GameBehavior` class could use a little of its magic right now.

You may have noticed that we set the progress text and timescale in two separate places, but we could easily make ourselves a utility method to do this for us in a single place.

To refactor the existing code, you'll need to update `GameBehavior.cs` as follows:

```
public class GameBehavior: MonoBehaviour
{
    // 1
    public void UpdateScene(string updatedText)
    {
        ProgressText.text = updatedText;
        Time.timeScale = 0f;
    }

    private int _itemsCollected = 0;
    public int Items
    {
        get { return _itemsCollected; }
        set
        {
            _itemsCollected = value;
            ItemText.text = "Items Collected: " + Items;

            if (_itemsCollected >= MaxItems)
            {
                WinButton.gameObject.SetActive(true);
```

```
            // 2
            UpdateScene("You've found all the items!");
        }
        else
        {
            ProgressText.text = "Item found, only " + (MaxItems -
_itemsCollected) + " more to go!";
        }
    }
}

private int _playerHP = 10;
public int HP
{
    get { return _playerHP; }
    set
    {
        _playerHP = value;
        HealthText.text = "Player Health: " + HP;

        if (_playerHP <= 0)
        {
            LossButton.gameObject.SetActive(true);

            // 3
            UpdateScene("You want another life with that?");
        }
        else
        {
            ProgressText.text = "Ouch... that's got hurt.";
        }

        Debug.LogFormat("Lives: {0}", _playerHP);
    }
}
}
```

Let's break down the code:

1. We declared a new method called `UpdateScene`, which takes in a string parameter that we want to assign to `ProgressText` and sets `Time.timeScale` to `0`.

2. We deleted our first instance of duplicated code and used our new method to update our scene when the game is won.
3. We deleted our second instance of duplicated code and update the scene when the game is lost.

There's always more to refactor if you look in the right places.

# Summary

With that, our enemy and player interactions are complete. We can dish out damage as well as take it, lose lives, and fight back, all while updating the on-screen GUI. Our enemies use Unity's navigation system to walk around the arena and change to attack mode when within a specified range of the player. Each GameObject is responsible for its behavior, internal logic, and object collisions, while the game manager keeps track of the variables that govern the game's state. Lastly, we learned about simple procedural programming and how much cleaner code can be when repeated instructions are abstracted out into their methods.

You should feel a sense of accomplishment at this point, especially if you started this book as a total beginner. Getting up to speed with a new programming language while building a working game is no easy trick. In the next chapter, you'll be introduced to some intermediate topics in C#, including new type modifiers, method overloading, interfaces, and class extensions.

# Pop quiz – AI and navigation

1. How is a NavMesh component created in a Unity scene?
2. What component identifies a GameObject to a NavMesh?
3. Executing the same logic on one or more sequential objects is an example of which programming technique?
4. What does the DRY acronym stand for?

# 10

# Revisiting Types, Methods, and Classes

Now that you've programmed the game's mechanics and interactions with Unity's built-in classes, it's time to expand our core C# knowledge and focus on the intermediate applications of the foundation we've laid. We'll revisit old friends—variables, types, methods, and classes—but we'll target their deeper applications and relevant use cases. Many of the topics we'll be covering don't apply to *Hero Born* in its current state, so some examples will be standalone rather than being applied directly to the game prototype.

I'll be throwing a lot of new information your way, so if you feel overwhelmed at any point, don't hesitate to revisit the first few chapters to solidify those building blocks. We'll also be using this chapter to break away from gameplay mechanics and features specific to Unity by focusing on the following topics:

- Intermediate modifiers
- Method overloading
- Using the `out` and `ref` parameters
- Working with interfaces
- Abstract classes and overriding
- Extending class functionality
- Namespace conflicts
- Type aliasing

Let's get started!

# Access modifiers

While we've gotten into the habit of pairing the public and private access modifiers with our variable declarations, like we did with player health and items collected, there remains a laundry list of modifier keywords that we haven't seen. We can't go into detail about every one of them in this chapter, but the five that we'll focus on will further your understanding of the C# language and give your programming skills a boost.

This section will cover the first three modifiers in the following list, while the remaining two will be discussed later on in the *Intermediate OOP* section:

- `const`
- `readonly`
- `static`
- `abstract`
- `override`

> You can find a full list of available modifiers at `https://docs.microsoft.com/en-us/dotnet/csharp/language-reference/keywords/modifiers`.

Let's start with the first three access modifiers provided in the preceding list.

# Constant and read-only properties

There will be times when you need to create variables that store constant, unchanging values. Adding the `const` keyword after a variable's access modifier will do just that, but only for built-in C# types. For example, you couldn't mark an instance of our `Character` class as a constant. A good candidate for a constant value is `MaxItems` in the `GameBehavior` class:

```
public const int MaxItems = 4;
```

The above code would essentially lock the value of `MaxItems` at `4`, making it unchangeable. The problem you'll run into with constant variables is that they can only be assigned a value in their declaration, meaning we can't leave `MaxItems` without an initial value. As an alternative, we can use `readonly`, which won't let you write to the variable, meaning it can't be changed:

```
public readonly int MaxItems;
```

Using the `readonly` keyword to declare a variable will give us the same unmodifiable value as a constant, while still letting us assign its initial value at any time. A good place for this would be the `Start()` or `Awake()` methods in one of our scripts.

# Using the static keyword

We've already gone over how objects, or instances, are created from a class blueprint, and that all properties and methods belong to that particular instance, like we had with our very first `Character` class instance. While this is great for object-oriented functionality, not all classes need to be instantiated, and not all properties need to belong to a specific instance. However, static classes are sealed, meaning they cannot be used in class inheritance.

Utility methods are a good case for this situation, where we don't necessarily care about instantiating a particular `Utility` class instance since all its methods wouldn't be dependent on a particular object. Your task is to create just such a utility method in a new script.

Let's create a new class to hold some of our future methods that deal with raw computations or repeated logic that doesn't depend on the gameplay:

1. Create a new C# script in the `Scripts` folder and name it `Utilities`.
2. Open it up and add the following code:

```
using System.Collections;
using System.Collections.Generic;
using UnityEngine;

// 1
using UnityEngine.SceneManagement;

// 2
public static class Utilities
{
    // 3
    public static int PlayerDeaths = 0;

    // 4
    public static void RestartLevel()
    {
        SceneManager.LoadScene(0);
        Time.timeScale = 1.0f;
    }
}
```

3. Delete the code inside `RestartLevel()` from `GameBehavior` and instead call the new `utility` method with the following code:

```
// 5
public void RestartScene()
{
    Utilities.RestartLevel();
}
```

Let's break down the code:

1. First, it adds the `using SceneManagement` directive so that we can access the `LoadScene()` method.
2. Then, it declares `Utilities` as a public `static` class that does not inherit from `MonoBehavior` because we won't need it to be in the game scene.
3. Next, it creates a public `static` variable to hold the number of times our player has died and restarted the game.
4. After, it declares a public `static` method to hold our level restart logic, which is currently hardcoded in `GameBehavior`.
5. Finally, our update to `GameBehavior` calls `RestartLevel()` from the static `Utilities` class when the win or the lose button is pressed. Notice that we didn't need an instance of the `Utilities` class to call the method because it's static—it's just dot notation.

We've now extracted the restart logic from `GameBehavior` and put it into its static class, which makes it easier to reuse across our codebase. Marking it as `static` will also ensure that we never have to create or manage instances of the `Utilities` class before we use its class members.

> Non-static classes can have properties and methods that are static and non-static. However, if an entire class is marked as static, all properties and methods must follow suit.

That wraps up our second visit of variables and types, which will enable you to build out your own set of utilities and tools when managing larger and more complex projects down the road. Now it's time to move on to methods and their intermediate capabilities, which includes method overloading and `ref` and `out` parameters.

# Revisiting methods

Methods have been a big part of our code since we learned how to use them in *Chapter 3, Diving into Variables, Types, and Methods*, but there are two intermediate use cases we haven't covered yet: method overloading and using the `ref` and `out` parameter keywords.

# Overloading methods

The term **method overloading** refers to creating multiple methods with the same name but with different signatures. A method's signature is made up of its name and parameters, which is how the C# compiler recognizes it. Take the following method as an example:

```
public bool AttackEnemy(int damage) {}
```

The method signature of `AttackEnemy()` is written as follows:

```
AttackEnemy(int)
```

Now that we know the signature of `AttackEnemy()`, it can be overloaded by changing the number of parameters or the parameter types themselves, while still keeping its name. This provides added flexibility when you need more than one option for a given operation.

The `RestartLevel()` method in `Utilities` is a great example of a situation where method overloading comes in handy. Right now, `RestartLevel()` only restarts the current level, but what happens if we expand the game so that it includes multiple scenes? We could refactor `RestartLevel()` to accept parameters, but that often leads to bloated and confusing code.

The `RestartLevel()` method is, once again, a good candidate for testing out our new knowledge. Your task is to overload it to take in different parameters.

Let's add an overloaded version of `RestartLevel()`:

1. Open up `Utilities` and add the following code:

```
public static class Utilities
{
    public static int PlayerDeaths = 0;

    public static void RestartLevel()
    {
        SceneManager.LoadScene(0);
        Time.timeScale = 1.0f;
    }

    // 1
    public static bool RestartLevel(int sceneIndex)
    {
        // 2
        SceneManager.LoadScene(sceneIndex);
```

```
            Time.timeScale = 1.0f;

            // 3
            return true;
        }
    }
```

2. Open `GameBehavior` and update the call to the `Utilities.RestartLevel()` method to the following:

```
    // 4
    public void RestartScene()
    {
        Utilities.RestartLevel(0);
    }
```

Let's break down the code:

1. First, it declares an overloaded version of the `RestartLevel()` method that takes in an `int` parameter and returns a `bool`.
2. Then, it calls `LoadScene()` and passes in the `sceneIndex` parameter instead of manually hardcoding that value.
3. Next, it returns `true` after the new scene is loaded and the `timeScale` property has been reset.
4. Finally, our update to `GameBehavior` calls the overloaded `RestartLevel()` method and passes in `0` as the `sceneIndex`. Overloaded methods are automatically detected by Visual Studio and are displayed by number, as shown here:

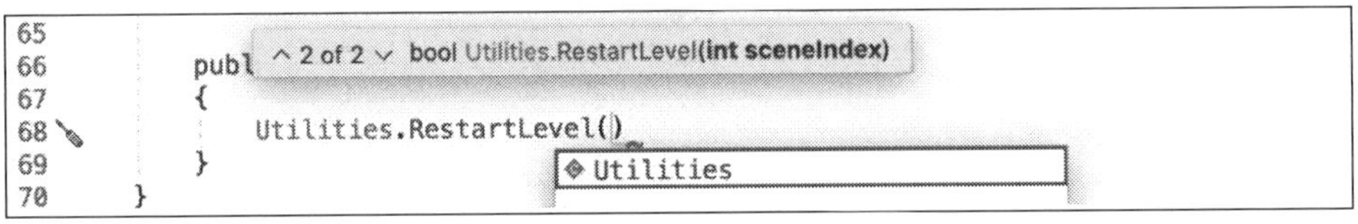


Figure 10.1: Multiple method overloads in Visual Studio

The functionality in the `RestartLevel()` method is now much more customizable and can account for additional situations you may need later. In this case, it is restarting the game from any scene we choose.

> Method overloading is not limited to static methods—this was just in line with the previous example. Any method can be overloaded as long as its signature differs from the original.

Next up, we're going to cover two additional topics that can take your method game to a whole new level—`ref` and `out` parameters.

# ref parameters

When we talked about classes and structs back in *Chapter 5, Working with Classes, Structs, and OOP*, we discovered that not all objects are passed the same way: value types are passed by copy, while reference types are passed by reference. However, we didn't go over how objects, or values, are used when they're passed into methods as parameter arguments.

By default, all arguments are passed by value, meaning that a variable passed into a method will not be affected by any changes that are made to its value inside the method body. This protects us from making unwanted changes to existing variables when we use them as method parameters. While this works for most cases, there are situations where you'll want to pass in a method argument by reference so that it can be updated and have that change reflected in the original variable. Prefixing a parameter declaration with either the `ref` or `out` keyword will mark the argument as a reference.

Here are a few key points to keep in mind about using the `ref` keyword:

- Arguments have to be initialized before being passed into a method.
- You don't need to initialize or assign the reference parameter value before ending the method.
- Properties with get or set accessors can't be used as `ref` or `out` arguments.

Let's try this out by adding some logic to keep track of how many times a player has restarted the game.

Let's create a method to update `PlayerDeaths` to see the method arguments that are being passed by reference in action.

Open up `Utilities` and add the following code:

```
public static class Utilities
{
    public static int PlayerDeaths = 0;

    // 1
    public static string UpdateDeathCount(ref int countReference)
    {
        // 2
        countReference += 1;
        return "Next time you'll be at number " + countReference;
    }
```

```
    public static void RestartLevel()
    {
       // ... No changes needed ...
    }

    public static bool RestartLevel(int sceneIndex)
    {
        // 3
        Debug.Log("Player deaths: " + PlayerDeaths);
        string message = UpdateDeathCount(ref PlayerDeaths);
        Debug.Log("Player deaths: " + PlayerDeaths);
        Debug.Log(message);

        SceneManager.LoadScene(sceneIndex);
        Time.timeScale = 1.0f;

        return true;
    }
}
```

Let's break down the code:

1. First, it declares a new `static` method that returns a `string` and takes in an `int` passed by reference.
2. Then, it updates the reference parameter directly, incrementing its value by `1` and returning a string that contains the new value.
3. Finally, it debugs the `PlayerDeaths` variable in `RestartLevel(int sceneIndex)` before and after it is passed by reference to `UpdateDeathCount()`. We also store a reference to the returned string value from `UpdateDeathCount()` in the `message` variable and print it out.

If you play the game and lose, the debug log will show that `PlayerDeaths` has increased by 1 inside `UpdateDeathCount()` because it was passed by reference and not by value:

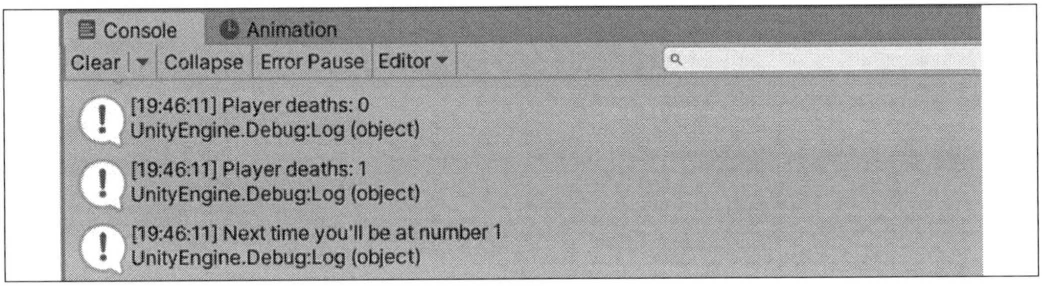


Figure 10.2: Example output from ref parameters

For clarity, we could have updated the player death count without a `ref` parameter because `UpdateDeathCount()` and `PlayerDeaths` are in the same script. However, if this wasn't the case and you wanted the same functionality, `ref` parameters are super useful.

> We're using the `ref` keyword in this situation for the sake of our example, but we could have also updated `PlayerDeaths` directly inside `UpdateDeathCount()` or added logic inside `RestartLevel()` to only fire `UpdateDeathCount()` when the restart was due to a loss.

Now that we know how to use a `ref` parameter in our project, let's take a look at the `out` parameter and how it serves a slightly different purpose.

## out parameters

The `out` keyword does the same job as `ref` but with different rules, which means they're similar tools but they're not interchangeable—each has its own use cases:

- Arguments do not need to be initialized before being passed into a method.
- The referenced parameter value does need to be initialized or assigned in the calling method before it's returned.

For instance, we could have replaced `ref` with `out` in `UpdateDeathCount()` as long as we initialized or assigned the `countReference` parameter before returning from the method:

```
public static string UpdateDeathCount(out int countReference)
{
     countReference = 1;
     return "Next time you'll be at number " + countReference;
}
```

Methods that use the `out` keyword are better suited to situations where you need to return multiple values from a single function, while the `ref` keyword works best when a reference value only needs to be modified. It's also more flexible than the `ref` keyword because the initial parameter values don't need to be set before they're used in the method. The `out` keyword is especially useful if you need to initialize the parameter value before you change it. Even though these keywords are a little more esoteric, it's important to have them in your C# toolkit for special use cases.

With these new method features under our belts, it's time to revisit the big one: **object-oriented programming** (**OOP**). There's so much to this topic that it's impossible to cover everything in a chapter or two, but there are a few key tools that will come in handy early on in your development career. OOP is one of those topics that you're encouraged to follow up on after finishing this book.

# Intermediate OOP

An object-oriented mindset is crucial to creating meaningful applications and understanding how the C# language works behind the scenes. The tricky part is that classes and structs by themselves aren't the end of the line when it comes to OOP and designing your objects. They'll always be the building blocks of your code, but classes are limited to single inheritance, meaning they can only ever have one parent or superclass, and structs can't inherit at all. So, the question you should be asking yourself right about now is simple: "*How can I create objects from the same blueprint and have them perform different actions based on a specific scenario?*"

To answer this question, we'll be learning about interfaces, abstract classes, and class extensions.

## Interfaces

One of the ways to gather groups of functionality together is through interfaces. Like classes, interfaces are blueprints for data and behaviors, but with one important difference: they can't have any actual implementation logic or stored values. Instead, they contain the implementation blueprint, and it's up to the adopting class or struct to fill in the values and methods outlined in the interface. You can use interfaces with both classes and structs, and there's no upper limit to how many interfaces a single class or struct can adopt.

Remember, a single class can only have one parent class, and structs can't subclass at all. Breaking out functionality into interfaces lets you build up classes like building blocks, picking and choosing how you want them to behave like food from a menu. This would be a huge efficiency boost to your code base, breaking away from long, messy subclassing hierarchies.

For example, what if we wanted our enemies to be able to shoot back at our player when they're in close range? We could create a parent class that both the player and enemy could derive from, which would base them both on the same blueprint. The problem with that approach, however, is that enemies and players won't necessarily share the same behaviors and data.

The more efficient way to handle this would be to define an interface with a blueprint for what shootable objects need to do, and then have both the enemy and player adopt it. That way, they have the freedom to be separate and exhibit different behaviors while still sharing common functionality.

Refactoring the shooting mechanic into an interface is a challenge I'll leave to you, but we still need to know how to create and adopt interfaces in code. For this example, we'll create an interface that all manager scripts might need to implement for sharing a common structure.

Create a new C# script in the `Scripts` folder, name it `IManager`, and update its code as follows:

```
using System.Collections;
using System.Collections.Generic;
using UnityEngine;

// 1
public interface IManager
{
    // 2
    string State { get; set; }

    // 3
    void Initialize();
}
```

Let's break down the code:

1. First, it declares a public interface called `IManager` using the `interface` keyword.
2. Then, it adds a `string` variable to `IManager` named `State` with `get` and `set` accessors to hold the current state of the adopting class.

> All interface properties need at least a get accessor to compile but can have both get and set accessors if necessary.

3. Finally, it defines a method named `Initialize()` with no return type for the adopting class to implement. However, you could absolutely have a return type for a method inside an interface; there's no rule against it.

You've now created a blueprint for all manager scripts, meaning that each manager script adopting this interface needs to have a state property and an initialize method. Your next task is to use the `IManager` interface, which means it needs to be adopted by another class.

To keep things simple, let's have the game manager adopt our new interface and implement its blueprint.

Update `GameBehavior` with the following code:

```
// 1
public class GameBehavior : MonoBehaviour, IManager
{
    // 2
    private string _state;

    // 3
    public string State
    {
        get { return _state; }
        set { _state = value; }
    }

    // ... No other changes needed ...

    // 4
    void Start()
    {
        Initialize();
    }

    // 5
    public void Initialize()
    {
        _state = "Game Manager initialized..";
        Debug.Log(_state);
    }
}
```

Let's break down the code:

1. First, it declares that `GameBehavior` adopts the `IManager` interface using a comma and its name, just like with subclassing.

2. Then, it adds a private variable that we'll use to back the public `State` value we have to implement from `IManager`.
3. Next, it adds the public `State` variable declared in `IManager` and uses `_state` as its private backing variable.
4. After that, it declares the `Start()` method and calls the `Initialize()` method.
5. Finally, it declares the `Initialize()` method declared in `IManager` with an implementation that sets and prints out the public `State` variable.

With this, we specified that `GameBehavior` adopts the `IManager` interface and implemented its `State` and `Initialize()` members, as shown here:

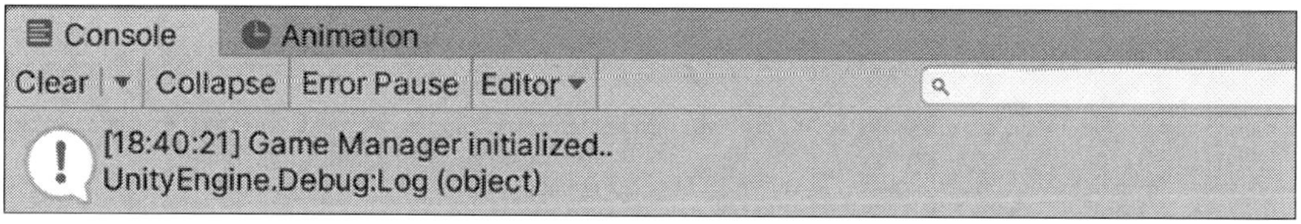


Figure 10.3: Example output from an interface

The great part of this is that the implementation is specific to `GameBehavior`; if we had another manager class, we could do the same thing but with different logic. Just for fun, let's set up a new manager script to test this out:

1. In the **Project**, right-click inside the **Scripts** folder and choose **Create** | **C# Script**, then name it `DataManager`.
2. Update the new script with the following code and adopt the `IManager` interface:

```
using System.Collections;
using System.Collections.Generic;
using UnityEngine;

public class DataManager : MonoBehaviour, IManager
{
    private string _state;
    public string State
    {
        get { return _state; }
        set { _state = value; }
    }

    void Start()
    {
        Initialize();
```

```
    }

    public void Initialize()
    {
        _state = "Data Manager initialized..";
        Debug.Log(_state);
    }
}
```

3. Drag and drop the new script onto the **Game_Manager** object in the **Hierarchy** panel:

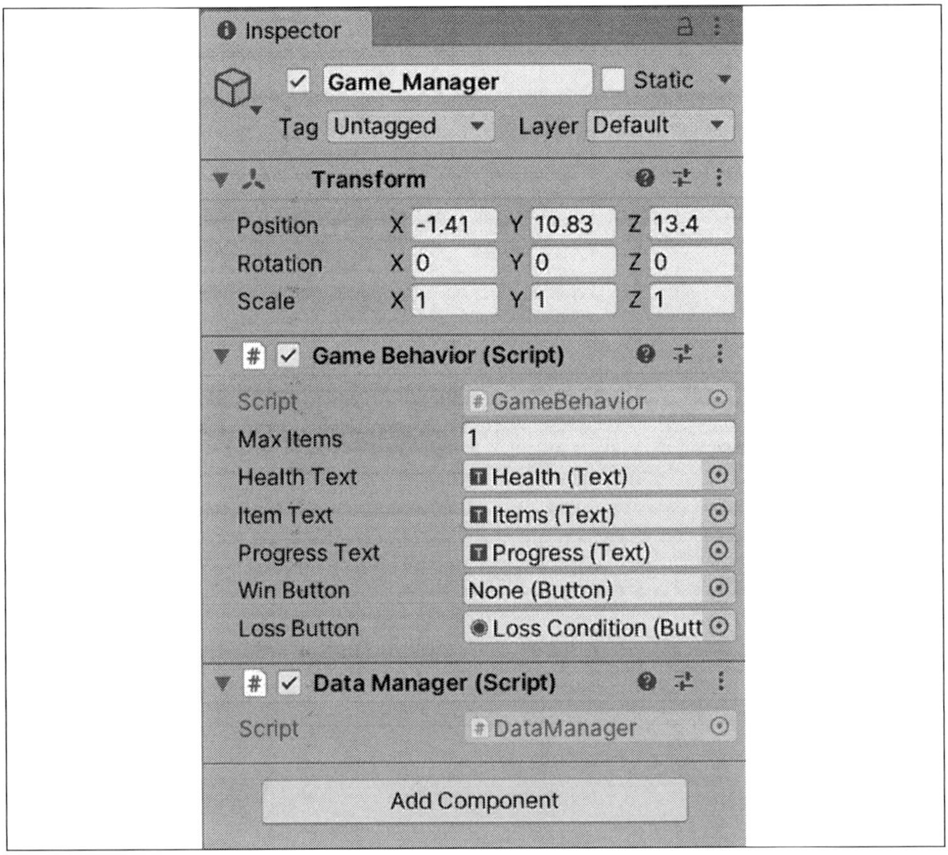


Figure 10.4: Data manager script attached to a GameObject

4. Then click play:

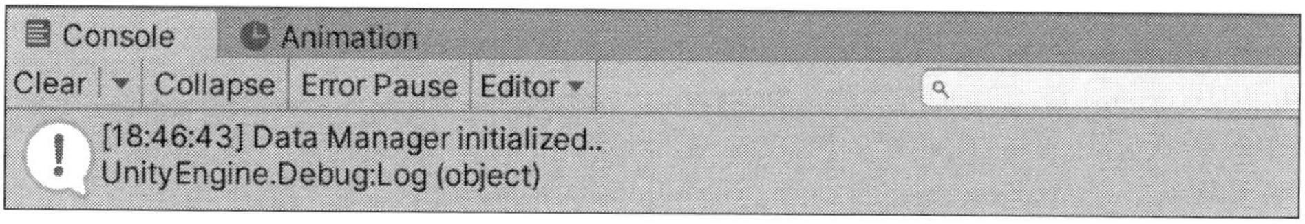


Figure 10.5: Output from data manager initialization

While we could have done all of this with subclassing, we'd be limited to one parent class for all our managers. Instead, we have the option of adding new interfaces if we choose. We'll revisit this new manager script in *Chapter 12, Saving, Loading, and Serializing Data*. This opens up a whole world of possibilities for building classes, one of which is a new OOP concept called abstract classes.

# Abstract classes

Another approach to separating common blueprints and sharing them between objects is the abstract class. Like interfaces, abstract classes cannot include any implementation logic for their methods; they can, however, store variable values. This is one of the key differences from interfaces—in situations where you might need to set initial values, an abstract class would be the way to go.

Any class that subclasses from an abstract class must fully implement all variables and methods marked with the `abstract` keyword. They can be particularly useful in situations where you want to use class inheritance without having to write out a base class's default implementation.

For example, let's take the `IManager` interface functionality we just wrote and see what it would look like as an abstract base class. *Don't change any of the actual code in our project*, as we still want to keep things working as they are:

```
// 1
public abstract class BaseManager
{
    // 2
    protected string _state = "Manager is not initialized...";
    public abstract string State { get; set; }

    // 3
    public abstract void Initialize();
}
```

Let's break down the code:

1. First, it declares a new class named `BaseManager` using the `abstract` keyword.
2. Then, it creates two variables: A `protected string` named `_state` that can only be accessed by classes that inherit from `BaseManager`. We've also set an initial value for `_state`, something we couldn't do in our interface.
    - We also have an abstract string named `State` with `get` and `set` accessors to be implemented by the subclass.
3. Finally, it adds `Initialize()` as an `abstract` method, also to be implemented in the subclass.

In doing so, we have created an abstract class that does the same thing as an interface. In this setup, `BaseManager` has the same blueprint as `IManager`, allowing any subclasses to define their implementations of `state` and `Initialize()` using the `override` keyword:

```
// 1
public class CombatManager: BaseManager
{
    // 2
    public override string State
    {
        get { return _state; }
        set { _state = value; }
    }

    // 3
    public override void Initialize()
    {
        _state = "Combat Manager initialized..";
        Debug.Log(_state);
    }
}
```

If we break down the preceding code, we can see the following:

1. First, it declares a new class called `CombatManager` that inherits from the `BaseManager` abstract class.
2. Then, it adds the `State` variable implementation from `BaseManager` using the `override` keyword.
3. Finally, it adds the `Initialize()` method implementation from `BaseManager` using the `override` keyword again and sets the protected `_state` variable.

Even though this is only the tip of the iceberg of interfaces and abstract classes, their possibilities should be jumping around in your programming brain. Interfaces will allow you to spread and share pieces of functionality between unrelated objects, leading to a building block-like assembly when it comes to your code.

Abstract classes, on the other hand, will let you keep the single-inheritance structure of OOP while separating a class's implementation from its blueprint. These approaches can even be mixed and matched, as abstract classes can adopt interfaces just like non-abstract ones.

> As always with complicated topics, your first stop should be the documentation. Check it out at `https://docs.microsoft.com/en-us/dotnet/csharp/language-reference/keywords/abstract` and `https://docs.microsoft.com/en-us/dotnet/csharp/language-reference/keywords/interface`.

You won't always need to build a new class from scratch. Sometimes, it's enough to add the feature or logic you want to an existing class, which is called a class extension.

# Class extensions

Let's step away from custom objects and talk about how we can extend existing classes so that they fit our own needs. The idea behind class extensions is simple: take an existing built-in C# class and add on any functionality that you need it to have. Since we don't have access to the underlying code that C# is built on, this is the only way to get custom behavior out of objects the language already has.

Classes can only be modified with methods—no variables or other entities are allowed. However limiting this might be, it makes the syntax consistent:

```
public static returnType MethodName(this ExtendingClass localVal) {}
```

Extension methods are declared using the same syntax as normal methods, but with a few caveats:

- All extension methods need to be marked as `static`.
- The first parameter needs to be the `this` keyword, followed by the name of the class we want to extend and a local variable name:
    - This special parameter lets the compiler identify the method as an extension, and gives us a local reference for the existing class.

    - Any class methods and properties can then be accessed through the local variable.

- It's common to store extension methods inside a static class, which, in turn, is stored inside its namespace. This allows you to control what other scripts have access to your custom functionality.

Your next task is to put class extensions into practice by adding a new method to the built-in C# `String` class.

Let's take a look at extensions in practice by adding a custom method to the `String` class. Create a new C# script in the `Scripts` folder, name it `CustomExtensions`, and add the following code:

```
using System.Collections;
using System.Collections.Generic;
using UnityEngine;

// 1
namespace CustomExtensions
{
    // 2
    public static class StringExtensions
    {
        // 3
        public static void FancyDebug(this string str)
        {
            // 4
            Debug.LogFormat("This string contains {0} characters.",
str.Length);
        }
    }
}
```

Let's break down the code:

1. First, it declares a namespace named `CustomExtensions` to hold all the extension classes and methods.
2. Then, it declares a `static` class named `StringExtensions` for organizational purposes; each group of class extensions should follow this setup.
3. Next, it adds a `static` method named `FancyDebug` to the `StringExtensions` class:

- The first parameter, `this string str`, marks the method as an extension.
- The `str` parameter will hold a reference to the actual text value that `FancyDebug()` is called from; we can operate on `str` inside the method body as a stand-in for all string literals.

4. Finally, it prints out a debug message whenever `FancyDebug` is executed, using `str.Length` to reference the string variable that the method is called on.

In practice, this will let you add any of your own custom functionality to existing C# classes or even your own custom ones. Now that the extension is part of the `String` class, let's test it out. To use our new custom string method, we'll need to include it in whatever class we want to have access to it.

Open up `GameBehavior` and update the class with the following code:

```
using System.Collections;
using System.Collections.Generic;
using UnityEngine;

// 1
using CustomExtensions;

public class GameBehavior : MonoBehaviour, IManager
{
    // ... No changes needed ...

    void Start()
    {
        // ... No changes needed ...
    }

    public void Initialize()
    {
        _state = "Game Manager initialized..";

        // 2
        _state.FancyDebug();

        Debug.Log(_state);
    }

}
```

Let's break down the code:

1. First, it adds the `CustomExtensions` namespace with a `using` directive at the top of the file.
2. Then, it calls `FancyDebug` on the `_state` string variable with dot notation inside `Initialize()` to print out the number of individual characters its value has.

Extending the entire `string` class with `FancyDebug()` means that any string variable has access to it. Since the first extension method parameter has a reference to whatever `string` value that `FancyDebug()` is called on, its length will be printed out properly, as shown here:

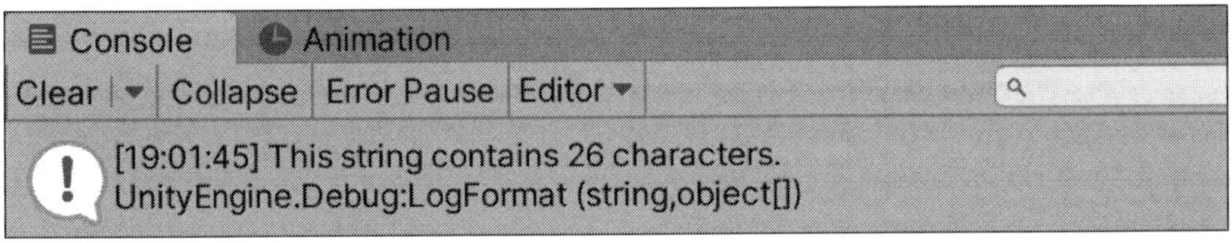


Figure 10.6: Example output from custom extension

> A custom class can also be extended using the same syntax, but it's more common to just add extra functionality directly into the class if it's one you control.

The last topic we'll explore in this chapter is namespaces, which we briefly learned about earlier in the book. In the next section, you'll learn about the larger role that namespaces play in C# and how to create your type alias.

# Namespace conflicts and type aliasing

As your applications get more complicated, you'll start to section off your code into namespaces, ensuring that you have control over where and when it's accessed. You'll also use third-party software tools and plugins to save on time implementing a feature from the ground up that someone else has already made available. Both of these scenarios show that you're progressing with your programming knowledge, but they can also cause namespace conflicts.

**Namespace conflicts** happen when there are two or more classes or types with the same name, which happens more than you'd think.

Good naming habits tend to produce similar results, and before you know it, you're dealing with multiple classes named `Error` or `Extension`, and Visual Studio is throwing out errors. Luckily, C# has a simple solution to these situations: **type aliasing**.

Defining a type alias lets you explicitly choose which conflicting type you want to use in a given class, or create a more user-friendly name for a long-winded existing one. Type aliases are added at the top of the class file with a `using` directive, followed by the alias name and the assigned type:

```
using AliasName = type;
```

For instance, if we wanted to create a type alias to refer to the existing `Int64` type, we could say the following:

```
using CustomInt = System.Int64;
```

Now that `CustomInt` is a type alias for the `System.Int64` type, the compiler will treat it as an `Int64`, letting us use it like any other type:

```
public CustomInt PlayerHealth = 100;
```

You can use type aliasing with your custom types, or existing ones with the same syntax, as long as they're declared at the top of script files with the other `using` directives.

> For more information on the `using` keyword and type aliasing, check out the C# documentation at `https://docs.microsoft.com/en-us/dotnet/csharp/language-reference/keywords/using-directive`.

# Summary

With new modifiers, method overloading, class extensions, and object-oriented skills under our belts, we are only one step away from the end of our C# journey. Remember, these intermediate topics are intended to get you thinking about more complex applications of the knowledge you've been gathering throughout this book; don't think that what you've learned in this chapter is all that there is to know on these concepts. Take it as a starting point and continue from there.

In the next chapter, we'll discuss the basics of generic programming, get a little hands-on experience with delegates and events, and wrap up with an overview of exception handling.

# Pop quiz – leveling up

1. Which keyword would mark a variable as unmodifiable but requires an initial value?
2. How would you create an overloaded version of a base method?
3. What is the main difference between classes and interfaces?
4. How would you solve a namespace conflict in one of your classes?

# 11

# Introducing Stacks, Queues, and HashSets

In the last chapter, we revisited variables, types, and classes to see what they had to offer beyond the basic features introduced at the beginning of the book. In this chapter, we'll take a closer look at new collection types and learn about their intermediate-level capabilities. Remember, being a good programmer isn't about memorizing code, it's about choosing the right tool for the right job.

Each of the new collection types in this chapter has a specific purpose. For most scenarios where you need a collection of data, a list or array works just fine. However, when you need temporary storage or control over the order of collection elements, or more specifically, the order they are accessed, look to stacks and queues. When you need to perform operations that depend on every element in a collection to be unique, meaning not duplicated, look to HashSets.

Before you start on the code in the following section, let's lay out the topics you'll be learning about:

- Introducing stacks
- Peeking and popping elements
- Working with queues
- Adding, removing, and peeking elements
- Using HashSets
- Performing operations

# Introducing stacks

At its most basic level, a stack is a collection of elements of the same specified type. The length of a stack is variable, meaning it can change depending on how many elements it's holding. The important difference between a stack and a list or array is how the elements are stored. While lists or arrays store elements by index, stacks follow the **last-in-first-out** (**LIFO**) model, meaning the last element in the stack is the first accessible element. This is useful when you want to access elements in reverse order. You should note that they can store `null` and duplicate values. A helpful analogy is a stack of plates—the last plate you put on the stack is the first one you can easily get to. Once it's removed, the next-to-last plate you stacked is accessible, and so on.

> All the collection types in this chapter are a part of the `System.Collections.Generic` namespace, meaning you need to add the following code to the top of any file that you want to use them in:
>
> ```
> using System.Collections.Generic;
> ```

Now that you know what you're about to work with, let's take a look at the basic syntax for declaring stacks.

A stack variable declaration needs to meet the following requirements:

- The `Stack` keyword, its element type between left and right arrow characters, and a unique name
- The `new` keyword to initialize the stack in memory, followed by the `Stack` keyword and element type between arrow characters
- A pair of parentheses capped off by a semicolon

In blueprint form, it looks like this:

```
Stack<elementType> name = new Stack<elementType>();
```

Unlike the other collection types you've worked with, stacks can't be initialized with elements when they're created. Instead, all elements have to be added after the stack is created.

> C# supports a non-generic version of the stack type that doesn't require you to define the type of element in the stack:
>
> ```
> Stack myStack = new Stack();
> ```
>
> However, this is less safe and more costly than using the preceding generic version, so the generic version above is recommended. You can read more about Microsoft's recommendation at `https://github.com/dotnet/platform-compat/blob/master/docs/DE0006.md`.

Your next task is to create a stack of your own and get hands-on experience with working with its class methods.

To test this out, you're going to modify the existing item collection logic in *Hero Born* by using a stack to store possible loot that can be collected. A stack works nicely here because we won't have to worry about supplying indexes to get loot items, we can just get the last one added every time:

1. Open `GameBehavior.cs` and add in a new stack variable named `LootStack`:

   ```
   // 1
   public Stack<string> LootStack = new Stack<string>();
   ```

2. Update the `Initialize` method with the following code to add new items to the stack:

   ```
   public void Initialize()
   {
       _state = "Game Manager initialized..";
       _state.FancyDebug();
       Debug.Log(_state);

       // 2
       LootStack.Push("Sword of Doom");
       LootStack.Push("HP Boost");
       LootStack.Push("Golden Key");
       LootStack.Push("Pair of Winged Boots");
       LootStack.Push("Mythril Bracer");
   }
   ```

3. Add a new method to the bottom of the script to print out the stack information:

```
// 3
public void PrintLootReport()
{
    Debug.LogFormat("There are {0} random loot items waiting
       for you!", LootStack.Count);
}
```

4. Open `ItemBehavior.cs` and call `PrintLootReport` from the `GameManager` instance:

```
void OnCollisionEnter(Collision collision)
{
    if(collision.gameObject.name == "Player")
    {
        Destroy(this.transform.parent.gameObject);
        Debug.Log("Item collected!");

        GameManager.Items += 1;

        // 4
        GameManager.PrintLootReport();
    }
}
```

Breaking this down, it does the following:

1. Creates an empty stack with elements of type string to hold the loot items we'll add in next
2. Uses the `Push` method to add string elements to the stack (which are loot item names), increasing its size each time
3. Prints out the stack count whenever the `PrintLootReport` method is called
4. Calls `PrintLootReport` inside `OnCollisionEnter` every time an item is collected by the player, which we set up in earlier chapters with Collider components

Hit play in Unity, collect an item Prefab, and take a look at the new loot report that's printed out.

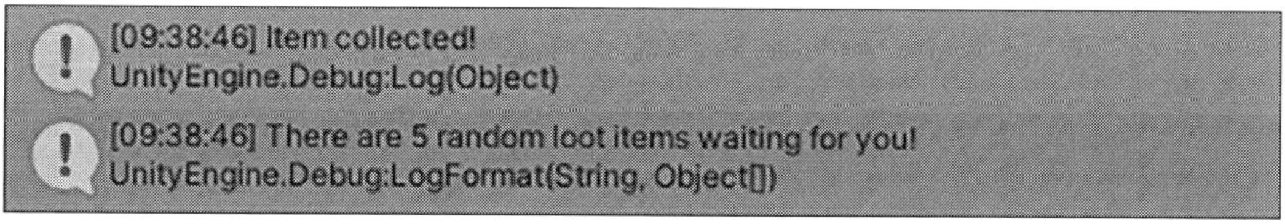


Figure 11.1: Output from using stacks

Now that you have a working stack holding all the game loot, you're ready to experiment with how items are accessed using the stack class's `Pop` and `Peek` methods.

# Popping and peeking

We've already talked about how stacks store elements using the LIFO method. Now, we need to look at how elements are accessed in a familiar but different collection type—by peeking and popping:

- The `Peek` method returns the next item on the stack without removing it, letting you "peek" at it without changing anything
- The `Pop` method returns and removes the next item on the stack, essentially "popping" it off and handing it to you

Both of these methods can be used by themselves or together depending on what you need. You'll get hands-on experience with both methods in the following section.

Your next task is to grab the last item added to `LootStack`. In our example, the last element is determined programmatically in the `Initialize` method, but you could always programmatically randomize the order the loot items were added to the stack in `Initialize`. Either way, update `PrintLootReport()` in `GameBehavior` with the following code:

```
public void PrintLootReport()
{
    // 1
    var currentItem = LootStack.Pop();

    // 2
    var nextItem = LootStack.Peek();
```

```
    // 3
    Debug.LogFormat("You got a {0}! You've got a good chance of finding
a {1} next!", currentItem, nextItem);

    Debug.LogFormat("There are {0} random loot items waiting for you!",
LootStack.Count);
}
```

Here's what's going on:

1. Calls `Pop` on `LootStack`, removes the next item on the stack, and stores it. Remember, stack elements are ordered by the LIFO model.
2. Calls `Peek` on `LootStack` and stores the next item on the stack without removing it.
3. Adds a new debug log to print out the item that was popped off and the next item on the stack.

You can see from the console that a **Mythril Bracer**, the last item added to the stack, was popped off first, followed by a **Pair of Winged Boots**, which was peeked at but not removed. You can also see that `LootStack` has four remaining elements that can be accessed:

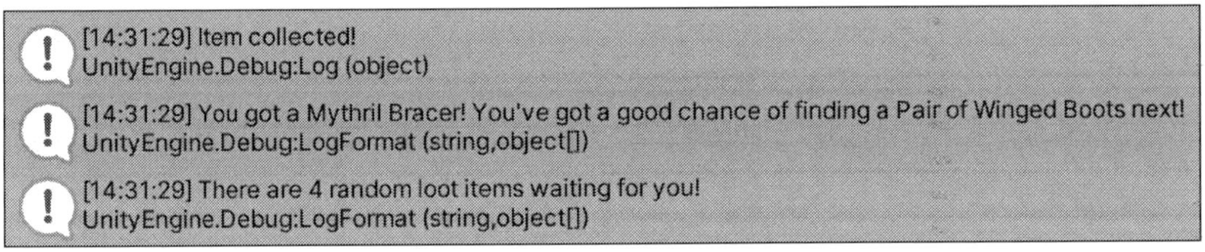


Figure 11.2: Output from popping and peeking on a stack

Our player can now pick up loot items in the reverse order that they were added to the stack. For instance, the first item picked up will always be a **Mythril Bracer**, followed by a **Pair of Winged Boots**, then a **Golden Key**, and so on.

Now that you know how to create, add, and query elements from a stack, we can move on to some common methods that you have access to through the stack class.

# Common methods

Each of the methods in this section are for example purposes only, they are not included in our game as we don't need the functionality.

First, you can use the `Clear` method to empty out or delete the entire contents of a stack:

```
// Empty the stack and reverting the count to 0
LootStack.Clear();
```

If you want to know whether an element exists in your stack, use the `Contains` method and specify the element you're looking for:

```
// Returns true for "Golden Key" item
var itemFound = LootStack.Contains("Golden Key");
```

If you need to copy the elements of a stack to an array, the `CopyTo` method will let you specify the destination and the starting index for the copy operation. This feature is helpful when you need to insert stack elements at a specific place in an array. Note that the array you want to copy the stack elements to must already exist:

```
// Creates a new array of the same length as LootStack
string[] CopiedLoot = new string[5];

/*
Copies the LootStack elements into the new CopiedLoot array at index 0.
The index parameter can be set to any index where you want the copied
elements to be stored
*/
LootStack.CopyTo(copiedLoot, 0);
```

If you need to convert a stack into an array, simply use the `ToArray()` method. This conversion creates a new array out of your stack, which is different than the `CopyTo()` method, which copies the stack elements to an existing array:

```
// Copies an existing stack to a new array
LootStack.ToArray();
```

> You can find the entire list of stack methods in the C# documentation at `https://docs.microsoft.com/dotnet/api/system.collections.generic.stack-1?view=netcore-3.1`.

That wraps up our introduction to stacks, but we're going to talk about its cousin, the queue, in the following section.

# Working with queues

Like stacks, queues are collections of elements or objects of the same type. The length of any queue is variable just like a stack, meaning its size changes as elements are added or removed. However, queues follow the **first-in-first-out** (**FIFO**) model, meaning the first element in the queue is the first accessible element. You should note that queues can store `null` and duplicate values but can't be initialized with elements when they're created. The code in this section is for example purposes only, and is not included in our game.

A queue variable declaration needs to have the following:

- The `Queue` keyword, its element type between left and right arrow characters, and a unique name
- The `new` keyword to initialize the queue in memory, followed by the `Queue` keyword and element type between arrow characters
- A pair of parentheses capped off by a semicolon

In blueprint form, a queue looks as follows:

```
Queue<elementType> name = new Queue<elementType>();
```

C# supports a non-generic version of the queue type that doesn't require you to define the type of element it stores:

```
Queue myQueue = new Queue();
```

However, this is less safe and more costly than using the preceding generic version. You can read more about Microsoft's recommendation at `https://github.com/dotnet/platform-compat/blob/master/docs/DE0006.md`.

An empty queue all by itself isn't all that useful; you want to be able to add, remove, and peek at its elements whenever you need, which is the topic of the following section.

# Adding, removing, and peeking

Since the `LootStack` variable in the previous sections could easily be a queue, we'll keep the following code out of our game scripts for efficiency. However, feel free to explore the differences, or similarities, of these classes in your own code.

To create a queue of string elements, use the following:

```
// Creates a new Queue of string values.
Queue<string> activePlayers = new Queue<string>();
```

To add elements to the queue, call the `Enqueue` method with the element you want to add:

```
// Adds string values to the end of the Queue.
activePlayers.Enqueue("Harrison");
activePlayers.Enqueue("Alex");
activePlayers.Enqueue("Haley");
```

To see the first element in the queue without removing it, use the `Peek` method:

```
// Returns the first element in the Queue without removing it.
var firstPlayer = activePlayers.Peek();
```

To return and remove the first element in the queue, use the `Dequeue` method:

```
// Returns and removes the first element in the Queue.
var firstPlayer = activePlayers.Dequeue();
```

Now that you know how to work with the basic features of a queue, feel free to explore the more intermediate and advanced methods that the queue class offers.

## Common methods

Queues and stacks share almost the exact same features, so we won't go over them a second time. You can find a complete list of methods and properties in the C# documentation at `https://docs.microsoft.com/dotnet/api/system.collections.generic.queue-1?view=netcore-3.1`.

Before closing out the chapter, let's take a look at the HashSet collection type and the mathematical operations it's uniquely suited for.

# Using HashSets

The last collection type we'll get our hands on in this chapter is the HashSet. This collection is very different from any other collection type that we've come across: it cannot store duplicate values and is not sorted, meaning its elements are not ordered in any way. Think of HashSets as dictionaries with just keys, instead of key-value pairs.

They can perform set operations and element lookups extremely fast, which we'll explore at the end of this section, and are best suited to situations where the element order and uniqueness are a top priority.

A HashSet variable declaration needs to meet the following requirements:

- The `HashSet` keyword, its element type between left and right arrow characters, and a unique name
- The `new` keyword to initialize the HashSet in memory, followed by the `HashSet` keyword and element type between arrow characters
- A pair of parentheses capped off by a semicolon

In blueprint form, it looks as follows:

```
HashSet<elementType> name = new HashSet<elementType>();
```

Unlike stacks and queues, you can initialize a HashSet with default values when declaring the variable:

```
HashSet<string> people = new HashSet<string>();

// OR

HashSet<string> people = new HashSet<string>() { "Joe", "Joan",
"Hank"};
```

To add elements, use the `Add` method and specify the new element:

```
people.Add("Walter");
people.Add("Evelyn");
```

To remove an element, call `Remove` and specify the element you want to delete from the HashSet:

```
people.Remove("Joe");
```

That's it for the easy stuff, and this should start to feel pretty familiar at this point in your programming journey. Set operations are where the HashSet collection really shines, which is the topic of the following section.

# Performing operations

Set operations need two things: a calling collection object and a passed-in collection object.

The calling collection object is the HashSet you want to modify based on which operation is used, while the passed-in collection object is used for comparison by the set operation. We'll get into this in more detail in the following code, but first, let's go over the three main set operations that crop up in programming scenarios the most often.

In the following definitions, `currentSet` refers to the HashSet calling an operation method and `specifiedSet` refers to the passed-in HashSet method parameter. The modified HashSet is always the current set:

```
currentSet.Operation(specifiedSet);
```

There are three main operations that we'll be working with in the rest of this section:

- `UnionWith` adds the elements of the current and specified sets together
- `IntersectWith` stores only the elements that are in both the current and specified sets
- `ExceptWith` subtracts the elements of the specified set from the current set

> There are two more groups of set operations that deal with subset and superset computations, but these are targeted at specific use cases that are beyond the scope of this chapter. You can find all the relevant information for these methods at `https://docs.microsoft.com/dotnet/api/system.collections.generic.hashset-1?view=netcore-3.1`.

Let's say we have two sets of player names—one for active players and one for inactive players:

```
HashSet<string> activePlayers = new HashSet<string>() { "Harrison",
"Alex", "Haley"};

HashSet<string> inactivePlayers = new HashSet<string>() { "Kelsey",
"Basel"};
```

We would use the `UnionWith()` operation to modify a set to include all the elements in both sets:

```
activePlayers.UnionWith(inactivePlayers);

/* activePlayers now stores "Harrison", "Alex", "Haley", "Kelsey",
"Basel"*/
```

Now, let's say we have two different sets—one for active players and one for premium players:

```
HashSet<string> activePlayers = new HashSet<string>() { "Harrison",
"Alex", "Haley"};

HashSet<string> premiumPlayers = new HashSet<string>() { "Haley",
"Basel"};
```

We would use the `IntersectWith()` operation to find any active players that are also premium members:

```
activePlayers.IntersectWith(premiumPlayers);
// activePlayers now stores only "Haley"
```

What if we wanted to find all active players that are not premium members? We would do the opposite of what we did with the `IntersectWith()` operation by calling `ExceptWith`:

```
HashSet<string> activePlayers = new HashSet<string>() { "Harrison",
"Alex", "Haley"};

HashSet<string> premiumPlayers = new HashSet<string>() { "Haley",
  "Basel"};

activePlayers.ExceptWith(premiumPlayers);
// activePlayers now stores "Harrison" and "Alex" but removed "Haley"
```

> Notice that I'm using brand-new instances of the two example sets for each operation because the current set is modified after each operation is executed. If you keep using the same sets throughout, you will get different results.

Now that you've learned how to perform fast mathematical operations with HashSets, it's time to close our chapter and drive home what we've learned.

# Intermediate collections roundup

Before you move on to the summary and the next chapter, let's drive home some key points from what we've just learned. Topics that don't always have a 1-to-1 relationship with the actual game prototype we're building need a little extra love sometimes.

The one question I'm sure you're asking yourself at this point is: why use any of these other collection types when I could just use lists for everything? And that's a perfectly valid question. The easy answer is that stacks, queues, and HashSets offer better performance than lists when applied in the correct circumstances. For example, when you need to store items in a specific order, and access them in a specific order, a stack would be more efficient than a list.

The more complicated answer is that using different collection types enforces how your code is allowed to interact with them and their elements. This is a mark of good code design, as it removes any ambiguity on how you're planning to use a collection. With lists everywhere, things get confusing when you don't remember what functions you're asking them to perform.

As with everything we've learned in this book, it's always best to use the right tool for the job at hand. More importantly, you need to have different tools available for that to be an option.

# Summary

Congratulations, you're almost at the finish line! In this chapter, you learned about three new collection types, and how they can be used in different situations.

Stacks are great if you want to access your collection elements in the reverse order that they were added, queues are your ticket if you want to access your elements in sequential order, and both are ideal for temporary storage. The important difference between these collection types and lists or arrays is how they can be accessed with popping and peeking operations. Lastly, you learned about the almighty HashSet and its performance-based mathematical set operations. In situations where you need to work with unique values and perform additions, comparisons, or subtractions on large collections, these are key.

In the next chapter, you'll be taken a little deeper into the intermediate world of C# with delegates, generics, and more as you approach the end of this book. Even after all you've learned, the last page is still just the beginning of another journey.

# Pop quiz – intermediate collections

1. Which collection type stores its elements using the LIFO model?
2. Which method lets you query the next element in a stack without removing it?
3. Can stacks and queues store `null` values?
4. How would you subtract one HashSet from another?

# 12

# Saving, Loading, and Serializing Data

Every game you've ever played works with data, whether it's your player stats, game progress, or online multiplayer scoreboards. Your favorite game also manages internal data, meaning the programmers used hardcoded information to build levels, keep track of enemy stats, and write helpful utilities. In other words, data is everywhere.

In this chapter, we're going to start with how both C# and Unity handle the filesystem on your computer, and move on to reading, writing, and serializing our game data. Our focus is on working with the three most common data formats you'll likely come across: text files, XML, and JSON.

By the end of this chapter, you'll have a foundational understanding of your computer's filesystem, data formats, and basic read-write functionality. This will be the foundation you build your game data on, creating a more enriching and engaging experience for your players. You'll also be in a good position to start thinking about what game data is important enough to save, and how your C# classes and objects will look in different data formats.

Along the way, we will cover the following topics:

- Introducing text, XML, and JSON formats
- Understanding the filesystem
- Working with different stream types
- Reading and writing game data
- Serializing objects

# Introducing data formats

Data can take different forms in programming, but the three formats you should be familiar with at the beginning of your data journey are:

- **Text**, which is what you're reading right now
- **XML (Extensible Markup Language)**, which is a way of encoding document information so it's readable for you and a computer
- **JSON (JavaScript Object Notation)**, which is a human-readable text format made up of attribute-value pairs and arrays

Each of these data formats has its own strengths and drawbacks, as well as applications in programming. For instance, text is generally used to store simpler, non-hierarchical, or nested information. XML is better at storing information in a document format, while JSON has a more diverse range of capabilities, specifically with database information and server communication with applications.

> You can find more information about XML at `https://www.xml.com` and JSON at `https://www.json.org`.

Data is a big topic in any programming language, so let's start off by breaking down what XML and JSON formats actually look like in the next two sections.

# Breaking down XML

A typical XML file has a standardized format. Each element of the XML document has an opening (<element_name>), a closing tag (</element_name>), and supports tag attributes (<element_name attribute= "attribute_name"></element_name>). A basic file will start with the version and encoding being used, then the starting or root element, followed by a list of element items, and finally the closing element. As a blueprint, it would look like this:

```
<?xml version="1.0" encoding="utf-8"?>
<root_element>
    <element_item>[Information goes here]</element_item>
    <element_item>[Information goes here]</element_item>
    <element_item>[Information goes here]</element_item>
</root_element>
```

XML data can also store more complex objects by using child elements. For example, we'll be turning a list of weapons into XML using the `Weapon` class we wrote earlier in the book. Since each weapon has properties for its name and damage value, that will look like this:

```
// 1
<?xml version="1.0"?>
// 2
<ArrayOfWeapon>
     // 3
    <Weapon>
     // 4
        <name>Sword of Doom</name>
        <damage>100</damage>
     // 5
    </Weapon>
    <Weapon>
        <name>Butterfly knives</name>
        <damage>25</damage>
    </Weapon>
    <Weapon>
        <name>Brass Knuckles</name>
        <damage>15</damage>
    </Weapon>
// 6
</ArrayOfWeapon>
```

Let's break down the example above to make sure we've got it right:

1. The XML document starts with the version being used
2. The root element is declared with an opening tag named `ArrayOfWeapon`, which will hold all our element items
3. A weapon item is created with an opening tag named `Weapon`
4. Its child properties are added with opening and closing tags on a single line for `name` and `damage`
5. The weapon item is closed, and two more weapon items are added
6. The array is closed, marking the end of the document

The good news is our application doesn't have to manually write our data in this format. C# has an entire library of classes and methods to help us translate simple text and class objects directly into XML.

We'll dive into practical code examples a little later on, but first we need to understand how JSON works.

# Breaking down JSON

The JSON data format is similar to XML, but without the tags. Instead, everything is based on attribute-value pairs, like the **Dictionary** collection type we worked with back in *Chapter 4, Control Flow and Collection Types*. Each JSON document starts with a parent dictionary that holds as many attribute-value pairs as you need. Dictionaries use open and closed curly braces ( `{ }` ), a colon separates each attribute and value, and each attribute-value pair is separated by a comma:

```
// Parent dictionary for the entire file
{
    // List of attribute-value pairs where you store your data
    "attribute_name": value,
    "attribute_name": value
}
```

JSON can also have child or nested structures by setting the value of an attribute-value pair to an array of attribute-value pairs. For instance, if we want to store a weapon, it would look like this:

```
// Parent dictionary
{
    // Weapon attribute with its value set to an child dictionary
    "weapon": {
          // Attribute-value pairs with weapon data
          "name": "Sword of Doom",
          "damage": 100
    }
}
```

Finally, JSON data is often made up of lists, or arrays, or objects. Continuing our example, if we wanted to store a list of all the weapons our player could choose, we would use a pair of square brackets to denote an array:

```
// Parent dictionary
{
    // List of weapon attribute set to an array of weapon objects
    "weapons": [
```

```
        // Each weapon object stored as its own dictionary
        {
            "name": "Sword of Doom",
            "damage": 100
        },
        {
            "name": "Butterfly knives",
            "damage": 25
        },
        {
            "name": "Brass Knuckles",
            "damage": 15
        }
    ]
}
```

You can mix and match any of these techniques to store any kind of complex data you need, which is one of JSON's main strengths. But just like with XML, don't be overtaken by the new syntax - C# and Unity both have helper classes and methods to translate text and class objects into JSON without us having to do any heavy lifting. Reading XML and JSON is sort of like learning a new language—the more you use it the more familiar it becomes. Soon it'll be second nature!

Now that we've dipped our toes into data formatting basics, we can start talking about how the filesystem on your computer works and what properties we can access from our C# code.

# Understanding the filesystem

When we say filesystem, we're talking about something you're already familiar with - how files and folders are created, organized, and stored on your computer. When you create a new folder on your computer, you can name it and put files or other folders inside it. It's also represented by an icon, which is both a visual cue and a way to drag, drop, and move it anywhere you like.

Everything you can do on your desktop you can do in code. All you need is the name of the folder, or directory as it's called, and a location to store it. Anytime you want to add a file or subfolder, you reference the parent directory and add your new content.

To drive the filesystem home, let's start building out the `DataManager` class:

1. Right-click in the **Hierarchy** and choose **Create Empty**, then name it **Data_Manager**:

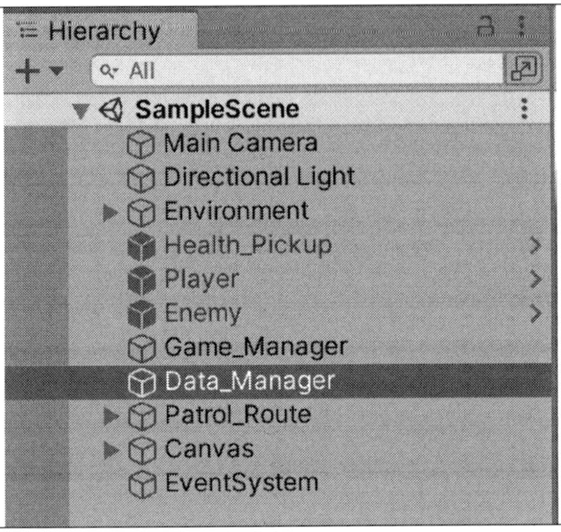


Figure 12.1: Data_Manager in the Hierarchy

2. Select the **Data_Manager** object in the **Hierarchy** and drag the `DataManager` script we created in *Chapter 10, Revisiting Types, Methods, and Classes*, from the **Scripts** folder into the **Inspector**:

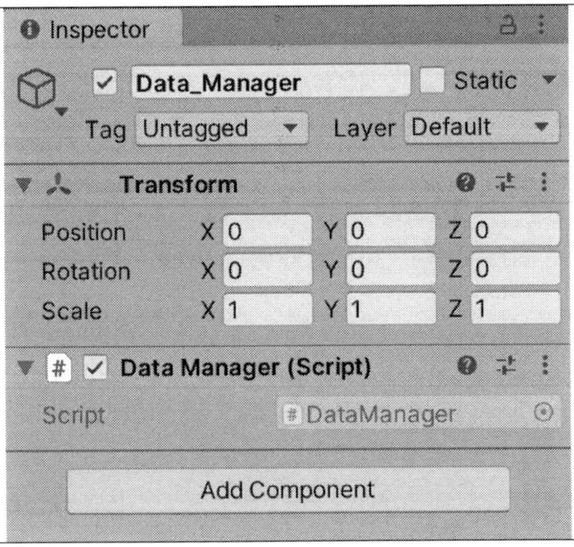


Figure 12.2: Data_Manager in the Inspector

3. Open the `DataManager` script and update it with the following code to print out a few filesystem properties:

```
using System.Collections;
using System.Collections.Generic;
using UnityEngine;

// 1
using System.IO;

public class DataManager : MonoBehaviour, IManager
{
    // ... No variable changes needed ...

    public void Initialize()
    {
        _state = "Data Manager initialized..";
        Debug.Log(_state);

        // 2
        FilesystemInfo();
    }

    public void FilesystemInfo()
    {
        // 3
        Debug.LogFormat("Path separator character: {0}",
          Path.PathSeparator);

        Debug.LogFormat("Directory separator character: {0}",
          Path.DirectorySeparatorChar);

        Debug.LogFormat("Current directory: {0}",
          Directory.GetCurrentDirectory());

        Debug.LogFormat("Temporary path: {0}",
          Path.GetTempPath());
    }
}
```

Let's break down the code:

1. First, we add the `System.IO` namespace, which has all the classes and methods we need to work with the filesystem.
2. We call the `FilesystemInfo` method we create in the next step.
3. We create the `FilesystemInfo` method to print out a few filesystem properties. Every operating system handles its filesystem paths differently—a path is the location of a directory or file written in a string. On Macs:
    - Paths are separated by a colon (`:`)
    - Directories are separated by a forward slash (`/`)
    - The current directory path is where the *Hero Born* project is stored
    - The temporary path is the location of your filesystem's temporary folder

If you're on other platforms and operating systems, make sure to check the `Path` and `Directory` methods for yourself before working with the filesystem.

Run the game and take a look at the output:

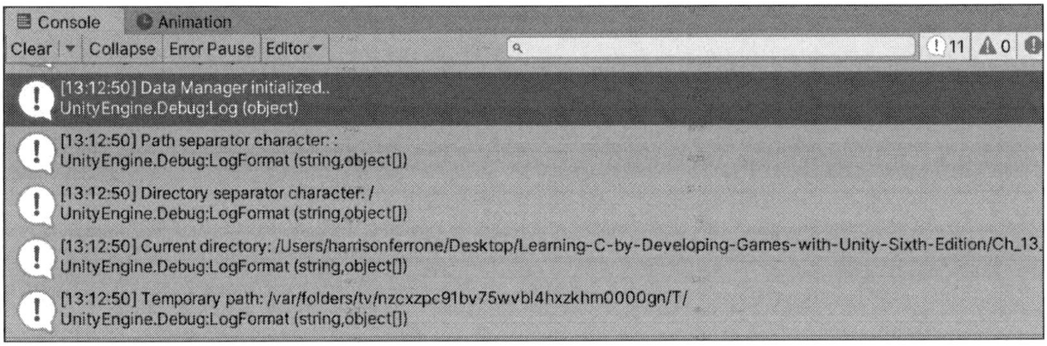


Figure 12.3: Console messages from Data Manager

The `Path` and `Directory` classes are the foundation we're going to be building on to store our data in the following sections. However, they're both large classes, so I encourage you to look into their documentation as you continue your data journey.

> You can find more documentation for the Path class at `https://docs.microsoft.com/en-us/dotnet/api/system.io.path` and the Directory class at `https://docs.microsoft.com/en-us/dotnet/api/system.io.directory`.

Now that we have a simple example of filesystem properties printed out in our `DataManager` script, we can create a filesystem path to the location where we want to save our data.

# Working with asset paths

In a purely C# application, you would have to choose what folder to save your files in and write out the folder path in a string. However, Unity provides a handy pre-configured path as part of the `Application` class where you can store persistent game data. Persistent data means the information is saved and kept each time the program runs, which makes it ideal for this kind of player information.

> It's important to know that the path to Unity's persistent data directory is cross-platform, meaning that it's different whether you're building a game for iOS, Android, Windows, and more. You can find out more information in the Unity documentation at `https://docs.unity3d.com/ScriptReference/Application-persistentDataPath.html`.

The only update we need to make to `DataManager` is creating a private variable to hold our path string. We're making this private because we don't want any other script to be able to access or change the value. That way, `DataManager` is responsible for all data-related logic and nothing else.

Add the following variable to `DataManager.cs`:

```
public class DataManager : MonoBehaviour, IManager
{
    // ... No other variable changes needed ...

    // 1
    private string _dataPath;

    // 2
    void Awake()
    {
        _dataPath = Application.persistentDataPath + "/Player_Data/";

        Debug.Log(_dataPath);
    }

    // ... No other changes needed ...
}
```

Let's break down our code update:

1. We created a private variable to hold the data path string
2. We set the data path string to the application's `persistentDataPath` value, added a new folder name called **Player_Data** using open and closed forward slashes, and printed out the complete path:
    - It's important to note that `Application.persistentDataPath` can only be used in a `MonoBehaviour` method like `Awake()`, `Start()`, `Update()`, and so on and the game needs to be running for Unity to return a valid path.

Figure 12.4: File path for Unity persistent data files

Since I'm using a Mac, my persistent data folder is nested inside my `/Users` folder. Remember to check out `https://docs.unity3d.com/ScriptReference/Application-persistentDataPath.html` to find out where your data is stored if you're using a different device.

When you're not working with a predefined asset path like Unity's persistent data directory, C# has a handy method called `Combine` in the `Path` class for automatically configuring path variables. The `Combine()` method can take up to four strings as input parameters or an array of strings representing the path components. For example, a path to your `User` directory might look like:

```
var path = Path.Combine("/Users", "hferrone", "Chapter_12");
```

This takes care of any potential cross-platform issues with separating characters and back or forward slashes in paths and directories.

Now that we have a path to store our data, let's create a new directory, or folder, in the filesystem. This will let us store our data securely and between game runs, as opposed to temporary storage where it would be deleted or overwritten.

# Creating and deleting directories

Creating a new directory folder is straightforward—we check to see if one already exists with the same name at the same path, and if not, we tell C# to create it for us. Everyone has their own ways of dealing with duplicates in their files and folders, so we'll be repeating a fair bit of duplicate checking code in the rest of the chapter.

I'd still recommend following the **DRY** (**Don't Repeat Yourself**) principle in real-world applications; the duplicate checking code is only repeated here to make the examples complete and easy to understand:

1. Add the following method to `DataManager`:

```
public void NewDirectory()
{
    // 1
    if(Directory.Exists(_dataPath))
    {
        // 2
        Debug.Log("Directory already exists...");
        return;
    }

    // 3
    Directory.CreateDirectory(_dataPath);
    Debug.Log("New directory created!");
}
```

2. Call the new method inside `Initialize()`:

```
public void Initialize()
{
    _state = "Data Manager initialized..";
    Debug.Log(_state);

    NewDirectory();
}
```

Let's break down what we did:

1. First, we check if the directory folder already exists using the path we created in the last step
2. If it's already been created, we send ourselves a message in the console and use the `return` keyword to exit the method without going any further
3. If the directory folder doesn't exist, we pass the `CreateDirectory()` method our data path and log that it's been created

Run the game and make sure that you see the right debug logs in the console, as well as the new directory folder in your persistent data folder.

If you can't find it, use the `_dataPath` value we printed out in the previous step.

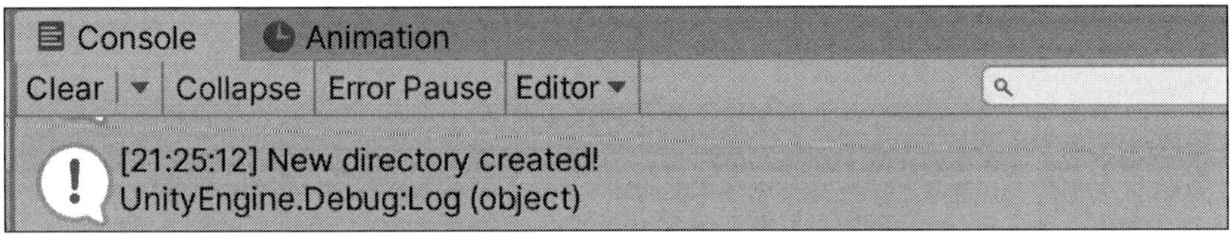


Figure 12.5: Console message for new directory creation

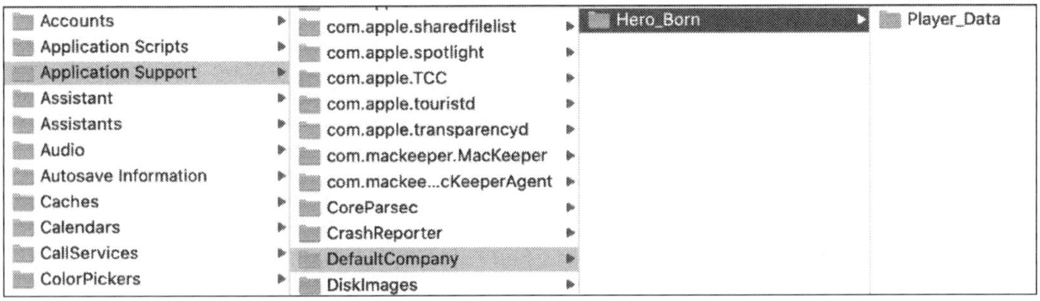


Figure 12.6: New directory created on the desktop

If you run the game a second time, no duplicate directory folder will be created, which is exactly the kind of safe code we want.

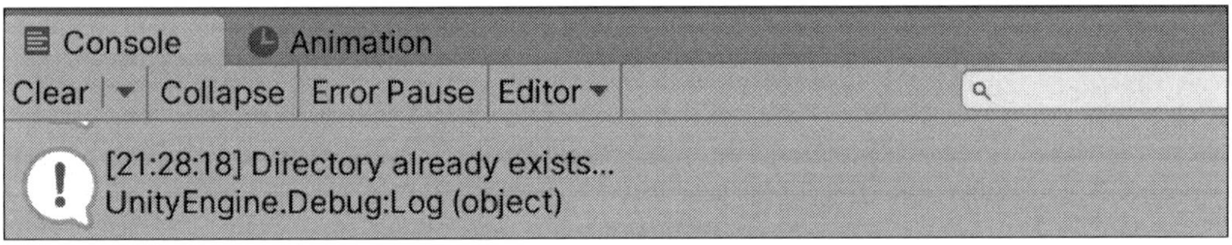


Figure 12.7: Console message for duplicate directory folders

Deleting a directory is very similar to how we created it – we check if it exists, then we use the `Directory` class to delete whatever folder is at the path we pass in.

Add the following method to `DataManager`:

```
public void DeleteDirectory()
{
    // 1
    if(!Directory.Exists(_dataPath))
    {
        // 2
        Debug.Log("Directory doesn't exist or has already been
```

```
deleted...");

            return;
        }

        // 3
        Directory.Delete(_dataPath, true);
        Debug.Log("Directory successfully deleted!");
    }
```

Since we want to keep the directory we just created, you don't have to call this function right now. However, if you want to try it out all you need to do is replace `NewDirectory()` with `DeleteDirectory()` in the `Initialize()` function.

An empty directory folder isn't super useful, so let's create our first text file and save it in our new location.

# Creating, updating, and deleting files

Working with files is similar to creating and deleting a directory, so we already have the basic building blocks we need. To make sure we don't duplicate data, we'll check if the file already exists, and if not, we'll create a new one in our new directory folder.

> We'll be working with the `File` class for this section, which has a ton of helpful methods to help us implement our features. You can find the entire list at `https://docs.microsoft.com/en-us/dotnet/api/system.io.file`.

An important point to drive home about files before we start is that they need to be opened before you can add text, and they need to be closed after you're finished. If you don't close the file you're programmatically working with, it will stay open in the program's memory. This both uses computation power for something you're not actively editing and can create potential memory leaks. More on them later in the chapter.

> We're going to be writing individual methods for each action we want to perform (create, update, and delete). We're also going to check if the files we're working with exist or not in each case, which is repetitive. I've structured this part of the book so you can get a solid grasp of each of the procedures. However, you can absolutely combine them into more economical methods after you've learned the basics.

Take the following steps:

1. Add a new private string path for the new text file and set its value in `Awake`:

```
private string _dataPath;
private string _textFile;

void Awake()
{
    _dataPath = Application.persistentDataPath + "/Player_Data/";

    Debug.Log(_dataPath);

    _textFile = _dataPath + "Save_Data.txt";
}
```

2. Add a new method to `DataManager`:

```
public void NewTextFile()
{
    // 1
    if (File.Exists(_textFile))
    {
        Debug.Log("File already exists...");
        return;
    }

    // 2
    File.WriteAllText(_textFile, "<SAVE DATA>\n\n");

    // 3
    Debug.Log("New file created!");
}
```

3. Call the new method in `Initialize()`:

```
public void Initialize()
{
    _state = "Data Manager initialized..";
    Debug.Log(_state);

    FilesystemInfo();
    NewDirectory();
    NewTextFile();
}
```

Let's break down our new code:

1. We check if the file already exists, and if it does we `return` out of the method to avoid duplicates:
    - It's worth noting that this approach works well for new files that aren't going to be changed. We'll cover updating and overwriting data to files in the next exercise.
2. We use the `WriteAllText()` method because it does everything we need all in one:
    - A new file is created using our `_textFile` path
    - We add a title string that says `<SAVE DATA>` and add two new lines with the `\n` characters
    - Then the file is closed for us automatically
3. We print out a log message to let us know everything went smoothly

When you play the game now, you'll see the debug log in the console and the new text file in your persistent data folder location:

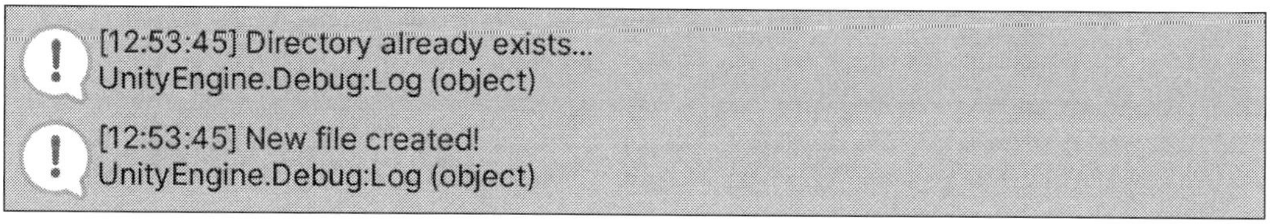


Figure 12.8: Console messages for new file creation

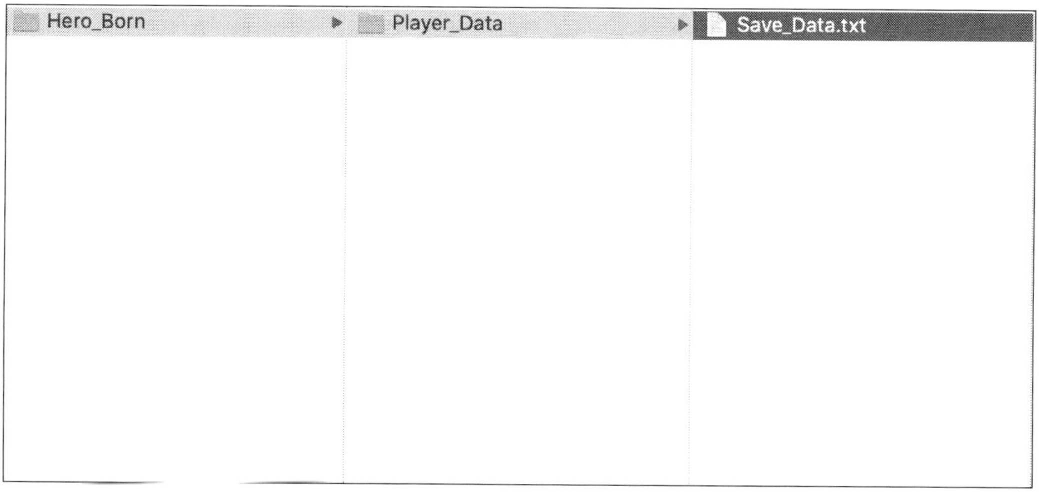


Figure 12.9: New file created on desktop

To update our new text file, we'll do a similar set of operations. It's always nice to know when a new game is started, so your next task is to add a method to write that information to our save data file:

1. Add a new `using` directive to the top of `DataManager`:

```
using System.Collections;
using System.Collections.Generic;
using UnityEngine;
using System.IO;
using System;
```

2. Add a new method to `DataManager`:

```
public void UpdateTextFile()
{
    // 1
    if (!File.Exists(_textFile))
    {
        Debug.Log("File doesn't exist...");
        return;
    }

    // 2
    File.AppendAllText(_textFile, $"Game started: {DateTime.
Now}\n");

    // 3
    Debug.Log("File updated successfully!");
}
```

3. Call the new method in `Initialize()`:

```
public void Initialize()
{
    _state = "Data Manager initialized..";
    Debug.Log(_state);

    FilesystemInfo();
    NewDirectory();
    NewTextFile();
    UpdateTextFile();
}
```

Let's break down the above code:

1. If the file exists, we don't want to duplicate it so we just exit out of the method without any further action
2. If the file does exist, we use another all-in-one method called `AppendAllText()` to add the game's start time:
    - This method opens the file
    - It adds a new line of text that's passed in as a method parameter
    - It closes the file
3. Print out a log message to let us know everything went smoothly

Play the game again and you'll see our console message and a new line in our text file with the new game's date and time:

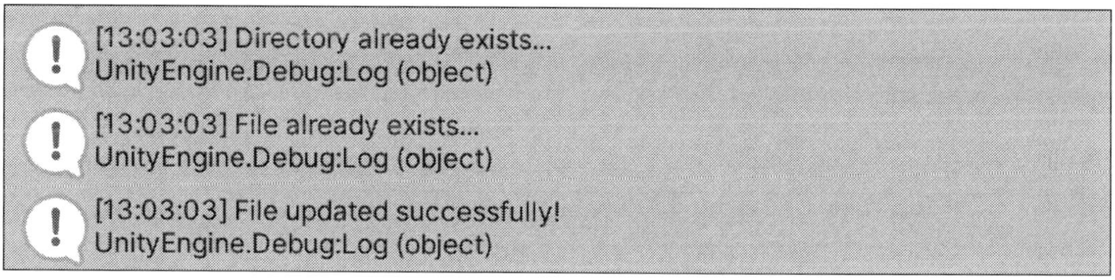


Figure 12.10: Console messages for updating the text file

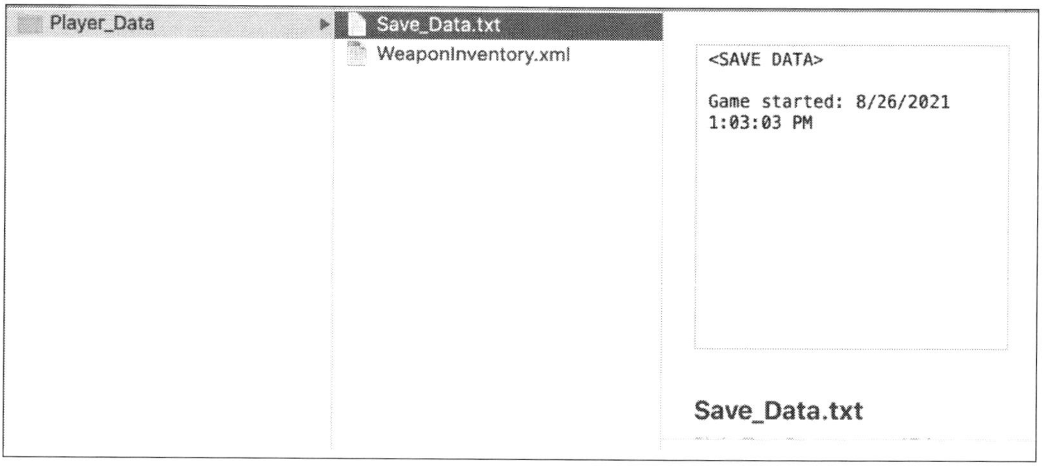


Figure 12.11: Text file data updated

In order to read our new file data, we need a method to grab all the file's text and hand it back to us in a string. Luckily, the `File` class has methods to do just that:

1. Add a new method to `DataManager`:

```
// 1
public void ReadFromFile(string filename)
{
    // 2
    if (!File.Exists(filename))
    {
        Debug.Log("File doesn't exist...");
        return;
    }

    // 3
    Debug.Log(File.ReadAllText(filename));
}
```

2. Call the new method in `Initialize()` and pass in the `_textFile` as a parameter:

```
public void Initialize()
{
    _state = "Data Manager initialized..";
    Debug.Log(_state);

    FilesystemInfo();
    NewDirectory();
    NewTextFile();
    UpdateTextFile();
    ReadFromFile(_textFile);
}
```

Let's break down the new method's code below:

1. We create a new method that takes in a string parameter for the file we want to read
2. If the file doesn't exist, there's no action needed so we exit out of the method
3. We use the `ReadAllText()` method to get all the file's text data as a string and print it out to the console

Play the game and you'll see a console message with our previous save and a new one!

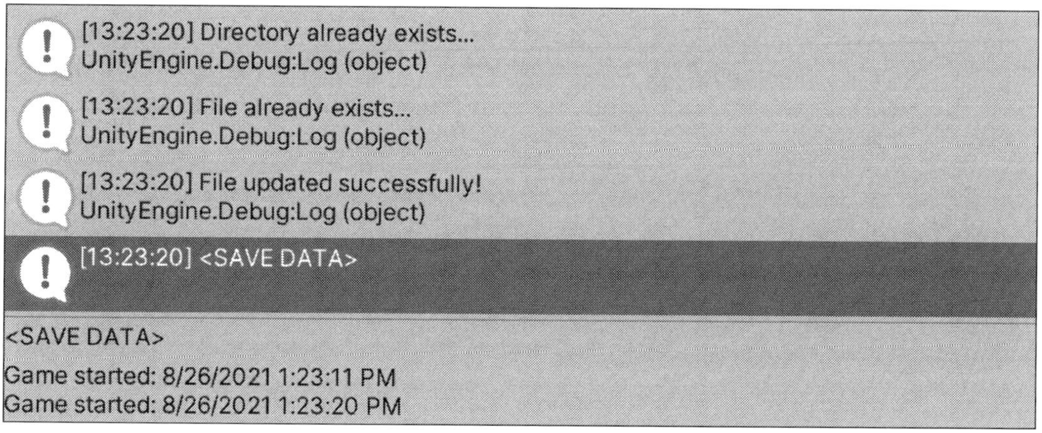


Figure 12.12: Console message with saved text data read from file

Lastly, let's add a method to delete our text file if we wanted. We're not actually going to use this method, as we want to keep our text file as is, but you can always try it out for yourself:

```
public void DeleteFile(string filename)
{
    if (!File.Exists(filename))
    {
        Debug.Log("File doesn't exist or has already been deleted...");

        return;
    }

    File.Delete(_textFile);
    Debug.Log("File successfully deleted!");
}
```

Now that we've dipped our toes a little deeper into the filesystem waters, it's time to talk about a slightly upgraded way of working with information — data streams!

# Working with streams

So far, we've been letting the `File` class do all of the heavy lifting with our data. What we haven't talked about is how the `File` class, or any other class that deals with reading and writing data, does that work under the hood.

For computers, data is made up of bytes. Think of bytes as the computer's atoms, they make up everything—there's even a C# `byte` type. When we read, write, or update a file, our data is converted into an array of bytes, which are then streamed to or from the file using a `Stream`. The data stream is responsible for carrying the data as a sequence of bytes to or from a file, acting as a translator or intermediary for us between our game application and the data files themselves.

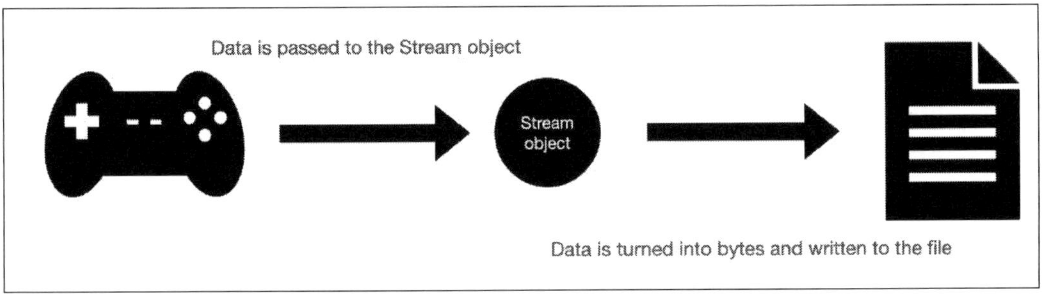


Figure 12.13: Diagram of streaming data to a file

The `File` class uses `Stream` objects for us automatically, and there are different `Stream` subclasses for different functionality:

- Use a `FileStream` to read and write data to your files
- Use a `MemoryStream` to read and write data to memory
- Use a `NetworkStream` to read and write data to other networked computers
- Use a `GZipStream` to compress data for easier storage and downloading

In the coming sections, we'll get into managing stream resources, using helper classes called `StreamReader` and `StreamWriter` to create, read, update, and delete files. You'll also learn how to format XML more easily using the `XmlWriter` class.

# Managing your Stream resources

One important topic we haven't talked about yet is resource allocation. What that means is some processes in your code will put computing power and memory on a sort of layaway plan where you can't touch it. These processes will wait until you explicitly tell your program or game to close and return the layaway resources to you so you're back to full power. Streams are one such process, and they need to be closed after you're done using them. If you don't properly close your streams, your program will keep using those resources even though you're not.

Luckily, C# has a handy interface called `IDisposable` that all `Stream` classes implement. This interface only has one method, `Dispose()`, which tells the stream when to give you back the resources it's been using.

You don't have to worry too much about this, as we'll cover an automatic way to make sure your streams are always closed correctly. Resource management is just a good programming concept to understand.

We'll be using a `FileStream` for the rest of the chapter, but we'll be doing so with convenience classes called `StreamWriter` and `StreamReader`. These classes leave out the manual conversion of data to bytes, but still use `FileStream` objects themselves.

# Using a StreamWriter and StreamReader

Both the `StreamWriter` and `StreamReader` classes serve as helpers for using objects belonging to `FileStream` to write and read text data to a specific file. These classes are a big help because they create, open, and return a stream you can use with minimal boilerplate code. The example code we've covered so far is fine for small data files, but streams are the way to go if you're dealing with large and complex data objects.

All we need is the name of the file we want to write to or read from and we're all set. Your next task is to use a stream to write text to a new file:

1. Add a new private string path for the new streaming text file and set its value in `Awake()`:

```
private string _dataPath;
private string _textFile;
private string _streamingTextFile;

void Awake()
{
    _dataPath = Application.persistentDataPath + "/Player_
Data/";
    Debug.Log(_dataPath);

    _textFile = _dataPath + "Save_Data.txt";
    _streamingTextFile = _dataPath + "Streaming_Save_Data.txt";
}
```

2. Add a new method to `DataManager`:

```
public void WriteToStream(string filename)
{
    // 1
    if (!File.Exists(filename))
    {
        // 2
```

```
        StreamWriter newStream = File.CreateText(filename);

        // 3
        newStream.WriteLine("<Save Data> for HERO BORN \n\n");
        newStream.Close();
        Debug.Log("New file created with StreamWriter!");
    }

    // 4
    StreamWriter streamWriter = File.AppendText(filename);

    // 5
    streamWriter.WriteLine("Game ended: " + DateTime.Now);
    streamWriter.Close();
    Debug.Log("File contents updated with StreamWriter!");
}
```

3. Delete or comment out the methods in `Initialize()` that we used in the previous section and add in our new code:

```
public void Initialize()
{
    _state = "Data Manager initialized..";
    Debug.Log(_state);

    FilesystemInfo();
    NewDirectory();
    WriteToStream(_streamingTextFile);
}
```

Let's break down the new method in the above code:

1. First, we check if the file doesn't exist
2. If the file hasn't been created yet, we add a new `StreamWriter` instance called `newStream`, which uses the `CreateText()` method to create and open the new file
3. Once the file is open, we use the `WriteLine()` method to add a header, close the stream, and print out a debug message
4. If the file already exists and we just want to update it, we grab our file through a new `StreamWriter` instance using the `AppendText()` method so our existing data doesn't get overwritten

5. Finally, we write a new line with our game data, close the stream, and print out a debug message:

Figure 12.14: Console messages for writing and updating text with a stream

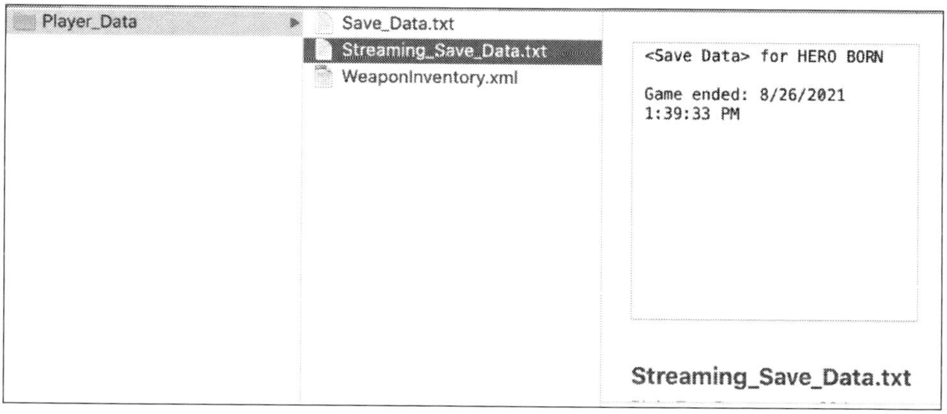


Figure 12.15: New file created and updated with a stream

Reading from a stream is almost exactly like the `ReadFromFile()` method we created in the last section. The only difference is that we'll use a `StreamReader` instance to open and read the information. Again, you want to use streams when you're dealing with big data files or complex objects instead of manually creating and writing to files with the `File` class:

1. Add a new method to `DataManager`:

```
public void ReadFromStream(string filename)
{
    // 1
    if (!File.Exists(filename))
    {
        Debug.Log("File doesn't exist...");
        return;
    }

    // 2
```

```
        StreamReader streamReader = new StreamReader(filename);
        Debug.Log(streamReader.ReadToEnd());
    }
```

2. Call the new method in `Initialize()` and pass in the `_streamingTextFile` as a parameter:

```
    public void Initialize()
    {
        _state = "Data Manager initialized..";
        Debug.Log(_state);

        FilesystemInfo();
        NewDirectory();
        WriteToStream(_streamingTextFile);
        ReadFromStream(_streamingTextFile);
    }
```

Let's break down our new code:

1. First, we check if the file doesn't exist, and if it doesn't then we print out a console message and exit the method
2. If the file does exist, we create a new `StreamReader` instance with the name of the file we want to access and print out the entire contents using the `ReadToEnd` method:

Figure 12.16: Console printing out saved data read from a stream

As you'll start to notice, a lot of our code is starting to look the same. The only difference is our use of stream classes to do the actual reading-writing work. However, it's important to keep in mind how different use cases will determine which route you take. Refer back to the beginning of this section to review how each stream type is different.

So far, we've covered the basic features of a **CRUD** (**Creating**, **Reading**, **Updating**, **and Deleting**) application using text files. But text files aren't the only data format you'll be using in C# games and applications. You're likely to see lots of XML and JSON in the wild once you start working with databases and your own complex data structures, which text can't compare to in efficiency or storage.

In the next section, we'll work with some basic XML data, then talk about an easier way to manage streams.

# Creating an XMLWriter

Sometimes you won't just have plain old text to write and read from a file. Your project might require XML-formatted documents, in which case you'll need to know how to use a regular `FileStream` to save and load XML data.

Writing XML data to a file isn't all that different from what we've been doing with text and streams. The only difference is we'll explicitly create a `FileStream` and use it to create an instance of an `XmlWriter`. Think of the `XmlWriter` class as a wrapper that takes our data stream, applies XML formatting, and spits out our information as an XML file. Once we have that, we can structure the document in the proper XML format using methods from the `XmlWriter` class and close the file.

Your next task is to create a file path for a new XML document and add the ability to write XML data to that file using the `DataManager` class:

1. Add the highlighted `using` directive to the top of the `DataManager` class:

```
using System.Collections;
using System.Collections.Generic;
using UnityEngine;
using System.IO;
using System;
using System.Xml;
```

2. Add a new private string path for the new XML file and set its value in `Awake()`:

```
// ... No other variable changes needed ...

private string _xmlLevelProgress;

void Awake()
{
     // ... No other changes needed ...
     _xmlLevelProgress = _dataPath + "Progress_Data.xml";
}
```

3. Add a new method at the bottom of the `DataManager` class:

```
public void WriteToXML(string filename)
{
    // 1
    if (!File.Exists(filename))
    {
        // 2
        FileStream xmlStream = File.Create(filename);

        // 3
        XmlWriter xmlWriter = XmlWriter.Create(xmlStream);

        // 4
        xmlWriter.WriteStartDocument();

        // 5
        xmlWriter.WriteStartElement("level_progress");

        // 6
        for (int i = 1; i < 5; i++)
        {
            xmlWriter.WriteElementString("level", "Level-" + i);
        }

        // 7
        xmlWriter.WriteEndElement();

        // 8
        xmlWriter.Close();
        xmlStream.Close();
    }
}
```

4. Call the new method in `Initialize()` and pass in `_xmlLevelProgress` as a parameter:

```
public void Initialize()
{
    _state = "Data Manager initialized..";
    Debug.Log(_state);

    FilesystemInfo();
```

```
        NewDirectory();
        WriteToXML(_xmlLevelProgress);
    }
```

Let's break down our XML writing method:

1. First, we check if the file already exists
2. If the file doesn't exist, we create a new `FileStream` using the new path variable we created
3. We then create a new `XmlWriter` instance and pass it our new `FileStream`
4. Next, we use the `WriteStartDocument` method to specify XML version 1.0
5. Then we call the `WriteStartElement` method to add the opening root element tag named `level_progress`
6. Now we can add individual elements to our document using the `WriteElementString` method, passing in `level` as the element tag and the level number using a `for` loop and its index value of `i`
7. To close the document, we use the `WriteEndElement` method to add a closing `level` tag
8. Finally, we close the writer and stream to release the stream resources we've been using

If you run the game now, you'll see a new `.xml` file in our **Player_Data** folder with the level progress information:

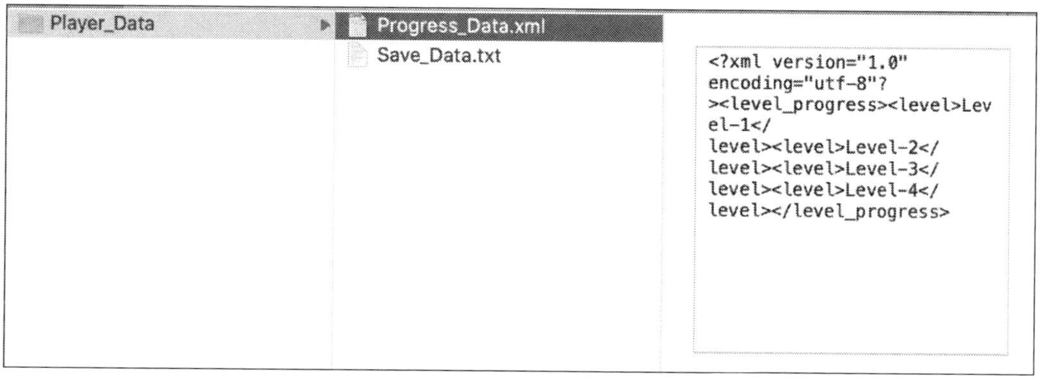


Figure 12.17: New XML file created with document data

You'll notice that there is no indenting or formatting, which is expected because we didn't specify any output formatting. We're not going to use any of them in this example because we'll be talking about a more efficient way of writing XML data in the next section, on serialization.

> You can find the list of output formatting properties at `https://docs.microsoft.com/dotnet/api/system.xml.xmlwriter#specifying-the-output-format`.

The good news is that reading an XML file is no different than reading any other file. You can call either the `readfromfile()` or `readfromstream()` methods inside `initialize()` and get the same console output:

```
public void Initialize()
{
    _state = "Data Manager initialized..";
    Debug.Log(_state);

    FilesystemInfo();
    NewDirectory();
    WriteToXML(_xmlLevelProgress);
    ReadFromStream(_xmlLevelProgress);
}
```

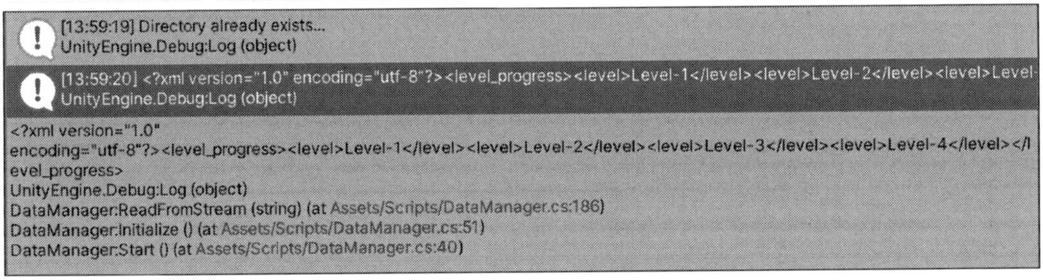


Figure 12.18: Console output from reading the XML file data

Now that we've written a few methods using streams, let's take a look at how to efficiently, and more importantly automatically, close any stream.

# Automatically closing streams

When you're working with streams, wrapping them in a `using` statement automatically closes the stream for you by calling the `Dispose()` method from the `IDisposable` interface we mentioned earlier.

This way, you never have to worry about unused allocated resources your program might be keeping open for no reason.

The syntax is almost exactly the same as what we've already done, except we use the `using` keyword at the beginning of the line, then reference a new stream inside a pair of parentheses, followed by a set of curly braces. Anything we want the stream to do, like read or write data, is done inside the curly braces block of code. For example, creating a new text file as we did in the `WriteToStream()` method would look like this:

```
// The new stream is wrapped in a using statement
using(StreamWriter newStream = File.CreateText(filename))
{
    // Any writing functionality goes inside the curly braces
    newStream.WriteLine("<Save Data> for HERO BORN \n");
}
```

As soon as the stream logic is inside the code block, the outer `using` statement automatically closes the stream and returns the allocated resources to your program. From here on out, I'd recommend always using this syntax to write your streaming code. It's more efficient, much safer, and will demonstrate your understanding of basic resource management!

With our text and XML stream code working, it's time to move on. If you're wondering why we didn't stream any JSON data, it's because we need to add one more tool to our data toolbox—serialization!

# Serializing data

When we talk about serializing and deserializing data, what we're really talking about is translation. While we've been translating our text and XML piecemeal in previous sections, being able to take an entire object and translate it in one shot is a great tool to have.

By definition:

- The act of **serializing** an object translates the object's entire state into another format
- The act of **deserializing** is the reverse, taking the data from a file and restoring it to its former object state

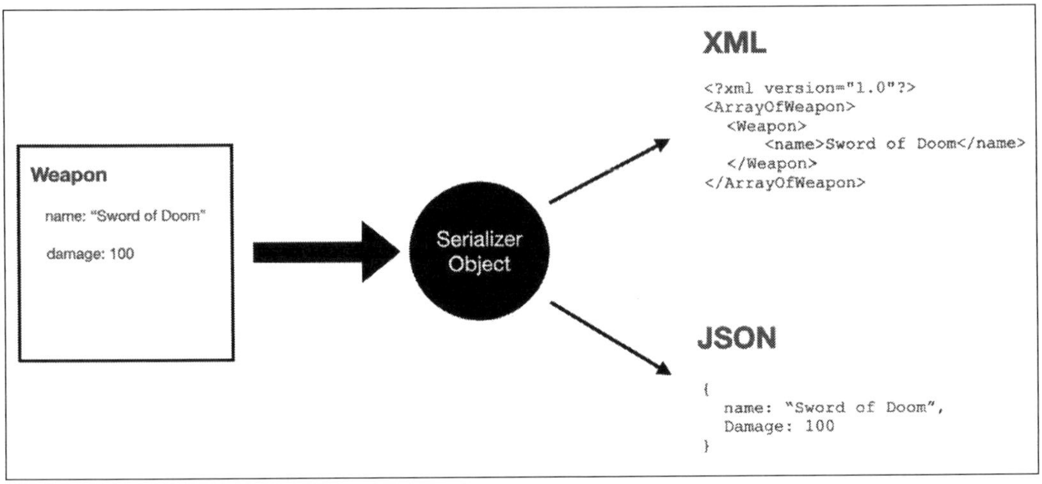


Figure 12.19: Example of serializing an object into XML and JSON

Let's take a practical example from the above image — an instance of our `Weapon` class. Each weapon has its own name and damage properties and associated values, which is called its state. The state of an object is unique, which allows the program to tell them apart.

An object's state also includes properties or fields that are reference types. For instance, if we had a `Character` class that had a `Weapon` property, C# would still recognize the weapon's `name` and `damage` properties when serializing and deserializing. You might hear objects with reference properties referred to as object graphs out in the programming world.

Before we jump in, it's worth noting that serializing objects can be tricky if you're not keeping a close eye on making sure the object properties match the data from a file, and vice versa. For example, if there's a mismatch between your class object properties and the data being deserialized, the serializer will return an empty object. We'll cover this in more detail when we try to serialize a C# list into JSON later in the chapter.

To really get the hang of this, let's take our `Weapon` example and turn it into working code.

# Serializing and deserializing XML

Your task for the rest of this chapter is to serialize and deserialize a list of weapons into XML and JSON, with XML going first!

1. Add a new `using` directive to the top of the `DataManager` class:

```
using System.Collections;
using System.Collections.Generic;
using UnityEngine;
using System.IO;
using System;
using System.Xml;
using System.Xml.Serialization;
```

2. Add a serializable attribute to the `Weapon` class so Unity and C# know the object can be serialized:

```
[Serializable]
public struct Weapon
{
    // ... No other changes needed ...
}
```

3. Add two new variables, one for the XML file path and one for the list of weapons:

```
// ... No other variable changes needed ...

private string _xmlWeapons;

private List<Weapon> weaponInventory = new List<Weapon>
{
    new Weapon("Sword of Doom", 100),
    new Weapon("Butterfly knives", 25),
    new Weapon("Brass Knuckles", 15),
};
```

4. Set the XML file path value in `Awake`:

```
void Awake()
{
    // ... No other changes needed ...

    _xmlWeapons = _dataPath + "WeaponInventory.xml";
}
```

5. Add a new method at the bottom of the `DataManager` class:

```
public void SerializeXML()
{
    // 1
```

```
        var xmlSerializer = new XmlSerializer(typeof(List<Weapon>));

        // 2
        using(FileStream stream = File.Create(_xmlWeapons))
        {
            // 3
            xmlSerializer.Serialize(stream, weaponInventory);
        }
    }
```

6. Call the new method in `Initialize`:

```
    public void Initialize()
    {
        _state = "Data Manager initialized..";
        Debug.Log(_state);

        FilesystemInfo();
        NewDirectory();
        SerializeXML();
    }
```

Let's break down our new method:

1. First, we create an `XmlSerializer` instance and pass in the type of data we're going to be translating. In this case, the `_weaponInventory` is of type `List<Weapon>`, which is what we use in the `typeof` operator:
    - The `XmlSerializer` class is another helpful formatting wrapper, just like the `XmlWriter` class we used earlier
2. Then, we create a `FileStream` using the `_xmlWeapons` file path and wrapped in a `using` code block to make sure it's closed properly.
3. Finally, we call the `Serialize()` method and pass in the stream and the data we want to translate.

Run the game again and take a look at the new XML document we created without having to specify any additional formatting!

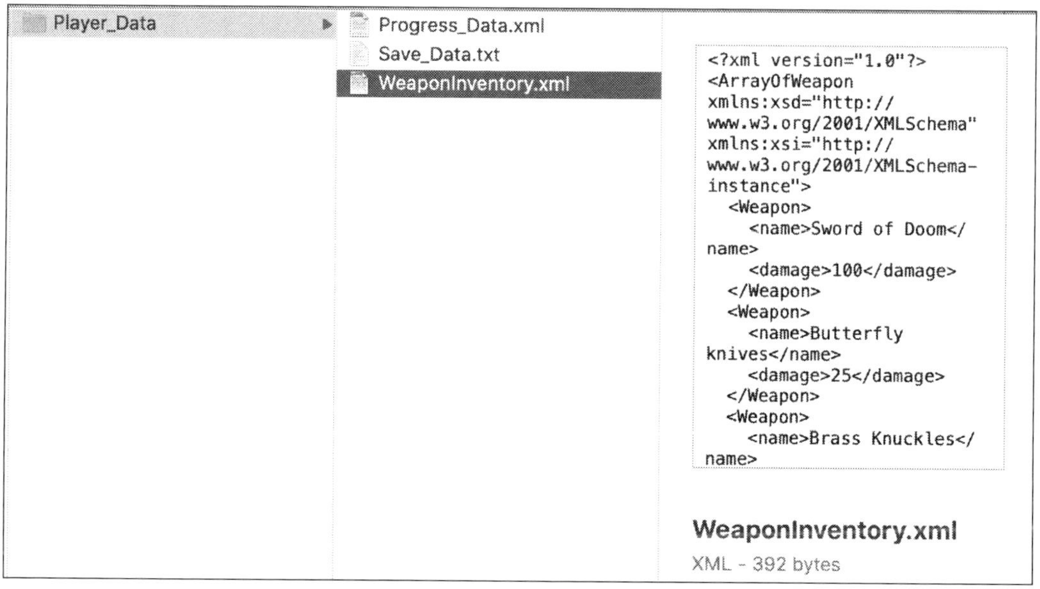


Figure 12.20: XML output in the weapon inventory file

To read back our XML into a list of weapons, we set up everything almost exactly same except we use the `Deserialize()` method from the `XmlSerializer` class instead:

1. Add the following method to the bottom of the `DataManager` class:

```
public void DeserializeXML()
{
    // 1
    if (File.Exists(_xmlWeapons))
    {
        // 2
        var xmlSerializer = new XmlSerializer(typeof(List<Weapon>
));

        // 3
        using (FileStream stream = File.OpenRead(_xmlWeapons))
        {
            // 4
```

```
            var weapons = (List<Weapon>)xmlSerializer.
Deserialize(stream);

            // 5
            foreach (var weapon in weapons)
            {
                Debug.LogFormat("Weapon: {0} - Damage: {1}",
                  weapon.name, weapon.damage);
            }
        }
    }
}
```

2. Call the new method in `Initialize` and pass in the `_xmlWeapons` as a parameter:

```
public void Initialize()
{
    _state = "Data Manager initialized..";
    Debug.Log(_state);

    FilesystemInfo();
    NewDirectory();
    SerializeXML();
    DeserializeXML();
}
```

Let's break down the `deserialize()` method:

1. First, we check if the file exists
2. If the file exists, we create an `XmlSerializer` object and specify that we're going to put the XML data back into a `List<Weapon>` object
3. Then, we open up a `FileStream` with the `_xmlWeapons` file name:
    - We're using `File.OpenRead()` to specify that we want to open the file for reading, not writing
4. Next, we create a variable to hold our deserialized list of weapons:
    - We put the explicit `List<Weapon>` cast in front of the call to `Deserialize()` so that we get the correct type back from the serializer
5. Finally, we use a `foreach` loop to print out each weapon's name and damage values in the console

When you run the game once again, you'll see that we get a console message for each weapon we deserialized from the XML list.

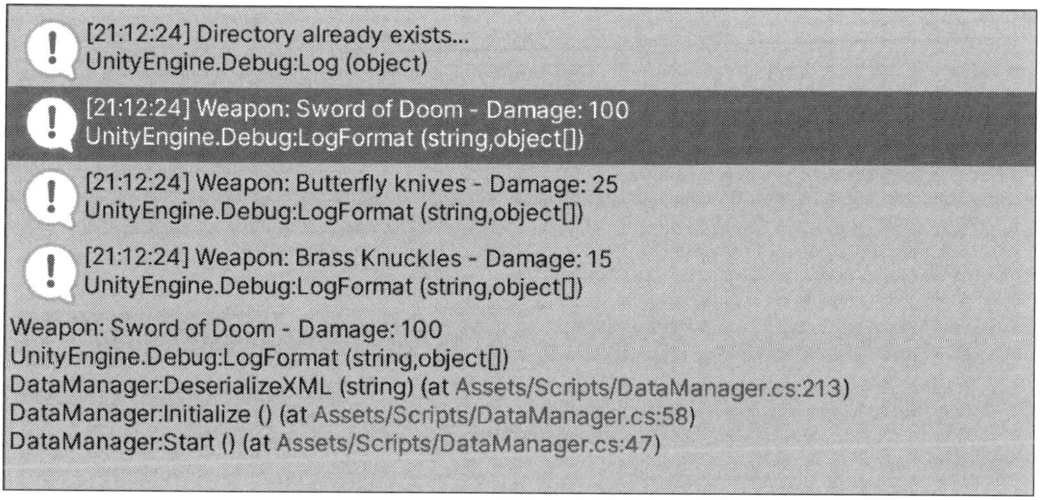


Figure 12.21: Console output from deserializing XML

That's all we need to do for XML data, but before we finish out the chapter we still need to learn how to work with JSON!

# Serializing and deserializing JSON

When it comes to serializing and deserializing JSON, Unity and C# aren't completely in sync. Essentially, C# has its own `JsonSerializer` class that works the exact same way as the `XmlSerializer` class we used in the previous examples.

In order to access the JSON serializer, you need the `System.Text.Json using` directive. Here's the rub—Unity doesn't support that namespace. Instead, Unity uses the `System.Text` namespace and implements its own JSON serializer class called `JsonUtility`.

Because our project is in Unity, we're going to work with Unity's supported serialization class. However, if you're working with a non-Unity C# project, the concepts are the same as the XML code we just wrote.

> You can find a complete how-to that includes code from Microsoft at `https://docs.microsoft.com/en-us/dotnet/standard/serialization/system-text-json-how-to#how-to-write-net-objects-as-json-serialize`.

Your next task is to serialize a single weapon to get the hang of the `JsonUtility` class:

1. Add a new `using` directive to the top of the `DataManager` class:

```
using System.Collections;
using System.Collections.Generic;
using UnityEngine;
using System.IO;
using System;
using System.Xml;
using System.Xml.Serialization;
using System.Text;
```

2. Add a new private string path for the new XML file and set its value in `Awake()`:

```
private string _jsonWeapons;

void Awake()
{
    _jsonWeapons = _dataPath + "WeaponJSON.json";
}
```

3. Add a new method at the bottom of the `DataManager` class:

```
public void SerializeJSON()
{
    // 1
    Weapon sword = new Weapon("Sword of Doom", 100);

    // 2
    string jsonString = JsonUtility.ToJson(sword, true);

    // 3
    using(StreamWriter stream = File.CreateText(_jsonWeapons))
    {
        // 4
        stream.WriteLine(jsonString);
    }
}
```

4. Call the new method in `Initialize()` and pass in the `_jsonWeapons` as a parameter:

```
public void Initialize()
{
```

```
        _state = "Data Manager initialized..";
        Debug.Log(_state);

        FilesystemInfo();
        NewDirectory();
        SerializeJSON();
    }
```

Here's the breakdown of the serialize method:

1. First, we need a weapon to work with, so we create one with our class initializer
2. Then we declare a variable to hold the translated JSON data when it's formatted as a string and call the `ToJson()` method:
    - The `ToJson()` method we're using takes in the `sword` object we want to serialize and a Boolean value of `true` so the string is pretty printed with proper indenting. If we didn't specify a `true` value, the JSON would still print out, it would just be a regular string, which isn't easily readable.
3. Now that we have a text string to write to a file, we create a `StreamWriter` stream and pass in the `_jsonWeapons` file name
4. Finally, we use the `WriteLine()` method and pass it the `jsonString` value to write to the file

Run the program and look at the new JSON file we created and wrote data into!

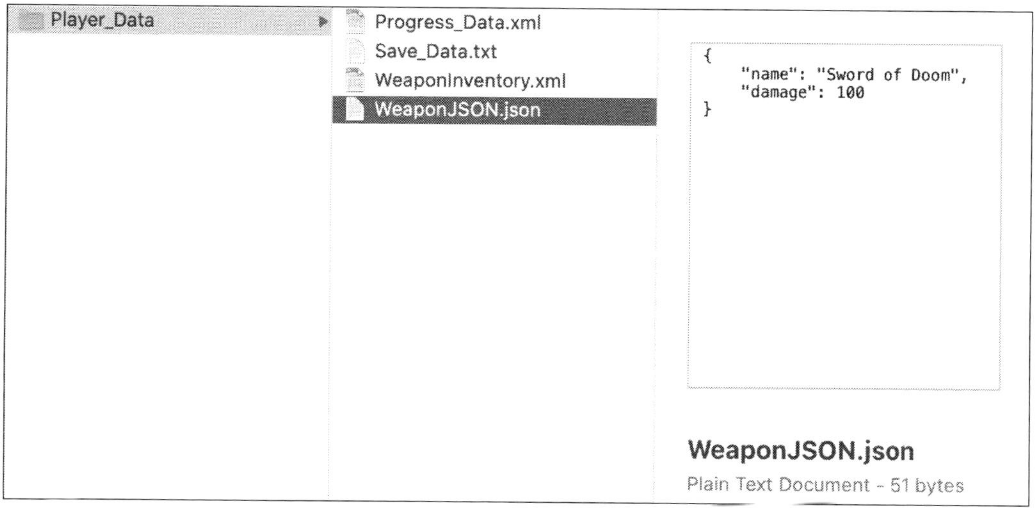


Figure 12.22: JSON file with weapon properties serialized

Now let's try and serialize our list of weapons we used in the XML examples and see what happens.

Update the `SerializeJSON()` method to use the existing list of weapons instead of the single `sword` instance:

```
public void SerializeJSON()
{
    string jsonString = JsonUtility.ToJson(weaponInventory, true);

    using(StreamWriter stream =
      File.CreateText(_jsonWeapons))
    {
        stream.WriteLine(jsonString);
    }
}
```

When you run the game again, you'll see the JSON file data was overwritten and all we ended up with is an empty array:

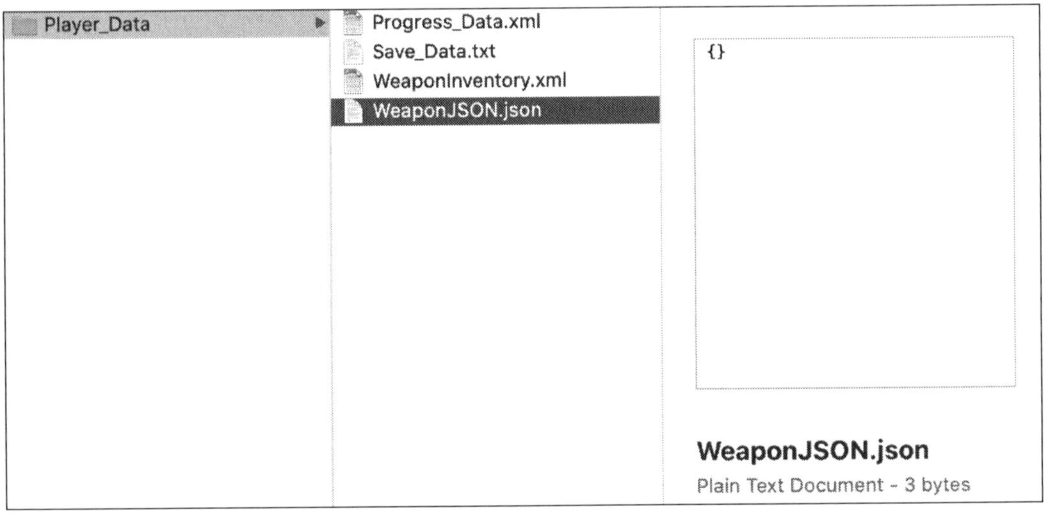


Figure 12.23: JSON file with an empty object after serialization

Again, this is because the way Unity handles JSON serialization doesn't support lists or arrays by themselves. Any list or array needs to be part of a class object for Unity's `JsonUtility` class to recognize and handle it correctly.

Don't panic, if we think about this, it's a fairly intuitive fix—we just need to create a class that has a weapons list property and use that when we serialize our data into JSON!

1. Open `Weapon.cs` and add the following serializable `WeaponShop` class to the bottom of the file. Be super careful to put the new class outside the `Weapon` class curly braces:

```
[Serializable]
public class WeaponShop
{
    public List<Weapon> inventory;
}
```

2. Back in the `DataManager` class, update the `SerializeJSON()` method with the following code:

```
public void SerializeJSON()
{
    // 1
    WeaponShop shop = new WeaponShop();

    // 2
    shop.inventory = weaponInventory;

    // 3
    string jsonString = JsonUtility.ToJson(shop, true);

    using(StreamWriter stream = File.CreateText(_jsonWeapons))
    {
        stream.WriteLine(jsonString);
    }
}
```

Let's break down the changes we just made:

1. First, we create a new variable called `shop`, which is an instance of the `WeaponShop` class
2. Then we set the `inventory` property to the `weaponInventory` list of weapons we already declared
3. Finally, we pass the `shop` object to the `ToJson()` method and write the new string data to the JSON file

Run the game again and look at the pretty printed list of weapons we've created:

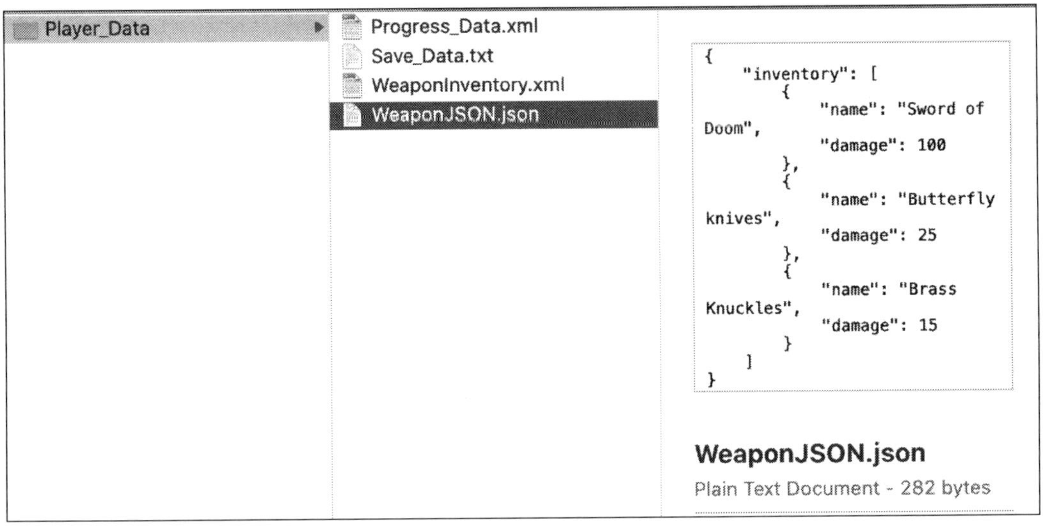


Figure 12.24: List object properly serialized into JSON

Deserializing JSON text back into an object is the reverse process of what we just did:

1. Add a new method at the bottom of the `DataManager` class:

```
public void DeserializeJSON()
{
    // 1
    if(File.Exists(_jsonWeapons))
    {
        // 2
        using (StreamReader stream = new StreamReader(_
jsonWeapons))
        {
            // 3
            var jsonString = stream.ReadToEnd();

            // 4
            var weaponData = JsonUtility.FromJson<WeaponShop>
              (jsonString);
```

```
                // 5
                foreach (var weapon in weaponData.inventory)
                {
                    Debug.LogFormat("Weapon: {0} - Damage: {1}",
                      weapon.name, weapon.damage);
                }
            }
        }
    }
```

2. Call the new method in `Initialize()` and pass `_jsonWeapons` in as a parameter:

```
public void Initialize()
{
    _state = "Data Manager initialized..";
    Debug.Log(_state);

    FilesystemInfo();
    NewDirectory();
    SerializeJSON();
    DeserializeJSON();
}
```

Let's break down the `DeserializeJSON()` method below:

1. First, we check if the file exists
2. If it does exist, we create a stream with the `_jsonWeapons` file path wrapped in a `using` code block
3. Then, we use the stream's `ReadToEnd()` method to grab the entire JSON text from the file
4. Next, we create a variable to hold our deserialized list of weapons and call the `FromJson()` method:
    - Notice that we specify that we want to turn our JSON into a `WeaponShop` object with the `<WeaponShop>` syntax before passing in the JSON string variable
5. Finally, we loop through the weapon shop's `inventory` list property and print out each weapon's name and damage values in the console

Run the game one last time and you'll see a console message printed out for each weapon in our JSON data:

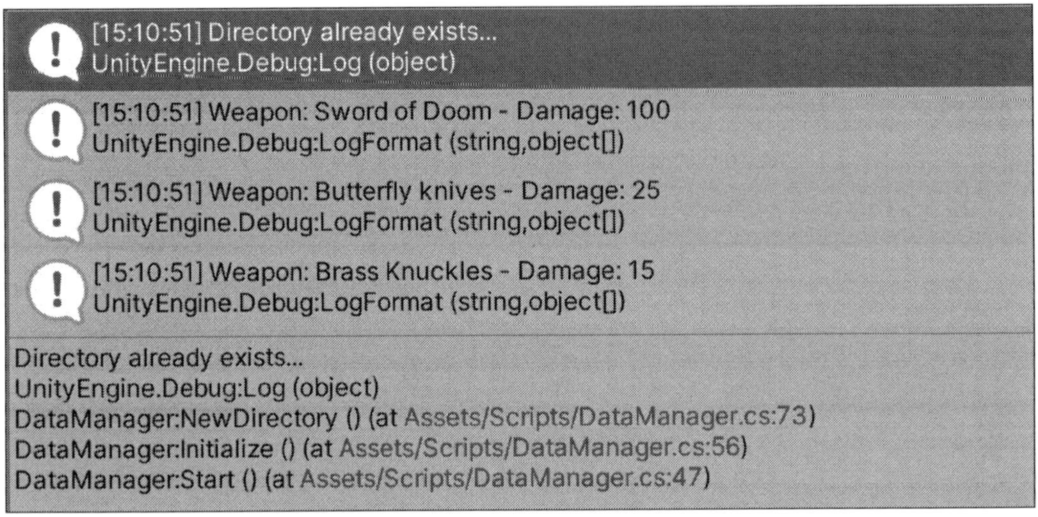


Figure 12.25: Console output from deserializing a list of JSON objects

# Data roundup

Every individual module and topic we've covered in this chapter can be used by itself or combined to suit your project's needs. For example, you could use text files to store character dialogue and only load it when you need to. This would be more efficient than having the game keep track of it every time it runs, even when the information isn't being used.

You could also put character data or enemy statistics into either an XML or JSON file and read from the file anytime you need to level up a character or spawn a new monster. Finally, you could fetch data from a third-party database and serialize it into your own custom classes. This is a super common scenario with storing player accounts and external game data.

> You can find a list of data types that can be serialized in C# at `https://docs.microsoft.com/en-us/dotnet/framework/wcf/feature-details/types-supported-by-the-data-contract-serializer`. Unity handles serialization a little differently, so make sure you check the available types at `https://docs.unity3d.com/ScriptReference/SerializeField.html`.

The point I'm trying to make is that data is everywhere, and it's your job to create a system that handles it the way your game needs, brick by brick.

# Summary

And that's a wrap on the basics of working with data! Congratulations on making it through this monster chapter intact. Data in any programming context is a big topic, so take everything you've learned in this chapter as a jumping-off point.

You already know how to navigate the filesystem, and create, read, update, and delete files. You also learned how to effectively work with text, XML, and JSON data formats, as well as data streams. And you know how to take an entire object's state and serialize or deserialize it into both XML and JSON. All in all, learning these skills was no small feat. Don't forget to review and revisit this chapter more than once; there's a lot here that might not become second nature on the first run-through.

In the next chapter, we'll discuss the basics of generic programming, get a little hands-on experience with delegates and events, and wrap up with an overview of exception handling.

# Pop quiz – data management

1. Which namespace gives you access to the `Path` and `Directory` classes?
2. In Unity, what folder path do you use to save data between runs of your game?
3. What data type do `Stream` objects use to read and write information to files?
4. What happens when you serialize an object into JSON?

# 13
# Exploring Generics, Delegates, and Beyond

The more time you spend programming, the more you start thinking about systems. Structuring how classes and objects interact, communicate, and exchange data are all examples of systems we've worked with so far; the question now is how to make them safer and more efficient.

Since this will be the last practical chapter of the book, we'll be going over examples of generic programming concepts, delegation, event creation, and error handling. Each of these topics is a large area of study in its own right, so take what you learn here and expand on it in your projects. After we complete our practical coding, we'll finish up with a brief overview of design patterns and how they'll play a part in your programming journey going forward.

We'll cover the following topics in this chapter:

- Generic programming
- Using delegates
- Creating events and subscriptions
- Throwing and handling errors
- Understanding design patterns

# Introducing generics

All of our code so far has been very specific in terms of defining and using types. However, there will be cases where you need a class or method to treat its entities in the same way, regardless of its type, while still being type-safe. Generic programming allows us to create reusable classes, methods, and variables using a placeholder, rather than a concrete type.

When a generic class instance is created at compile time or a method is used, a concrete type will be assigned, but the code itself treats it as a generic type. Being able to write generic code is a huge benefit when you need to work with different object types in the same way, for example, custom collection types that need to be able to perform the same operations on elements regardless of type, or classes that need the same underlying functionality. While you might be asking yourself why we don't just subclass or use interfaces, you'll see in our examples that generics help us in a different way.

> We've already seen this in action with the `List` type, which is a generic type. We can access all its addition, removal, and modification functions regardless of whether it's storing integers, strings, or individual characters.

## Generic objects

Creating a generic class works the same as creating a non-generic class but with one important difference: its generic type parameter. Let's take a look at an example of a generic collection class we might want to create to get a clearer picture of how this works:

```
public class SomeGenericCollection<T> {}
```

We've declared a generic collection class named `SomeGenericCollection` and specified that its type parameter will be named `T`. Now, `T` will stand in for the element type that the generic list will store and can be used inside the generic class just like any other type.

Whenever we create an instance of `SomeGenericCollection`, we need to specify the type of values it can store:

```
SomeGenericCollection<int> highScores = new
SomeGenericCollection<int>();
```

In this case, `highScores` stores integer values and `T` stands in for the `int` type, but the `SomeGenericCollection` class will treat any element type the same.

> You have complete control over naming a generic type parameter, but the industry standard in many programming languages is a capital `T`. If you are going to name your type parameters differently, consider starting the name with a capital `T` for consistency and readability.

Let's create a more game-focused example next with a generic `Shop` class to store some fictional inventory items with the following steps:

1. Create a new C# script in the `Scripts` folder, name it `Shop`, and update its code to the following:

```
using System.Collections;
using System.Collections.Generic;
using UnityEngine;

// 1
public class Shop<T>
{
    // 2
    public List<T> inventory = new List<T>();
}
```

2. Create a new instance of `Shop` in `GameBehavior`:

```
public class GameBehavior : MonoBehaviour, IManager
{
    // ... No other changes needed ...


    public void Initialize()
    {
        // 3
        var itemShop = new Shop<string>();

        // 4
        Debug.Log("There are " + itemShop.inventory.Count + "
items for sale.");
    }
}
```

Let's break down the code:

1. Declares a new generic class named IShop with a T type parameter
2. Adds an inventory List<T> of type T to store whatever item types we initialize the generic class with
3. Creates a new instance of Shop<string> in GameBehavior and specifies string values as the generic type
4. Prints out a debug message with the inventory count:

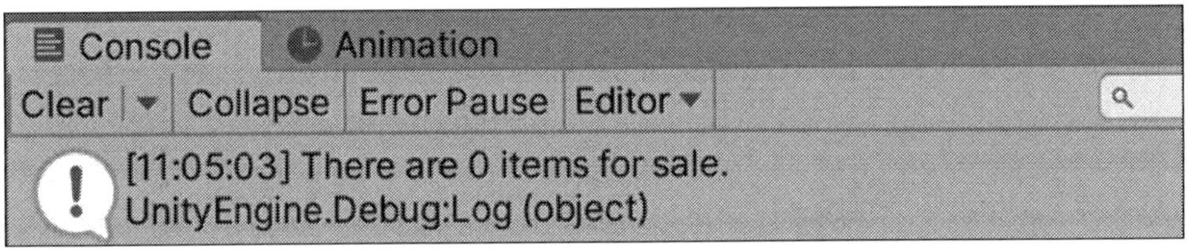


Figure 13.1: Console output from a generic class

Nothing new has happened here yet in terms of functionality, but Visual Studio recognizes Shop as a generic class because of its generic type parameter, T. This sets us up to include additional generic operations like adding inventory items or finding how many of each item is available.

> It's worth noting here that generics aren't supported by the Unity Serializer by default. If you want to serialize generic classes, like we did with custom classes in the last chapter, you need to add the Serializable attribute to the top of class, like we did with our Weapon class. You can find more information at https://docs.unity3d.com/ScriptReference/SerializeReference.html.

# Generic methods

A standalone generic method can have a placeholder type parameter, just like a generic class, which allows it to be included inside either a generic or non-generic class as needed:

```
public void GenericMethod<T>(T genericParameter) {}
```

The T type can be used inside the method body and defined when the method is called:

```
GenericMethod<string>("Hello World!");
```

If you want to declare a generic method inside a generic class, you don't need to specify a new `T` type:

```
public class SomeGenericCollection<T>
{
    public void NonGenericMethod(T genericParameter) {}
}
```

When you call a non-generic method that uses a generic type parameter, there's no issue because the generic class has already taken care of assigning a concrete type:

```
SomeGenericCollection<int> highScores = new SomeGenericCollection
<int> ();

highScores.NonGenericMethod(35);
```

> Generic methods can be overloaded and marked as static, just like non-generic methods. If you want the specific syntax for those situations, check out `https://docs.microsoft.com/en-us/dotnet/csharp/programming-guide/generics/generic-methods`.

Your next task is to create a method that adds new generic items to the inventory and use it in the `GameBehavior` script.

Since we already have a generic class with a defined type parameter, let's add a non-generic method to see them working together:

1. Open up `Shop` and update the code as follows:

```
public class Shop<T>
{
    public List<T> inventory = new List<T>();

    // 1
    public void AddItem(T newItem)
    {

        inventory.Add(newItem);
    }
}
```

2. Go into `GameBehavior` and add an item to `itemShop`:

```
public class GameBehavior : MonoBehaviour, IManager
{
    // ... No other changes needed ...

     public void Initialize()
    {
        var itemShop = new Shop<string>();

        // 2
        itemShop.AddItem("Potion");
        itemShop.AddItem("Antidote");

       Debug.Log("There are " + itemShop.inventory.Count + "
items for sale.");
    }
}
```

Let's break down the code:

1. Declares a method for adding `newItems` of type `T` to the inventory
2. Adds two string items to `itemShop` using `AddItem()` and prints out a debug log:

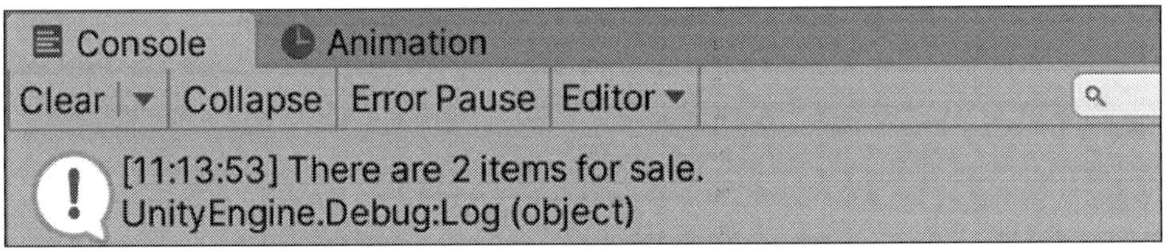


Figure 13.2: Console output after adding an item to a generic class

We wrote `AddItem()` to take in a parameter of the same type as our generic `Shop` instance. Since `itemShop` was created to hold string values, we add the `"Potion"` and `"Antidote"` string values without any issues.

However, if you try and add an integer, for example, you'll get an error saying that the generic type of the `itemShop` doesn't match:

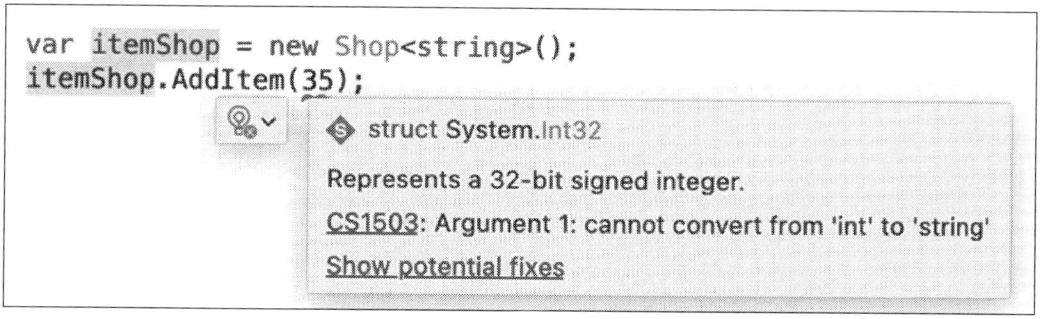


Figure 13.3: Conversion error in a generic class

Now that you've written a generic method, you need to know how to use multiple generic types in a single class. For example, what if we wanted to add a method to the `Shop` class that finds out how many of a given item are in stock? We can't use type `T` again because it's already been defined in the class definition. So what do we do?

Add the following method to the bottom of the `Shop` class:

```
// 1
public int GetStockCount<U>()
{
    // 2
    var stock = 0;

    // 3
    foreach (var item in inventory)
    {
        if (item is U)
        {
            stock++;
        }
    }

    // 4
    return stock;
}
```

Let's break down our new method:

1. Declares a method that returns an int value for how many matching items of type `U` we find in the inventory
    - Generic type parameter naming is completely up to you, just like naming variables. Conventionally, they start at `T` and continue in alphabetical order from there.
2. Creates a variable to hold the number of matching stock items we find and eventually return from the inventory
3. Uses a `foreach` loop to go through the inventory list and increase the stock value every time a match is found
4. Returns the number of matching stock items

The problem here is that we're storing string values in our shop, so if we try and look up how many string items we have, we'll get the full inventory:

```
Debug.Log("There are " + itemShop.GetStockCount<string>() + " items for
sale.");
```

This will print something like the following to the console:

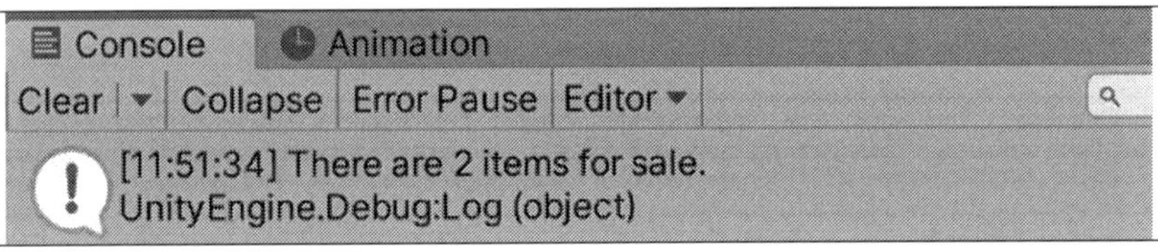


Figure 13.4: Console output from using multiple generic string types

On the other hand, if we tried to look up integer types in our inventory, we'd get no results because we're only storing strings:

```
Debug.Log("There are " + itemShop.GetStockCount<int>() + " items for
sale.");
```

This will print something like the following to the console:

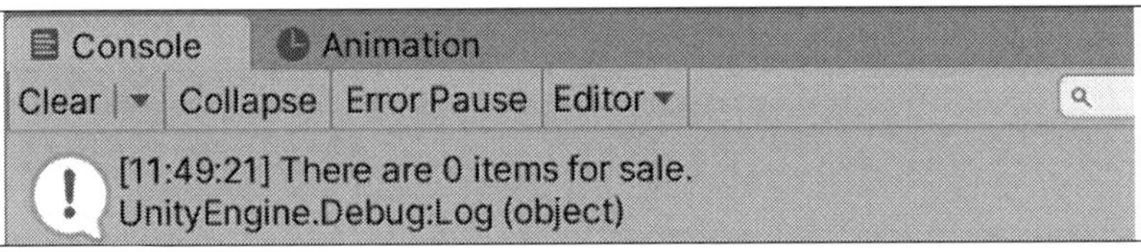


Figure 13.5: Console output using multiple non-matching generic types

Neither of these scenarios is ideal since we can't make sure our shop inventory is storing AND can be searched for the same item type. But here's where generics really shine—we can add rules for our generic classes and methods to enforce the behavior we want, which we'll cover in the next section.

# Constraint type parameters

One of the great things about generics is that their type parameters can be limited. This might contradict what we've learned about generics so far, but just because a class *can* contain any type, doesn't mean it should be allowed to.

To constrain a generic type parameter, we need a new keyword and a syntax we haven't seen before:

```
public class SomeGenericCollection<T> where T: ConstraintType {}
```

The `where` keyword defines the rules that `T` must pass before it can be used as a generic type parameter. It essentially says `SomeGenericClass` can take in any `T` type as long as it conforms to the constraining type. The constraining rules aren't anything mystical or scary; they're concepts we've already covered:

- Adding the `class` keyword would constrain `T` to types that are classes
- Adding the `struct` keyword would constrain `T` to types that are structs
- Adding an interface, such as `IManager`, as the type would limit `T` to types that adopt the interface
- Adding a custom class, such as `Character`, would constrain `T` to only that class type

> If you need a more flexible approach to account for classes that have subclasses, you can use `where T : U`, which specifies that the generic `T` type must be of, or derive from, the `U` type. This is a little advanced for our needs, but you can find more details at `https://docs.microsoft.com/en-us/dotnet/csharp/programming-guide/generics/constraints-on-type-parameters`.

Just for fun, let's constrain `Shop` to only accept a new type called `Collectable`:

1. Create a new script in the `Scripts` folder, name it `Collectable`, and add the following code:

```
using System.Collections;
using System.Collections.Generic;
using UnityEngine;
```

```
public class Collectable
{
    public string name;
}

public class Potion : Collectable
{
    public Potion()
    {
        this.name = "Potion";
    }
}

public class Antidote : Collectable
{
    public Antidote()
    {
        this.name = "Antidote";
    }
}
```

All we've done here is declare a new class called `Collectable` with a name property, and created subclasses for potions and antidotes. With this structure, we can enforce our `Shop` to only accept `Collectable` types, and our stock finding method to only accept `Collectable` types as well so we can compare them and find matches.

2. Open up `Shop` and update the class declaration:

```
public class Shop<T> where T : Collectable
```

3. Update the `GetStockCount()` method to constrain `U` to equal whatever the initial generic `T` type is:

```
public int GetStockCount<U>() where U : T
{
    var stock = 0;
    foreach (var item in inventory)
    {
        if (item is U)
        {
            stock++;
        }
    }
    return stock;
}
```

4. In GameBehavior, update the itemShop instance to the following code:

```
var itemShop = new Shop<Collectable>();

itemShop.AddItem(new Potion());
itemShop.AddItem(new Antidote());

Debug.Log("There are " + itemShop.GetStockCount<Potion>() + "
items for sale.");
```

This will result in output like the following:

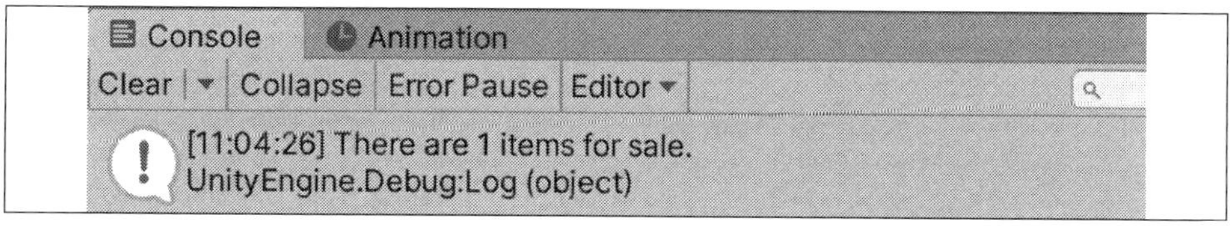


Figure 13.6: Output from updated GameBehavior script

In our example, we can ensure only collectable types are allowed in our shops. If we accidentally try and add non-collectable types in our code, Visual Studio will alert us about trying to break our own rules!

# Adding generics to Unity objects

Generics also work with Unity scripts and GameObjects. For example, we can easily create a generic destroyable class to use on any MonoBehaviour or object Component we want to delete from the scene. If this sounds familiar, it's what our BulletBehavior does for us, but it's not applicable to anything other than that script. To make this more scalable, let's make any script that inherits from MonoBehaviour destroyable.

1. Create a new script in the Scripts folder, name it Destroyable, and add the following code:

```
using System.Collections;
using System.Collections.Generic;
using UnityEngine;

public class Destroyable<T> : MonoBehaviour where T :
MonoBehaviour
{
    public int OnscreenDelay;

    void Start()
    {
```

```
            Destroy(this.gameObject, OnscreenDelay);
        }
    }
```

2. Delete all the code inside `BulletBehavior` and inherit from the new generic class:

```
public class BulletBehavior : Destroyable<BulletBehavior>
{

}
```

We've now turned our `BulletBehavior` script into a generic destroyable object. Nothing changes in the Bullet Prefab, but we can make any other object destroyable by inheriting from the generic `Destroyable` class. In our example, this would boost code efficiency and reusability if we created multiple projectile Prefabs and wanted them all to be destroyable, but at different times.

Generic programming is a powerful tool in our toolbox, but with the basics covered it's time to talk about an equally important topic as you progress in your programming journey—delegation!

# Delegating actions

There will be times when you need to pass off, or delegate, the execution of a method from one file to another. In C#, this can be accomplished through delegate types, which store references to methods and can be treated like any other variable. The only caveat is that the delegate itself and any assigned method need to have the same signature—just like integer variables can only hold whole numbers and strings can only hold text.

Creating a delegate is a mix between writing a function and declaring a variable:

```
public delegate returnType DelegateName(int param1, string param2);
```

You start with an access modifier followed by the `delegate` keyword, which identifies it to the compiler as a `delegate` type. A `delegate` type can have a return type and name as a regular function, as well as parameters if needed. However, this syntax only declares the `delegate` type itself; to use it, you need to create an instance as we do with classes:

```
public DelegateName someDelegate;
```

With a `delegate` type variable declared, it's easy to assign a method that matches the delegate signature:

```
public DelegateName someDelegate = MatchingMethod;
public void MatchingMethod(int param1, string param2)
{
    // ... Executing code here ...
}
```

Notice that you don't include the parentheses when assigning `MatchingMethod` to the `someDelegate` variable, as it's not calling the method at this point. What it's doing is delegating the calling responsibility of `MatchingMethod` to `someDelegate`, which means we can call the function as follows:

```
someDelegate();
```

This might seem cumbersome at this point in your C# skill development, but I promise you that being able to store and execute methods as variables will come in handy down the road.

# Creating a debug delegate

Let's create a simple delegate type to define a method that takes in a string and eventually prints it out using an assigned method. Open up `GameBehavior` and add the following code:

```
public class GameBehavior : MonoBehaviour, IManager
{
    // ... No other changes needed ...

    // 1
    public delegate void DebugDelegate(string newText);

    // 2
    public DebugDelegate debug = Print;


    public void Initialize()
    {
        _state = "Game Manager initialized..";
        _state.FancyDebug();
```

```
        // 3
        debug(_state);

    // ... No changes needed ...
    }

    // 4
    public static void Print(string newText)
    {
        Debug.Log(newText);
    }
}
```

Let's break down the code:

1. Declares a `public delegate` type named `DebugDelegate` to hold a method that takes in a `string` parameter and returns `void`
2. Creates a new `DebugDelegate` instance named `debug` and assigns it a method with a matching signature named `Print()`
3. Replaces the `Debug.Log(_state)` code inside `Initialize()` with a call to the `debug` delegate instance instead
4. Declares `Print()` as a `static` method that takes in a `string` parameter and logs it to the console:

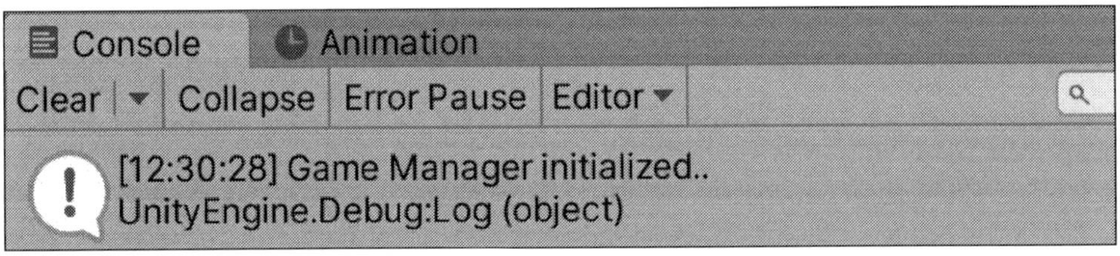


Figure 13.7: Console output from a delegate action

Nothing in the console has changed, but instead of directly calling `Debug.Log()` inside `Initialize()`, that operation has been delegated to the `debug` delegate instance. While this is a simplistic example, delegation is a powerful tool when you need to store, pass, and execute methods as their types.

In Unity, we've already worked with examples of delegation by using the `OnCollisionEnter()` and `OnCollisionExit()` methods, which are methods that are called through delegation. In the real world, custom delegates are most useful when paired with events, which we'll see in a later section of this chapter.

# Delegates as parameter types

Since we've seen how to create delegate types for storing methods, it makes sense that a delegate type could also be used as a method parameter itself. This isn't that far removed from what we've already done, but it's a good idea to cover our bases.

Let's see how a delegate type can be used as a method parameter. Update GameBehavior with the following code:

```
public class GameBehavior : MonoBehaviour, IManager
{
    // ... No changes needed ...


    public void Initialize()
    {
        _state = "Game Manager initialized..";
        _state.FancyDebug();

        debug(_state);

        // 1
        LogWithDelegate(debug);
    }


    // 2
    public void LogWithDelegate(DebugDelegate del)
    {
        // 3
        del("Delegating the debug task...");
    }

}
```

Let's break down the code:

1. Calls LogWithDelegate() and passes in our debug variable as its type parameter
2. Declares a new method that takes in a parameter of the DebugDelegate type

3. Calls the delegate parameter's function and passes in a string literal to be printed out:

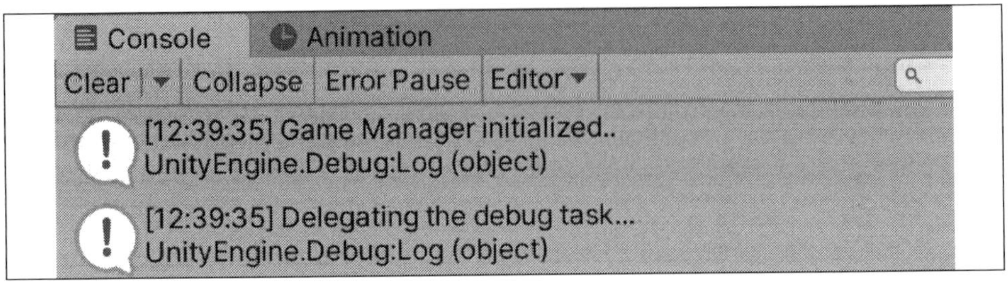


Figure 13.8: Console output of a delegate as a parameter type

We've created a method that takes in a parameter of the `DebugDelegate` type, which means that the actual argument passed in will represent a method and can be treated as one. Think of this example as a delegation chain, where `LogWithDelegate()` is two steps removed from the actual method doing the debugging, which is `Print()`. Creating a delegation chain like this isn't always a common solution in a game or application scenario, but when you need to control levels of delegation it's important to understand the syntax involved. This is especially true in scenarios where your delegation chain is spread across multiple scripts or classes.

> It's easy to get lost with delegation if you miss an important mental connection, so go back and review the code from the beginning of the section and check the docs at `https://docs.microsoft.com/en-us/dotnet/csharp/programming-guide/delegates/`.

Now that you know how to work with basic delegates, it's time to talk about how events can be used to efficiently communicate information between multiple scripts. Honestly, the best use case for a delegate is being paired with events, which we'll dive into next.

# Firing events

C# events allow you to essentially create a subscription system based on actions in your games or apps. For instance, if you wanted to send out an event whenever an item is collected, or when a player presses the spacebar, you could do that. However, when an event fires, it doesn't automatically have a subscriber, or receiver, to handle any code that needs to execute after the event action.

Any class can subscribe or unsubscribe to an event through the calling class the event is fired from; just like signing up to receive notifications on your phone when a new post is shared on Facebook, events form a kind of distributed-information superhighway for sharing actions and data across your application.

Declaring events is similar to declaring delegates in that an event has a specific method signature. We'll use a delegate to specify the method signature we want the event to have, then create the event using the `delegate` type and the `event` keyword:

```
public delegate void EventDelegate(int param1, string param2);
public event EventDelegate eventInstance;
```

This setup allows us to treat `eventInstance` as a method because it's a delegate type, which means we can send it out at any time by calling it:

```
eventInstance(35, "John Doe");
```

Your next task is to create an event of your own and fire it off in the appropriate place inside `PlayerBehavior`.

# Creating and invoking events

Let's create an event to fire off any time our player jumps. Open up `PlayerBehavior` and add the following changes:

```
public class PlayerBehavior : MonoBehaviour
{
    // ... No other variable changes needed ...

    // 1
    public delegate void JumpingEvent();

    // 2
    public event JumpingEvent playerJump;

    void Start()
    {
        // ... No changes needed ...
    }

    void Update()
```

```
    {
        // ... No changes needed ...
;
    }

    void FixedUpdate()
    {
        if(IsGrounded() &&  _isJumping)
        {
            _rb.AddForce(Vector3.up * jumpVelocity,
               ForceMode.Impulse);

            // 3
            playerJump();
        }
    }

    // ... No changes needed in IsGrounded or OnCollisionEnter
}
```

Let's break down the code:

1. Declares a new `delegate` type that returns `void` and takes in no parameters
2. Creates an event of the `JumpingEvent` type, named `playerJump`, that can be treated as a method that matches the preceding delegate's `void` return and no parameter signature
3. Calls `playerJump` after the force is applied in `Update()`

We have successfully created a simple delegate type that takes in no parameters and returns nothing, as well as an event of that type to execute whenever the player jumps. Each time the player jumps, the `playerJump` event is sent out to all of its subscribers to notify them of the action.

After the event fires, it's up to its subscribers to process it and do any additional operations, which we'll see in the *Handling event subscriptions* section, next.

# Handling event subscriptions

Right now, our `playerJump` event has no subscribers, but changing that is simple and very similar to how we assigned method references to delegate types in the last section:

```
someClass.eventInstance += EventHandler;
```

Since events are variables that belong to the class they're declared in, and subscribers will be other classes, a reference to the event-containing class is necessary for subscriptions. The += operator is used to assign a method that will fire when an event executes, just like setting up an out-of-office email. Like assigning delegates, the method signature of the event handler method must match the event's type. In our previous syntax example, that means `EventHandler` needs to be the following:

```
public void EventHandler(int param1, string param2) {}
```

In cases where you need to unsubscribe from an event, you simply do the reverse of the assignment by using the `-=` operator:

```
someClass.eventInstance -= EventHandler;
```

> Event subscriptions are generally handled when a class is initialized or destroyed, making it easy to manage multiple events without messy code implementations.

Now that you know the syntax for subscribing and unsubscribing to events, it's your turn to put this into practice in the `GameBehavior` script.

Now that our event is firing every time the player jumps, we need a way to capture that action:

1. Go back to `GameBehavior` and update the following code:

```
public class GameBehavior : MonoBehaviour, IManager
{
    // 1
    public PlayerBehavior playerBehavior;

    // 2
    void OnEnable()
    {
        // 3
        GameObject player = GameObject.Find("Player");

        // 4
        playerBehavior = player.GetComponent<PlayerBehavior>();

        // 5
        playerBehavior.playerJump += HandlePlayerJump;
        debug("Jump event subscribed...");
```

```
        }

        // 6
        public void HandlePlayerJump()
        {
            debug("Player has jumped...");
        }

        // ... No other changes ...
    }
```

Let's break down the code:

1. Creates a public variable of type `PlayerBehavior`
2. Declares the `OnEnable()` method, which is called whenever the object the script is attached to becomes active in the scene

> `OnEnable` is a method in the `MonoBehaviour` class, so all Unity scripts have access to it. This is a great place to put event subscriptions instead of `Awake` because it only executes when the object is active, not just in the process of loading.

3. Finds the `Player` object in the scene and stores its `GameObject` in a local variable
4. Uses `GetComponent()` to retrieve a reference to the `PlayerBehavior` class attached to the `Player` and stores it in the `playerBehavior` variable
5. Subscribes to the `playerJump` event declared in `PlayerBehavior` with a method named `HandlePlayerJump` using the += operator
6. Declares the `HandlePlayerJump()` method with a signature that matches the event's type and logs a success message using the debug delegate each time the event is received:

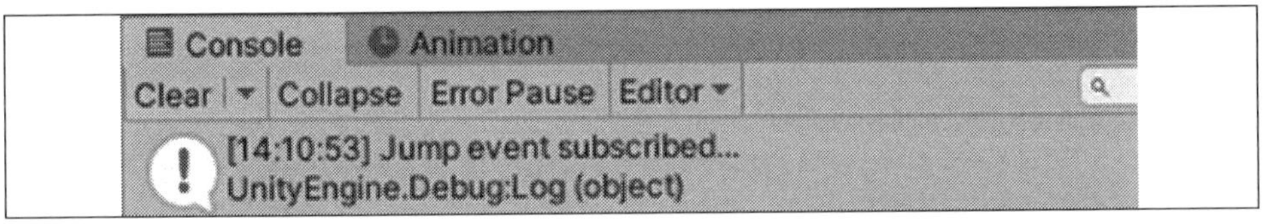


Figure 13.9: Console output from a delegate event subscription

To correctly subscribe and receive events in `GameBehavior`, we had to grab a reference to the `PlayerBehavior` class attached to the player. We could have done this all in one line, but it's much more readable when it's split up. We then assigned a method to the `playerJump` event that will execute whenever the event is received, and complete the subscription process.

Now each time you jump, you'll see a debug message with the event message:

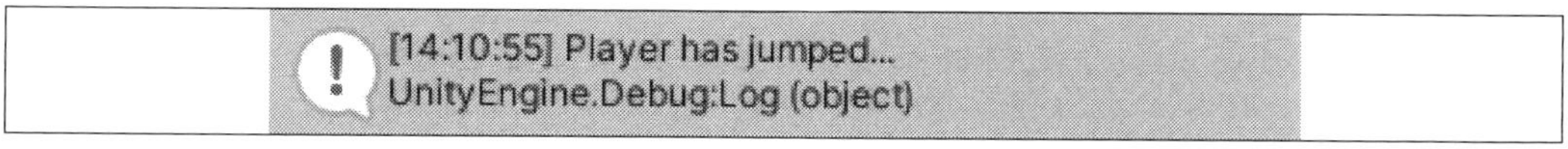


Figure 13.10: Console output from a delegate event firing

Since event subscriptions are configured in scripts, and scripts are attached to Unity objects, our job isn't done yet. We still need to handle how we clean up subscriptions when the object is destroyed or removed from the scene, which we'll cover in the next section.

# Cleaning up event subscriptions

Even though our player is never destroyed in our prototype, that's a common feature in games when you lose. It's always important to clean up event subscriptions because they take up allocated resources, as we discussed with streams in *Chapter 12, Saving, Loading, and Serializing Data.*

We don't want any subscriptions hanging around after the subscribed object has been destroyed, so let's clean up our jumping event. Add the following code to `GameBehavior` after the `OnEnable` method:

```
// 1
private void OnDisable()
{
    // 2
    playerBehavior.playerJump -= HandlePlayerJump;
    debug("Jump event unsubscribed...");
}
```

Let's break down our new code addition:

1. Declares the `OnDisable()` method, which belongs to the `MonoBehavior` class and is the companion to the `OnEnable()` method we used earlier
    - Any cleanup code you need to write should generally go in this method, as it executes when the object the script is attached to is inactive

2. Unsubscribes the `playerJump` event from `HandlePlayerJump` using the `-=` operator and print out a console message

Now our script properly subscribes and unsubscribes to an event when the GameObject is enabled and disabled, leaving no unused resources in our game scene.

That wraps up our discussion on events. Now you can broadcast them to every corner of your game from a single script and react to scenarios like a player losing life, collecting items, or updating the UI. However, we still have to discuss a very important topic that no program can succeed without, and that's error handling.

# Handling exceptions

Efficiently incorporating errors and exceptions into your code is both a professional and personal benchmark in your programming journey. Before you start yelling "Why would I add errors when I've spent all this time trying to avoid them?!", you should know that I don't mean adding errors to break your existing code. It's quite the opposite—including errors or exceptions and handling them appropriately when pieces of functionality are used incorrectly makes your code base stronger and less prone to crashes, not weaker.

## Throwing exceptions

When we talk about adding errors, we refer to the process as *exception throwing*, which is an apt visual analogy. Throwing exceptions is part of something called defensive programming, which essentially means that you actively and consciously guard against improper or unplanned operations in your code. To mark those situations, you throw out an exception from a method that is then handled by the calling code.

Let's take an example: say we have an `if` statement that checks whether a player's email address is valid before letting them sign up. If the email entered is not valid, we want our code to throw an exception:

```
public void ValidateEmail(string email)
{
    if(!email.Contains("@"))
    {
        throw new System.ArgumentException("Email is invalid");
    }
}
```

We use the `throw` keyword to send out the exception, which is created with the `new` keyword followed by the exception we specify. `System.ArgumentException()` will log the information about where and when the exception was executed by default, but can also accept a custom string if you want to be more specific.

`ArgumentException` is a subclass of the `Exception` class and is accessed through the `System` class shown previously. C# comes with many built-in exception types, including subclasses for checking for null values, out or range collection values, and invalid operations. Exceptions are a prime example of using the right tool for the right job. Our example only needs the basic `ArgumentException`, but you can find the full descriptive list at `https://docs.microsoft.com/en-us/dotnet/api/system.exception#Standard`.

Let's keep things simple on our first foray into exceptions and make sure that our level only restarts if we provide a positive scene index number:

1. Open up `Utilities` and add the following code to the overloaded version of `RestartLevel(int)`:

```
public static class Utilities
{
    // ... No changes needed ...

    public static bool RestartLevel(int sceneIndex)
    {
        // 1
        if(sceneIndex < 0)
        {
            // 2
            throw new System.ArgumentException("Scene index cannot be negative");
        }

        Debug.Log("Player deaths: " + PlayerDeaths);
        string message = UpdateDeathCount(ref PlayerDeaths);
        Debug.Log("Player deaths: " + PlayerDeaths);
        Debug.Log(message);

        SceneManager.LoadScene(sceneIndex);
        Time.timeScale = 1.0f;

        return true;
    }
}
```

2. Change `RestartLevel()` in `GameBehavior` to take in a negative scene index and lose the game:

```
// 3
public void RestartScene()
{
    Utilities.RestartLevel(-1);
}
```

Let's break down the code:

1. Declares an `if` statement to check that `sceneIndex` is not less than 0 or a negative number
2. Throws an `ArgumentException` with a custom message if a negative scene index is passed in as an argument
3. Calls `RestartLevel()` with a scene index of `-1`:

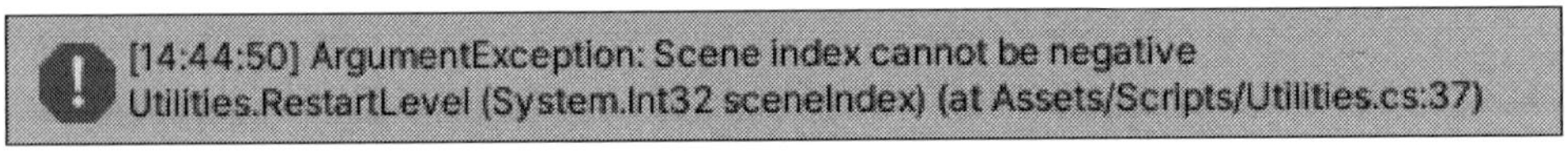


Figure 13.11: Console output when an exception is thrown

When we lose the game now, `RestartLevel()` is called, but since we're using `-1` as the scene index argument, our exception is fired before any of the scene manager logic is executed. We don't have any other scenes configured in our game at the moment, but this defensive code acts as a safeguard and doesn't let us take an action that might crash the game (Unity doesn't support negative indexes when loading scenes).

Now that you've successfully thrown an error, you need to know how to handle the fallout from the error, which leads us to our next section and the `try-catch` statement.

# Using try-catch

Now that we've thrown an error, it's our job to safely handle the possible outcomes that calling `RestartLevel()` might have because at this point, this is not addressed properly. The way to do this is with a new kind of statement, called `try-catch`:

```
try
{
    // Call a method that might throw an exception
}
catch (ExceptionType localVariable)
{
    // Catch all exception cases individually
}
```

The `try-catch` statement is made up of consecutive code blocks that are executed on different conditions; it's like a specialized `if/else` statement. We call any methods that potentially throw exceptions in the `try` block—if no exceptions are thrown, the code keeps executing without interruption. If an exception is thrown, the code jumps to the `catch` statement that matches the thrown exception, just like `switch` statements do with their cases. `catch` statements need to define what exception they are accounting for and specify a local variable name that will represent it inside the `catch` block.

You can chain as many `catch` statements after the `try` block as you need to handle multiple exceptions thrown from a single method, provided they are catching different exceptions. For example:

```
try
{
    // Call a method that might throw an exception
}
catch (ArgumentException argException)
{
    // Catch argument exceptions here
}
catch (FileNotFoundException fileException)
{
    // Catch exceptions for files not found here
}
```

There's also an optional `finally` block that can be declared after any `catch` statements that will execute at the very end of the `try-catch` statement, regardless of whether an exception was thrown:

```
finally
{
    // Executes at the end of the try-catch no matter what
}
```

Your next task is to use a `try-catch` statement to handle any errors thrown from restarting the level unsuccessfully. Now that we have an exception that is thrown when we lose the game, let's handle it safely. Update `GameBehavior` with the following code and lose the game again:

```
public class GameBehavior : MonoBehaviour, IManager
{
    // ... No variable changes needed ...
```

```
    public void RestartScene()
    {
        // 1
        try
        {
            Utilities.RestartLevel(-1);
            debug("Level successfully restarted...");
        }
        // 2
        catch (System.ArgumentException exception)
        {
            // 3
            Utilities.RestartLevel(0);
            debug("Reverting to scene 0: " + exception.ToString());
        }
        // 4
        finally
        {
            debug("Level restart has completed...");
        }
    }
}
```

Let's break down the code:

1. Declares the `try` block and moves the call to `RestartLevel()` inside with a `debug` command to print out if the restart is completed without any exceptions.
2. Declares the `catch` block and defines `System.ArgumentException` as the exception type it will handle and `exception` as the local variable name.
3. Restarts the game at the default scene index if the exception is thrown:
    - Uses the `debug` delegate to print out a custom message, plus the exception information, which can be accessed from `exception` and converted into a string with the `ToString()` method

   Since `exception` is of the `ArgumentException` type, there are several properties and methods associated with the `Exception` class that you can access. These are often useful when you need detailed information about a particular exception.
4. Adds a `finally` block with a debug message to signal the end of the exception-handling code:

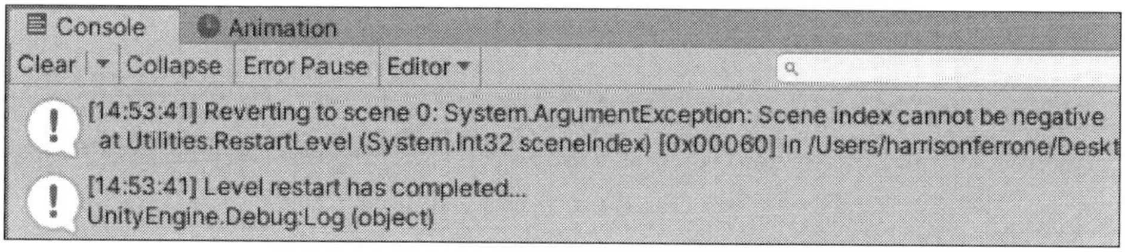


Figure 13.12: Console output of a complete try-catch statement

When `RestartLevel()` is called now, our `try` block safely allows it to execute, and if an error is thrown, it's caught inside the `catch` block. The `catch` block restarts the level at the default scene index and the code proceeds to the `finally` block, which simply logs a message for us.

It's important to understand how to work with exceptions, but you shouldn't get into the habit of putting them everywhere in your code. This will lead to bloated classes and might affect the game's processing time. Instead, you want to use exceptions where they are most needed—invalidation or data processing, rather than game mechanics.

C# allows you the freedom to create your exception types to suit any specific needs your code might have, but that's beyond the scope of this book. It's just a good thing to remember for the future: `https://docs.microsoft.com/en-us/dotnet/standard/exceptions/how-to-create-user-defined-exceptions`.

# Summary

While this chapter brings us to the end of our practical adventure into C# and Unity 2020, I hope that your journey into game programming and software development has just begun. You've learned everything from creating variables, methods, and class objects to writing your game mechanics, enemy behavior, and more.

The topics we've covered in this chapter have been a level above what we dealt with for the majority of this book, and with good reason. You already know your programming brain is a muscle that you need to exercise before you can advance to the next plateau. That's all generics, events, and design patterns are: just the next rung up the programming ladder.

In the next chapter, I will leave you with resources, further reading, and lots of other helpful (and, dare I say, cool) opportunities and information about the Unity community and the software development industry at large.

Happy coding!

# Pop quiz – intermediate C#

1. What is the difference between a generic and non-generic class?
2. What needs to match when assigning a value to a delegate type?
3. How would you unsubscribe from an event?
4. Which C# keyword would you use to send out an exception in your code?

# 14

# The Journey Continues

If you started this book as a complete newcomer to the world of programming, congratulations on your achievement! If you came in knowing a bit about Unity or another scripting language, guess what? Congratulations to you as well. If you began with all the topics and concepts we covered already firmly solidified in your head, you guessed it: congratulations. There is no such thing as an insignificant learning experience, no matter how much or how little you may think you came away with. Revel in the time you spent learning something new, even if it only turned out to be a new keyword.

As you reach the end of this journey, it's important to look back at the skills you've acquired along the way. As with all instructional content, there's always more to learn and explore, so this chapter will focus on cementing the following topics and giving you resources for your next adventure:

- Diving deeper
- Object-oriented programming and beyond
- Design patterns
- Approaching Unity projects
- C# and Unity resources
- Unity certifications
- Next steps and future learning

# Diving deeper

While we've done a good amount of work with variables, types, methods, and classes throughout this book, there are still areas of C# that were left unexplored.

Learning a new skill shouldn't be a simple bombardment of information without context; it should be a careful stack of bricks, one on top of the other, each building on the foundational knowledge already acquired.

Here are some of the concepts you'll want to look into as you progress in your programming journey with C#, regardless of whether it's with Unity:

- Optional and dynamic variables
- Debugging approaches
- Concurrent programming
- Networking and RESTful APIs
- Recursion and reflection
- Design patterns
- LINQ
- Functional programming

As you revisit the code we've written throughout this book, don't just think about what we accomplished, but also about how the different parts of our project work together. Our code is modular, meaning actions and logic are self-contained. Our code is flexible because we've used **object-oriented programming** (**OOP**) techniques, which makes it easy to improve and update. Our code is clean and doesn't repeat, making it readable to anyone who looks at it down the line, even if that's us.

The takeaway here is that digesting basic concepts takes time. Things don't always sink in on the first try, and the "Aha!" moments don't always come when you expect. The key is to keep learning new things, but always with one eye on your foundation.

Let's take our own advice and revisit the tenets of OOP in the next section.

# Remembering your object-oriented programming

OOP is a vast field of expertise, and its mastery requires not only study but also time spent applying its principles to real-life software development.

With all the foundational information you learned in this book, it might seem like a mountain you're just better off not even attempting to climb. However, when you feel that way, take a step back and revisit these concepts:

- Classes are blueprints for objects you want to create in code
- They can contain properties, methods, and events
- They use constructors to define how they are instantiated
- Instantiating objects from a class blueprint creates a unique instance of that class
- Classes are reference types, meaning when the reference is copied it's not a new instance
- Structs are value types, meaning when the struct is copied a brand-new instance is created
- Classes can use inheritance to share common behavior and data with subclasses
- Classes use access modifiers to encapsulate their data and behaviors
- Classes can be composed of other class or struct types
- Polymorphism allows subclasses to be treated the same as their parent class
- Polymorphism also allows subclass behaviors to be changed without affecting the parent class

Once you've mastered OOP, there are other programming paradigms to explore, such as functional and reactive programming. A simple online search will get you going in the right direction.

# Design patterns primer

Before we wrap up the book, I want to talk about a concept that will play a huge part in your programming career: **design patterns**. Googling design patterns or software programming patterns will give you a host of definitions and examples, which can be overwhelming if you've never encountered them before. Let's simplify the term and define a design pattern as follows:

A template for solving programming problems or situations that you'll run into on a regular basis during any kind of application development. These are not hardcoded solutions—they're more like tested guidelines and best practices that can be adapted to fit a specific situation.

There's a lot of history behind how design patterns became an integral part of the programming lexicon, but that excavation is up to you.

If this concept strikes a chord with your programming brain, start with the book *Design Patterns: Elements of Reusable Object-Oriented Software* and its authors, the *Gang of Four*: Erich Gamma, Richard Helm, Ralph Johnson, and John Vlissides.

This barely scratches the surface of what design patterns can do in real-world programming situations. I highly encourage you to dig into their history and application—they'll be one of your best resources going forward.

Next, even though the goal of this book has been to teach you C#, we can't forget about everything we've learned about Unity.

# Approaching Unity projects

Even though Unity is a 3D game engine, it still has to follow the principles set down by the code it's built on. When you think of your game, remember that the GameObjects, components, and systems you see on screen are just visual representations of classes and data; they're not magical or unknown—they're the result of taking the programming foundations you've learned in this book to their advanced conclusion.

Everything in Unity is an object, but that doesn't mean all C# classes have to work within the engine's `MonoBehaviour` framework. Don't be limited to thinking only about in-game mechanics; branch out and define your data or behavior the way your project needs.

Lastly, always ask yourself how you can best separate code out into pieces of functionality instead of creating huge, bloated, thousand-line classes. Related code should be responsible for its behavior and stored together. That means creating separate `MonoBehaviour` classes and attaching them to the GameObjects they affect. I said it at the beginning of this book and I'll say it again: programming is more a mindset and contextual framework than syntax memorization. Keep training your brain to think like a programmer and eventually, you won't be able to see the world any differently.

# Unity features we didn't cover

We managed to briefly cover many of Unity's core features in *Chapter 6, Getting Your Hands Dirty with Unity*, but there is still so much more the engine has to offer. These topics aren't in any particular order of importance, but if you're going forward with Unity development, you'll want to have at least a passing familiarity with the following:

- Shaders and effects
- Scriptable objects

- Editor extension scripting
- Non-programmatic UI
- ProBuilder and Terrain tools
- PlayerPrefs and saving data
- Model rigging
- Animator states and transitions

You should also go back and dive into the Lighting, Navigation, Particle Effects, and Animation features in the editor.

# Next steps

Now that you have a basic level of literacy in the C# language, you're ready to seek out additional skills and syntax. This most commonly takes the form of online communities, tutorial sites, and YouTube videos, but it can also include textbooks, such as this one. Transitioning from being a reader to an active member of the software development community can be tough, especially with the abundance of options out there, so I've laid out some of my favorite C# and Unity resources to get you started.

## C# resources

When I'm developing games or applications in C#, I always have the Microsoft documentation open in a window I can get to easily. If I can't find an answer to a specific question or problem, I'll start checking out the community sites I use most often:

- C# Corner: `https://www.c-sharpcorner.com`
- Dot Net Perls: `http://www.dotnetperls.com`
- Stack Overflow: `https://stackoverflow.com`

Since most of my C# questions relate to Unity, I tend to gravitate toward those kinds of resources, which I've laid out in the next section.

## Unity resources

The best Unity learning resources are at the source; video tutorials, articles, free assets, and documentation are all available from `https://unity3d.com`.

However, if you're looking for community answers or a specific solution to a programming problem, give the following sites a visit:

- Unity Forum: `https://forum.unity.com`
- Unity Learn: `https://learn.unity.com`
- Unity Answers: `https://answers.unity.com`
- Unity Discord channel: `https://discord.com/invite/unity`
- Stack Overflow: `https://stackoverflow.com`

There is also a huge video tutorial community on YouTube if that's more your speed; here are my top five:

- Brackeys: `https://www.youtube.com/user/Brackeys`
- Sykoo: `https://www.youtube.com/user/SykooTV/videos`
- Renaissance Coders: `https://www.youtube.com/channel/UCkUIs-k38aDaImZq2Fgsyjw`
- BurgZerg Arcade: `https://www.youtube.com/user/BurgZergArcade`

The Packt library also has a wide variety of books and videos on Unity, game development, and C#, available at `https://www.packtpub.com/all-products`.

# Unity certifications

Unity now offers various levels of certification for programmers and artists that will lend a certain amount of credibility and empirical skill ranking to your resume. These are great if you're trying to break into the game industry as a self-taught or non-computer science major, and they come in the following flavors:

- Certified Associate
- Certified User: Programmer
- Certified Programmer
- Certified Artist
- Certified Expert - Gameplay Programmer
- Certified Expert - Technical Artist: Rigging and Animation
- Certified Expert - Technical Artist: Shading and Effects

> Unity also provides preparatory courses in-house and through third-party providers to help you get ready for the various certifications. You can find all the information at `https://certification.unity.com`.

Never let a certification, or the lack of one, define your work or what you put out into the world. Your last hero's trial is to join the development community and start making your mark.

# Hero's trial – putting something out into the world

The last task I'll offer you in this book is probably the hardest, but also the most rewarding. Your assignment is to take your C# and Unity knowledge and create something to put out into the software- or game-development communities. Whether it's a small game prototype or a full-scale mobile game, get your code out there in the following ways:

- Join GitHub (`https://github.com`)
- Get active on Stack Overflow, Unity Answers, and Unity Forums
- Sign up to publish custom assets on the Unity Asset Store (`https://assetstore.unity.com`)

Whatever your passion project is, put it out into the world.

# Summary

You might be tempted to think that this marks the end of your programming journey, but you couldn't be more wrong. There is no end to learning, only a beginning. We set out to understand the building blocks of programming, the basics of the C# language, and how to transfer that knowledge into meaningful behaviors in Unity. If you've gotten to this last page, I'm confident you've achieved those goals, and you should be too.

One last word of advice that I wish someone had told me when I first started: you're a programmer if you say you are. There will be plenty of people in the community that will tell you that you're an amateur, that you lack the experience necessary to be considered a "real" programmer, or, better yet, that you need some kind of intangible professional stamp of approval. That's false: you're a programmer if you practice thinking like one regularly, aim to solve problems with efficiency and clean code, and love the act of learning new things. Own that identity; it'll make your journey one hell of a ride.

# Pop Quiz Answers

## Chapter 1 – Getting to Know Your Environment

### Pop quiz – dealing with scripts

| | |
|---|---|
| Q1 | Unity and Visual Studio have a symbiotic relationship |
| Q2 | The Reference Manual |
| Q3 | None, as it is a reference document, not a test |
| Q4 | When the new file appears in the **Project** tab with the filename in edit mode, which will make the class name the same as the filename and prevent naming conflicts |

## Chapter 2 – The Building Blocks of Programming

### Pop quiz – C# building blocks

| | |
|---|---|
| Q1 | Storing a specific type of data for use elsewhere in a C# file |
| Q2 | Methods store executable lines of code for fast and efficient reuse |
| Q3 | By adopting `MonoBehaviour` as its parent class and attaching it to a GameObject |
| Q4 | To access variables and methods of components or files attached to different GameObjects |

# Chapter 3 – Diving into Variables, Types, and Methods

## Pop quiz #1 – variables and methods

| | |
|---|---|
| Q1 | Using camelCase |
| Q2 | Declare the variable as `public` |
| Q3 | `public`, `private`, `protected`, and `internal` |
| Q4 | When an implicit conversion doesn't already exist |
| Q5 | The type of data returned from the method, the name of the method with parentheses, and a pair of curly brackets for the code block |
| Q6 | To allow parameter data to be passed into the code block |
| Q7 | The method will not return any data |
| Q8 | The `Update()` method is called every frame |

# Chapter 4 – Control Flow and Collection Types

## Pop quiz #1 – if, and, or but

| | |
|---|---|
| Q1 | True or false |
| Q2 | The NOT operator, written with the exclamation mark symbol (!) |
| Q3 | The AND operator, written with double ampersand symbols (&&) |
| Q4 | The OR operator, written with double bars (\|\|) |

## Pop quiz #2 – all about collections

| | |
|---|---|
| Q1 | The location where data is stored |
| Q2 | The first element in an array or list is 0, as they are both zero-indexed |
| Q3 | No – when an array or a list is declared, the type of data it stores is defined, making it impossible for elements to be of different types |
| Q4 | An array cannot be dynamically expanded once it is initialized, which is why lists are a more flexible choice as they can be dynamically modified |

# Chapter 5 – Working with Classes, Structs, and OOP

## Pop quiz – all things OOP

| | |
|---|---|
| Q1 | The constructor |
| Q2 | By copy, rather than by reference like classes |
| Q3 | Encapsulation, inheritance, composition, and polymorphism |
| Q4 | `GetComponent` |

# Chapter 6 – Getting Your Hands Dirty with Unity

## Pop quiz – basic Unity features

| | |
|---|---|
| Q1 | Primitives |
| Q2 | The *z* axis |
| Q3 | Drag the GameObject into the `Prefabs` folder |
| Q4 | Keyframes |

# Chapter 7 – Movement, Camera Controls, and Collisions

## Pop quiz – player controls and physics

| | |
|---|---|
| Q1 | `Vector3` |
| Q2 | `InputManager` |
| Q3 | A `Rigidbody` component |
| Q4 | `FixedUpdate` |

# Chapter 8 – Scripting Game Mechanics

## Pop quiz – working with mechanics

| | |
|---|---|
| Q1 | A set or collection of named constants that belong to the same variable |
| Q2 | Using the `Instantiate()` method with an existing Prefab |
| Q3 | The `get` and `set` accessors |
| Q4 | `OnGUI()` |

# Chapter 9 – Basic AI and Enemy Behavior

## Pop quiz – AI and navigation

| | |
|---|---|
| Q1 | It's generated automatically from the level geometry |
| Q2 | `NavMeshAgent` |
| Q3 | Procedural programming |
| Q4 | Don't repeat yourself |

# Chapter 10 – Revisiting Types, Methods, and Classes

## Pop quiz – leveling up

| | |
|---|---|
| Q1 | `Readonly` |
| Q2 | Change the number of method parameters or their parameter types |
| Q3 | Interfaces cannot have method implementations or stored variables |
| Q4 | Create a type alias to differentiate conflicting namespaces |

# Chapter 11 – Introducing Stacks, Queues, and HashSets

## Pop quiz – intermediate collections

| | |
|---|---|
| Q1 | Stacks |
| Q2 | Peek |
| Q3 | Yes |
| Q4 | `ExceptWith` |

# Chapter 12 – Saving, Loading, and Serializing Data

## Pop quiz – data management

| | |
|---|---|
| Q1 | The `System.IO` namespace |
| Q2 | `Application.persistentDataPath` |
| Q3 | Streams read and write data as bytes |
| Q4 | The entire C# class object is converted into JSON format |

# Chapter 13 – Exploring Generics, Delegates, and Beyond

## Pop quiz – intermediate C#

| | |
|---|---|
| Q1 | Generic classes need to have a defined type parameter |
| Q2 | The `values` method and the `delegates` method signature |
| Q3 | The `-=` operator |
| Q4 | The `throw` keyword |

Packt>

packt.com

Subscribe to our online digital library for full access to over 7,000 books and videos, as well as industry leading tools to help you plan your personal development and advance your career. For more information, please visit our website.

# Why subscribe?

- Spend less time learning and more time coding with practical eBooks and Videos from over 4,000 industry professionals
- Improve your learning with Skill Plans built especially for you
- Get a free eBook or video every month
- Fully searchable for easy access to vital information
- Copy and paste, print, and bookmark content

At www.packt.com, you can also read a collection of free technical articles, sign up for a range of free newsletters, and receive exclusive discounts and offers on Packt books and eBooks.

# Other Books You May Enjoy

If you enjoyed this book, you may be interested in these other books by Packt:

**C# 10 and .NET 6 – Modern Cross-Platform Development, Sixth Edition**

Mark J. Price

ISBN: 9781801077361

- Build single project cross-platform apps using .NET MAUI and XAML
- Build your own types with object-oriented programming
- Write, test, and debug functions
- Query and manipulate data using LINQ
- Integrate and update databases in your apps using Entity Framework Core, Microsoft SQL Server, and SQLite

- Build rich web experiences using Blazor, Razor Pages, the Model-View-Controller (MVC) pattern, and other features of ASP.NET Core
- Build and consume powerful services using all the latest technologies, including gRPC and GraphQL

**Game Development Patterns with Unity 2021, Second Edition**

David Baron

ISBN: 9781800200814

- Structure professional Unity code using industry-standard development patterns
- Identify the right patterns for implementing specific game mechanics or features
- Develop configurable core game mechanics and ingredients that can be modified without writing a single line of code
- Review practical object-oriented programming (OOP) techniques and learn how they're used in the context of a Unity project
- Build unique game development systems such as a level editor
- Explore ways to adapt traditional design patterns for use with the Unity API

# Packt is searching for authors like you

If you're interested in becoming an author for Packt, please visit `authors.packtpub.com` and apply today. We have worked with thousands of developers and tech professionals, just like you, to help them share their insight with the global tech community. You can make a general application, apply for a specific hot topic that we are recruiting an author for, or submit your own idea.

# Share your thoughts

Now you've finished *Learning C# by Developing Games with Unity 2021, Sixth Edition*, we'd love to hear your thoughts! Scan the QR code below to go straight to the Amazon review page for this book and share your feedback or leave a review on the site that you purchased it from.

https://packt.link/r/1801813949

Your review is important to us and the tech community and will help us make sure we're delivering excellent quality content.

# Index

# D



# E

# F



# G

## N



## O



## P

## U



## V



## W

# X

Made in the USA
Middletown, DE
13 December 2021

55401924R00239